Brains Confounded by the Ode of Abū Shādūf Expounded

Volume Two

WITH

Risible Rhymes

Letter from the General Editor

The Library of Arabic Literature makes available Arabic editions and English translations of significant works of Arabic literature, with an emphasis on the seventh to nineteenth centuries. The Library of Arabic Literature thus includes texts from the pre-Islamic era to the cusp of the modern period, and encompasses a wide range of genres, including poetry, poetics, fiction, religion, philosophy, law, science, travel writing, history, and historiography.

Books in the series are edited and translated by internationally recognized scholars. They are published as hardcovers in parallel-text format with Arabic and English on facing pages, as English-only paperbacks, and as downloadable Arabic editions. For some texts, the series also publishes separate scholarly editions with full critical apparatus.

The Library encourages scholars to produce authoritative Arabic editions, accompanied by modern, lucid English translations, with the ultimate goal of introducing Arabic's rich literary heritage to a general audience of readers as well as to scholars and students.

The Library of Arabic Literature is supported by a grant from the New York University Abu Dhabi Institute and is published by NYU Press.

Philip F. Kennedy
General Editor, Library of Arabic Literature

About this Paperback

This paperback edition differs in a few respects from its dual-language hardcover predecessor. Because of the compact trim size the pagination has changed. Material that referred to the Arabic edition has been updated to reflect the English-only format, and other material has been corrected and updated where appropriate. For information about the Arabic edition on which this English translation is based and about how the LAL Arabic text was established, readers are referred to the hardcover.

Brains Confounded by the Ode of Abū Shādūf Expounded

Volume Two

BY

Yūsuf al-Shirbīnī

with Risible Rhymes
by Muḥammad ibn Maḥfūẓ al-Sanhūrī

TRANSLATED BY
Humphrey Davies

VOLUME EDITORS
James E. Montgomery
Geert Jan van Gelder

NEW YORK UNIVERSITY PRESS
New York

NEW YORK UNIVERSITY PRESS
New York

Library of Congress Cataloging-in-Publication Data
Names: Shirbīnī, Yūsuf ibn Muḥammad, active 1665–1687, author. | Davies, Humphrey T. (Humphrey Taman), editor translator. | Shirbīnī, Yūsuf ibn Muḥammad, active 1665–1687. Hazz al-quḥūf fī sharḥ qaṣīd Abī Shādūf. English. | Shirbīnī, Yūsuf ibn Muḥammad, active 1665–1687. Hazz al-quḥūf fī sharḥ qaṣīd Abī Shādūf.
Title: Brains confounded by the ode of Abu Shaduf expounded / Yusuf al-Shirbini ; translated by Humphrey Davies ; foreword by Youssef Rakha.
Description: New York : New York University Press, [2019] | Originally published in hardback in 2016. | Includes bibliographical references and index. | In English with original Arabic text.
Identifiers: LCCN 2018052779 (print) | LCCN 2018055775 (ebook) | ISBN 9781479879847 (ebook) | ISBN 9781479852949 (ebook) | ISBN 9781479840212 (pbk. : alk. paper)
Subjects: LCSH: Villages—Egypt—Early works to 1800. | Egypt—Rural conditions—Early works to 1800. | Social problems in literature—Early works to 1800. | Satire, Arabic—Egypt—Early works to 1800. | Arabic literature—Egypt—Early works to 1800.
Classification: LCC HN786.A8 (ebook) | LCC HN786.A8 S5513 2019 (print) | DDC 307.720932—dc23
LC record available at https://lccn.loc.gov/2018052779

New York University Press books are printed on acid-free paper, and their binding materials are chosen for strength and durability.

Series design and composition by Nicole Hayward
Typeset in Adobe Text

Manufactured in the United States of America

10 9 8 7 6 5 4 3 2 1

Contents

Brains Confounded by the Ode of Abū Shādūf Expounded

Part Two

In the Name of God,
the Merciful, the Compassionate

Praise be to God, Lord of the Worlds, and blessings and peace upon our master Muḥammad, noblest of prophets, and upon his family and companions, one and all! To proceed. The humble slave of the Almighty, Yūsuf ibn Muḥammad ibn ʿAbd al-Jawād ibn Khiḍr al-Shirbīnī declares (and may God be for him and have mercy on his forebears): after frigid determination and sluggish lucubration had bestirred themselves for a few days and been constrained to produce a book that's now on paper contained, on the conditions of the people of the countryside as it may be, and on their love and longing and their prose and poetry, which work became a Part in coarseness without peer, to which no man of virtue and discerning scholarship would ever give ear, which was to serve as an introduction to the coming Ode, which motifs like the prickly ends of palm fronds included and with an *urjūzah*—a summary of all that's in it of poetry and prose—concluded and which, to cut the story short, was a dollop of my inspired thought, I determined to add thereto this second part and unravel the meanings of the Ode, which are the point from which its formal constructions depart; so I set my lethargic brain to work, allowing my pen on the elucidation of the matters therein to go berserk and to unravel the motifs that the Ode contains, descending upon it like a downpour on Upper Egypt when it rains, with expressions whose sense wafts about like a fart, and motifs thrown together without method or art. And indeed, my brain assisted me in that for which I strove and bestirred itself with me to attain the goal at which I drove; and now's the moment to set out in pursuit of that thing, with the help of God, the Worshipped King. I therefore declare: 9.1

An Account of the Lineage of the Poet and Its Components, and of the Place That Took Him to Its Bosom and Gave Him Shelter from His Earliest Moments, and of the Origins of His Fortune and How It Was Brought, and of the Nature of His Beard, Whether It Was Long or Short, and of How, at the End, by Fate He Was O'erthrown, as a Result of Which He Composed This Ode for Which He Became Famous and Well Known

His Lineage

We declare: opinions differ concerning his lineage. Some state that he was Abū Shādūf son of Abū Jārūf son of Shaqādif son of Laqāliq (Storks) son of Baḥlaq (Goggle-Eye) son of ʿAflaq (Big Flabby Vagina) son of ʿAfr (Dust) son of Duʿmūm son of Falḥas[1] son of Kharā Ilḥas (Lick-Shit). If you ingest these words with your rational faculty, you will realize that this is the end of his ancestry. Others, however, say he was Abū Shādūf son of Abū Jārūf son of Bardaʿ (Donkey Saddle) son of Zawbaʿ (Dust Storm) son of Baḥlaq son of ʿAflaq son of Bahdal (Disheveled) son of ʿAwkal son of ʿAmrah[2] son of Kul Kharā (Eat-Shit). Thus, according to the first version, his genealogy ends with "son of Lick-Shit" and according to the second with "son of Eat-Shit"; however, the second is more correct because to eat shit is more eloquent than to lick it. 10.1

His Village

10.2 As for his village, it is a matter of dispute. Some say that he was from Tall Fandarūk and others from Kafr Shammirṭāṭī,[3] the latter being correct, for the poet himself says so in some verses of his, to wit:

10.2.1 Me, good people, my words are a guide
And my verses speak true, no tomfooleries hide.
Abū Shādūf am I. My dad told me the tale,
And likewise my grandma, old Umm Nāyil,
Of how, good folk, I was raised
In a hamlet known since olden days
Called Kafr Shammir-lī wa-Ṭāṭī[4]—
So, Fasāqil,[5] be a wise laddie!
These are my verses, Abū Shādūf's my name,
And any who comes to inquire my verse can claim.

10.2.2 And I heard verses by a country person that indicate that he was from Tall Fandarūk, as follows:

We have heard in days old and new
Speech strong as iron and as true—
Of Abū Shādūf they did us tell,
In words very trusty and confirmed as well,
That Tall Fandarūk was his childhood abode,
And there he lived, good people, and composed an ode.
These are my verses, Ghindāf's my name,
And verse far-fetched is the name of my game!

The two versions may be reconciled by saying that he was born in Kafr Shammirṭāṭī and raised in Tall Fandarūk.

The Shape of His Beard

10.3 As for the shape of his beard, some say it was very long, while others say it was moderate in both length and shortness. The two accounts may be reconciled by saying that, at the beginning of his life—when, as we shall see, he enjoyed perfect good fortune and abundant blessings—his beard was long because he groomed it frequently with chicken fat and linseed oil and combed it and tended its hairs and so on; however, when he grew old and his fortunes changed and care and sorrows overtook him, it became less commode-ious[6] because of his eating dirt and nits and so on. In other words, it grew long at first and then later it grew wide, with the result that its width rendered its length odious, and, as such, there is no contradiction between the two versions. As the poet says:

A beard grew long and got quite nasty,
So that its length became quite odious.
They cut it short and it got much nicer,
When its length was less commode-ious.

Some say that it is sign of a lack of brains when a man's head is small and his beard long, and if his name is Yaḥyā as well, he hasn't a hope of brains at all; and the proverb says, "Long beard, little brain." Thus it came about that a man had a friend with a long beard who was a teacher of young children.[7] On one occasion, after he had failed to see him for some days, the man asked after his friend and was told, "He has shut himself up in his house to grieve." The man thought that he must have lost a child or one of his relatives, so he went to see him and found him grief-stricken and weeping and wailing. "My brother," said the first, "may God make great your recompense and make good your consolation and have mercy on the departed! Every soul must taste death!" "Think you that one of mine has died?" said the other. "What then?" said the first. "Know," said the shaykh, "that I was sitting one day when I heard a man recite the following verses: 10.4

O Umm ʿAmr, God reward you well,
Give me back my heart, wherever it may be![8]
Don't take my heart to make of it your toy—
How can a girl with a young man's heart make free?

"—so I said to myself, 'Were not this Umm 'Amr one of the best and most beautiful of people, these verses would not have been said of her!' and I fell madly in love with her and shut myself away with her love. Then one day I sat for a while and I heard someone say:

> When the donkey went off with Umm 'Amr,
> She never came back, and neither did the donkey

"—so I thought, 'If Umm 'Amr were not dead, they would not have made up this verse about her' and I was overcome with grief and afflicted by sorrow." This made his friend realize how stupid the man was and he left him and went his way.

10.5 And the story is told that one extremely cold day a certain person was going along when he saw a man with a small head and long beard wearing nothing but a shift and shivering from the cold. Noticing that the man had a white woolen mantle folded under his arm, he asked him, "Why don't you put on the mantle to protect yourself from the cold?" The man replied, "I'm afraid that the rain will get on it and make it wet, and then it won't be lovely and new-looking anymore." This made the man realize how stupid he was and he left him and went his way.

10.6 The finest beard is middling, with hairs of even length, neither long nor short. If it be said, "Pharaoh's beard was longer than he was tall, by one or two spans, or so it is reported, and even so he was wise and full of insight," we respond, "The explanation is that the Almighty gave him three miraculous signs, one of them being the length of his beard, which was also green and the like of which was vouchsafed to no other of his sort. He also had a steed that placed its front foot at the farthest point that it could see and raised its hind legs when it ascended and its front legs when it descended. Or it may be said that, even though he possessed extraordinary knowledge, he was effectively bereft of intelligence because he claimed to be divine and perpetrated heinous acts and so on. Thus what we have said is correct as stated above. End."

It is said that the most quick-witted and devilishly clever of men are those who have no beard at all. Anyone associating with them must be on guard, because of their great intelligence, breadth of knowledge, and finesse. Thus it happened that a certain king once asked his minister, "Who are the most devilishly clever and quick-witted of men?" and the minister answered, "Those who have no beard." "I want you," said the king, "to demonstrate the truth of that for me." Said the minister, "You must prepare some food and make spoons for the food, each spoon three cubits in length, and order people to come and eat. When the people have come and sat down, order them to eat with nothing but those spoons and tell them that no one may touch the spoon except by the handle and that he may eat in no other way. Then watch what happens." The king did as the minister instructed him, and the people came for the food. When they sat down, he ordered that they eat only with the spoons and told them that no one should touch any part of the spoon but the handle, as described. They wanted to eat but could not, and they wanted to leave, but the king stopped them and ordered them to sit. One of them would fill the spoon and try to put what was in it in his mouth, but it would miss his mouth and stick out over his shoulder, and no one knew what to do. While they were thus engaged, a man with no beard entered. "How is it that you are not eating the food?" he asked, so they told him the problem. "That's easy," he said, "I will show you a stratagem that will allow you to eat without disobeying the king's command: each one of you will feed the man sitting opposite him, and that man likewise will feed the one who feeds him. That way you will eat your fill with the spoons as they are." So this man started feeding morsels to that one and likewise that man to this one till all had eaten their fill. The king was amazed at the beardless man's stratagem and the force of his cunning and his great insight and ordered that he be given a gift and bestowed a robe of honor on the minister. 10.7

10.8 And once a beardless man stood before a certain king and brought a complaint against an opponent. The king said to him, "I am amazed at your complaint. After all, you are beardless, and no one should be able to get the better of you." "Pardon, O king," replied the man, "but my face has the odd hair, while my opponent is completely smooth, without a single hair on his face!" The king laughed and gave the man his due against his opponent and ordered that he be given a gift.

The Origins of His Good Fortune in His Early Days and How Fate Came to Turn Against Him

10.9 As for the origins of the poet's good fortune in his early days and how fate came to turn against him, accounts differ. One says that, when he was grown and had reached ten years of age, he was strong, lusty, and well versed in pasturing flocks, gamboling in fields, and walking barefoot and naked in the heat, and that he would haul wet manure on his head from the field to his house in the shortest time imaginable, so that the liquid released would run over his face, and from this, if he ever got thirsty, he would drink; and sometimes what ran down from it would cover the rest of his body, as is typically the case among country boys. And he would go for a month or even two without giving his face a wash, unless he should happen to get doused in urine by a calf or a cow as he was on his way to or from the fields, in which case he would rub it in with his hand, using it in place of water to wash his face. Despite this fatuous cleanliness, he never passed up an opportunity to beat up the other children, play ball around the village quarters, gambol on the dung heaps and threshing floors, play at *dārah* and on the drums and *zummārah*, making a tumult and wild sounds, and beating the hounds, and other crud and crap, to the point that he was the one among his companions who knew best how to make two days of every one and of every month two. As the Bard of the Two Villages[9] put it:

10.9.1 Abū Shādūf from day one's been cocky—
Like a puppy he bounces all over

And goes to Abū Maʿrah's field and gathers
Fresh dung on a platter.
He'll be naked, with a load on his head,
And his face like the face of an ogre,
And the wet dung that's gone runny
Will have run down upon him, and there's nothing brave in his manner.
He goes for a month without washing his face,
Or for two, and his body's still got power:
After sweeping the threshing floors all morning long, 10.9.2
He'll still dash about like our bitch Umm Ṣarwah.
How fine you look, Abū Shādūf (when
He comes to the buffaloes and falls into ordure
And gets down and wallows there behind them).
You'd say you were the afreet of some cloister!
All his life Abū Shādūf's been pampered:
Like a puppy dog he grew up among us and scampered.
Abū Shādūf, God grant him ease,
Put on a cap and today has a sheepskin fur.
Today his father's shaykh of the hamlet and sits
Knee to sandal with the tax collector.
The first says, "Master!" The other, "You pimp! 10.9.3
Cough up the taxes or I'll use you others to deter."
This is from the likes of Abū Shādūf and his grandfather[10]
And his father and his father's sister, Umm Faswah's[11] daughter,
And we close our words with praise for Muḥammad—
How many a calamity he has swept away, God's Messenger!
On him, O Lord, pour blessings and peace,
As on his noble companions, of knightly order!

Indeed, people used to envy his father for having a son so strong and so smart and such an expert at banging the drum and playing the *zummārah*. Now, his father had acquired, in the course of his life, a lame donkey, two goats, a share in the ox that turned the 10.10

waterwheel, half a cow, ten hens with their rooster, four bushels of bran, and two quarterns of barley. He also owned about four hundred dung cakes and a bin in which he stored chicken droppings during the winter, and he had a broken water jug, a striped earthenware water butt, a besom to sweep the threshing floor, and a dog to guard the house. Once he had achieved this state of luxury, he died and passed into the mercy of the Almighty, in keeping with the common rule that the day a poor man gets rich, he dies—a point well made by the poet[12] who said:

When a thing's complete, decline sets in.
  Expect extinction when men say, "Done!"

10.11 So his son Abū Shādūf wrapped him in a cloak of combed linen and buried him in a grave known as "the grave of Ibn Kharūf" at the acacia trees of Kafr Shammirṭāṭī, or, as some say, at Kafr Tall Fandarūk; but the two statements may be combined, in which case one would say, "He died in Kafr Shammirṭāṭī and was buried in Kafr Tall Fandarūk." His grave is now known as "the grave of Abū Jārūf," and the peasants visit it and play ball next to it, and the animals urinate on it from time to time. A country poet elegized him in the following lines:

10.11.1 Ah come, good people, to my aid,
  And weep, *mushāh*, time and again!
Abū Jārūf today away from us has turned,
  While his goat and cow remain.
He's left his father's brother's daughter, Umm Falḥas,[13]
  In an empty chamber today to weep and complain,
And Abū Shādūf bawls fit to burst,
  "My father's dead and it's all gone awful again!"
Gone is the hamlet's shaykh who ruled
  O'er the brave lads and all those men!

10.11.2 And when, to go raiding, he used to mount
  His dog and primp and preen,

And put his cap atop his head—
His beard sticking out and looking mean—
And about him were Jarw Ibn Kharā Inta Falḥas[14]
And the *mushāh* of the hamlet, none worth a bead,
You'd have said he was head of a band of musicians,
Or the buffoon who'd come to plead!
Gone now is his fart, God bless his bones
And moisten his head-brick[15] time and again!
As to Abū Shādūf, God preserve his youth 10.11.3
And make him our shaykh, to rule to our gain,
Like his father mounted, and may his army
Troop after troop after troop contain,
And may he buck like a donkey and set off around noon
And lounge about pompously and sit in the *shirāʿah*.[16]
Thus we end our words, and God alone endures,
And death's a cup from which none may abstain!
And I'm a smart guy and all my life a poet,
And I string together verses that shimmer and shine.
These I've made so all who behold them may mourn, 10.11.4
And today with my words I've sent him off fine,
And for the rest of my days I'll praise the Beauteous,
God's Prophet, and pray his intercession to gain.
Now the blessing's done, so hear what I say:
I hope you're all snuffed by a clot on the brain!

And when the wake was over and the dust had settled and Abū Shādūf had received the condolences of the shaykhs and the brave lads, and he had distributed bran-and-barley pastries as alms for the repose of his father's soul and had plastered his grave with mud and dung, and built the calf's trough next to it, he put his cudgel over his shoulder and stepped out like a fine steed, and played the shaykh over the hamlet, and every Zayd and ʿAmr[17] obeyed, and he sat on his ass with one knee up and one knee on the ground, and shouted and jumped, both up and down, and sang and made up poetry, of which he was proud, declaiming and saying out loud: 10.12

10.12.1 Me, Abū Shādūf—O Salāmah[18]—
All my life I've made up verses and I'm a bright guy,
And now my father's in his grave[19]
I'm shaykh of the hamlet, which none can decry!
And I rule the foot soldiers and come and go,
And I wade in the river up to my thigh,
And I saddle my donkey and mount, around me
A company like to a candle in the night sky,
With Abū ʿUntūz and Abū Buzbūz[20] and ʿAflaq,
While Blood-Lick-the-Back-of-Your-Neck and Abū *ʿimāmah*[21] are nigh.

10.12.2 These days the world doesn't hold my like,
And I'll boss you forever and go on being a helluva guy,
And with my cudgel I'll break the bones and smash the pate
Of any who disobey.
My father before me was shaykh over you,
So let me be, and be on your way!
And we close our words with praise of Muḥammad
And his dandy companions, the people of generosity!

10.13 At this the shaykhs and the brave lads envied him the shaykhdom of the hamlet, to which he had succeeded after his father's death, and they incited the authorities against him, and the latter sent for him and deprived him of a part or, as some say, of all of it, and he had nothing to fall back on but the binful of droppings, which he had kept out of sight and which had been the source of his prosperity after his father's death, or so they say. However, he set about sucking up to people and flattering them, until the matter was forgotten and the winter came and he opened the bin one night and sold the droppings and made a good living, according to this version of events. Others, however, say that he borrowed twenty silver pieces and bought eggs with them and went to Cairo, where he happened to arrive on the feast of the Christians,[22] so he sold the eggs for more than they were worth, and this was the source of his prosperity. The two versions may be reconciled by saying that he sold the droppings and bought eggs with the proceeds, so that his prosperity was the sum of the price of the droppings and the price of the eggs, and from this perspective there is no contradiction. And he took to handing out money and dispensing hospitality, and poets and men of letters from the farthest hamlets sought him out. One poet he rewarded with fifty eggs and a measure of barley, and to another he gave a hundred dung cakes, and yet another brought him a sack, which he filled with droppings from top to bottom and gave him in payment. He became even richer than his father, for he had two geese, twenty roosters, a chicken hutch made out of palm ribs, a crooked staff, a felt cap, a tattered blue shift, a basket full of bran, ten bunches of dry carrots, and other stuff too, and he continued thus, with the Lord blessing his prosperity—for prosperity comes from the Almighty alone.

In illustration of which, we might mention that it happened that a certain righteous man was very poor. Once, while asleep, he heard a voice say to him of a sudden, "You! Go to such-and-such a place and take from there a thousand dinars!" "Has the Lord blessed them?" he asked. "No," said the voice. "Leave me!" said the man. Then the voice came to him again and said, "Go to such-and-such a place and take from there five hundred dinars!" "Has the Lord blessed them?" he asked. "No," said the voice. "Leave me!" said the man. The voice kept coming to him again and again, until it said to him, "Go to such-and-such a place and take from there one dinar!" "Has the Lord blessed it?" he asked. "Yes," said the voice. "Then I will take it," said the man, and he went and he took the dinar and was blessed in it and obtained great ease and abundant riches, for if a man is content with what he has he will not suffer want, and the little he has will be blessed. As says the Righteous Saint and Initiate of the Almighty, My Master Yaḥyā al-Buhlūl,[23] may the Almighty be pleased with him and benefit us and all Muslims through him, amen: 10.14

Be content with the little you have
And God will give you much!

And he says:

How many a cloud after sprinkling
Lets fall a heavy shower!

10.15 And al-Shāfiʿī,[24] may God be pleased with him, has said:

I found acceptance of my lot a treasure house of riches,
And to its skirts began to cling.
Now no man finds me at his door
Or chasing him for anything.
I move among mankind without a single cent
And have no wants, just like a king.

10.16 Thus it was till fate and fortune against him turned, and he was by relatives and boon companions spurned, and all that he had owned was spent, and he found himself in the greatest woe and severest predicament, of all friends and helpers bereft, no wealth remaining but what his father'd left, and those who were once his servants took over the shaykhdom of the hamlet, while he could find neither helper nor friend—for such is the way of Fate: it raises up the lowly, and brings down the noble and exemplary, it being like a balance in its action, or like a sieve in its working and extraction—as the poet[25] says in the following verses:

I see Fate lifts every scoundrel high
And humbles those with noble traits—
Just like the sea, which drowns all living things
While every stinking carcass to its surface levitates,
Or like the scale, which raises all that's light
But sinks with weights.

10.17 And another has said:

Fate's like a sieve in how it works,
So wonder at what the sieve achieves—
The densest grains it puts below,
And on the top the husks and chaff it leaves

—for the accidents of Fate may be cause for alarm, and drive a man into the way of harm.

In the opening lines of an ode of mine on the same theme I say: 10.18

The accidents of Fate may be to your peril—
So beware their outcome and escape any harm that might transpire.
Prepare against them an ample coat of mail from patience,
To protect you from their fierceness when showered with their fire
And leave behind the time of youth—its boughs have dried
That in the verdant nursery once were full of juice.
They were nights bowed down with pleasures
From which, when young, I gathered glory's fruits

—and so on to the end of these verses.

Nothing but "patience fair"[26] against the accidents of Fate can 10.19
remedy afford—that, and submission to the Majestic Lord; and apropos of those caught unawares by fate's blows and abandoned by kin and fellows, is the story that is told of how a certain envious person slandered the vizier and calligrapher Ibn Muqlah—who was unique in his age for the sublime beauty of his hand—claiming that he had cheated the king in some matter. The king, in consequence, ordered Ibn Muqlah's hand cut off. After the command had been carried out, Ibn Muqlah kept to his house, while his friends and dear ones abandoned him and up to the middle of the day no one came to see him. Then the king discovered that the accusation against him was false, ordered that the man who had slandered him be killed, and restored Ibn Muqlah to his previous position, repenting that he had had his hand cut off. When Ibn Muqlah's brethren saw that

he was returned to favor, they came back to him and visited him to make their excuses, at which he recited the following verses:[27]

Man and time succeed each other in reciprocity,
So, as time is, man must too be.
Fate savaged me for half a day,
And man's nature was thus revealed and made clear to me.
O you who turned away,
Return, for time itself's turned back to me.

It is said that he continued to write with his left hand for the rest of his life, and his writing did not change to the day he died.

10.20 A curious anecdote attesting to Ibn Muqlah's mastery of the language relates that a man once wrote something on a scrap of paper and tossed it to him in the presence of the king for him to read to him, and every word contained the letter r, which Ibn Muqlah could not pronounce. The message read as follows: "The ruler of rulers requires a spring drilled right by the road so every transient and traveler may drink." After glancing at it, Ibn Muqlah changed the words and kept the meaning, saying: "The king of kings commands that a well be dug next to the wadi, so all who come and go may wet their whistles." This was an example of his extraordinary skill with words, may the Almighty have mercy on him. It is said there are four men whose qualities have become proverbial: Ḥassān ibn Thābit for eloquence, Luqmān for wisdom, Ibn Adham for self-denial, and Ibn Muqlah for beauty of writing and script. Said the poet, describing these four:

Ḥassān's tongue and Ibn Muqlah's hand,
The wisdom of Luqmān and the self-denial of Ibn Adham,
Were these brought together in one bankrupt,
And he were hawked for sale, he'd not bring in one dirham.

10.21 As for the opposites of these four,[28] how well the poet put it in the following lines:

Uṭrūsh is odious, Ibn Qaynah discourteous,
Qarnān's credulous, and Ibn Ayham's obstreperous.

Were all these faults combined in one with wealth endowed,
He'd be "the people's orator" whenever he made a sound!

Concerning another who was caught unawares by Fate's blows 10.22
and overcome by oppression and woes—so that after he was exalted he became debased, and after riches saw his wealth effaced—is the story that is told of a man who was burdened with debts and left his children and wandered aimlessly until he came to a high-walled city, mightily built. He entered, abject and broken in spirit, devoured by hunger and exhausted by travel, and was walking along one of its streets when he saw a company of eminent persons proceeding together. He joined them and they came to a place like a king's palace, and they entered, the man following, and they continued until they came to a man sitting in great state, with pages and servants around him, as though he were the son of a viceroy, and this man, when he saw them, rose to greet them and paid them great honor. The subject of our tale was overcome with amazement and taken aback by the magnificence of the place and the servants and retainers, and he retired in a state of perplexity and apprehension, afraid for his safety, and sat down in a spot far removed from the people, where none could catch sight of him. While he was thus seated, a man came towards him with four hunting dogs dressed in silks and brocades and with gold collars and silver chains around their necks. The man tied each dog in its appointed place and disappeared and returned with four golden dishes filled with sumptuous food and placed before each dog its own dish. Then he went away and left them. The man was so hungry that he started to eye the food, and wanted to go up to one of the dogs and eat with it, but fear prevented him from approaching them. One of the dogs, however, looked at him, understood his plight, and, ceasing to eat, signaled to him to approach. The man drew near, and again the dog made a sign, as though to say, "Eat from this dish," and drew back from the dish, so the man ate until he was full and wanted to leave. At this, the dog made a sign to him as if to say, "Take this dish with the remaining food," so the man picked it up and put it in his sleeve and

waited a while, but no one came looking for the dish, so he took it and went his way. Then he journeyed to another city and sold the dish and bought goods with the proceeds and made his way to his own town, where he sold what he had and paid off his debts, and his business increased and he found himself in a state of the greatest ease and general good fortune. When some time had passed, he said to himself, "You must make a journey to the city of the owner of the dish and take with you a splendid gift in recompense and pay him back the price of the dish, even though one of his dogs made you a present of it." So he took a gift befitting the man's standing and took with him the price of the dish, and he journeyed by day and by night until he came to that city and went up into it, hoping to meet with the man. However, on approaching that place, he nothing saw but crumbling ruins and cawing ravens, dwellings reduced to desolation and all things in deterioration, a sight to leave the heart in a state of agitation and a place turned by Fate into «a scene of devastation».[29] As the poet[30] says:

Suʿdā's ghost agliding came and woke me in alarm
At break of dawn, my fellows in their homes yet still asleep,
But when aroused by that night phantom gliding,
I found the house bereft, the tryst too far to keep.

10.23 When the man observed that wasted debris, and beheld what fate had wrought for all to see, perplexity assailed him for sure, and, turning, a pitiful man he saw, his state fit to make the skin creep, the sight of him enough to make a stone weep. "You there!" he said. "What have Fate and time made of the master of this facade? Where are those suns that shimmered and stars that glimmered? What blow upon his edifice could fall that would leave nothing standing but the wall?" That pitiful man responded for his part, moaning from a grieving heart, "Is there not guidance in the Messenger's words for those who follow his example and heed his admonition that 'It is God's right to raise up naught in this Abode that He does not then subject to demolition'? If your question be for good reason and cause, know that there is nothing in the vicissitudes of Fate that calls for pause. I am the master of this place and its erector, its occupant and its constructor, the owner of its shimmering suns and overwhelming sums and master of this place replete with so many a brilliant bauble and slave girl adorable—but Fate turned its back, put servants and money to the sack, and drove me to this present state, catching me unawares with concealed blows with which it lies in wait. However, your question surely is for good cause and reason raised, so inform me of what they may be and cease to be amazed!" The other then related to him his tale, with a lump in his throat and great travail, telling him, "I have brought you a gift such as any might desire, plus the price of your golden dish that I did acquire, for it was a cause of my becoming rich after poverty and of my relief from dire straits and misery." The man then wagged his head and wailed, and moaned and railed, and he said, "You are crazy, sir, it seems to me, for such a thing can never be. A dog of ours made you a gift of a dish of gold, and I should now go back on that? Never, though I were subject to woe and misery untold! By God, I will not take from you one fingernail sliver, so return in peace to the place whence you came hither!" The man then kissed his feet and hands, and, extolling the other's worth, set off for his native lands, and, as he left him and was bidding him good-bye, spoke this verse on which the ear must love to dwell:

Gone are the men and the dogs together,
So to men and dogs alike, farewell!

Likewise the author of this book from fortune's plots has suffered blows, after the nights had shot him with woe's arrows from disaster's bows, so that he found himself, after companionship, on his own, after sweet intimacy, alone, conversing with the stars, wrestling with his cares, over the departure of his dear ones pouring his lament, and hoping—faint hope!—that Fate might yet relent. As the poet says: 10.24

Would that I knew—for the world tears friends apart
And the stars of men both wax and wane—
Will the house, after parting, fill once more with cheer,
And will those first days of ours return again?

10.25 However, patience with life's perfidies is a mark of the noble man:

Patience! You'd rush to thank the Lord of Every Boon
If you but knew what benefits in patience lie!
And know that should you not endure with grace
What by the Pen is writ, you will, perforce, comply!

The Ode of Abū Shādūf with Commentary

All of which paves the way for the woes that on our own poet were inflicted, and the accidents of fate, both overt and covert, with which he was afflicted and which were the reason for his composing this ode, and of his complaint, profuse and extended, against all that fate on him bestowed. Thus he says: 11.0

TEXT

yaqūlu abū shādūfi[31] *min ʿuẓmi mā shakā* 11.1
mina l-qilli jismū mā yaḍāl naḥīf

Says Abū Shādūf: from all he has suffered
of want, his body's ever skinny

COMMENTARY

These words are metered[32] and tuned,[33] have feet, and may be crooned.[34] The meter's the one that's both "Long" and "Extended"[35]—and impaired and distended. Those who claim its meter's "the Perfect" say it goes "without intellect, without intellect (*mutahābilun mutahābilun*)," [36] while those who compare it to that called "the Exuberant" say, "This is the meter luxuriant!" and those who assign it to "the Diffused" say, "It's flabby and confused!" while those who compare it to the Meter of the Chain[37] say it goes "featherbrain, featherbrain (*halhalah halhalah*)," [38] and those who compare it to other metrical clocks use, to represent it, "You're a *donkey* or an 11.1.1

ox." Its usual tune goes to the measure "If you chew a bit of soap, it'll make you like leather."[39] Its feet, of which we've already made mention, appear as follows, when in articulation:[40]

yaqūlu	*abū shā*	*dūfi min*	*ʿuẓmi mā*	*shakā*
nabūlu	*ʿalayhā*	*fī l-ḍuḥā*	*maʿ ghurū*	*bihā*

and the whole of the Ode is in the same mode, namely:

nabūlu ʿalayhā fī l-ḍuḥā maʿ ghurūbihā
We urinate upon it in the forenoon and at sunset.

Now that you know the meter and tune, the feet and the croon, let me embark on the exposition of the verse according to its rhythmic pattern, or in firecracker fashion.

11.1.2 Thus we declare:

yaqūlu ("Abū Shādūf says")—i.e., he intends to initiate speech (*qawl*) external to himself that will contain an explanation of his state and evidence of the accidents of Time with which he was inflicted, and the occasions for woe and grief with which he was inflicted. The word *qawl* has paradigms and etymologies. The paradigm is *qāla*, *yaqūlu*, *qawlan*, and *maqālatan*, to which may be added *qullatan* ("water pitcher")[41] and *qaylūlatan* ("midday snooze").[42] It is derived from *qaylūlah* or from *qulal* ("water pitchers") or from *aqwāl* ("sayings") or from *qālū* ("they said") or *qulnā* ("we said").[43]

11.1.3 I have added these facetious paradigms and silly etymologies simply as a point of departure for the account that I shall relate to you of an encounter I once had with one of those persons who claim learning while in fact they are ignorant, to wit that, when I went on pilgrimage to God's Holy House[44] in the year 1074[45] and had reached the port of al-Quṣayr and was waiting there for the ships to leave, I stayed for a few days at a hostel on the sea, preaching to the people. One day, as I was reciting the Qur'an there, explaining the words and their meanings to the people to make them clear, a sorry sight to see, accoutered for travel by sea, engaged in buffoonery and deliration, and cant and speechification,[46] there came towards me—let no one doubt my say-so!—a man round as a halo, tall and cretinous, gross and hebetudinous, with a turban huge as the Primordial Lump, and a woolen shawl draped over his chump. Clearly up to no good, he sat himself down and fixed me with a frown, while his determination to involve me in trouble and contention plainly could be read, since he could barely wait for me to say the word "Said . . ." And so it was as I've described, and in the manner that I've implied, for no sooner had I begun to give my lesson, and declared, "Said the Prophet, upon him peace and benison . . ." than he asked me in tones unrefined, "What's the meaning of 'said' *when it's declined*?" When I heard his query, and understood his ignorance and inanity, I realized that in learning he was so far from an adept as to be quite unaware of the difference between word and concept. So I said to him, "From *qāl* both nouns and verbs we may decline: *qāla*, *yaqūlu*, *qawlan*, and *maqālatan* or *qullatan* or *qaylūlatan* in fine—and if you like I'll make you up, for sure, in addition to these six, thirty more!" Said he to me, "In what standard text is this declension shown?" Said I, "In the collected works of Ibn Sūdūn!" Then he accepted my words—he was that ignorant and benighted—and I realized that he couldn't tell the name from the thing cited. Thenceforth, after all the pretension and bluster, he followed me as a sheep its master, and submitted in his comings and goings to my sway, till he departed and went his way.

If it be said, "How come you set out to confuse this inquirer 11.1.4
with such paradigms and etymologies, and you gave him such good measure of imbecilities, when you should have stuck to what they'd say in a grammar book, instead of ladling out such gobbledygook?" we reply, "All well and good, but that only goes for those who understand scholarship as one should. As for the dumb ignoramus, who's gross and pertinacious, his ignorance calls for nothing better than whatever nonsense one may churn out, and the haughtiness befitting the condition of such a lout. Thus the reply that I have given above—taken as it came—was quite appropriate

to a question so inane. The problem's now revealed, the silliness no longer concealed."

11.1.5 A Silly Topic for Debate: What's the explanation for the fact that the poet starts his verse in the present tense and does not use the past, unlike, for example, the author of *The Thousand Lines on Grammar*,[47] God have mercy on him, when he writes, "Muḥammad, Mālik's son, *has said* . . . etc.?"[48] The Facetious Answer: It is the past tense of the verb, namely, *qāla*, from which the present tense, namely, *yaqūlu*, is generated, and from *yaqūlu* comes the verbal noun *qawl*, as already noted in tracing the origins of these verbs and nouns; thus the poet simply settled for using the derived rather than the base form. Or it may be that he wanted to enumerate the changes and vicissitudes of fate that had befallen him and, not having mentioned them earlier using past-tense forms, he determined to narrate them using the present-tense form, namely, *yaqūlu*, albeit this has past meaning formally speaking and present meaning in reality. As the poet says:

So *qāla*'s past, *yaqūlu*'s present,
Though the last is its past in reality.[49]

And Abū l-Ṭayyib al-Mutanabbī,[50] may God excuse him his sins, says:

If what he intended were a present verb,
It would be past before any could negate it

—meaning, "If he intends to do something in the future, he completes the action before anything can 'negate' it," that is, can intervene between him and its doing and silence the vowels of his verb.[51] End. Also, if he were to introduce the past form, the meter would be broken, even if the meaning remained as before. Thus the answer now is right; the truth has loomed into sight.

11.1.6 *Abū Shādūfi*: this is his *kunyah*, but it took him over and became his primary name, as happened in the case of Maʿdīkarib, Baʿlabakk, Baraqa Naḥruhu, and so on.[52] His real name was ʿUjayl, diminutive of *ʿijl* ("calf"), or so it is reported, the reason for his being so named being that, when his mother gave birth to him, she threw him in the cow's trough, and then the calf came along and licked him, so they called him that for a few days, until he became known by the *kunyah* in question. The reason for his becoming known by the latter is variously explained. One version has it that when the times turned against him, as described above, he hired himself out to water the crops using the device made by the country people, called the Abū Shādūf.[53] The way this works is that they construct two pillars of mud next to the river and excavate a hole like a small pit between them; on the two pillars they place a small beam and also, at right angles, another, resembling the arm of a pair of scales; to the land end of the last they attach a weight, and to the river end, a bucket or scoop,[54] with which they raise the water. A man stands on the riverside and pulls the end of the crossbeam downward, and the bucket or scoop falls and scoops up the water; then he lets go, the other end descends under its weight, and the bucket or scoop rises and, with the aid of the man, empties into the pit; the water then runs on to the crops and so on, as we have ourselves observed on numerous occasions. The whole assemblage, consisting of the device itself with the pillars, is called *abū shādūf*, which is derived from *shadf*, which means "scooping" (*gharf*). It says in *The Blue Ocean and Piebald Canon*, *shadafa, yashdufu, shadfan* means *gharafa, yaghrifu, gharfan*. As the poet says:

> If you see water, scoop (*ushduf*) carefully,
> For that, to the thirsty, more comfortable is and more pleasant!

Thus the poet, because he cleaved to this device and became almost inseparable from it, came to be known by its name, according to the rule of "naming the condition after the position." Another version has it that his mother gave birth to him next to an *abū shādūf* and he was therefore named after it, but this is refuted by what has already been said, to the effect that his original name was ʿUjayl. The two versions may be reconciled by saying that after his mother 11.1.7

had given birth to him next to the *abū shādūf*, she took him and placed him in the trough and the calf licked him and he became known as described above. Thus there is no contradiction between the accounts. It is also said that he was so named because he did so much scooping of water with this device—so much, indeed, that it got to the point that anyone who asked after him would be told, "he's busy *shadf*-ing" that is, "scooping"; then they added the *alif* and *waw* to the word and said *shādūf*.[55] With constant repetition, they have come to think of the crossbeam as though it were the child and the pillars as though they were the father, so that now they call the device "the father of the crossbeam (*abū shādūf*)"; and they applied the name to the poet himself because he was always next to the device and they identified him with it, and thus it became a proper name by which he was addressed, as already explained. End.

11.1.8 A Silly Debate: What is to be learned from the fact that the bucket or scoop never leaves the beam, which resembles the arm of a pair of scales; and does the latter play the role of father to the former, just as, as pointed out earlier, the two pillars play the role of father to the crossbeam of the *shādūf*; and is it the case that the bucket or scoop adheres to the beam merely out of necessity and, once disconnected from it, ceases to perform its function; and, as such, may it be said to be attached to it only when needed and not otherwise? We declare: the fatuous response is that the beam cannot dispense with the bucket or the scoop and neither can dispense with the beam, and so together they play the role of child to the beam, and the beam plays the role of father for the reason given, since both of them—the bucket and the scoop—are in a stable relationship with the beam. Now the contention's straightened out, the silliness shown up for what it's about.

11.1.9 A Useful Note: the word *ab* ("father") is derived from *āba*, meaning "he returned."[56] Ibn Zurayq,[57] God have mercy on him, says in an ode:

He never returns (*āba*) from one journey but feels an urge
To be on his way again, that only his will can purge.

That is, "he never comes back from one journey but the urge to undertake a second disturbs him." It is the same with a father, because he is always coming back to his child and missing him and looking about for him. Others say that the word is derived from *ubuwwah* ("fatherhood"), just as *akh* ("brother") is derived from *ukhuwwah* ("brotherhood"). Says the poet:

A man's *ab* from *āba* derives,
And a man's *akh* from *ukhuwwah* likewise.

The paradigm is *āba, ya'ūbu, awban,* active participle *ābin.*[58]

11.1.10 Ibn Sūdūn[59] claims that *abū,* the construct form of *ab,* is really a perfect-tense defective verb,[60] being originally *abūsu* ("I would kiss"), and he cites as evidence the verse that says:

"They said, 'Your sweetie hides his mouth affectedly from view;
What would you attempt, if he should show it?' Said I, '*abū*. . .'[61]

"that is, *abūs* ('I would kiss'), the *s* having been dropped for two reasons, the first being to deceive the listener, this being the proper thing to do in literary opinion and the more conducive to safety from tattletales and nosy parkers, and the second because its numerical value is sixty,[62] and sixty kisses, according to some, is excessive."

These are his words as explicitly stated in his collected works. End.

11.1.11 Personally, I would say that the opinion of such people, as transmitted by Ibn Sūdūn, is invalid, because, once the lover succeeds in winning his beloved, his heart will never be satisfied with sixty or even a hundred kisses, especially if the beloved in question is graceful of form, comely of feature, to his lover obedient, sincere, and compliant, whose genial body has not been denied, and who to his lover has been gathered like a bride, the lover of his beloved being thus fully possessed, the place free of tattletale, nosy parker or other pest. Then for kissing there is no number firm—it knows no bounds nor any term. As the poet says:

"One kiss!" I asked the full moon high in the sky.
"By Him who draped the clouds,"[63] he said, "I will comply!"
But when we met with none about,
I reckoned wrong and lost all count!

11.1.12 And I myself said on the same theme:[64]

I saw upon his cheek a stippled mark that beauty held—
He whom an earring had made yet sweeter to behold.
"I want a kiss," I said. Said he, "When we're alone!"
And on that "stipulation" I kissed a thousandfold!

—unless the place be unsuitable for a lover and the object of his adoration, in that there's a fear of tattletales or of observation, in which case any hugging and kissing will depend on how comfortable the lover feels—as to whether it be quite a lot or almost completely missing—though there are a few who have, in this regard, no doubt or fear and will kiss their loved ones in front of anyone who's there, and, even though the latter turn and flee, chase after him relentlessly. As the poet says:

Would that you'd seen me and my darling
When, like a deer, he from me fled
And ran away, and I gave chase;
Would you'd seen us when after hot pursuit he said,
"Will you not leave me be?" and I said, "No!"
And he, "What would you of me?" and I, "You know!"
And he then stayed aloof and shyly turned his back,
And proudly turned, not to me, but away—
For then I almost kissed him, right in front of everyone.
Ah, would I now could do what then I should have done!

11.1.13 An amusing story has it that Abū Nuwās was one day walking in the streets of Baghdad when he saw a beautiful youth and kissed him in front of everyone. He and the youth were brought before the judge Yaḥyā ibn Aktham, and the youth brought charges against Abū Nuwās. After bowing his head in silence for a moment, the judge recited:[65]

If you object to being groped and kissed
    Don't go to market without a veil;
Don't lower lashes o'er a forelock
    And don't display upon your temple a scorpion curl,
For as you are, you slay the weak, drive the lover to delirium,
    And leave the Muslims' judge in dire travail!

The youth in turn bowed his head in silence for a while and then recited:[66]

We had hoped to see justice between us,
    But after hope there followed despair.
When will the world and its people go right
    If the judge of the Muslims fucks boys in the rear?

min ʿuẓmi mā shakā ("from all that he has suffered"): that is, from the thing, or indeed the things, he has to complain of. He expresses his complaint out loud in the hope that the Almighty will release him from his sufferings and restore him to his former life of ease, for when things are at their worst they are not far from getting easier, and though the gate be strait, it opens onto larger spaces. Says the poet: 11.1.14

How many a night of woes like ulcers
    I have tended, till I won through to day!
The blows of fate pass young men lightly by
    And dissipate, and in their thoughts they do not stay.

There are different categories of complaint. There is the complaint to God, which is praiseworthy, and the complaint to one of His creation, which is blameworthy, unless the complainer place his trust entirely in the Almighty and rely on Him, seeking His help to repel whatever misfortunes may have befallen him—in which case there is no harm, though it is preferable for him to have patience and resign himself to God's will, in which case God will grant him relief. The Almighty has said, «And give good tidings to the patient!»[67] and also, «Verily, along with hardship there shall be ease.»[68] Among the verses of Master Yaḥyā al-Buhlūl,[69] may the Almighty benefit us through him, are:

When things get tough,
Think on «Have we not dilated . . .?»![70]
Remember one "hardship" between two "eases"[71]
And neither mourn nor feel elated!

11.1.15 Next the poet decided to enumerate the things that had befallen him, one after another, beginning with the worst and the most important, so he says:

11.1.16 *min al-qilli* ("of want"), with an *i* after the *q* and no vowel after the *l*;[72] that is, my gravest and greatest complaint is of *qill* ("want"), which is a paucity (*qillah*) of food and drink (the *ah* having being dropped for the meter)[73] and also of inadequate clothing and of the great toil and exhaustion required by the struggle to make a living. In the Tradition it says, "Poverty may bring one to the verge of denying one's faith," meaning that it may come close to forcing one to deny his faith because it leads to dissatisfaction with providence and displeasure with his material state and this may drag him into denying his faith. Ibn Daqīq al-ʿĪd, God have mercy upon him, said of poverty:

By my life, poverty has dealt me a cruel stroke,
And reduced me with it to confusion and dismay.
If I go public with my plaint, I violate my privacy;
But if I don't confess my need, I fear I'll die!

And it is said that four sayings were written on the crown of Chosroes Anūshirwān: "Justice If It Lasts Brings Prosperity"; "Injustice

If It Lasts Brings Ruin"; "The Blind Man Is as Dead Though He Be Not Buried"; and "Poverty Is the Red Death."[74] The people of the countryside use the word to cast aspersions on a poor man. They say that so-and-so is *fī qill* ("in a state of want"), and sometimes they add another word and say *fī qill wa-ʿatrah*, that is, in a state of struggle and exhaustion and the performance of foul deeds and awful doings. It is an expression used by the people of the countryside. One of their poets says:

> Abū Jāmūs—his state
> Makes people weep; he's quite lost face:
> He runs around and finds nothing,
> And lives in want and disgrace (*fī qillah wa-fī ʿatrah*).

The word *qill* is of the measure of *ghill* ("rancor, spite") or *ẓill* ("shadow") and derives from *qalqalah* ("agitation, convulsion") or from *qullah* ("water pitcher"), with *u* after the *q*, or from *qawlaq* ("leather money pouch"). The word *ʿatrah*, with *a* after the ʿ and no inflectional vowel at the end, is of the measure of *zubrah* ("small penis"); take a *zubrah* and weigh it against a *ʿatrah*, and you'll see there's no difference at all. The word means "the performance of acts of corruption and deficiency in religion" and so on. They say, "So-and-so is an *ʿitr*," that is, one who does such things.[75] As for *ʿathrah*, with *th*, it is the singular of *ʿatharāt* ("slips, mistakes, sins"), which belongs to the chaste language, in which case the meaning would be that the sins of one who is mired in such a state are many; thus the sense is the same. *Qill* occurs in the language of the Arabs, as in the anecdote that a city man invited a Bedouin to a meal, and brought him out a bowl of food and a little bread. As often as the Bedouin took a mouthful, the city man would say to him, "Say, Bedouin, 'In the Name of God, the Merciful, the Compassionate!'" and he kept repeating the same until the Bedouin was abashed and got up without eating his fill and left. Then, a few days later, the Bedouin left his dwelling and saw his city friend, so he took him and sat him down in his house and brought out a large bowl full of bread and meat with 11.1.17

broth and said to him, "Eat, city man, and knock it back! There's no blessing in paucity (*qillah*)!" that is, "there's no blessing in paucity of food when accompanied by stinginess, whether you say 'In the name of God' or not, even though He be the source of that blessing, for what matters is an ungrudging spirit, even though its owner be poor," for generosity comforts the heart and covers many a flaw. As the poet says:[76]

If your flaws are become well known to men,
And you're inclined to find for them a cover,
Assume a mantle of liberality, for any flaw,
They say, by liberality may be covered over

—and, as the common saying has it, "Whatever the flaw, generosity covers it."

11.1.18 A Silly Debate: What is the wisdom in deriving *qill* from *qawlaq*, or from *qullah*, or from *qalqalah*, and how do they fit with one another, and what do these words mean? The Fatuous Response: *qawlaq*[77] is the name for a leather thing that is made to keep money in and tied onto the belt on the right thigh; some coffee waiters and others use it. The derivation of *qill* from *qawlaq* comes from the latter's crampedness and its lack of room, since *qill* denotes a cramped life and lack of ease; thus it fits the meaning from that perspective. As for its derivation from *qullah* ("water pitcher"), with *u* after the *q*, this could be for one of several reasons. It may be because water is retained within it, in which case want and lack of good fortune are analogous to the presence or absence of the water. Alternatively, the fit may lie in the actual narrowness of the *qullah* and the fact that the water has to pass through narrow holes in order to come out,[78] and that, when submerged in water, it makes a gurgling sound, as though it were complaining to the water. As the poet says:

The mug makes a gurgle because it's in pain:
It protests to the water what it suffered from the flame.

This process of firing implies distress and hardship, so it fits with the derivation of *qill* from that perspective. The third opinion states that it is derived from *qalqalah* ("agitation, convulsion"). From this point of view *qill* would be from the agitatedness (*qalqalah*) of events, that is, the speed with which they move, their intensity, and the distressing circumstances to which they give rise and so on. As the poet[79] says:

> Stir (*qalqil*) your stirrups in the steppes (*falā*)
> And leave the pretty girls at home.
> Like dwellers in the grave to me are those
> Who never from their homelands roam.

—that is, move your stirrups "in the *falā*," which means the wide-open spaces. The meaning is: "Go east and west, and acquire whatever will relieve you of having to beg from others, and be not a burden upon them, and do not humiliate yourself before them, and leave the *ghawānī*—plural of *ghāniyah*, which means 'a female possessed of beauty'; that is, abandon any such and do not allow yourself to be distracted by her from seeking your livelihood, for that distraction may lead to inactivity and idleness, in which case you will not find the wherewithal to spend on her and her heart will turn to someone else, with all sorts of evil consequences. If, on the other hand, you bestir yourself and leave her and then come back with all the things she needs to assuage her hunger and clothe her nakedness, she will stay with you just as your heart would desire and in perfect felicity. And even if you benefit little from your efforts and journeys, what you get will still be better for you than doing nothing." As the poet says:

> Man must work for what he needs,
> And Fate is not obliged to help.

In one of the Revealed Books, the Almighty says, "My slave, I created you from motion; move and I will provide for you!" and the proverb says, “In activity is blessing,”[80] and the Imam al-Shāfiʿī,[81] may the Almighty be pleased with him, says:

Leave your lands and seek advancement!
  Go abroad, for there are five good things in travel:
Escape from care and a way to earn your living,
  Knowledge, savoir faire, and the friendship of the noble.
Though some say travel means abjection in exile,
  And loss of one’s friends and meeting with trouble,
Still better a young man die than live
  In ignominy ’midst jealousy and tittle-tattle.

Thus the answer now is clear, all can agree, and the nature of this derivation’s plain to see.

11.1.19 *jismū* (“his body”): the pronoun suffix refers to the poet, that is, “his body” means “his person,” the word being derived from *tajassum* (“corporeality”) or from *al-mujassimah* (“the Corporealists”), which is a sect that holds to the doctrine of incarnation and corporealization,[82] may the Almighty disfigure them, or from *jism al-ʿāshiq* (“the body of the lover”), when the latter is worn thin by separation from the beloved and the poet can find neither medicine nor doctor for it.

11.1.20 *mā yaḍāl* (“is ever”): a rural phrase, meaning *mā yazālu*, as discussed in Part One.[83] That is, his body is never free of want, toil, and discomfort.

11.1.21 *naḥīf* (“thin”): of the measure of *raghīf* (“loaf”); it is properly *naḥīfan*, with an *alif* of prolongation, the latter having been dropped for the meter.[84] The meaning is that his body became weak and thin from the succession of cares that afflicted it, and the injury and hardship that it had to put up with in the course of making a living and so on—for care weakens and sickens the body, unlike ease and abundance of comforts, from which it will be evident that the bodies of the rich and affluent are in general vigorous, attractive, and graceful, because of the excellence of their food and drink and the cleanliness and fineness of their clothes, and they do not, as a result, suffer any of the ill effects of care. Imam al-Shāfiʿī, may the Almighty be pleased with him, said, "He whose garments are clean has few worries," and it says in the Tradition, "One's garments should give glory to God"; if they get dirty, this glorification is brought to a halt. The body, in fact, is like a crop of plants: so long as its owner is careful to water it and tend it and clean out the weeds, it remains full of vigor and glows with good looks, but when he ceases to attend to it, diseases attack it and things take a turn for the worse. In the absence of sickness, on the other hand, slenderness and trimness of the body are desirable characteristics in both women and men, and one possessed of such characteristics is referred to as *ahyaf* ("slender waisted"). As the poet[85] says:

Two slender-waisted creatures,
 One girl, one boy,
At backgammon played.
 Said she, "I am a turtledove!"
"Hush!" said I. "You are the moon above!"

—and even more expressive are the words of the poet who said:

A slender-waisted lass—should she tread on the lids of one with eyes inflamed,
 No pain from her footfall would he feel.
Light-spirited—should she, of her levity, desire
 To dance on water, not a drop would wet her heel.

A Silly Topic for Debate: "Why did the poet say *naḥīf* rather than 11.1.22
saqīm ('sick'), though the latter is more appropriate in meaning and more elegant in expression and is found in the Mighty Qur'an, in the words of the Almighty, «And he cast a glance at the stars, then said, 'Lo! I feel sick (*saqīm*)!'»[86] that is, 'I feel sick at your worship of idols'?" We declare, the fatuous response is that the poet avoided the latter word because it includes the meaning of the word that

rhymes with it, namely, *qaṭīm*, and *qaṭīm* is, in the language of the country people, a passive sodomite, and, in another dialect, an unmarried man;[87] if he had used the word in the verse, they might have attributed passive sodomy to him, with harmful consequences. Or it may be said that, in this, he was following the rules of rhyme for poetry, so there is no problem. Our words are now clear, the silliness made to appear.

11.1.23 Next the poet sought to tell of a further misfortune by which he was smitten and which was a product of the aforementioned want, abasement, and lack of wherewithal. He says:

TEXT

11.2 *anā l-qamlu wa-l-ṣībānu fī ṭawqi jubbatī*
shabīhu l-nukhālah yajrufūhū jarīf

Me, the lice and nits in the yoke of my gown
are like bran that they shovel willy-nilly

COMMENTARY

11.2.1 *anā* ("me"): meaning "Me, Abū Shādūf, I inform you in addition, good friends, and I complain to you" of

11.2.2 *(a)l-qaml* ("lice")—the well-known type that makes the rounds among people, not the type mentioned in the Mighty Qur'an, for the latter is a type of worm or tick, according to some of the commentators.[88] (Useful note: al-Damīrī, in his *Life of Animals*,[89] mentions, on someone's authority, that the tick lives seven hundred years, which is remarkable. End.) [90] Lice are born from the sweat and dirt of the body. The word is derived from *taqammul* ("infestation with lice") or from the *taqmīl* ("licing") of yarn, when the latter is dyed and sized and placed in the hottest sun, so that it dries and develops white spots that look like lice; thus one speaks of "liced yarn." The paradigm is *qamila, yaqmalu, qamlan* ("to be infested with lice"); *qaml* is a collective noun, the female being a *qamlah* ("a louse");[91] the male is perhaps called a *qāmil*. The poet says:

I never had a male louse (*qāmil*) in my clothes but it seemed to me
To creep like a male scorpion (*ʿuqrubān*) as it moved.

The word *ʿuqrubān* is of the pattern of *thuʿlubān*, which means "fox" (*thaʿlab*). As the poet says:

Is there a lord on whose face the dog-foxes pee?
Contemptible indeed is he on whom the foxes pee!

The dual[92] may be used as a form of address, as it is in the Mighty Qur'an when the Almighty addresses the Guardian of the Fire, saying, «Throw (dual) into Hell . . .»[93] and as in the words of al-Ḥājjaj, "Boy, strike (dual) his neck!."[94] As for the poet's words in the first verse, "creep like a male scorpion," this is the case because the louse is conventionally likened to the scorpion and the flea to the elephant, because the former stings while the flea bites. If it be said, "If the louse resembles the scorpion and the flea resembles the elephant, why is the louse not as large as the scorpion and its sting like the scorpion's sting, and, by the same token, why is the flea not the size of the elephant and why does it not behave like one?" the reply would be that, because the louse is generated by and never leaves the human body for a specific beneficial purpose ordained by the Divine Wisdom, namely, the removal by sucking of corrupt blood, even though it may sometimes do harm too, it is in accord with the wisdom of the Almighty that it should be small and also that its sting should cause hardly any pain, because, were the louse the size of a scorpion, a human would have to be the size of a camel and would live in dread of seeing one and being tortured by its sting—but Almighty God is generous to mankind. Likewise, the flea, given that the Almighty has formed it to live in the creases of clothes and other tight places, is small like the louse because, if it were the size of an elephant, a human would have to be the size of a mountain. The word *burghūth* ("flea") is the singular of *barāghīth*, and the female is a *burghūthah*; it is derived from *birr* ("charity") plus *ghawth* ("help").[95] Al-Jalāl al-Suyūṭī,[96] God have mercy on him, said:

Hate not the flea—
    Its name is Charity,
And though you know it not
    It also helps a lot:
In sucking bad blood
    Its charity lies;
By rousing you at dawn for prayer
    Its help it supplies.

The poet's mention of the louse spares him the need to mention the flea, because the latter is subordinate to the former.

11.2.3 A Question: "Where is the wisdom in the fact that the flea can jump while the louse cannot?" The answer: "The louse, being born of the sweat and effluvia of the body, is correspondingly weak, and it is, moreover, female,[97] and the female is weaker than the male. The flea, however, being born of the earth, is of a stronger clay, which is why it resembles the elephant, which is the animal with the largest body. Thus, its strength is inborn, which allows it to jump." The situation's now revealed, the problem no more concealed.

11.2.4 Some say the flea is more harmful than the louse. The poet says:

I complain to you of certain fleas with which I am afflicted.
    On my heart a choking cup these have inflicted.
While I chase one, another comes to bug me,
    And so goes the night, in hunting and ven'ry.

And how well the poet put it, when he said:

Gnats, fleas, and bedbugs clung tight to me:
    They thought my blood wine and held its taste most dear.
The fleas would dance to the piping of a gnat,
    While the bedbugs kept mum so the others could hear.

11.2.5 One of our hashish-eating brethren—may God prolong through the eating of hashish their conviviality and stifle with a jar of wine on sleeping their raucous hilarity—informed me that, if one drops a little hashish before sleeping, followed by a few jars, and then sleeps, he doesn't feel the pain of fleas, or anything else, especially if he uses candy after eating the hashish, for hashish produces strange reactions and creates amazing effects, and the only thing that spoils it is eating sour things. As the poet says, incorporating words of Ibn al-Fāriḍ's, may God be pleased with him:

O you who're stoned on dope for lack of wine
(That vap'rous draft around whose fires men meet),
When you are high, I do advise you, Don't
Consume what's sour, do eat what's sweet!

My mother, may God excuse her sins, told me a riddle about fleas that I didn't understand until I had mastered the sciences and spent time among people with a command of the best language. It goes as follows: *yā shī min shī aḥmar ḥimmayr waraq al-jimmayr jarū warāh khamsah miskūh itnayn* ("Something from something else![98] Red as red can be, red as the leaves of the heart of the palm tree! Five ran after it, two caught it!"). It may be interpreted as follows: *yā shī* ("O thing"): *yā* ("O") is the vocative particle, that is, "O man, interpret to us a name that comes from something obscure and is" *aḥmar ḥimmayr* ("dark, dark red"): *ḥimmayr* (with double *m*, *i* following the *ḥ*, and no vowel on the *y*) being the diminutive of *aḥmar* ("red"), and meaning "of intense redness";[99] *waraq al-jimmayr* ("leaves of palm hearts"): that is, like the leaves of palm hearts in color, *jimmayr* being the diminutive of *jummār* ("palm hearts"), which are the core of the palm tree, while the "leaves" are the fibrous integument that is wrapped around them; *jarū warāh khamsah* ("five ran behind it"): namely, the fingers; *miskūh itnayn* ("two caught it"): two of the latter, namely, the index finger and the thumb. There is diacritical paronomasia between *ḥimmayr* and *jimmayr*.[100] End. 11.2.6

The noxious effects of fleas may be prevented by using incense mixed with dried bitter-orange peel on sleeping. Lice may be killed with a woolen thread pounded with henna and mercury and hung around the neck. As for the beneficial qualities of lice, the author 11.2.7

of *The Book of the Physick of the Poor*[101] mentions that, if a migraine sufferer takes a louse from a head that is free of pain and puts it in a grilled bean and seals the latter with wax and hangs it at the point of the migraine, his head will get better, if the Almighty wills.

11.2.8 *wa-l-ṣībānu* ("and nits"): joined to *al-qaml* ("the lice") by the conjunction *wa-* ("and"), these being the seeds that are born of the latter; in other words, the poet joined the branch to the root, since the former is a concomitant of the latter. They are generally found in the greatest numbers on the heads of children, because children's bodies are tender and should be treated with fats and henna and by combing the hair and so forth. They are very prone to cause itching in the body but are less harmful than lice, because they are weaker and have softer bodies. The origin of the word is *ṣibyān* ("boys") (with the *b* before the *y*), plural of *ṣabī*.[102] Subsequently, they decided to avoid that plural, lest nits be confused with human children; so they put the *y* after the *b* and said *ṣibyān*. The word is derived from *ṣābūn* ("soap") because of the whiteness of the creatures, or from *muṣībah* ("disaster"), or from the Bridges of al-Ṣābūnī. The paradigm is *ṣabyana, yuṣabyinu, ṣibyānan*.[103]

11.2.9 The poet is silent on another form of the offspring of the louse, namely, the *nimnim* (with *i* after the two *n*'s and no vowel after the two *m*'s),[104] the latter, too, being a concomitant of the former and the branch being subordinate to the root, as previously stated. The word *nimnim* is of the measure of *simsim* ("sesame") and is a derivative of *namnamah* ("wren") or of *nammām*, a sweet-smelling plant.[105] If, on the other hand, we spell it as *namnam*, it would be a compound made of an imperative verb, as though one were ordering someone to go to sleep twice.[106] Al-Ḥarīrī,[107] God excuse him his sins, said in similar vein:

Perform an act for whose same seed you will be praised,
Thanking Him who gives, be it but a sesame seed!

This is close to the art of word puzzles[108] such as *ṭājin* and *ṭāfiyah* and *yāsamīn*[109] and the verse that says:

I saw a marvel in your houses—
An old man and a maiden in the stomach of a bird![110]

And another says:

Red of cheek, of a crimson
That all rouge to emulate must try;
Fangless, eyeless,
But with fang and eye.[111]

The word *namnam*[112] is used in the language of small children:[113] 11.2.10
when a child wants to eat, he says *namnam*, or *buff* (with *u* after the *b* and no vowel after the *f*), for children utter different words from those used by adults, as may be observed. As for the language children use *before* they start to talk, some say it is Syriac. When a child wants water, he says *unbūh* (with *u* at the beginning, no vowel after the *n*, *ū* after the *b*, and no vowel after the *h*). If he puts out his hand to something dirty to take it, he is scolded with the word *kukhkh* (with *k* and *kh*), and if he is on the point of taking something that might harm him, he is rebuked with the word *aḥḥ* (with *alif* and *ḥ*). If he takes something that pleases him and plays with it, they call it (or he calls it) *daḥḥ* (with *d* and *ḥ*) with no following vowels.[114] They call (or he himself calls) food when he has had enough of it *baḥḥ* (with *b* and *ḥ*). If his mother wants to scare him or stop him from bawling, she says, "Quiet, or the *biʿbiʿ* ('bogeyman') will eat you!" (with *i* or *u* after the two *b*s and no vowel after the *ʿ*s). *Biʿbiʿ* is derived from *baʿbaʿah*, which is the sound of the camel.[115] Among *aḥḥ* and *daḥḥ* and *baḥḥ* there is mutational paronomasia of the first letter.[116] The child addresses his mother as *māmā*, his father as *bābā*, his little brother as *wāwā*,[117] and so on. A poet has gathered these expressions together in a verse from a *mawāliyā* in which he flirtatiously addresses a little boy:

You who stole my heart and soul, Ouch! It hurts!
You make friends with others, but when it's me, your love's "all gone!"?

I feed you din-dins and tidbits and you say "All gone!"
Am I a "Bogeyman"? Am I "Yuck," little baby, while another's "Yumyum"?[118]

And Ibn Sūdūn, may the Almighty have mercy on him, says, in similar vein:[119]

Because of my mother's death I find sorrows wring me (*taḥnīnī*).
How often she suckled me tenderly (*taḥnīnī*),
And, as she brought me up, how often she indulged me,
So that I turned out just as she made me.
If I said *namnam*, she'd bring food and feed me.
If I said *unbūh*, she'd bring water to give me.

The words *taḥnīnī* ("wring me")[120] and *taḥnīnī* ("tenderly") constitute "perfect paronomasia,"[121] the first being from *inḥinā'* ("bending"), the second from *taḥannun* ("tenderness") and "having pity" (*shafaqah*), as is clear.

11.2.11 One also speaks of *'idhār munamnim* ("creeping fuzz") on a young man's cheek, meaning that the down resembles the creeping of the *nimnim* or of the *nammām* plant as it sprouts. Comparing it to the creeping of the *nimnim*, I wrote:

The down crept o'er his cheeks; it seemed to me
To be *nimnim* moving lazily.

11.2.12 Some have added a fourth type of vermin and named it *liḥḥīs* (with *i* after the *l* and double *ḥ*), of the measure of *ba'bīṣ* or *liqqīs*, *ba'bīṣ* being taken from *ba'baṣah*, which is "the insertion of a digit between the buttocks of another," while *liqqīs* is from *liqāsah* ("licking"); one says, "The dog licked (*laqisa*) the dish," meaning "it licked it clean (*laḥisahu*) with its tongue."[122] Thus there is a kind of resemblance to the *liḥḥīs*; or it may be that the word is formed according to the analogy of Fuṭays.[123] The words *liḥāsah* and *najāsah* are of the same pattern; one says, "So-and-so is *laḥis*," that is, "one who has committed something resembling impurity (*najāsah*) or who talks a great deal to no effect."[124] Thus *liḥāsah* and *najāsah* have the same underlying meaning. In *The Blue Ocean and Piebald Canon* it says, "There is no difference between *liqāsah* and *liḥāsah*, and undoubtedly *najāsah* enters into it too," and this is the more correct formulation. One also says, "You are *taʿīs laḥis*," that is, you resemble a dog licking a dish, or you lick shit with your tongue, or you talk raving nonsense (*tatalaḥḥas bi-l-kalam*) and cannot tell a thing from its name. *Taʿīs* has the same meaning, making all of them closely similar expressions, which is why the *liḥḥīs* are so harmful.[125] In *The Blue Ocean and Piebald Canon* it says:

> And I suffer torments from the harm the *liḥḥīs* do to my head,
> And a boiling and an itching in my clothes and in my body.

The paradigm[126] is *laḥḥasa, yulaḥḥisu, talḥīsan.*

If it be said, "This *liḥḥīs* added by the people you refer is insignificant, almost to the point of nonexistence, and this is why the poet, like others, leaves it out, so why do you raise the issue at all?" we would reply, "True. However, even if we grant that it is so minute that it barely exists, nevertheless it becomes, in bulk, unmitigated harm and injury and on this basis is to be associated with lice, and indeed it should be counted among the latter's offspring, just like the nits and the *nimnim* mentioned above. Alternatively, the issue is raised by analogy to those who add a fourth category to the parts of speech and name it 'the residual,' meaning by this the verbal substantive, namely, *ṣah* ('Hush!') in the sense of *uskut* ('Be silent!')."[127] Thus the situation now's revealed, the silliness no more concealed. 11.2.13

fī ṭawqi jubbatī ("in the yoke of my *jubbah*"): that is, I speak of those lice and nits that are existing or well established in its yoke. *Ṭawq* ("yoke") is of the pattern of *jawq* ("band of musicians"), as used in the expressions *jawq al-ṭabbālah* ("the band of drummers") and *jawq al-maghānī* ("the singing band") and so on. It is the name given to anything that encircles the neck, of a garment or of anything else, be it made of iron, silver, gold, brass, or the like.[128] The Almighty says, «That which they hoard will be their collar on the day of resurrection,»[129] meaning that the wealth that they store up in this world 11.2.14

and on which they do not pay tithes and which they do not use for good works will be placed around their necks like a collar, and they will be tormented by it in the Fire. The word *ṭawq* is derived from *ṭāqah* ("aperture") or from *ṭawāqī* ("skullcaps"), because of its roundness, or from the Khān of Abū Ṭaqiyyah in Cairo. The paradigm[130] is *ṭawwaqa, yuṭawwiqu, taṭwīqan.* The women of the countryside make their neck rings of silver, calling them also *ḍāmin,* and they regard them as the best of ornaments. The type of collar that is placed on the necks of men in prison is called a *ḍāminah*; one says, "So-and-so is in the *ḍāminah*" meaning that this iron device that is on his neck is a guarantee (*ḍāminah*) for him that he will not be able to get away, just like the man who acts as a guarantor (*ḍāmin*) for another and produces him when he is summonsed.

11.2.15 *jubbatī* ("my *jubbah*"): of the measure of *shakhkhatī* ("my pissing") and *liḥyatī* ("my beard"), or so it is if the form refers to oneself; but, if it refers to someone else, you say *jubbatak* ("your *jubbah*") on the pattern of *shakhkhatak* ("your pissing") or *liḥyatak* ("your beard"), for example. If you were describing it and said *jubbatak ḥamrah* ("Your *jubbah* is red"), you could change the dots and it would become *khanatak Ḥamzah,* meaning "a man named Ḥamzah fucked you."[131] *jubbah* is the singular of *jubab,* derived from *jabb,* which means "cutting," because the tailor tailors (*yajubbu*) the *jubbah,* that is, cuts (*yaqṭaʿu*) it and pieces it together. One also says *jāba l-fayāfī* ("he traversed open country"),[132] meaning "he cut across it (*qaṭaʿahā*)," and in this vein I said:

> I traverse (*ajūbu*) the open spaces, greedy for your arms,
> And cross (*aqṭaʿu*) a land of which I have no knowledge.

The paradigm is *jabba, yajubbu, jabban,* and *jubbatan.*[133]

11.2.16 There are two types: the rural and the urban. The rural type is of thick, coarse wool, closed in front like a *thawb.* They make the sleeves wide, especially their poets. Indeed, they are known for the excessive width of their sleeves, for the men's sleeves are made of cut-off sacks and are as wide as those of poets, or wider.[134] As for their women, their sleeves are wide enough to accommodate a man, who can go in through one and come out by the other; thus a man may have intercourse with his wife via her sleeve without needing to raise the rest of her shift, as I myself have experienced, for I married one of these women and had intercourse with my wife via her sleeve on several occasions—so glory to Him who made them unkempt, even with regard to their sleeves and other raiment, for these are things by them desired, and consistency is required. As the proverb has it, "They saw an ape getting drunk on a dung heap and said, 'For so pellucid a wine what better match than a youth so fine?' And they saw a buffalo blinkered with a reed mat and said, 'For so elegant a girl, what better match than so divine a veil?'"[135] As the poet says:

I saw a leper deep down in a well
And another with vitiligo whose shit on him fell.
Said I, "Behold what your Lord hath wrought—
The like of a thing attracts its own sort!"

The urban sort is the one used by the people of the cities, especially scholars and sophisticates. It is of soft, fine wool, and they make it tight at the armpits and open in front. They call it a *jubbah mufarrajah* ("an open *jubbah*") (with double *r*) because it has been opened (*infarajat*) at the wearer's front and what is beneath may be seen. They add a silk or other trimming, so that the beholder is amazed by the sight and the wearer finds it a true delight—glory be to Him who has embellished such people with elegant raiment, bestowed on them every kind of pleasant form as adornment, and made their women an embellishment! As the proverb has it, "The foundation is according to the builder, and all things resemble their owner," for men grow up according to their God-given natures to be as they ought, and the like of a thing attracts its own sort. In the same vein, I myself said:

I saw on his cheek both water and fire[136]
And, strewn about, those roses fair.
Said I, "Behold what my Lord hath wrought—
The like of a thing attracts its own sort!"

11.2.17 Next, the poet, realizing that the lice, nits, and other vermin present in the yoke of his *jubbah* were too many to be counted, decided to liken them to something resembling them in quantity and color, so he said:

11.2.18 *shabīhu l-nukhālah* ("are like bran"), which is the husks of wheat and barley that come to the top of the sieve when they are bolted. More information on this, and the etymology, are to come. This simile yields the likeness of the comparator from two perspectives. The first is that lice are white, and so is bran. The second is that, when they accumulate in heaps, they appear to the eye to be a lot, just as bran does. In other words, this is an appropriate comparison. The word *nukhālah* is derived from *nakhl* ("palm trees") or from *munkhal* ("sieve"). In *The Blue Ocean and Piebald Canon* it says:

The noun *nukhālah* is derived, as they recall,
From *munkhal* and *nakhīl*[137] and, finally, from *minkhāl*.[138]

Barley bran is the best for one because, if it is steeped in water and heated and someone suffering from chest pains drinks it, it will cure him, if the Almighty so wills.

11.2.19 *yajrufuhū* ("they shovel"): that is, the lice and the nits and their aforementioned relatives.

11.2.20 *jarīf* ("willy-nilly"): originally *jarfan*, because it is a verbal noun with the *alif* omitted, the *ī* being added for the sake of the rhyme; or it may be a rural form; in either case there can be no objection.[139] It is derived from *jarf* or from *mijrafah* ("shovel") or from *jarrāfah* ("shovel-sledge"). If it be said, "The poet ought to have referred the pronominal suffix of *yajrufuhū* to the nearest antecedent, namely, *nukhālah*,[140] and this would have been more appropriate," we say,

"He may have avoided using a feminine pronominal suffix for the meter, because, if he had used one, the line would no longer have scanned;[141] or it may be a case of truncation,[142] as in the line[143]

Gently now, Fāṭim![144] A little less disdainful:
Even if you would cut my rope, do it kindly!

"—or he may have been referring it to the 'husks of wheat and barley,' which are called collectively *nukhālah,* in which case it should be taken as an example of the suppression of the first term of a genitive construct,[145] so there can be no objection." And if it also be said, "One might understand from the poet's words that the lice and nits were confined exclusively to the yoke of his *jubbah* and there were none of them whatsoever on his body, in which case what would be the point in his complaining about them?" we would reply, "The answer may be that one might say that his words 'in the yoke of my *jubbah*' mean that *most* of the lice were accumulated in and had risen to the yoke of his *jubbah* and then, in their abundance, came to resemble bran when shoveled and that it does not necessarily follow from this wording that the rest of his body was free of them. Indeed, if they were present in the yoke of his *jubbah* in such quantities, then, a fortiori, there should be some on the rest of his body, for the body is where they live and derive their nourishment, by sucking blood and imbibing the body's wastes. In fact, it is the way of lice to spread first in the clothes, then expand throughout the body, sucking out the bad blood; and those that have had their fill climb up to the top of the body and stay there to take the air and rest, just as humans, for example, having eaten their fill, rest by keeping quiet and sleeping. This is their habitual way of behaving, according to custom, so the answer now is clear."

Question: How come the poet does not raise a complaint against bedbugs, ants, and gnats and omits all mention of them, despite the fact that each of these is responsible for great harm and injury? This question may be answered from several perspectives. The first is 11.2.21

that bedbugs, though plentiful—as the proverb has it, "The bedbug gives birth to a hundred and says, 'So few children!'"—in general favor only cities because of their tall buildings, the large quantities of timber there, and the plaster and lime with which they are coated, because it is in these things that they live and breed; whereas the country villages have no tall, costly construction. If they were to be found in a village, it would be in the house of the bailiff or the tax farmer, for example, to which the poet would never have access and in which he would never sleep. In fact, their houses are mostly made out of slabs of dung mixed with urine and of daub, to which dung cakes are sometimes added. As a result, they are unacquainted with bedbugs and do not see them and tend not to frequent the same places. Ants, though found in the villages of the countryside, nevertheless favor only those places in which there are fatty things such as clarified butter and oil, and they like sweet things, such as honey and sugar; they come to these and feed off them simply by smelling them, as mentioned by the author of *The Life of Animals*,[146] resembling in this the cumin plant, which can live simply on the prospect of being watered. As the poet[147] says:

> Don't treat me like the cumin in its plot,
> Whom promises content though it be watered not!

Our poet never saw any trace of ants in his house because it contained so few fats and sweets, or, rather, because there were none of these whatsoever. As a result, ants would have no way of getting to him, whether via his clothes or his home, and this would be the reason for their failure to affect him. As for gnats, though these are found in the villages of the countryside, they come just on certain days and then go away again, unlike lice and nits, whose harm is constant and unremitting, in clothes and elsewhere, as mentioned above; and the harm done by something that hurts a little and is absent a lot is insignificant, and this may be the reason for his omitting to complain about the lot of them. Thus the answer's clear.

Useful Note: If colocynth is steeped in water in which yarn has been thoroughly soaked and the place is sprinkled with that water while it is hot, it will kill the bedbugs and not one will be left, and if ants appear in a place where there are bedbugs, they eat them. As the poet says: 11.2.22

My body couldn't take another bug,
Their bite was giving me such pain.
I brought the ants. They helped me out—
They spared not one and let not one remain.[148]

Ants are repelled by the smell of tar, gnats by the smoke made by burning bran.

A Silly Topic for Debate: What is the wisdom in the fact that, if a louse bites a man or a flea or any other harmful creature stings him, the pain spreads through the body, outside and in, until it comes to embrace the liver, the lungs, the heart, and so on, even though the louse, the flea, and the rest do not have access to the inside of the body, unless one of them should enter through one of the orifices; and if, on some rare occasion, it should enter, it usually dies immediately, even before it reaches the interior of the body, as indeed a flea has often entered my own ear and stayed a while moving about and doing damage and then quickly come out or died? What is the explanation for this? The fatuous reply to this silly enquiry is: it may be said that the body experiences pain to the same degree internally and externally because the spirit circulates within it the way sap circulates in a green branch. Thus, if any damage is done to the body's surface, the spirit feels pain and the pain spreads to the whole body, outside and in. Let me draw you a facetious example, to wit, if a man is imprisoned in a small closet, for example, that is too small to hold anyone else and has no outlet and the man is locked up there for a long time, his body weakens, changes, and sickens and he feels pain both externally and internally, especially if he is pressed by the urge to urinate and does so until he fills the place, or if he farts there too 11.2.23

and the resulting odors rise upwards and then, finding no escape, come back down on his beard and mustache, causing him grievous harm, especially if he is the owner of a long, broad beard (as long as its breadth has not rendered its length odious, in which case the damage will be less, or it has not become less commode-ious, in which instance it is the same for both cases).[149] Thus the situation's now revealed, the silliness no more concealed.

11.2.24 Next the poet embarks on the description of another disaster that afflicted him—one yet more damaging, taken as a whole, than lice and nits, for it comes to him from the direction of his relatives. He says:

TEXT

11.3 *wa-lā ḍarranī ʾillā-bnu ʿammī Muḥaylibah*
yawmin tajī l-wajbah ʿalayya yaḥīf

And none has harmed me as much as the son of my paternal uncle, Muḥayliba—
the day the *wajbah* comes, he heaps upon me more than my lot.

COMMENTARY

11.3.1 *wa-lā ḍarranī* ("and none has harmed me"): that is, harmed me over and above what has already been mentioned.

11.3.2 *ʾillā-bnu ʿammī* ("as much as the son of my paternal uncle"): that is, my father's brother, *ʿamm* ("paternal uncle"), being derived from *ʿumūm* ("generality") because his competence encompasses both his own children and those of his brother, for he is like a father to them, if their actual father is not present. This is why the Arabs call the paternal uncle "father." One of the commentators on the words of the Almighty «When Ibrahim said unto his father Āzar,»[150] says, "What is meant is 'his paternal uncle.'" Or the word is derived from *ʿimāmah* ("turban") because of the latter's being high above the head, like a crown—as it says in the Tradition, "Turbans are the crowns of the Arabs"—for the paternal uncle has an exalted position with regard to his brother's children because of his responsibility for and guardianship of them.

Muḥaylibah: diminutive of *maḥlabah*, which is a vessel made of red earthenware with a concave belly and a narrow neck; it has one handle but is sometimes made with two, if it is large.[151] It is so called because milk is milked (*ḥalb*) into it, according to the rule of "naming the container after the thing contained." 11.3.3

A Brief Overview: Vessels prepared for milking are of different sorts. There is the *maḥlabah*, and there is the *miḥlāb*, which is itself of three sorts—small, large, and medium; the *miḥlāb* is taller than the *maḥlabah* and has a wider mouth and more slender belly; its bottom is like that of the jar in which the water is raised on a waterwheel (*qādūs*),[152] being very small. There is also the *rubʿ*, which is a small vessel that holds, as a unit of measurement, one quarter of a *maḥlabah*. And there is the *qarrūfih* (with *a* after the *q*, double *r*, *i* after the *f*, and no vowel on the *h* at the end).[153] This resembles the *miḥlāb* in having a small base, but has a narrow neck and a very wide belly, like the *maḥlabah*; it has either one or two handles. The largest of the milk vessels is the *qisṭ*, which is a large jar. There is also another vessel, called the *kūz*, with which milk is sold in the cities, as we have observed; it is crudely made and holds little. *Muḥaylibah* is of the measure of *mudawlibah* ("causing to go round and round"), *miḥlāb* of the measure of *dūlāb* ("waterwheel"), and *qisṭ* of the measure of *qibṭ* ("Copts"). It is called a *qisṭ* because it is divided up (*muqassaṭ*) by weight or volume. The word *rubʿ* is of the pattern of *surʿ* ("reins"), and *kūz* is of the pattern of *būz* ("muzzle") because its wide mouth resembles the muzzle of a cow or a calf; *kūz* is derived from *kazz* which means "to bite" (*ʿaḍḍa*);[154] one says the earth "bit" (*kazzat*) on the plow, when it seizes (*ʿaḍḍat*) it with the share, and the child "bit" (*kazza*) on his finger, when it takes it between its teeth (*ʿaḍḍahu*); so I find in *The Blue Ocean and Piebald Canon*. If milk or water is put in the *kūz*, it gurgles and moans, complaining 11.3.4

of the pain of the fire and all that it suffered when being turned into pottery.

> The mug makes a gurgle because it's in pain:
> It protests to the water what it suffered from the flame.

This would be according to the analogy of Fuṭays.[155] These vessels are well known to the people of the countryside, as are others, among them the *zīr* ("water jar")[156] and the *tumnah* ("one-eighth measure") and so on.

11.3.5 If it be said, "The definition and, in some cases, the etymologies of the names *maḥlabah* and *miḥlāb* and the rest such as *qisṭ*, *rubʿ*, and *kūz* have been given, but what is the meaning of *qarrūfih*, and how did this strange word come to be applied to this vessel and what was the occasion for that?" we reply that this question may be answered from a number of perspectives. The first is that this vessel was made at the time of the *qirr* (with *i* after the *q* and no vowel after the *r*),[157] which means "extreme cold"; then they completed (*wafaw*) its firing in the summer, and so it was called *qirrwafih*, that is, the firing of this vessel was accomplished (*wafiya*) and it was finished; then they put a *ū* after the double *r* of *qirr* and made a name for it out of all these letters and said *qarrūfih*. In this case it would be composed of a noun and a verb.[158] The second is that, when it had just been invented and the milker put it between his legs and directed the milk into it, the milk started to rise and make a lot of froth, so the milkman became afraid that the milk would overflow the vessel and called out to the milk *qarr fīh qarr fīh* ("Stay in it! Stay in it!"), that is, "Remain in it and be settled!" Then they added a *w* to the word between the imperative verb and the prepositional phrase, omitted the *ī* because it was awkward to pronounce, realized the *w* as *ū*,[159] and said *qarrūfih*, and that became its name. The third perspective is that the clay of which it was made was originally taken from a place close to the Qarāfah ("cemetery") of Cairo, so they started saying "a *qarāfī* vessel,"[160] then derived this name for it from that sense and said *qarrūfih*. The fourth is that it is derived from *qirfah* ("cinnamon") (with *i* after the *f*), which is a spice with a delicious taste and smell that is used in fine dishes and sumptuous foods, for milk too, when fresh from the cow, has an appetizing smell and sweet taste—as the Almighty has said, «pure milk, palatable to the drinkers»;[161] then they added a *ū* to it and made that its name. And fifthly, names cannot be etymologized, so there is no need for these fatuous investigations and inane fabulations. Thus the answer now's clear, the truth made to appear.

Various accounts are given for how the poet's paternal cousin came by this name. The first is that, when his mother gave birth to him, she heard one person say to another, "Fetch the milk crock!" so she named him thus, taking a good omen from the word and making it into a diminutive, seeing that the child was small. A second version has it that his mother had borne another boy before him and called him Miḥlāb, but he died. When she gave birth to this child, she did not want to call him by his brother's name, so she made the word feminine[162] and made it a diminutive and said *muḥaylibah*, and by this he was known. A third account has it that someone visited her with a new milk crock (*maḥlabah*) at the moment when she gave birth, so she took this as a good omen and said, "I shall call him Muḥaylibah." This is the extent of what I have learnt from these fatuous investigations and inane fabulations. 11.3.6

yawmin ("on the day when"): with *in* following the *m*, for the meter.[163] *Yawm* ("day") is a name for the whiteness of daylight that is illumined by the rays of the sun and during which one may undertake a legally meaningful fast, as is well known.[164] 11.3.7

tajī ("comes"): from the verbal noun *majī'* ("coming"), which means arriving at a place. 11.3.8

al-wajbah ("the *wajbah*"): this takes effect from the moment of the coming, or arrival, of the bailiff or the tax farmer or the Christian in the hamlet or the village, at which time it is distributed among the peasants on the basis of how many carats or feddans, etc., of land 11.3.9

each one works. Some are obligated to provide it one day a month, others once a week, and still others once every three days, etc., according to how many or few are the peasants and how extensive or limited is the land. It must be provided every day throughout the stay. Under this system, a man sees to the provisioning of the bailiff and the Christian, if the latter is present, and of all those belonging to the tax farmer's entourage, and undertakes to provide them with their food and drink and everything they need in the way of fodder for their animals and whatever dishes of meat or fowl they may have a liking for. If the man is poor, they impose this on him by force, or else the bailiff imprisons him and beats him severely. Sometimes a man will flee because he does not have enough to offer, and the bailiff then sends for his children and his wife and demands it from them with threats. A wife may pawn some of her jewelry or her clothes for a little money and use the proceeds to buy poultry or meat, and cook it and prevent her children from touching it for fear of what will happen to her if it is not enough for them. Sometimes a peasant will raise chickens and eat none of them and make himself and his children go without for fear of being beaten or imprisoned, and things such as chickens and butter and flour he will keep aside in readiness for this disaster, doing his own cooking with sesame oil and eating barley bread, and he may put his seed wheat aside for them and eat salty cottage cheese and put himself to the expense of buying sweet fresh cheese and send this with the *wajbah*, all for fear of what may happen to him because of these matters.

11.3.10 It is called *wajbah* because it has come to be like a duty (*wājib*) that the tax farmers impose on the peasants, for it has to be done for the bailiff in the village or the Christian or the tax farmer, if he comes, as stated above. While some tax farmers have waived it, they have replaced it with an agreed sum of money and added that to the land tax, forcing them to pay it to the bailiff in the village, the money being taken from them annually. It is a form of injustice, and eating such food is forbidden by religion so long as the peasants do not give it of their own free will and cheerfully,[165] the tax farmer keeping them happy by granting them a little land or something else in return. Some tax farmers have given it up altogether and impose nothing on them, neither for the bailiff nor anyone else, although they may volunteer something of their own free will. In that case, it is not forbidden and it is permitted to eat it. Similar to the *wajbah* is the fine imposed on the landless and putting them to work without pay, as long as this is without their consent, in return for covering their lodging and compensation for leaving their crops and so on. Anything that involves injury to others is forbidden. The poet says:

Be as you wish, for God is kind—
  No harm shall befall you if you sin.
Two things alone you must eschew in full—
  Ascribing partners to God[166] and doing injury to men.

If it be said, "If an emir, or someone else, on assuming the right to farm the taxes of a village, finds the *wajbah* or the fine on the landless or any other form of injustice on the ledgers of those who held the tax farm before him and so imposes that on the people of the village as was done under earlier determinations by the surveyors according to established custom, is the sin then his or that of the person who introduced the practice before him, or both of theirs together?" the answer is to be found in the Tradition of the Prophet, upon whom blessings and peace, that says, "He who introduces into this affair of ours that which is not in it is rejected," meaning, whoever introduces something that was not present in the time of the Prophet, upon whom blessings and peace—such things being called "innovation"—is rejected, that is, refused, meaning invalid and not to be taken as an example. This shows clearly that there is no difference between someone's introducing the practice himself and someone else having preceded him in this. Thus the sin pertains to everyone who acts in accordance with this practice or orders others to act in accordance with it, for everyone who performs an act that is not stipulated by the Law is a sinner, as stated in the words of the Prophet, blessings and peace upon him, "He who introduces into it 11.3.11

an innovation or provides accommodation for an innovator, upon him be the curse of God." The substance of the Tradition constitutes a response to those whose minds are corrupt and to government accompanied by ignorance, oppression, and other things of the same sort that are not in accordance with the Law. Thus the answer now is clear, the truth made to appear.

11.3.12 The poet's words *tajī l-wajbah* contain an elegant literary device called "distribution," which consists of the poet's "distributing" one of the letters of the alphabet in each, or most of, the words of a line of verse, as in the following verse by al-Ṣafī al-Ḥillī, may God have mercy on him, from his *Embellished Ode in the Prophet's Praise* (*Al-Badī'iyyah*):[167]

Muḥammadu l-muṣṭafā l-mukhtāru man khutimat
Bi-majdihī mursalū l-raḥmāni li-l-umamī

Muḥammad, the Named, the Nominated,
With whose majesty the messengers of the Merciful to men were made complete

—where he repeats the letter *m* in every word of the line. Our poet managed to work the letter *j* into just two words.

11.3.13 In the same vein is what happened once concerning a man who was a fryer of fish by trade. He was in love with a beautiful woman and had a young servant boy who was extremely quick-witted and a master of correct speech. One day he sent this boy to her to ask her to come to his home. The boy went to her home and told her that his boss wanted her. She accepted and was about to set off with him when her husband turned up. The boy made himself inconspicuous, took off without anyone noticing him, and made his way back to his boss, whom he found frying fish, as was his wont, with people all around him placing their orders. So as to make the man understand the situation while concealing it from those present the boy accosted him with words rhymed and metered. He said to him, *Yā mu'allimī fuq lī, min dha l-samak fa-qlī. Jat tajī fa-jā. Law lam yajī la-jat. Wa-lākin tartajī lammā yarūḥ tajī* ("Boss, hear my cry! Of this fish now fry! She was going to come, but he came. Had he not come, she would have come. But she hopes, when he goes, to come").

These words are to be explained as follows: 11.3.14

yā muʿallimī fuq lī ("Boss, hear my cry!"): that is, "Boss, hearken to what I say, and listen well to it and understand it!"

min dha l-samak fa-qlī ("Of this fish now fry!"): he came up with these words to make the people around think that he wanted a portion of fish or that he was asking him to hurry up with the frying (note the "augmentative consonantal paronomasia" between the words *fuq lī* ("hear my cry") and *fa-qlī* ("now fry")!).[168] 11.3.15

jat tajī ("She was about to come"): that is, she wanted to come and obey your summons 11.3.16

fa-jā ("but he came"): that is, her husband, at the moment that she wanted to go; then he said 11.3.17

law lam yajī ("Had he not come"): that is, her husband, 11.3.18

la-jat ("she would have come"), which is originally *la-jāʾat*, which the boy elided for the meter; that is, she would have presented herself and not disobeyed your order. He continues by saying: 11.3.19

wa-lākin tartajī ("But she hopes"): that is, her coming will be in accordance with her hope (*rajāʾ*), which means the occurrence of a thing agreeably to the will of the one who requests it 11.3.20

lamma yarūḥ ("when he goes"), meaning her husband, and leaves the place free 11.3.21

tajī (ilayk) ("to come (to you)"); and what you want will come to pass. The relevant citation lies in his words *jat tajī fa-jā*, etc., for he repeats the letter *j* in every word, as you can see. 11.3.22

If it be asked, "Is it forbidden by religion for the peasants to honor the Christian by coming and entertaining him and sending him the *wajbah* when he comes to a village to collect its taxes, 11.3.23

abasing themselves in front of him and obeying his every command and prohibition, most of them indeed being at his service, and are they sinning in so doing, or what is the situation?" we reply, "The response is that a Muslim is forbidden to serve an infidel, just as he is forbidden to honor him, submit to him, or abase himself before him, and the one who does so sins in that respect, unless he does so out of fear of some harm or injury from him as a result of the infidel's being set in authority over him and given charge of his affairs, or is compelled to have recourse to him in a matter such as the Christian's collection of taxes in the villages of the countryside and elsewhere, for they monopolize this business; indeed, some tax farmers hand control of everything to do with the village to the Christian, who rules it through beating and imprisonment and the like, so that the peasants are so frightened that they never come before him without trembling.

11.3.24 "As it happened in the days of the Master and Initiate of the Almighty, Shaykh Taqī al-Dīn Ibn Daqīq al-ʿĪd, God benefit us through him, when the sultan handed over control of the entire province of Egypt to a certain Christian for the collection of taxes. The latter used to visit the province with a great procession of servants and retainers and pass through the settlements collecting their taxes. He would ride his horse and dismount only when he had to eat and drink and stop for the night, so evil was he and so great the harm he brought. His horse had stirrups of steel plated with gold, to which he had attached two iron spikes that projected about a hand's breadth. He would summon someone and the man would come, trembling with fright, and stand next to his horse, while the Christian, from the back of his horse, would speak roughly and brutally to him, telling him, 'Pay the taxes you owe this minute!' If the man did as he was told that was that, but if he did not he would strike him with the spikes, stabbing him or slashing his sides, so that he died. Such was his way with Muslims, God's curse upon him! It happened that this same Christian went to the village of Shaykh Ibn Daqīq al-ʿĪd, God have mercy upon him, and summoned one of the shaykh's followers who had a balance to pay on the tax on land that he cultivated. When the man came before him, he said to him, 'Pay what you owe!' but the man replied, 'Give me till the end of the day.' The Christian was about to put his stirrups to work and strike him with the spikes and kill him when the man turned and fled, the Christian in hot pursuit, until he came to the shaykh and threw himself down before him. The shaykh, who at the time was burning lime in a kiln (for that was his profession when he was young), asked what was the matter and the man told him the story. Before he knew what was happening, the Christian was towering over him. 'Give him till the end of the day!' the shaykh told him. However, the Christian replied to the shaykh with angry words, at which the shaykh became filled with fury and zeal for the defense of the Muslims and attacked him, grabbing him by the neck of his garments, so that he became like a sparrow in the shaykh's hand. Then he said to him, 'Accursed wretch! Your life has been long and the harm you do to the Muslims has become excessive. Now your name is expunged and every trace of you obliterated!' and he bore down on him until his back snapped and he threw him into the oven of the kiln, where he was consumed. Then he directed a look of fury at the men who were with the Christian and God cast terror into their hearts and they turned and ran till they reached the sultan and told him of the matter. Incensed, the latter sent for the shaykh, who proceeded until he reached the audience chamber. When he presented himself before him, the sultan said to him, 'What drove you to burn the Christian?' 'And what,' replied the shaykh, 'drove you to put him in authority over the Muslims and order him to do them harm?' At this the sultan's fury increased, and he was about to strike the shaykh a blow on the head, when the shaykh made a sign to the chair on which the sultan was seated and it moved beneath him and he was spilled onto the ground in a swoon, and the chair itself started to spin through the Citadel with a humming sound, rumbling like thunder. The soldiers leapt up in confusion and the Citadel with all the troops that were in it shook, while they cried,

'Spare us! Spare us!' Then the shaykh made a sign with his hand, and everything returned to its place, after which he gestured towards the king, who awoke from his swoon and, when he had revived, kissed the shaykh's hands and said to him, 'Pardon, My Master! Ask of me what you will!' The shaykh replied, 'All I want from you is that you never again set a Christian in authority over the Muslims. Should you do so, you will perish.' 'I hear and obey!' said the sultan. Then the shaykh descended from his presence, to the accompaniment of the utmost honor and love, and proceeded to his village. Thereafter, this practice remained in abeyance for a while, and no Christian was set in authority over the Muslims with regard to the collection of taxes or other matters, until the rulers were forced to have recourse to them for their acuteness and talent for accounting; so they put them in charge of these matters up to our day. Similarly, the Jews have taken over the practice of medical science, so that the two groups have come to hold sway over our money and our lives. How well the poet put it when he said:

A curse on both Christians and Jews!
They've got what they wanted by stealth:
They've made themselves doctors and clerks
To divide up our lives and our wealth!

11.3.25 "Thus one is permitted to associate with them and obey them if he fears that they might harm him or his dependents in any matter, religious or secular, that depends on such contact and that he is compelled to undertake. Under such circumstances, there is no harm in making friends with them. Master 'Abd al-'Azīz al-Dīrīnī, God benefit us through him, was punished for frequenting the Christian of his village, and he said:

They blame me, my friends, for befriending Copts,
Though never, by God, did I love them in my heart!
But I'm one of those who hunts for his living in their land,
And hunter and dogs cannot live apart!

"On the other hand, the person who has intercourse with them on the basis of affection and friendship for no compelling worldly objective or fear of any harm that they might do should probably be counted among those referred to in the words of the Prophet, may God bless him and give him peace, 'He who loves a people shall be marshaled with them on the Day of Judgment.'"

'alayya ("to me"): meaning to himself and no other. 11.3.26

yaḥīf ("he does wrong (to me)"): that is, he turns against me and treats me unjustly, charging me with more than I can bear. This injury was more severe for him than the others, namely, the previously described harm caused by the lice and the nits and so on, because it originated with his relatives. The poet says: 11.3.27

> Relatives (*aqārib*) are like scorpions (*'aqārib*), so avoid them,
> And depend not on father's or mother's brothers.
> How many of the first will bring you grief
> And how devoid of good are the others!

Observe how this clever poet used *'amm* ("father's brother") and *khāl* ("mother's brother"), changing the letters on the first to make it into *ghamm* ("grief") and employing the second to mean that they are "devoid" (*khālī*) of boons, and how he managed to work in both paronomasia and punning.[168]

Another poet said:

> The enmity of kith and kin
> Is like a fire in a forest when there's wind.

'Alī,[170] God honor his face, said, "Enmity is among relatives, envy among neighbors, and affection among brothers." The origin of the enmity among relatives is to be found in the story of Qābīl's murdering Hābīl,[171] as a result of which enmity among brethren and relatives has continued down to these days of ours, the root cause of it all being envy—and "may the envious not prevail!"[172] In the Tradition it says, "Two alone are to be envied: a man on whom 11.3.28

God bestows wealth and who uses it to defeat his perdition through good works, and a man on whom God bestows knowledge and who instructs others in it." The poet says:

Though they envy me, I blame them not—
  Good men before me have felt the evil eye.
Let me keep mine and them keep theirs,
  And he who is the more vexed by what he finds can die!

And another said:

May your enemies not die but live
  Till you have had the chance to make them livid,
And may Fate not deprive you of an envier,
  For the best are those who've been envied!

11.3.29 Next the poet moves on from complaining about his paternal cousin Muḥaylibah to complaining about the latter's nephew Khanāfir, who brings him even more trouble than his cousin. He says:

TEXT

11.4 *wa-'ayshamu minnū 'ibnu-khūhu Khanāfir*
  yuqarriṭ'alā bayḍī bi-khulbat līf

And more inauspicious than him is the son of his brother Khanāfir.
He draws tight around my balls a palm-fiber knot

COMMENTARY

11.4.1 *wa-'ayshamu* ("and more inauspicious"): from *shu'm* ("calamity") or from *tayshimah*.[173] The word is originally *ash'am*,[174] on the pattern of *ablam* ("more/most stupid") or *aqṭam* ("more/most given to passive sodomy"). The proverb says, "More of a jinx (*ash'am*) than Ṭuways,"[175] and one says, "So-and-so is *mayshūm* ('possessed of the power to jinx')" or *dhū tayshimah*, that is, possessed of strength and tyrannical powers and capable of doing great harm to others. *Shūm* wood[176] is so called because of its strength and hardness. The Arabs use “jinxing and infamy” (*al-shuʾm wa-l-luʾm*) in their flytings.

It is said that Jaʿfar al-Barmakī built a magnificent palace and embellished it with all kinds of silks and so on and stayed there some days. Gazing one day through one of its windows, he beheld a Bedouin writing on the wall of the palace two lines of verse, as follows: 11.4.2

Palace of Jaʿfar, may ill fortune and infamy engulf you,
Till the owls in your corners make their nest!
When the owls nest there, from sheer delight,
I'll be the first to offer condolences, if under protest![177]

—so Jaʿfar said, “Bring me that Bedouin!” When the man was in front of him, he asked him, “What has driven you to do as you have done, and what has made you call down ruin upon our palace?” The man told him, “Poverty and need have driven me to it, and a brood of young lads that I have sired, like the chicks of the sandgrouse,[178] that whimper from the pangs of hunger. I came to beseech your charity and plead for your favor and I have dwelt a month at the gate of this palace, unable to come in to you. When I despaired, I called ruin down upon it and said, ‘So long as it remains prosperous, I shall benefit nothing by it. But if it turns to ruins, I may pass by and take from it a piece of wood or some of its embellishments that I can make use of.’” Jaʿfar smiled and said, “Our ignorance of your presence has prolonged your waiting and caused harm to your children. Give him a thousand dinars for seeking us out, and a thousand dinars for dwelling so long at our gate, and a thousand dinars for calling ruin down upon our palace, and a thousand dinars for our clemency towards him, and a thousand dinars for a brood of young lads that he has sired, like the chicks of the sandgrouse!” And the Bedouin took the five thousand dinars and retired, giving thanks.

minnū (“than he”): with double *n*, for the meter;[179] that is, “stronger and more extreme than him” in the harm he does me and his oppression of me. 11.4.3

11.4.4 *ʾibnu-khūhu* ("is the son of his brother"): that is, of the brother of Muḥaylibah, the latter being his brother on both his mother's and his father's side. He should have said *akhīhi,* as a genitive construct, but his tongue gave him no help in producing such a form because he was from the countryside, and it would have broken the meter, too.[180]

11.4.5 Next he states his nephew's name, by saying

Khanāfir: derived from *khanfarah* ("snoring") of the measure of *kharkharah* ("snorting") or *barbarah* ("jabbering"). One says, "So-and-so slept and snored (*khanfar*)," meaning that he stored up the breath in his throat and expelled it through his nostrils in such a way as to make a loud breath accompanied with snoring and snorting. Said the poet:

> He snored on sleeping through his nostril
> And thus he got this name—Khanāfir.

He was so called because he snored so much when sleeping. The paradigm is *khanfara, yukhanfiru, khanfaratan,* active participle *khanfūr,*[181] of the measure of *khanshūr* ("tough guy"), while Khanāfir is of the measure of *ʿabāyir,* plural of *ʿabūrah* ("sheep"). His brother's[182] name was Qādūs ("waterwheel jar"), of the pattern of *buʿbūṣ* ("goosing"); this Qādūs fathered two boys, Muḥaylibah and Fasāqil, and this Khanāfir was the latter's son, meaning the poet suffered harm from both his paternal cousin[183] and his paternal cousin's son.[184]

11.4.6 Next the poet makes plain the harm that he suffered from the latter by saying: *yuqarriṭ* ("he draws tight"): with *u* after the *y*, of the measure of *yuḍarriṭ* ("he farts audibly and repeatedly").[185] *Yuḍarriṭ* has two forms, as already stated.[186]

As the poet has it:

> There the snitches all farted together,
> So their farts wafted everywhere about.

The word *yuqarriṭ* is used here in the sense of constricting (*taqrīṭ*) strongly and forcibly with a rope. *Qarṭ* with *a* after the *q* and no vowel after the *r* refers to the *qarṭ* of the crops, namely, taking the ears and leaving the roots in the ground. One says, "So-and-so cut off the ears of so-and-so's crop (*qaraṭa zarʿa fulān*)." With *u* after the *q*, it is the name of a small ring of silver that is put in the ear of a young boy—a praiseworthy custom, especially if the boy is beautiful, for it adds to his good looks and clothes him in cuteness. Abū Nuwās[187] says in the opening line of one of his odes:

> An earringed[188] boy who hastens to the drinking companions
> With a carnelian in a white pearl

—that is, this graceful beauty and charming form, adorned with and characterized by this silver earring, now hastens towards the drinking companions, with a wine in his hand whose color resembles that of a carnelian, in a cup resembling in purity of substance and refinement of form a white pearl, and gives them to drink from what is in his hand and passes the wine among them, beguiling them with his slender figure and charming talk . . . and so on to the end of the poem.

ʿalā bayḍī ("around my balls"): that is, the poet's balls, not those of the person actually reciting the verse, nor the "balls" of anything else such as a chicken, a bird, or the like.[189] Testicles are called "eggs" because they resemble them if you peel the skin off them. The word is derived from *bayāḍ* ("whiteness") or from *abū buyūḍ* ("the one with the eggs"), an animal resembling a spider,[190] or from *bayḍat al-qabbān* ("the 'egg' of the steelyard", i.e., the counterweight). 11.4.7

A Silly Topic for Discussion: What is the wisdom in *bayḍ* ("balls") also being called *khiṣyatān* ("testicles (dual)"),[191] and what points of resemblance are there between the two in name, and what is their etymology and what does it mean? The Facetious Answer is that the singular of *khiṣyatān* is *khiṣyah* with *i* after the *kh*; and likewise the dual of *khiṣā* ("testicles (plural)") is *khiṣwān*, and one of them 11.4.8

is a *khiṣy*/*khaṣī*,[192] and if you were to take one *khaṣiy*, for example, and add another, you would have taken a pair of balls (*khiṣwayn*), no doubt about it! Understand this well! The same thing may also be called *khiṣw*, with *w* instead of *a*, which is also a word for the penis,[193] for the latter is like a father to the two testicles, because it never leaves them, and they are as two daughters to it; thus its name is derived from that of the subordinate entity because it is never separated from the latter. From this it follows that the two testicles are in a position of permanent submission to the male organ, while the latter is in a position of high standing over them and they likewise are in a position of dependence while it is in a position of upward mobility; and, additionally, they are in the position of annexation, while it is in the position of the elevated and erected vowels.[194] Further, the male organ has the power to open locked doors, assault fortresses, and knock at smooth domes, while the testicles politely wait for him at the entrance, which is a sign of the filial piety due to a father. In illustration of which, it once came about that a certain poet sought out a king in order to plead for his charity and found him to be in his garden. The poet stood by the gate and tried to gain entrance, but the guard prevented him. The poet then looked behind the wall of the garden and found a water channel running towards, and ending at a point beneath, the wall, where it debouched into a large basin, next to which he beheld the king sitting. So he took a piece of paper and wrote on it this verse:[195]

Everyone else, like a penis, has gone in,
But this slave, like the testes, is left lying at the door.

Then he folded it and put it in a Persian reed, sealed it with wax, and threw it into the channel, whence the water carried it until it cast it at the feet of the king. The king picked it up, broke the seal, and pulled out the piece of paper. When he read the verse he smiled and called out to him, "Come in, testicles!" to which the poet replied, "This is just evidence of your great capacity, God preserve you!"[196] The king was well pleased with the aptness of the joke and rewarded him, and the poet retired, giving thanks.

Apropos of the aptness of these words, I am reminded of what happened once when Sultan Qānṣawh al-Ghawrī, God have mercy upon him, got angry with a man and wanted to kill him. Some of those present interceded on his behalf, and the sultan imposed on him instead a fine of three thousand dinars. The man left the sultan's presence to get them and one of his friends, encountering him as he was descending the steps from the audience chamber, said to him, "I hear that the sultan has fined you a thousand dinars." The other replied, "No, may I be divorced—times three!"[197] When the sultan heard of this bon mot of his and how he had used the same word to cover both divorce and money, he pardoned him, forgave him the three thousand dinars, and rewarded him, and the man went his way. 11.4.9

The word *khiṣā* may also be applied to the male organ, which is also called *duldūl* ("dangler"),[198] *dhanab* ("tail"), *zubb*,[199] *ayr*,[200] *ghurmūl*,[201] and other names too. However, the best known are five, which I have mentioned in my treatise *Meadows of Intimate Vim concerning What Transpired 'twixt the Prick and the Quim*, namely: 11.4.10

They give me different names, some quite popular:
Ayr, *zubb*, *duldul*,[202] and *dhakar* there are.[203]
The fifth of these names I'm called is *khiṣā*—
When I get stiff, you'd think I was a shillelagh!

It is given the nicknames the One-Eyed, the Snub-Nosed, the Plugger, the Extender, and the Demolisher of Donjons and Conqueror of Castles, along with the *kunyahs* of Father of Campaigns, Father of Collisions, Father of Disturbances, Father of Earthquakes, and so on. If a man gives it free rein and obeys its whims, it will propel him into the most terrible calamities. Says Ibn ʿArūs, God have mercy upon him:

The people in God are lost,
    And praise of noble men spreads far and wide.
Naught hurts me but my belly
    And this thing that's dangling by its side.

The testicles may be likened to two hens. A certain poet made up the following lines to make fun of his shaykh:

O Lord, relieve us of our woe—O Lord!
    O Lord, seize upon our shaykh, of facial hair galore!
His testes when he's bended o'er
    Are like two chickens pecking grain up off the floor.

11.4.11 To sum up, *khuṣā* with *u*[204] and *khiṣā* with *i*, and likewise with *w* instead of the *ā*,[205] are names common to the male organ and the testicles, this falling under the rubric of "naming a thing according to its neighbors." The word *khiṣyatayn* is of the pattern of *ḍarṭatayn* ("two audible farts") or *shakhkhatayn* ("two pisses"), so it contains both farts and pisses for sure. Both words[206] are derived from *khuṣṣ* ("hovel") with *u*, or from a village named al-Khuṣūṣ,[207] or, for example, from the word *ikhṣā* ("bad dog!") that they use for dogs. The paradigm is *khaṣā, yakhṣū, khaṣā'an.*[208] As the poet says:

Khaṣā, yakhṣū are the base forms of *khiṣyatayn.*
    khaṣā' is correct in the verse of al-Ṭunayn.[209]

This brings these fatuous discussions and inane problems to an end.

11.4.12 *bi-khulbat līf* ("a palm-fiber knot"): that is, a strong knot going twice around his balls with a rope made of plaited palm fiber (*līf*), which is so called because it is wrapped (*multaff*)[210] around the bases of palm fronds. This knot is called a *khulbah* because it grasps (*takhlibu*) a thing that can then only be released from it with difficulty. In the jargon of shepherds, if they want to tie something tightly, they say, "Secure it with a clove hitch (*khulbat watid*, literally, 'peg knot')", that is, wrap the rope around it twice and tie it tightly so that it cannot come undone. It is derived from the *khalb* ("reaping") of crops, or from the *mikhlāb* ("talon") of birds, or from "deceptive" lightning (*barq khullab*), with *u* after the *k* and double *l*, meaning lightning that brings no rain.[211] Says Ibn al-ʿArabī, God benefit us through him:

All those who seek Your favor have been granted rain;
Your lightning has failed in its promise to me alone.

Next the poet mentions the reason his hair has turned prematurely white. He says: 11.4.13

TEXT

wa-min nazlati l-kushshāfi shābat ʿawāriḍī 11.5
wa-ṣāra li-qalbī lawʿatun wa-rajīf

And from the descent of the Inspectors, my side whiskers have turned white
and my heart is afflicted with pangs and trembling.

COMMENTARY

wa-min nazlat ("And from the descent of"): *nazlah*[212] is the instance noun from *nuzūl* ("descending") and is applied to a large company if it alights at a place and remains there a while. Thus one speaks of *nazlat banī fulān* ("the settlement of the tribe of So-and-so") and *nazlat al-ʿarab* ("the settlement of the Bedouin") and *nazlat al-ghawāzī* ("the settlement of the Ghawāzī"); hence also the village known as al-Nazlah.[213] *Nuzūl* means "the descent of something from higher to lower" and its opposite is *ṣuʿūd*, which means "ascent from lower to higher"; one says, "He ascended (*ṣaʿada*) to the top of the mountain and descended (*nazala*) to the lowest part of the land." Describing a mettlesome steed, Imruʾ al-Qays[214] says: 11.5.1

At once wheeling and turning, advancing and retreating,
Match for a boulder that the flood throws down from above.

11.5.2 *al-kushshāfi* ("the Inspectors"): plural of *kāshif*, so called because he inspects (*yakshifu*) the region placed under his charge and does away with whatever corruption and unauthorized imposts may exist there, and dams the waterways, strengthens the dikes, and rids the place of robbers; such was the custom of every Inspector in former times. He would behave righteously and make a progress around the settlements, and when he approached a village the drums would beat and those who had introduced unsanctioned practices and the corrupt would feel frightened and run away in fear of him and sometimes fall into his hands, in which case he would punish them as they deserved, whether by execution, imprisonment, beating, or fines. Then he would descend on the village, if it was his custom to stop there, and its shaykhs would come and stand before him in the utmost terror and fear, while he interrogated them concerning their affairs and asked them who was corrupt and who had introduced unsanctioned practices, and enjoined them to apprehend the latter if they were not in the village. Afterward they would hurry to bring him the customary food, drink, and presents. If any conflict had arisen among them in a village, or any killing, or they had shown disobedience to their Master, he would attack them on the viceroy's orders, lay waste to the village, kill those of them who deserved to be killed, and destroy the rebels and tyrants.[215] However that may be,[216] his presence in charge of the provinces constitutes a mercy, a shield, and a discovery of afflictions, provided no injury is done to people at his hands or at the hands of his soldiers by way of seizure of their property, harassment, or commanding them to provide food and drink beyond their capacity to do so. Should such things occur, it should be considered injustice and, as such, forbidden by religion, and whatever is taken should be returned to its owner (unless he had provided it of his own free will in the first place, in which case there is no objection).

11.5.3 His saying "the Inspectors," even though there would not be more than one of them, should be taken as implying the suppression of the first term of a genitive annexation,[217] whose implied sense would be "from the continuous descents of inspector after inspector, accompanied by the terror and fear that afflict me as a result of the beating of the drums, the stamping of the horses' hoofs, the Inspector's awe-inspiring demeanor when on progress and descending on the village, and the thudding of my heart at the sight of the soldiers, the retainers, and the torturers, and my fear that he should cause me injury on this account."

shābat ʿawāriḍī ("my side whiskers have turned white"): because of my inability to face the Inspectors and my having nothing for them to take from my house such as dung cakes for the kitchen or anything else. Consequently, my limbs tremble, my heart flutters, and white hairs sprout before their time. White hairs are a sign of the Almighty's favor, with which He honors one of His slaves. The first to grow white hairs was Ibrāhīm the Beloved,[218] blessings and peace be upon him. Half his beard turned white, and he said, "Lord, what is this?" The Lord said, "It is a token of your venerability in this world, and a light for you in the next." So Ibrāhīm said, "Lord, give me more of this venerability!" and he awoke the next morning and the whole of his beard had turned white. In the Tradition it says, "Verily, God would feel ashamed to treat harshly hairs that had turned white in Islam." White hair has many virtues, among which are that it is a sign of venerability in a person, as already mentioned, and a sign of dignity for him, and that it reminds him of his approaching end, for it is the harbinger of death. A poet says: 11.5.4

When a man's skin turns black and his hair turns white,
And his robe's too long in front,
And he takes short steps as he walks along,
Tell him then that he's close to defunct.

And another, putting it excellently, said:[219]

The smile of white hairs on the young man's cheeks
Forced tears from his eyelids to race.

And who would not weep for himself
When white hairs laugh in his face?

11.5.5 The lines contain "antithesis" in the wording,[220] as you will have noticed. Women, however, dislike white hair. Hārūn al-Rashīd asked his wife, "What kind of men do you women find attractive?" She replied, "One whose cheek is like my cheek and whose member is like my forearm." "And if his beard grows?" he asked. "He should keep his eyes to himself, and be ready with his wealth!" she said. "And if his hair turns white?" he said. "He must either put up with strife, or offer to divorce his wife!" she said—for this is something they condemn and the company of pretty women is denied to such men, especially if their money's tight, in which case their outlook's not bright. As the poet[221] said:

Ask me how women are, for I'm
Well versed in women's ways, a physician.
When a man's hair turns white or his money runs out,
Let him abandon all hope of their affection.

11.5.6 How much worse, then, for the man who has both—white hair and poverty! Such a one might as well not exist, as far as they are concerned. Al-Qāḍī al-Fāḍil,[222] God have mercy on him, said:

She wondered, when my wealth took off
Right when my hair had lost its hue—
"This thing I see," she said, "what is't?
Is it dust from some mill that I have in view?"
Said I, "Be not amazed! This is
The powder that from time's mill does accrue."

—that is, her mood darkened when she saw that white hair resembling mill dust had appeared upon his face and altered his beard, and she wondered at its sudden onset, a wonderment that necessarily plunged her into gloom and "rolled up the carpet of her conviviality." Then he answered her by saying, "Be not amazed" at how fast it has appeared—for the wondrous events that the passing of time brings and the disasters that result from these, which may be likened in their turning to a mill, have caused the appearance of these flecks that you see; so do not blame me, and patiently endure this misfortune that has befallen you. A poet[223] has compared the onset of white hair in the beard to the bird called the vulture because of the latter's whiteness[224] and compared the remaining part, in its blackness, to the "Ibn Dāyah" ("Son of a Midwife"), which is the black crow. He says:

When I saw the vulture mourn Ibn Dāyah
And roost in its two nests,[225] my heart felt pain at his loss.

Others have likened its onset to the appearance of the light of morning and have said that the way it "catches fire" in the blackness is like fire catching in thick, dry firewood. Ibn Durayd, may the Almighty have mercy upon him, says at the start of his *maqṣūrah*:[226] 11.5.7

Ah Gazelle, so like the oryx
'Twixt al-ʿAqīq and al-Liwā grazing,[227]
See you not how my head's color has mimicked
The dawn's gleam 'neath the skirts of darkness trailing,
And how the whiteness in the blackness has caught
Just as fire in a saxaul log breaks out blazing?
Methought it was some pitch-dark night
In whose expanse the morn, unloosed, turns all to light!

Similes of this sort for white hair are legion. The word *shayb* ("white hair") is derived from the *shaybah* ("artemisia") that is sold at the druggist's, because of its whiteness and the fineness of its roots and the way its hairs become entangled with one another, which is why they say, "They saw impurity in the artemisia" as a proverb.[228] The paradigm is *shāba, yashību, shayban* ("to turn white (of hair)"). The fact that he mentions that the sides of his beard turned white first is an indication that he was a man of stature and nobility, for the first thing to turn white on a noble man is the sides of the beard, 11.5.8

and on an ignoble man the hair between the lower lip and the chin. The poet says:

White hairs on the noble start at the whiskers,
On the vile above the chin.
White hairs on the head by worry are fed
And white hairs on the chest are a sin!

11.5.9 However, his restriction of mention of white hairs to those on the sides of his beard is arbitrary: they would begin at the edges and then progress ineluctably to the rest of his beard. In other words, he stated the root and the secondary phenomena follow as a matter of course. As for his adding the feminine marker *-t* to the verb, he follows in this the language of the country people, of whom the poet was one; and, in addition, had he said *shāba ʿāriḍī* or *shābū ʿawāriḍī*, the meter would have been thrown off. Thus he acted in accord with both his own speech habits and the meter.[229]

11.5.10 A Silly Topic for Debate: What makes him refer to the *nazlah* ("descent") of the Inspectors instead of their *nuzūl*, when a slow-witted listener might imagine that the former refers to the *nazlah* that afflicts a person when he catches cold that is, "catarrh,"[230] and then descends (*yanzilu*) in the head and gives rise to sneezing and sickness and so on, the treatment for which is to anoint the forehead with egg white mixed with mastic, which alleviates it? And what is the wisdom in his immediately following a reference to the sides of the beard with one to the heart, which is located far from the former and has no meaningful connection with them? Should he not rather have talked about his mustache and the hair on his lower lip, after the manner of the poet who said:

Up the ass of an unleashed bitch
Shove your mustache, plus the tuft below your lip!
Then lick her shit, good Connoisseur,
And spoon it, sip by sip!?

We respond: the reply is that *nazlah* is of the measure of *ʿijlah* ("female calf") and *nuzūl* is of the measure of *ʿujūl* ("calves"), and *ʿujūl* is a plural, so he used the lesser to stand for the greater; likewise the female[231] is more refined in form and feature than the male (albeit the male is more honorable)—not to mention that, to a peasant, the female calf or cow is more useful than the male calf or the ox. From this it may be deduced that the poet loved females rather than males, in contrast to the school of reprobates like us—for we follow the words of Abū Nuwās:[232]

I wonder at one who has sex with girls
When there's a beardless boy in sight.
Aren't we all agreed from the start
Your stallion's the better mount in a fight?

As for his mentioning the heart in the same breath as the sides of the beard, this amounts to no more than a shift in wording while the meaning remains the same, from the perspective that the spirit diffuses itself throughout the body, so that, if the heart experiences anxiety and suffering, this is diffused throughout the body and white hairs sprout in response to it; in which case, it would be a matter of "what is in proximity to a thing lends it its own stamp." Or perhaps it should be taken in the sense that people use when they say "my heart's hairs turned white," in which case it would be a metaphorical whitening of the hair, and there would be no grounds for objection. Thus the problem is now revealed, such silliness no more concealed. 11.5.11

The word *ʿāriḍ* is derived from the *ʿarḍī* ("headcloth, turban")[233] that one wraps around the head or from the *ʿarīḍah* ("crossbar") of a door, or from the *ʿarūḍ* ("prosody, verse-making") that afflicts a person as a result of being touched by the jinn,[234] or from the *ʿāriḍ* ("bank of clouds") that brings rain, or from the *ʿāriḍ* ("flank") of a mountain. As the poet says: 11.5.12

Halt in the Qarāfah[235] 'neath the flanks of al-ʿĀriḍ
And say, "Peace be upon you, O Ibn al-Fāriḍ!"

Or it may be so called because of its being spread sideways (*taʿarruḍ*) on the face. The paradigm is *ʿaraḍa, yaʿriḍu, ʿarḍan*, active participle *ʿāriḍ* ("to happen, to present, to expose").

11.5.13 *wa-ṣāra* ("and (my heart) is"): of the measure of *fāra* ("it boiled over"), from *ṣayrurah* (verbal noun of *ṣāra*), or from the *ṣārī* ("mast") of a boat, or from the *ṣurr* ("purse") that is transferred every year to the Two Sanctuaries.[236]

11.5.14 *li-qalbī* ("(to) my heart"): meaning the poet's heart and not anyone else's, as will be obvious to anyone with a fatuous mind.

11.5.15 *lawʿatun* ("pangs"): these are an intense burning and yearning of the heart from the agony of passionate love, or fear, or separation from the beloved and so on. As I said in the same vein:

Woe is me and alack for my pangs! Enough
That I endure deep wrenching sighs in my sorrows!

11.5.16 *wa-rajīf* ("and trembling"): of the pattern of *raghīf* ("loaf"); that is, a trembling, the pain of which cannot be stilled and the motion of which cannot be quieted, resulting from the terror that has afflicted me from the descending of the Inspectors and my fear of them, as previously described.

The paradigm is *rajafa, yarjufu, rajfan* ("to tremble"), like *gharafa, yaghrufu, gharfan* ("to ladle").

11.5.17 Next, the poet begins to talk of another disaster with which he and his fellow peasants are afflicted and which is the most severe of the grave matters that affect them. He says:

TEXT

11.6 *wa-yawmin yajī l-dīwānu tabṭul mafāṣilī*
wa-hurru ʿalā rūḥī mina l-takhwīf

And on the day when the tax collectors come, my joints give way
and I void my loose bowels over myself from the terror
they're creating

COMMENTARY

wa-yawmin ("and on the day when"): with nunation[237] 11.6.1

yajī ("comes"): the time for the collection of the taxes by 11.6.2

al-dīwānu ("the tax collectors"): This is one of those things of which they say, «And ask the village!»[238] that is, the people of the village. What happens is that, when the Christian arrives at the village or hamlet and divides up the tax into individual portions among the peasants according to the determinations made by the surveyors and the laws that are customarily followed and starts collecting them, fear, beatings, and the imprisonment of those who are unable to pay their taxes mount. A peasant may borrow money at excessive interest or take money against his crop before its ripening at a lower price than it will fetch when it is ripe, or sell his animal that provides milk for his children, or take his wife's jewelry—by force if need be—to pawn or sell, and pay the proceeds to the Christian or whoever is charged with collecting the tax. If he cannot come up with anything and cannot find anyone to give it to him, and the tax farmer or the bailiff fears that his impoverishment may lead to his land going to ruin and being lost to the village tax rolls, the latter will take the peasant's son and keep him as a pledge until he pays his taxes, or, if he has no son, his brother, or any of his relatives, or he may be put in prison to be beaten and punished so that the ordinances of the Almighty may be implemented against him. Some save themselves and flee under cover of night and never return to their homes, leaving their family and birthplace because of the oppressiveness of the taxation and the difficulty of their lives. As a poet said: 11.6.3

Life's bane is separation
From loved ones and from birthplace.

11.6.4 There is no escape, in any case, from paying the tax, even if that results in affliction and woe, for, as the well-known and widespread proverb says, "The sultan's taxes are extracted from between the nail and the quick," and the peasant remains in severe distress so long as he has any tax to pay, and the day he pays it off is, in his eyes, a feast day.

11.6.5 To sum up, peasants are of two sorts, one blameless and noble, one feckless and false. The first is intelligent and prudent, skilled at choosing to whom to entrust his affairs and at exercising leadership. Sober minded, he is as regular in his prayers and other religious duties as he is in attending to his crops and fields. He has no time for lounging by the wall and is eager to defend the interests of his family, while avoiding all that is base and mean. He supervises the planting himself and is present in person at the harvesting and picking. He resorts to neither surveyor nor sharecropper, and has recourse to neither cowman nor hired laborer. On the contrary, he directs all his affairs himself and knows the problems and underlying causes involved in each case. He pays regular visits to the bailiff and his Master and does not busy himself with destruction or corruption. If he takes money from a moneylender, he doesn't spend it on something perverse but rather on the well-being of his crops and animals and on servicing his obligations. He makes it his purpose to pay back his creditors and has compassion for the poor and the humble. He looks out for the well-being of his oxen, and respects his neighbor's field. He makes it his purpose to pay his taxes, and puts his trust in the High, the Exalted. He shuns the twirling of mustaches and sitting about on stoops, is blessed by the Divine Reckoner, and pays his taxes to the sultan. If the moneylender comes to him he pays him his due in full, and if he asks for a second loan, the moneylender gives it to him. His children live in comfort, and his Master is pleased with him. He lives in ease and piety, and the Lord of the Worlds is pleased with him.

11.6.6 As for the second sort, he is brainless and of service to none, naked and destitute. He neither prays nor observes any religious practices, nor is he obedient to the Lord of the Worlds. He lacks taste and understanding, is ever on the lookout for what's evil and disgusting, plays *manqalah* by day, and by night takes out his crowbar.[239] He spends little time in the fields, preferring to loaf by the wall. He is a mustache-twirler, a low earner, a scrounger, a ranter, a . . .,[240] and a braggart. Should any money come his way, he distributes it to blackguards and clods. He spends no time with bailiff or Master, but is sunk in perversity and corruption. His oxen starve, his horses waste away. He spends all his money on hubbub and hullabaloo, and his crops aren't worth a fart. He spends without logic and is broke, penniless, indebted, detested by his Master, sunk in his error and corruption. Though his Master were to whip him and break his bones, he would not leave off gallivanting in the houses and alleys. If his Master exhorts him to do what's right, he sets his heart on decamping, allowing his land to go to ruin. Forever caught up in spite and sorrow, imprisonment and beating have no effect on him. Haughty and perverse, an instigator of evil as great as the War of al-Basūs, incapable of paying what he owes, ever a thousand or two in arrears, a source of strife in his community, all his life he's in woe and misery. He does not repay the moneylender, and his judgment is unsound. His children are naked and his ways demented. He is the object of general loathing and "the like of a thing attracts its own sort." Thus his life brings no good, and no one weeps for him on his death, for his sleeves are long and he is a braggart, one who brings little joy to his household, a blackguard, a shit eater, without prospects in this world or the other. As it has been said:

> This is one who, alive, is of interest to none
> And who goes unmourned by his kin when he dies.

The first to establish apparatuses for the collection of taxes was Our Master ʿUmar ibn al-Khaṭṭāb, may God be pleased with him, and the first such apparatus in Egypt was created at the direction of Our Master ʿAmr ibn al-ʿĀṣ when he conquered Egypt,[241] though it 11.6.7

was not organized in a uniform manner. In his time, the land tax was low and so, when he conquered it (whether by treaty or by force of arms, according to the different opinions),[242] he collected enormous wealth from it, beyond counting, in the form of treasures and other things. Hishām ibn Ruqayyah al-Lakhmī says[243] that when ʿAmr ibn al-ʿĀṣ conquered Egypt he said to the Copts of Egypt, "I will kill anyone who conceals from me a hoard of treasure that he possesses and that I subsequently manage to obtain." He also mentions that ʿAmr was told that a Copt from the Ṣaʿīd called Buṭrus was in possession of a hoard, so he summoned and questioned him but the man denied it. Then he imprisoned him and every so often ʿAmr would ask concerning him, "Have you heard him asking for anyone?" "No," they said. "But we have heard him ask about a monk from al-Ṭūr." So ʿAmr sent to Buṭrus and took his seal and wrote to the monk in Coptic as though he were Buṭrus, urging him to tell him about his money and the place in which it was kept. He wrote what he wanted and sent it with a Copt whom he trusted. The messenger returned with a Syrian pitcher sealed with lead, which ʿAmr opened, finding inside a sheet on which was written, "Your money is beneath the big fountain." He had the water blocked off and removed the tiles that were at the bottom, and there he found fifty-two sacks of red gold coined at the mint of Egypt. So he took the money and had Buṭrus beheaded at the door of the mosque. The End.

11.6.8 The poet's application of the term "the moneys collected" to the tax-collection apparatus (*dīwān*) because the latter is their destination is an example of "nomination by destination." It is called a *dīwān* because it is there that religion (*dīn*)[244] is upheld through the exposition of the Truth and the exaction of the rights of the oppressed from the oppressor; or because of the presence there of what the king has registered (*dawwanahu*); or because it brings together different types,[245] in the same way that a book bringing together the odes, strophic poems, and epigrams of an individual poet is called a *dīwān*. Whatever the case, the descent of the tax collectors on a village is a terrifying matter for the peasants and a disaster for the impoverished, and the poet, God have mercy on him, was one of the impoverished and penniless who are behind on the sultan's taxes, as will appear below in his words "Almost all my life on paying the taxes and their woes . . ." and Fate and Time had turned on him and driven him to this state, as already mentioned. Consequently, he says of himself, "If the tax collectors arrive, or are on the verge of arriving, fear enters into me, terror overwhelms me, the mightiest of disasters catches me by surprise, and a great agitation overtakes me because of my lack of any money to provide towards the sultan's taxes, or for fear of punishment and imprisonment." For this reason:

tabṭul ("give way"): that is, go loose, cease to function, and become almost useless. 11.6.9

mafāṣilī ("my joints"): plural of *mafṣil*, which denotes a little gap between two bones, held together by sinews; should these sinews cease to function and go loose, they no longer do their job and the limb becomes nearly useless. The term *mafṣil* was employed by Abū Nuwās[246] in the verses he composed on his deathbed: 11.6.10

Naught remains but a faltering breath
  And an eye with pupil pale
And a passionate lover whose heart with fire
  Still burns, yet cannot tell the tale.
No limb has he, no joint (*mafṣil*)
  Without travail.
His elegy is spoke by those who revel in his state—
  Alas for him whose elegy the malign orate!

Moving on, our poet draws attention to what befell him as a result of his inability to pay the tax that he owed, of the Christian's refusal to grant him a delay or take pity on him, and of the inevitable consequences in terms of the weakening of his joints from the great fear and agitation and the loosening of his bowels, as generally happens to certain people. 11.6.11

11.6.12 He says: *wa-ahurru ʿalā rūḥī* ("and I void my loose bowels over myself"): that is, over my own person, not over the spirit (*rūḥ*) that courses through my body,[247] from the great agitation and the affliction of

11.6.13 *al-takhwīf* ("the terror they're creating"): that is, the terror being created by the followers of the Christian or the bailiff, and the fear that affects me, meaning that my bowels go soft as a result of the spasms caused by this affliction and the severity of the resulting agitation, so that the excrement comes out soft, like semi-liquid mud, when before it was so hard that if you flung it against a wall it would bounce back in your face. As a result, it runs over my person and my clothes, and my fear is so acute that it makes it spurt out too rapidly for me to control its eruption. *Hirr* ("tomcat") is the singular of *hirār*,[248] of the pattern of *jirār*, plural of *jarrah* ("jar"), deriving from the expressions *harr ʿalayka al-ḥimār* ("The donkey voided its loose bowels all over you!") or *harr ʿalā liḥyatika al-kalbah* ("The bitch voided her loose bowels all over your beard!") or *harr ʿalā dhaqinika* ("He voided his loose bowels all over your beard!"), for example. One also says *harr al-turāb* ("The dust piles collapsed") and *harr al-raml* ("The sand piles collapsed"), when they accumulate in heaps and flow spontaneously downward. Thus, if you look at piles of sand, you will observe *hurār* there for sure.[249] Or it may be derived from the *hirrah* ("she-cat") that hunts the mouse and which in the Hijaz they call *bussah*, with *u* after the *b*, and in the language of the people of Egypt, *quṭṭah*. The paradigm is *harra, yahirru, hirāran*.[250]

11.6.14 Next, the poet calls attention to the fact that the only course left open to him after his joints have gone weak and his bowels loose because he is so scared is to flee from the events that afflict him and disappear. So he says:

TEXT

11.7 *wa-ahrab ḥidā l-niswān wa-ʾaltaffu bi-l-ʿabā*
wa-yabqā ḍurāṭī shibha ṭablin ʿanīf

And I flee next to the women and wrap myself in my cloak
    and my farts are like a loud drum

COMMENTARY

wa-ahrab ("And I flee"): that is, I and no other person 11.7.1

ḥidā ("next to"): originally with long *-ā'* and *dh*,[251] but used here in the form with *d* in accordance with the dialect of the countryside, but he has shortened it for the meter. To be *ḥidhā'* a thing means to be alongside it or facing it. 11.7.2

(a)l-niswān ("the women"): that is, with them or facing them. The word also has the plurals *nisā'* and *niswah*,[252] derived from *ta'annus* ("friendliness"), or *uns* ("friendliness"), or *mu'ānasah* ("intimacy"), since, when Adam, God's blessings and peace be upon him, saw Eve, he felt friendly towards her (*anisa ilayhā*) and ran to her. Consequently, one finds that men run after women and are drawn to them, for they are the acme of desire, the fragrant nosegays of men's hearts. It is said that a man once passed a beautiful woman and recited: 11.7.3

Women are devils created for us—
    God save us from those devils' ways!

To which the woman replied:

Women are nosegays created for you—
    And all of you love to sniff nosegays!

Niswān is of the pattern of *jirwān* ("puppies"), *niswah* of the pattern of *qahwah* ("coffee") or *'ajwah* ("pressed dates"), and *nisā'* of the pattern of *kisā'* ("clothes"); *fusā'* ("silent farting") may also be a contributing element.

The meaning is: "I am afraid for myself and am frightened at what has befallen me, so while in this state I go off quickly, and 'flee,' that is, make a quick departure, towards 'the womenfolk,' and hide myself among them" or "I sit next to them or facing them," as in 11.7.4

the proverb "Half of valor is knowing when to flee." Even ʿAntarah, for all his strength and courage, fled, saying, "I would rather be reproached for this than be killed!" for if anyone is in fear of an oppressor or of one who might do him harm and he is able to free himself from his clutches by fleeing, he may do so. The Almighty has said, «Cast not yourselves into perdition!»[253]

11.7.5 If it be said, why did the poet choose to take refuge with the women rather than the men, even though women are incapable of fending off harm and injury or of protecting any person who might be taken from their midst because of their weakness and inability to fight, we would reply that the answer may be from either of two perspectives. First, that, when this disaster took him by surprise and the tax collectors arrived unexpectedly and his joints went loose and he suffered an attack of the trots, he shat all over himself, as explained above, and was unable to stand up or make his way towards any man with whom he might hide himself or towards any place far from the village in which he might conceal himself, because he was so scared and was shitting on himself so much—and indeed farting on himself, the latter being, as we shall see, a concomitant of the former—and when he saw these women near him, or near the place where he was, he concealed himself among them. Second, it may be understood from what he says that he was weakhearted and a coward, incapable of standing up to or trading blows with others, or of any other type of men's business, and that he was afraid that if he went to any of the people or to any of his relatives, they would direct the Christian to him, and the latter would take him and use him ill, and take his revenge on him; for the peasants give one another no quarter and do not maintain kindly relations among themselves, especially where relatives are concerned, as previously noted[254]—and everything has a foe of its own kind. As the poet says:

> Everything has a foe of its own kind—
> Even iron is attacked by the file!

Additionally, women are not implicated in this business, so no one who saw them congregated in a place would suspect that they had a man in their midst, unless some circumstantial evidence should happen to give him away, and propriety would probably prevent anyone from searching them. Our Master Ḥassān,[255] God be pleased with him, hid among the women during certain raids because of his cowardice and lack of courage, as mentioned in the various biographies of the Prophet. Thus the answer now is clear. 11.7.6

Subsequently, since his taking refuge among the women required something to actually conceal him from his enemies and hide him from sight, he says:

wa-ltaffu bil-ʿabā ("and wrap myself in my cloak"): that is, "when I am seated in the midst of the women, or next to them, or opposite them, I wrap myself in my cloak (*ʿabā*), or I lie down after wrapping myself in it, in order by so wrapping myself to rid myself of my fears"—for one who is frightened will conceal himself in anything that he sees, be it a cloak or a robe or anything else that may hide him from sight. He may even go so far as to dress himself as a woman and so disappear from the sight of his enemies and be saved by the Almighty. 11.7.7

It once fell out that a certain king was searching everywhere for a rebellious subject in order to kill him and was told, "He is in such and such a village." So he sent one of his officers after him with a contingent of soldiers, who entered the village and surrounded it. When the man realized that they wanted to take him to the king, he put on women's clothing and went out among a throng of women, all of them wailing and weeping and shrieking. "What's the matter with those women?" asked the officer. "Ask them what they're doing!" So a company approached them and questioned them, and they replied, "A relative of ours has died in another village and we wish to go to him," and they allowed them then to pass and they proceeded—the fugitive, unknown to the officer, among them—until 11.7.8

the man had passed through the soldiers and gone his way and the Almighty saved him.

11.7.9 A similar incident once befell me when I was in a ship traveling from my town, Shirbīn, to Cairo.[256] We were passing by a village called Masīd al-Khiḍr[257] when a good-looking youth appeared, handsomely dressed in the uniform of an emir's servant, who cried out to the ship's captain, "Take me with you!" and beseeched and implored him in great distress to take him on board. The captain, however, refused, fearing that someone might be coming after him looking for him or following his tracks. At the same time, there were three women in the boat, one of them elderly. "Captain," said the last, "a young man in distress asks you to take him with you, and you do not accede to his plea or have mercy on him? Pull in to the shore, take him, and I'll come up with a trick to hide him from those who're looking for him. I'll conceal him among my daughters and no one will know who he is!" So the captain did as she said and took the youth on board. Once on the ship, he informed us that he was in the service of an emir and that he had duped him and fled and that he was certain to come after him. "Take off your clothes!" the woman told him, so he took them off. Then she took them and hid them among her things and dressed him in women's clothes and sat him next to her. While we were thus engaged, an emir appeared riding a horse, spurring it on for all he was worth, men and slaves behind him, till they drew abreast of the ship and he said to the captain, "Pull in to the shore so I can search you! A serving boy of mine has just now fled, taking with him a thousand dinars that he stole." The woman told the captain, "Pull in and don't be afraid!" so the captain pulled in to shore and everyone on the ship was frightened at what was going on. The emir and his helpers boarded and searched the ship, while the woman exclaimed, "We saw nothing of the sort! What we did see was a young man in the distance running in such and such a direction." Propriety and lack of grounds for suspicion prevented the emir from searching the women, so he left the boat empty-handed, but the young man stayed with us on the boat until it reached Cairo, and he went off to his family, safe and sound.

The poet, seeing this cloak (*ʿabāʾah*),[258] enveloped himself in it and wrapped it around himself. *Laff* ("wrapping") means enveloping oneself in something and wrapping it around oneself several times. In the language of the country people, the word is also applied to eating: one says, "So-and-so 'wrapped' (*laff*) a crock of lentils" or "a crock of *bīsār*," meaning "he ate it." And one says *dāhiyah taluffak* ("May a disaster consume you!"), for example. The poet enveloped himself in the aforementioned *ʿabāʾah* so as to trick anyone who saw it into thinking that it was just a folded cloak and not suspect that there was anyone inside it. The *ʿabāʾah* is a long, wide garment made of wool with varicolored stripes, which the country people use as something to lie on in summer and as a cover in winter.[259] Thus it is well suited to both seasons and is the most sumptuous bedding and covering that they have. The term *ʿabāʾ* is used in the verse of Our Master al-Ḥusayn, may the Almighty be pleased with him: 11.7.10

Wearers of the *ʿabāʾ* are we, the five of us;[260]
We hold sway over east and west!

ʿAbāʾah is derived from *ʿabb al-māʾ* ("he gulped the water") because it "gulps it up" (*taʿubbuhu*) if it is thrown into it, or from the *ʿubūb* ("billows") of the river in the days of the Nile flood,[261] or from the *abū ʿubayyah* ("the one with the little cloak"), a nickname that the women of the countryside give to certain small chicks. The paradigm is *ʿabba, yaʿubbu, ʿabban*. 11.7.11

wa-yabqā ("and (my farts) are"): that is, are while I am in this state in which I find myself, namely, that of having loose bowels and with my sloppy stools running all over me from the insecurity and the terror while I am wrapped and enveloped in that cloak . . . 11.7.12

ḍurāṭī ("my farts"): that is, the sounds made by the wind resounding harmoniously in the belly as a result of eating lentils and *bīsār*, 11.7.13

when expelled by the pounding of my members and the shaking of my heart, are . . .

11.7.14 *shibha* ("like"): that is, resemble the sounds made by the beating of . . .

11.7.15 *ṭablin* ("a drum"): meaning a hide mounted on wood or copper beaten during processions and on joining combat; it makes a loud noise and creates great terror and is permitted by religion in all its forms except for the *kūbah*, which is a small drum with a narrow neck also known as the *darābukkah* ("goblet drum"), and the *ṭabl al-riqq* ("tambourine"), which is used by singers—these belong to the category of instruments employed for frivolous purposes. Likewise, all types of wind instruments, except the trumpet, are forbidden by religion.[262]

11.7.16 *ʿanīf* ("loud"): that is, beaten hard; one says someone "dealt harshly with" (*ʿannafa*) another, meaning that he beat him or disciplined him. The meaning is that the sound of that wind that exits from his belly and is called farting resembles the sound of a drum beaten vigorously and forcefully, according to which analysis the adjective would refer to the one beating rather than the thing beaten.[263] Or it may be that by "a loud drum" he means a big one, such as the kettledrum or the like, since he knows no other.

11.7.17 To give a brief overview of this word, farts fall into four categories: first, the fart that emerges delicately, with a feeble sound, and is of extended duration; second, the fart that circulates, rumbling, in the belly, then emerges as wind with no sound; third, the fart that emerges mixed with feces and makes a sound like a water pitcher when it is full; and fourth, the fart that emerges violently, with a loud noise that strikes terror into the heart, this last being the one to which the poet so frankly draws our attention. And each of these four categories has a cause by which it is occasioned.

11.7.18 The first is caused by refined airs that are generated in a person's belly, then emerge, as per their particular state and degree of feebleness, from between the buttocks, with a sound as delicate as they are refined, their delicacy being attributable to the refinement of the dish consumed. As the poet says:

The fart of the beloved emerged delicately
And with refinement, for his food was refined.

This type of fart emanates from people with refined bodies and from eaters of light foods.

The second is the fart that circulates, rumbling, in the belly, and 11.7.19
sometimes comes to a stop right in the middle of it, not moving until the sufferer has almost perished, then proceeds with distentionary strength and loud rumbling to the extremities of the belly. This sort causes injury. It is known to physicians as an "unripened fart" and is generated by coarse foods. If it ripens, it emerges at speed, and if any part of it emerges before it has ripened, it does so as an inaudible fart, in which case the subsequent emergence of the audible fart is of rare occurrence. The poet says:

He eats any-old-how all day,
And at night you find his belly rumbles.

A man once went to a doctor and told him, "I feel the collywob- 11.7.20
bles and a rumbling in my belly." The doctor told him, "As to the collywobbles, I couldn't venture an opinion, but as to the rumbling, it's an unripened fart." If the wind circulates in the belly without rumbling but with acute pain, it is called colic and is treated by consuming a quantity of wormwood or thyme boiled with sugar for breakfast; it may last an entire day or an entire night. It happened that Ibn al-Rāwandī, may God excuse his sins, was afflicted by such a colic for an entire night and passed the time imploring the Almighty to send him relief in the form of a single fart, but such was not vouchsafed to him. First thing in the morning he went out supporting himself on a stick he had and heard a man saying, "Lord, send me a thousand dinars!" Ibn al-Rāwandī said to him, "You crass fool! All night long I've been asking Him for a single fart and He

didn't give it to me, and you think He's going to send you a thousand dinars?" Then he left him and went his way. For these reasons it is called "low-emission colic."

11.7.21 The third is the fart that emerges mixed with feces and is caused by the winds mixing and blending with the excreta just before they emerge, the two coming together as one relieves himself, especially if the bowels are loose. As a result, noises that are staccato and non-legato are to be heard, resembling the gurgling of a water pitcher when full. These are caused by emissions from the bloating of the stomach and relaxation of the bowels consequent to taking food that is too easily digested, followed by its copious, rapid descent. As the poet says:

When a man's in a shithouse all on his own,
  The emissions of his bloat will surely be heard.
Thus the man of good sense will pretend he heard naught,
  While the moron can have the farts up his beard!

11.7.22 Sometimes a fart will emerge with a delicate sound like the mewling and humming that a spindle makes as women spin with it. Such a sound once emerged from a certain poet and when his companions chided him for it he said:

This is a child of my belly who came out crying,
  "I've lost me a spindle. It's quite disappeared."
And if anyone says to me, "Stifle your farts!"
  I'll bury my shit deep in his beard!

The poet makes the stomach the mother and the fart within it the daughter who leaves her mother and who starts crying and mewling like a spindle on being separated from her. From this it is to be understood that he is to be excused, and he who does not excuse him is ignorant of his state and the poet's shit will be in his beard.

11.7.23 A fart may come without warning, as when one lifts something heavy, or makes a great leap, or stands up suddenly, but in such cases the sound is not as long as in the others, and such a fart is less harmful than the preceding. For instance, it happened that a Bedouin poet once let out a sudden loud fart, and his companions reproached him. The Bedouin then proceeded to recite the following:

I farted but by that did nothing unknown to mankind,
Nor did my anus commit some sin of which I should repent.
Since all the world's anuses are given to farting,
Who can reproach me for such an event?

And once two men went before a judge, and one of them stepped forward and made his complaint against his companion and presented his story. While he was speaking, however, he farted, so he turned to his backside and said to it, "Either I speak or you do!" 11.7.24

Nifṭawayh relates, on the authority of Ḥakīm ibn ʿAyyāsh al-Kalbī, that delegations from Quraysh and the Bedouins met with ʿAbd al-Malik. While the latter was holding audience, a Bedouin of whom ʿAbd al-Malik was particularly fond came in. ʿAbd al-Malik was delighted and said, "A happy day indeed!" and seating the man next to him called for a bow, with which he took a shot. Then he passed it on to the next man on his right, who in turn took a shot, until it came around to the Bedouin. When the Bedouin pulled hard on the bow, he farted, and threw it down in embarrassment. ʿAbd al-Malik said, "The Bedouin has put us to shame! We were too greedy for his company, but I know that the only thing that will settle his problem is food." Then he called for the food tray to be brought and said, "Come forward, Bedouin, and fart!" though what he meant to say was "and eat!" The Bedouin said to him, "I have already done so!" to which ʿAbd al-Malik responded, "We belong to God and to God we shall return! We have indeed been tested today! By God, I shall make it something to remember! Page, bring me ten thousand dirhams!" The page brought them, and ʿAbd al-Malik gave them to the Bedouin, who, when he received them, was consoled and rejoiced and forgot what he had let slip. At this Ḥakīm ibn ʿAyyāsh al-Kalbī recited: 11.7.25

A farter from ʿAbd Qays lets one rip,
And the Commander gives him a ten-thousand-dinar tip?
Some fart, to net so much!
Some fart, to make a pauper rich!
We all would happily fart as one
If that fart would net one tenth of that sum.
If a thousand per thousand's the going rate,
Just hear me fart, God set the Commander straight!

ʿAbd al-Malik smiled and rewarded Ḥakīm ibn ʿAyyāsh with a like amount.

11.7.26 And it is said that al-Ṣaghīrī[264] approached an emir when the latter was holding a salon and wanted to speak but farted instead and turned away in embarrassment. One of those who heard him then said:

Tell al-Ṣaghīrī when he turns away fast
At a fart like a flute playing to the oud,
"'Tis but a wind you cannot control,
Since you're not Sulaymān son of Dāʾūd!"[265]

11.7.27 These are all examples of savoir faire and of how to draw a veil over the faults of others and find excuses for a member of a gathering if he farts unavoidably, to spare him the embarrassment and the ridicule of the unforgiving that he would otherwise have to endure. This is why they tell the following riddle about a fart:

One newly born, whose mother never bled,
Who has no life and does not stir.
All guffaw, though she's not seen,
But her owner doesn't laugh—he's too ashamed of her.

If, on the other hand, the farting is a deliberate act on someone's part and not because of an indisposition or an illness, then it's disgusting and bad-mannered and shows contempt for those sitting in the gathering, and the one who farts there behaves inappropriately even if he is trying, for example, to be funny.

We have observed in the villages of the countryside that, if a person farts unexpectedly at a gathering, he suffers enormously at the others' hands, and they force him to prepare them food. Sometimes they make him a mark in whitewash or lime on the wall next to where he was sitting so that everyone may see and know that he farted on that spot. On occasion he may even leave the village because of the reproach they heap on him for what he did, all of which arises from the coarseness of their natures, the worthlessness of their characters, their intolerance of farters, and their indifference to their embarrassment. However that may be, anyone who farts involuntarily is to be excused, especially if stifling the wind would cause him discomfort, even if he is in company. In such circumstances there is nothing wrong with his farting there, and he should be forgiven by reason of his indisposition. 11.7.28

I saw in a book that the reason that Ḥātim, God benefit us through him, was given the nickname "the Deaf"[266] is that a woman came to ask him about something and, when she spoke, an audible wind came out, so she was embarrassed and fell silent. Ḥātim told her, "Raise your voice when you speak, for I am deaf!" as a way of sparing her embarrassment. The woman rejoiced and was convinced that he had not heard her fart. Then he became known for that, God be pleased with him. 11.7.29

And once it happened that I loved a youth,[267] comely of person, refined of personality, honeyed of tongue, tender of limb, most wonderful in beauty, most winsome in coquetry. Infatuated with his charms, hankering for his arms, ever alert to be alone with him for a space and for fortune to cast us together in some place, I happened across him in a meadow whose fragrant plants exuded balm, whose birds filled the air with song under many a towering palm, where proudly he strolled in garments of glory with to his gait a delectable twist—and how much sweeter a chance encounter than any tryst! I greeted him in open fashion, revealed to him my passion, and asked him to sit down, with which request he complied—and ah, how sweet it is when lovers sit side by side! Then, after we'd settled 11.7.30

ourselves and taken our place, and I wanted to take advantage of his compliant grace, among those meadows all in bloom, and all that fragrance and perfume, and to enjoy his converse sweet and pure, and accents of supreme allure, along came a bunch of those whose persons are coarse and natures gross, who sat down without invitation, and plunged without manners into conversation. The youth felt shy and hung his head, assailed by rage and dread, but as he made a move to flee a sound escaped, involuntarily. They mocked him then and left without more ado, making disparaging comments as they did so. He looked at me, his eye with kohl bright, his face a lovely sight, and said, "What say you to the chidings of those boors?" And thus did I recite:

11.7.31 They chided the beloved, unaware
Of what he meant by what he did
When he displayed his scorn for his companions,
Showing that from him their churlishness was no way hid,
And thought it best to speak sweetly with them,
Employing a subtle utterance, like honey,
Though this was lost on them, since they
Were men of coarseness and ennui.
He called out to them from his buttocks
With a delicate sound, unpremeditated—
11.7.32 Something to match their condition
And their most lowly state;
And so they left a gathering
That gazelle and ghazal did unite—
May we ne'er be deprived of a fart
That can put such ills to flight!
It came out sweetly, and cleared the place
Of censors and their displeasure,
So praise be to God for getting rid
Of a burden that's now gone forever!
11.7.33 So fart, sing, and be happy,
And roam, brave lad, and be gay,

In a meadow, oh so lovely,
  Where joy has come to stay!
So long as you're willing to have him,
  Your slave will ne'er avert his face—
But, by the Chosen One, swear
  That you'll take none else in my place!

At this he smiled, revealing teeth like a pearly line, his willowy body close to mine, and said, "Nay, by Him who split the grain[268] and planted in your heart love's tree, I'll never break this oath of mine—no third shall come between us till the end of time!" And so we remained, he with me, till he joined the Lord of Majesty.[269] 11.7.34

An amusing story relates how Sultan Qānṣawh al-Ghawrī was walking in disguise one day with his vizier in the streets of Cairo when he heard one singer say to another, "You dare to boast of your superiority to me, So-and-so, when I know how to produce the musical modes from my ass?" The sultan said to his vizier, "Bring the man to me!" So the vizier brought him before him and the sultan related to him what he had heard him say and said to him, "Seeing is believing! Make good your claim!" "Please let me off, Your Majesty," the man replied, "for in the heat of an argument a man may say anything!" However, the sultan answered, "Prove your claim or I'll kill you!" "Will you grant me immunity from punishment?" said the man. "That is yours," said the sultan. "Let it be in an empty place," said the man. "So be it," said the sultan. So the sultan decamped to the reception hall, had the man brought, spoke kindly to him, and told him, "Proceed at your leisure!" (Sultan al-Ghawrī was well-versed in this art and had written several treatises on it).[270] "What mode would you like?" said the man. "Ḥijāz,[271] for example," said the sultan. So the man worked his buttocks and produced it, and then continued to make one mode after another until he had run through them all, along with their transitions,[272] omitting none and leaving no room for criticism. The sultan was delighted and said, "Such as you must surely be the master of Egypt in this art!" Then he awarded him a thousand dinars and appointed him chief of 11.7.35

all the singers of Egypt, and it is said that he is the ancestor of the Awlād al-ʿAtr Troupe that is famous today.

11.7.36 Once I met a man called Māḍī the Farter, God have mercy on his soul. He was extremely meticulous in his religion and pious, as well as refined and musical, and he knew the Qur'an very well by heart. His farts were made by artifice, in that he did them with his armpit, but he could still make any mode whatsoever that way and work variations and so on on them. He was a source of amazement to all who saw him and hearing him would make a stone laugh. He was famous among the emirs and received by the mighty, may God excuse him his sins.

11.7.37 A bit of facetious useful knowledge that I heard from a profligate: Satan, God curse him, farts five farts every day and distributes them among five individuals. The first of these is the man who puts his wife on a mount and takes her around to visit the tombs of the saints and the cemeteries. The second is the man who sees two people delighting in one another's company and inserts himself between them; such people are known as a "parasites of friendship." The third is the man who sees two people fighting and inserts himself between them so that most of the blows fall on him, according to the proverb "The peacemaker gains nothing but torn clothes." The fourth is the man who walks in the highway looking this way and that for no reason. And the fifth is the man who is a prisoner of his wife. Many more could be added to the list.

11.7.38 If it be said that a fart is a sound, and sound has been defined as "air compressed between what is pulled and what it is pulled out of," or "between what strikes and what is struck"—while, in this case, there is no striker and nothing struck, the fart merely emerging from the anus at the parting and articulation of the buttocks—so what is the explanation, we would reply that it may be said that this phenomenon, namely, the fart, can be integrated only under a second definition, which is that sound is air that forms waves on the collision of two bodies. Thus the answer now is clear.

And if it be said that there is a problem with the poet's words, "and my farts are like a loud drum," to wit that, if his farts resembled the sound of heavy drumming, everyone who heard them would come to him and they would discover him, his presence would become known, and the Christian and others would be informed about it, so there would be no point in his hiding among the women or in wrapping himself in the *ʿabāʾah*, so what is the wisdom in this, we would reply that the poet mentions that he would fart in this manner only after wrapping himself in the *ʿabāʾah*. Thus, even if his farts were forceful and loud, nothing would be heard once he had wrapped himself in the *ʿabāʾah*. Thus the meaning is that, absent any envelopment and wrapping, his farting would be heard like the sound of drums. As it stands, however, the situation would be similar, for example, to that of a man imprisoned in a deep pit who has drums with him on which he beats: scarcely any of the sound would be heard, even if he were beating on them hard, for the ability to hear the sound would be confined to the man himself, or to those standing at the opening of the pit or close to it—the *ʿabāʾah* playing the role of the pit, albeit narrower, because he is enveloped and wrapped up in it—and even if the farting were strong on the inside, the noise would emerge only feebly to the outside. Or it may be that the whole thing should be treated under the rubric of "impossible rhetorical exaggeration," similar to the example given by al-Ṣafī al-Ḥillī in his *Embellished Ode in the Prophet's Praise* (*Al-Badīʿiyyah*), when he says:[273] 11.7.39

A champion so strong that were the night to seek his aid
Against the morn, mankind would live in darkness!

Or it may be said that, even if this farting were to be heard as described, no one would imagine that it was a man who was hiding; rather, it might be thought that it was a man or a woman relieving him or herself, in which case there would be no reason to think that there was anything suspicious. In any case, there is nothing problematic in the poet's words, and the answer now is clear. 11.7.40

And I would like to add that I am the only person to have set forth such an interpretation, made such a classification of farting, and defined it in such terms, so far as I am aware.

11.7.41 Next the poet draws attention to the fact that his life has been expended in puerility and passed in futility, because he is so poor and earns so little. He says:

TEXT

11.8 *wa-yā dawba ʿumrī fī l-kharāji wa-hammihī*
taqaḍḍā wa-lā lī fī l-ḥaṣād saʿīf

Almost all my life on the tax and its woes
Has been spent, and I have no helper when the harvest comes!

COMMENTARY

11.8.1 *wa-yā dawba* ("almost all"): *wa-* ("and") is the conjunction that coordinates the words with what goes before, *yā* is the vocative particle, and *dawb* is a term that has facetious etymologies[274] and a variety of meanings. It may derive from the *daʾb* ("ongoing concern") of a person, that is to say, his affairs, and the circumstances in which he is involved. Thus the meaning would be, "You are aware, my brethren, that my ongoing concern, throughout

11.8.2 "*ʿumrī* ('my life'): has lain (in addition to the worries that afflicted me previously) in the computation of, worrying over, and great suffering concerning how much

11.8.3 "of *al-kharāji* ('the tax') and what springs from *hammihī* ('its woes'), that is, the land tax (*kharāj al-arḍ*), namely, the tax that is entered against my name in payment for cultivation of the land and for what it produces every year, for these do not cover the tax I owe, because the latter is great, while farming produces little, and because I am so weak and poor and have few to help me in sowing and harvesting. Consequently, my life

11.8.4 "*taqaḍḍā* ('has been spent'): in this state," etc.

Or it (*yā dawba*) may be from nocturnal "creeping up" (*dab*) on a beardless youth, when he lies down in the midst of a throng, meaning that the profligate has not been able to get at him; in such cases, the man bides his time until the boy is asleep and then "creeps up" on him unawares, the boy feeling nothing until most, or all, of the penis has entered.[275] Then the boy submits until the profligate has gotten what he wants, either for fear of anyone stirring or because scared of causing strife. Sometimes the boy will then reproach him gently, or chide him lightly, and the other will say, "God has decreed it so, and I am your slave," for example, or "I'm dying for love of you" and so on, until things are sorted out to everyone's satisfaction. A poet has said in a *mawāliyā*: 11.8.5

I crept up at night on a boy most cute
And rode like a hawk with his back in my clutch.
Waking, he asked, "Who's this who's won his suit?"
Said I, "A blind man, poking with his crutch!"

The meaning would be "at any time, the worry and fatigue associated with the land tax and the calculation of it may creep up on me and deny me any ease in my daily life or pleasure in my days and so on as long as I live, just as the profligate creeps up on the beardless boy, who feels nothing until the man is on his back and has had his way with him, as described above." Or it may be from the spreading (*dabīb*) of the poison of the scorpion, in the sense that preoccupation with making this sort of calculation night and day engenders a depression that diffuses itself to the heart and spreads itself there, just as the scorpion's poison spreads throughout the entire body. Or it may be derived from *dubb* ("bear"), with *u* after the *d*, an animal with a massive body, thick hair, and slow reactions, than which there is no more slow-witted beast, albeit its powers of comprehension are greater than others'—as the proverb says, "Better the slowness of the bear than the quickness of the monkey." One of its remarkable traits is that, if it sees a hunting party coming, it rubs its hair against gum from trees so that the gum mixes with the 11.8.6

hair, then rolls in the sand until the hair becomes as hard as rock. Thereafter, neither arrow nor anything else has any effect on it, and the hair protects it.

There is a kind of ease and a way of testing people's thinking to be found in reacting slowly to things. As the poet says:

Affect slowness, weighing thus men's minds,
And these will reveal to you things you never knew!

11.8.7 In this case, the meaning would be "Excessive worry from calculating the money that I owe in tax and weighing out the tax in kind[276] have brought me to a state that resembles that of the bear in the slowness of its reactions and its sluggishness in bestirring itself, because of the low earnings and small profit that are to be gotten from farming and my extreme poverty and the unceasing demands upon me from one moment to the next, for I am denied the good things of this world and my situation benefits me nothing." As a certain poet[277] has said:

I'm left with neither work nor leisure—
Our earnings are from a bargain vexed;
And the outcome of it all and the upshot
Is naught in this life and naught in the next!

—for I can see no profit in farming, starting from the lack of seed and my inability to improve the land, for only the strong, affluent peasant can cultivate the land, especially in view of the abusive levies,[278] tax augmentations, and customary dues that are entered nowadays against the peasants, and the "obligations." For, though it is written that it is "nine-tenths of all blessing," farming falls short of such a yield because of the pervasive injustices. In earlier times, the peasant did not have "customary dues" or "charges" or "obligations" or any of the other things that exist today imposed upon him. On the contrary, a person would farm the land, the tax calculated on it would be light, and he would know nothing of the *wajbah*, the fine on the landless, and the rest. Blessing was unconfined, all the land was under cultivation, and the people enjoyed the greatest good fortune, affluence, and profit.

When al-Ma'mūn entered Egypt[279] and made a progress through 11.8.8
its villages, a foundation of crushed stone would be built for him in a day in each village on which his pavilion would be erected and this would be surrounded by troops, and he would stay a night and a day in each village. So he passed a village called Ṭā l-Naml[280] but did not enter it because it was so wretched. When he had gone by, an old woman known as Māriyah the Copt, the owner of the village, came after him, shouting. Al-Ma'mūn thought she was calling on him for help as a petitioner against some injustice, so he stopped for her. He had interpreters of every race on hand, and they told him that the Coptic woman said, "The Commander of the Believers has stayed at every estate and ignored mine and not alighted there, and the Copts are using this to mock me. I ask the Commander of the Believers to honor me by alighting at my estate, that he may honor me and my progeny, and that my enemies do not gloat over me," and she wept copiously. Al-Ma'mūn felt sorry for her, so he turned his horse back towards her and alighted. Her son came to the master of the kitchen and asked him, "What quantities of sheep and fowl and chickens and fish and spices and sugar and honey and perfume and candles and fruit and fodder and other customarily provided things do you need?" "Such and such amounts," he replied, and the man's mother provided everything he had mentioned, and more. Al-Ma'mūn's brother al-Mu'taṣim, his son al-'Abbās, his nephews al-Wāthiq and al-Mutawakkil, Yaḥyā ibn Aktham, and Judge Dā'ūd[281] were with him, and each of these she provided with his own supplies. Then she personally brought al-Ma'mūn such a large quantity of superb and delicious food that he wondered at it. When the morning came and he was about to set off, she came to him accompanied by ten serving women, each carrying a covered dish. When al-Ma'mūn spotted this and saw her, he said, "The Coptic woman has brought you all a country present!" When she placed the dishes in front of him and uncovered them, each one turned

out to be filled with gold. Impressed, he ordered her to take it all back to her house, but she said, "No, by God! This is a gift for you, Commander of the Believers." He looked at the gold, and behold, it was all of one year's minting. "This is a wonder," he said. "Our own treasury might not be able to come up with the like." She replied, "Commander of the Believers, do not break our hearts and treat us with contempt!"[282] He said, "You have done more than enough. There is no need to overburden anyone. Take your wealth back and keep it, and may God bless you in it!" Then she took a piece of the soil and said, "Commander of the Believers, this" (and she pointed to the gold) "is from this" (and she pointed to the earth that she had picked up from the ground) "and then from your justice and fairness, Commander of the Believers, and of the former I have much!" Then he gave an order and accepted the gold from her and awarded her many estates and exempted her from the tax on two hundred feddans of her own village of Ṭā l-Naml, and departed, wondering at her gallantry and affluence. See what bounty, blessing, and affluence the land used to give those who farmed it in the past, and all of it because of the absence of abusive levies, the abundance of justice, and the rarity of upheavals!

11.8.9 The first[283] to introduce a tax other than that on land was Aḥmad ibn al-Mudabbir, when he took charge of Egyptian taxation. He was a crafty rogue, who introduced many harmful innovations, among them a monopoly on caustic soda, which previously had been free for everyone to take. He also set a tax on animals, calling it "the pastures," and another on the food that God provides from the sea, calling it "the fisheries." From then on, the taxes of Egypt were divided into land-based and lunar, and the lunar taxes became known as "the new tax."[284]

11.8.10 *wa-lā lī fī l-ḥaṣādi saʿīf* ("and I have no helper when the harvest comes"): that is, "and I find no one to help me when the harvest is ready or to help me load it onto the camels and unload it on the threshing floor, thresh it, and winnow it." The harvesting of a crop consists of gathering it with an iron implement or pulling it up by the roots when it is ripe and the seeds have hardened and the ears are full and firm and about to fall; this is when they make haste to harvest it. Humans may be likened to a crop. When a crop starts to sprout, it is green, tender, and resplendent. Likewise, a person during his early childhood and youth grows larger and blossoms as described. And when the crop reaches maturity and the time comes for it to be harvested, its days are over; and likewise the human being, when he reaches maturity and gray hairs afflict him, has reached the end of his life, for gray hairs are the harbingers of death. This is why one says of a man afflicted with gray hairs "the crop has ripened," meaning death is approaching and the harvest is nigh. "Sowing a crop" may be used in both concrete and abstract senses: the concrete is that employed above; the abstract is, for example, the doing of good deeds. One says, for instance, "So-and-so 'sowed' good deeds," meaning he did good to others. The poet says:

> Sow good deeds, though in a barren spot—
> No good deed is ever wasted, wherever it be sown.
> In good deeds, though the wait be long,
> No man reaps any crop but his own.

And there is a wise saying that goes "As you make your bed, so shall you lie, and as you sow, so shall you reap," and every sower reaps what he has sown, be it of good or evil.

Next the poet, may God have mercy on him, draws attention to another of the disastrous varieties of injustice with which he has been afflicted, he and others among his brother peasants and the landless, and says: 11.8.11

TEXT

wa-yawmin tajī l-ʿawnah ʿalā l-nāsi fī l-balad 11.9
tukhabbiʾunī fī l-furni ʾUmmu Waṭīf

> And on the day when the corvée descends on the people in the village
> Umm Waṭīf hides me in the oven

11.9.1 *wa-yawmin* ("And on the day when"): with or without nunation in this verse.[285]

11.9.2 *tajī l-ʿawnah* ("the corvée descends"): this occurs when activities that require it, such as the excavation of pits for waterwheels, the gathering of crops, and the digging of canals, take place.[286] The corvée is found only in those tax farmers' villages that include demesne land. The system is that most tax farmers, when they take a village or one of the hamlets of the countryside, cultivate a parcel of land in the village or the hamlet and give the rest to the peasants against a fixed tax. This parcel cultivated by the tax farmer is called "the demesne." The tax farmer sends oxen, timber, plows, and whatever else is needed and appoints an agent to take charge of it and prepares a place for the timber and animals belonging to it, the latter being called "the demesne house." He also commissions someone to spend money on the upkeep of the animals, etc., and to keep careful accounts. If mud needs to be cleared out of the wells, or canals dug, or crops brought in, the bailiff of the village or hamlet gives an order to a man known as the watchman and the latter calls out, "Corvée, you peasants! Corvée, you landless!" and they leave in a body early in the morning and set off to dig or do whatever else he may order them to do, every day, without pay, until the digging or harvesting is done. Anyone who is slack or lazy about going to work is taken by the bailiff, who punishes him and takes from him a fine of a set amount. In some villages the corvée applies to a number of men, fixed by household, for example. Thus they say, "From such and such a household one man is to go, and from such and such two," according to the quota set for them in the distant or more recent past. A person subject to the corvée cannot be released from it, and if he dies they impose it on his sons, and so on. It is a great tribulation for the peasants and a huge disaster for the landless. Thank God that He has relieved our village of it! There the peasants are obligated for a fixed number of carats only and all the tax farmer concerns himself with is the tax on these, which he takes each year in full. Although they do have to pay the customary dues and abusive levies, it is not like the villages with demesnes, which are constantly caught up in hardship and distress, levies on the landless, corvée, and excessive affliction. The poet lived in a village with a demesne, which is why he says that if the corvée descends . . .

ʿalā l-nāsi fī l-balad ("on the people in the village"): that is, the poet's village, the "people" here being the ones in the village singled out for the corvée, not every inhabitant. It may be that the poet was one of those who used to set off to work on the corvée because his own acreage was so small and he was so poor, and that when he had been away from his dependents for a while without earning anything, they found themselves in need, though he could not leave the corvée and look for paid work. Consequently he says, 11.9.3

tukhabbiʾunī ("(she) hides me"): that is, hides me from people's eyes so that no one sees or hears me 11.9.4

fī l-furni ("in the oven"): that is, the oven of his house that is used for baking bread and cooking flaky pastry in the ashes and stewing *bīsār* and fava beans and so forth. 11.9.5

ʾUmmu Waṭīf: the name is properly Waṭfah, but he uses it in the masculine for the sake of the meter.[287] It derives from the *ṭayf*, which is the phantasm that appears in one's dreams—the poet says: 11.9.6

> Suʿdā's phantom came to me by night and woke me with a start
> At break of dawn, while my fellows in the desert sleeping lay;
> But, by that night-phantom woken,
> I find the dwelling desolate, while the place of tryst is far away

—or from *al-ṭūfān* ("the Flood") or from the *aṭwāf* ("small domes") of dung that the women make in the countryside,[288] for Umm Waṭīf used to work a lot at mashing the dung into cakes and making them into *aṭwāf*, for which they bestowed on her this honorific. Some say her real name was Zawbaʿah ("Whirlwind"), others that it was Khuṭayṭah or Muʿaykah. She was the poet's wife, or mother, or sister.[289] The *ʿawnah* ("corvée") is so called because it derives from *muʿāwanah* ("helping one another") because it consists of a group who go out to help one another in the tax farmer's work and so on. Or it may be that it is the name for a group that cooperates in doing something, which is why they say, "They fucked So-and-so last night *as a group* (*ʿawnah*)," that is, they all cooperated in fucking him at one go in the byre or the granary. Similarly, they mock a beardless boy by saying to him, "You, you faggot, you cow! You're always getting gangbanged by a hundred (*ʿawnatuka miʾah*)!" (meaning by a hundred persons). Or it is from *māʿūn*, a name for the big storage jar.[290] The paradigm is *ʿawwana, yuʿawwinu, taʿwīnan* or *ʿāna, yuʿīnu , iʿānatan*.[291] Said the poet:

> Thus *ʿawwana, taʿwīnan* and *ʿāna, iʿānatan*—
> Each has its true sense and attestation.

11.9.7 If it be said that the poet's words give the impression that, if he were to hide in the oven, they would leave him alone and no one would notice him, though this contradicts the preceding statement that there is no escaping going off to work on the corvée, especially if it has been imposed on a certain person since early times or since the days of his grandfathers, as explained above, so how do you explain this, we would reply that the explanation is that, when fate turned against the poet and he joined the ranks of the weak and the poor, he became as one who did not exist, and no one gave any further thought to him. The only reason he hid himself was for fear that his relatives should sic the tax farmer's followers on him to do him harm and beat him up. From this perspective, the words would indicate that the corvée was not applied to him because, in former times, he had been shaykh of the hamlet and administered its affairs, or because age had taken its toll on him and he had turned into an old man; thus, when the time for the corvée arrived, he hid in the oven simply for the sake of decorum and so that no one should see him, according to the maxims "Keep out of harm's way, and thumb your nose at it!" and "What the eye doesn't see the heart doesn't grieve for." The solution to this problem has now been correctly set forth.

When the poet is done with complaining about want, disgrace, lice, nits, the enmity of his relatives, and the distress caused him by the *wajbah*, the tax, the corvée, and so on, he turns his attention to longing for all kinds of foods, or at least to seeing them, because of the extreme straits he finds himself in as a result of the absence of such things and his great poverty and because he knows such victuals only from other people's houses and that is the only place he sees them. He longs that Fate might bungle his case and he might get to see such things and possess them, even in a small amount, before his life ends. He begins with wheat groats, as it is the country people's most sumptuous dish. He says: 11.9.8

TEXT

wa-lā haddanī min baʿdi hādah wa-hādihī 11.10
siwā l-kishki lammā yastaḥiqqu gharīf

And nothing has demolished me after this and that
but wheat groats when they're ready to ladle!

COMMENTARY

wa-lā haddanī ("and nothing has demolished me"): that is, nothing has demolished my stamina and my strength, taken from *hadd al-ḥāʾiṭ* ("he demolished the wall"), which is originally from *hadm* ("destruction"), with an additional *m*, which has been dropped from it in accordance with rural usage,[292] or as a case of "restraint," as in the verse: 11.10.1

"Queen of Beauty, grant a meeting of your kindness
To a lover whose heart melts for you in pain—
My heart you've ruined!" Said she, "Such is our way!
He to whom all glory says, «Lo! Kings, when . . .»"[293]

11.10.2 It is said that *hadd* combined with *hadd* makes *hudhud* ("hoopoe"), with *u* after the *h*, which would thus be a compound noun formed of two verbs.[294] The *hudhud* is a well-known bird mentioned by the Almighty in the Noble Qur'an when He says, quoting Our Master Sulaymān, upon whom be peace, «And he sought among the birds and said, "How is it that I see not the hoopoe, or is he among the absent?"»[295] referring to the fact that it is the messenger of the birds and guides them to water, for it can see water beneath the ground due to a special faculty created in it by Almighty God. Ibn ʿAbbās, may God be pleased with him, was asked, "What is the wisdom in the hoopoe's seeing the water beneath the ground but not seeing the trap, and falling into it?" and he replied, God be pleased with him, "When destiny falls, the eye is blinded." Or it may be derived from *hadiyyah* ("gift"), because it sounds similar.[296] In the Tradition it says, "Give one another gifts and you will love one another," and it is said that the source of love is a gift, the source of enmity a complaint, and the source of hatred maltreatment. A gift, even though small, touches the soul. In the proverb it says, "The gift of friends is on leaves of rue."[297] A poet says:

The lark on parade day[298] came to Sulaymān
  To give him a locust it had in its beak
And uttered the while these words, in nature's tongue:[299]
  "Gifts are proportionate to the giver, be he mighty or meek.
If each according to his worth were given,
  Your gift would be the World and all you therein seek!"

11.10.3 Or it is from *hadhayān* ("raving"), with *dh*, which is the correct form.[300] The paradigm is *hadda, yahuddu, haddan* or *hadama, yahdimu, hadman* according to the two forms, deriving from the expression *haddaka Allāhuan* ("May God demolish you utterly!") or *hadamaka hadman* ("May He destroy you utterly!"), meaning that He should weaken your powers and immobilize you, as a wall becomes profitless when demolished, and so on.

min baʿdi hādah wa-hādihī ("after this and that"): *hādah* being with *h* and *ā* and *d* and final *h*,[301] which means that its ends are "knotted together,"[302] with its beginning being the same as its end, as you will notice if you look closely. The origin of the word is *hādhā*, a demonstrative, but the tongues of the country people have changed it. The meaning is that this has demolished my stamina and weakened my powers after all that went before (namely, being bitten by lice and nits, and want and disgrace and so on) and what came after (namely, the injuries done by relatives and worries over the tax and the *wajbah* and fears over the arrival of the Inspectors and the corvée and demands for the sultan's taxes and scurrying about in the fields and so on, as set out above). As the poet says: 11.10.4

The worry of farming has put me in a dither
And all the while I'm losing more.
No sooner I escape the *wajbah*'s worries
Than the sultan's tax is at the door.

Indeed, you will find the peasant, if poor, is always on the verge of perishing from beatings, imprisonment, and a lack of delicious things to eat and drink, and finds no rest unless he has paid the sultan's tax; and, if he has a small balance owing, he will think about it all night long, and at daybreak and day's end, and exist in a state of frantic effort and exhaustion, unless the Almighty bless him in his planting—for much may come forth from little if his intentions at the time of sowing the land are good and if his purpose at the time be that he and others should benefit by what he is doing, as by providing food for the birds and the animals and so on, and if he places his trust in the Almighty for its growth and preservation from pests. In such a case God will bless him in it, with great reward, as witnessed by the fact that it is related of Our Master ʿUmar,[303] God be pleased with him, that one day he passed by some people sitting without work or gain and begging. "Who are you?" he asked. They said, "We are those who place our trust in God." "That you are 11.10.5

not," he said, "for those who place their trust in God are those who place the grain between the water and the soil. Go and be gainfully employed!" The cultivator is the person who puts the greatest faith in God, if he heeds what is prescribed above at the time of sowing.

11.10.6 A Useful Note: It is desirable that the cultivator should pray two prostrations at the time of sowing the grain in the earth and then say, "My God, I, Your feeble slave, have commended this seed to You, so bless me in it!" Then he should bless the Prophet, God bless him and grant him peace, for God will preserve the plants from infestations if he does so. Imam al-Zāhidī mentions this.

For our part, however, we thank God that he has relieved us of farming and its woes; it was never our father's or our grandfathers' occupation, for we are of the sort described by al-Buhlūl,[304] God have mercy on him, when he said:

When kings mount steeds
 After fixing their standards to lances frail,
I mount my reedling and don my cassock
 And travel as they do in every vale.
Then never can troopers demand from me taxes
 Nor the collectors over my assessment fail.

Agriculture is, in any case, a tribulation from which we pray God to spare us and our loved ones.

11.10.7 *siwā l-kishki* ("but *kishk*"): *kishk* ("wheat groats") is at base a mixture of wheat and milk; it is Coarse[305] and stimulates sickness. The poet says:

Kishk is Gross and Coarse.
 It activates what's still.
Its ingredients are milk and wheat—
 Noble forefathers, but still . . .[306]

—that is, "but still, what a horrible child!" with "quotation" and "restraint."

The recipe is to take *burr* ("wheat"), synonym *qamḥ*, wash it well, and soak it in water.[307] Then it is placed on the fire and heated until it goes soft and the grain swells and it is well boiled. Then it is dried in the sun and husked and put in a pot, and milk and strained *mishsh* is poured onto it and it is stirred, then left for several days, then stirred again and more milk is added and so on until it ferments and thickens and acquires a sour smell and a most excellent taste. More milk is added to cut the sourness and it is formed into small cakes and put in the sun to dry, and taken and stored until it is to be cooked. This is how they make the groats of the villages by the river, which is the best in quality and the finest to eat. As for the groats of the hamlets and the villages of the swamplands, which is the type referred to by the poet, God spare you such a disgusting sight! They make it with strained cottage-cheese culture and just a small quantity of milk, which makes it extremely sour, sharp to the taste, gross in nature compared to other types, and laxative. This is the sort that is brownish, and the whiter, purer, and less sour-smelling it gets, the better it is. The groats of Upper Egypt is the same, for it resembles that of the hamlets in its poor quality, though in Upper Egypt they form it into small balls, and they also have a type that is of good quality because it has high milk content and is very clean. 11.10.8

As for how to cook with it, this varies according to the place where that is done. The people of the villages on the river sometimes cook it with rice and fatty meat, other times with chicken or one of the other types of edible fowl, or make it with rice alone, and they make it thick. The people of al-Manzalah and Dimyāṭ cook it with fat mullet, and I have eaten it in Dimyāṭ many times. The Turks make it thin and runny, with a small quantity of rice, and it is drunk with a spoon, and they make a garnish for it by frying greens and fats and good clarified butter, and they cook it with fat mutton. This makes it extremely delicious to eat. Its nature is Moderate, especially when eaten with mutton, chicken, and rice. The bad kind that "activates what's still," as mentioned in the verses above, is the groats of the people of the hamlets and the villages of the swamplands, for 11.10.9

they neglect to wash it or strain it well when they cook it, and they put it in a crock or a kettle or a pan on the fire and add a handful of shelled fava beans and heat it until it thickens. Then they take it off the fire and mince an onion into it and add a little sesame oil and make it a fried garnish with these, and ladle it into earthenware kneading bowls or milk crocks and crumble maize or barley bread into it. Such people eat a crockful, chewing and gulping, and set off for the fields, where they stay until evening. By that time, what is left has gone hard, with bits of fava beans sticking out. This they gulp down till they are satisfied. This is what is called among them *hirāsh al-ʿajāʾiz* ("old women's butting")[308] and it is the most highly prized of their dishes. Most of them make it for their weddings, as stated above in Part One of this commentary.[309] They know nothing of cooking it with rice and meat, for rice is found among them only rarely and they only eat meat once a year, as we shall show. Another type in the same category they cook without fava beans and consists of just *kishk* and nothing else, without any kind of garnish; this they call *nayrab*, and that and the preceding generate wind and "move what is still" and are harmful to the stomach because they contain so many beans,[310] the latter being Gross in nature. Wheat is similar because it is Hot and Moist, and cottage cheese culture is Cold and Moist, and beans are Coarse and Heavy. Thus harm arises from the combination of these four.[311]

11.10.10 Groats, before it is cooked, has several beneficial qualities. For example, if dissolved in water and drunk by someone with heartburn, it brings relief and soothes the inflammation of the stomach. If a camel sickens from the heat and is given some to drink, it recovers. For the same reason, travelers such as pilgrims and others use it when the heat overcomes them and makes them feel unwell. As an ointment, it is good for the pain caused by whipping, and it has other beneficial properties mentioned in the medical books. The people of Upper Egypt cook it without straining it first, so that it resembles nothing so much as bran cooked with vinegar; there is no benefit to be had from it, and it has no taste or savor because their good properties are present only after they have been strained—but anyway their food consists mostly of okra and Jew's mallow, as we have observed in their villages. It is said that an Upper Egyptian from the region of Qinā and Qūṣ once came to Cairo to buy himself a girl to do the housework. He came across a girl who was for sale at an extremely high price because of her knowledge of different dishes. He stood in front of her and asked, "Do you cook well as they say?" She looked at him and asked him, "What country are you from?" "From Upper Egypt," he said. Then she said, "You have no need of fine food, for the diet of the people of Upper Egypt is six months a year okra and six months Jew's mallow. They have no need of finer foods than these." The man left her and went away amazed.

A Fatuous Question: What is the meaning of the name *kishk* and what is its etymology, and what is the meaning of the name of the cooked type that is called *hirāsh al-ʿajāʾiz* and the other type called *nayrab*, and what does the poet mean when he says that it "demolished" his stamina when he beheld it as it was about to be ladled out and he smelled its aroma? The Facetious Answer is that *kishk* is one of those back-to-front words that can be read forward and backward. Similar are *kaʿk* ("a type of short pastry"), *shāsh* ("muslin"), *bāb* ("door"), etc.[312] Similar too are *sir fa-lā kabā bi-ka al-faras* ("Go, and may the mare not stumble with you!") and *qilʿ murakkab bi-bakar muʿallaq* ("A sail set with a pulley suspended") and *ḥissak tatazawwaj ʿajūz tatakassaḥ* ("Mind you don't marry an old woman who hobbles!"). The same is also found in the Mighty Qurʾan in the words of the Almighty «*(wa-)rabbaka fa-kabbir*[313] ("(and) thy Lord magnify"),» «*kullun fī falak*[314] ("each in an orbit"),» and elsewhere, as in *kamālak taḥta kalāmak* ("Your words are the offspring of your perfection") and *kalb yabulluka* ("May a dog wet you!") and *ʿilq taḥta qilʿ* ("A faggot under a sail"). An example in verse is the words of al-Ḥarīrī:[315] 11.10.11

*Us armalan idhā ʿarā * wa-rʿa idhā l-marʾu asā*
*Uslu janāba ghāshimin * mushāghibin in jalasā*

Give to the pauper when he passes by
and stay friends with one who does you harm.
Avoid the abode of an unjust
scoundrel when he's at home!

Also, when they turn groats over in the sun, their bottoms are just like their tops, and the beginning of each ball of groats is the same as its end; from this perspective there is a certain appropriateness in their being a palindrome. Or the name may derive from the fact that when it is put in the sun it shrinks (*yakishshu*) and shrivels from the heat; or from the saying they have, "So-and-so 'ate *kishk*' (*kashshaka*) at So-and-so's house," meaning he ate a lot, so that his belly swelled till he looked like a crock full of *kishk*; or from *kishkish*, which they say to a dog—when they want to throw it something to eat, this is the word they use to call it. Or from *kushuk* ("kiosk, gazebo"), with *u* after the *k* and the *sh*, which is a place outside a large building, mounted on timbers, that the great erect to sit in. Or from the fact that the *kishkah* ("cake of *kishk*"), once formed into a ball, would resemble the *kuss* ("cunt"), with *s*, which is the vagina; later they changed the *s* (without dots) to the *sh* (with dots) because of the ugliness of the expression and added a *k* and said *kishk*.[316] The paradigm is *kashshaka, yukashshiku, takshīkan* ("to form *kishk* into balls").

11.10.12 As to the naming of one type, *hirāsh al-ʿajāʾiz, hirāsh* originally means the same as *niṭāḥ* ("butting"). One speaks of the *muhārashah* ("butting contests") of rams and the *niqār* ("pecking contests") of cocks.[317] It is known as "old women's" because it is generally they who cook it with relish and butt one another to get at it in a fashion most distressing that seems both perverse and depressing, not to mention that the old women of villages such as these belong to the ghoulish jinn species. Thus, the dish was given this name because of their butting one another to get at it. Or it may fall under the rubric of "wear and tear" (*harsh*) on the stomach.

11.10.13 And as to the other type being called *nayrab*, this may be because it derives from *nayrūb*, of the pattern of *daylūb*,[318] or because they trace it to a man called *nayrab*,[319] or to the *arnab* ("rabbit"), an animal that it is permitted to eat, but were afraid of confusion in the pronunciation, so they called it *nayrab*. Or because it is made at the season of Nayrūz, so first they said *nayrūz* and then its name and that of the season got mixed up, so they exchanged the letter *z* at the end of the word for a *b* and said *nayrab*.

The poet's statement that it demolished his strength when he beheld it, saw it, and smelled its aroma is attributable to the facts that he did not possess any, that it was so infrequently cooked at his house, and that he used to see it only at his neighbors' houses. Consequently, whenever he saw it ready for eating, he would grieve and mourn, especially . . . 11.10.14

lamma yastaḥiqqu gharīf ("when it's ready to ladle"): that is, when it's done cooking and they want to ladle it out, and its aroma, as it is being ladled, wafts here and there. It is originally "when it's ready for ladling (*gharf*) *with a ladling instrument*," but he shortened it and added the *ī* to *gharf* for the sake of the meter.[320] *Gharīf* is of the pattern of *kanīf* ("latrine"), the latter being a hole for shitting in, for sure. When he observed this situation and smelled that smell, his strength was demolished, for a person's greatest zeal, all his life long, is for his belly and his privates; as Ibn ʿArūs, God have mercy on him, says, in his collected works: 11.10.15

The people are lost in God,
    And praise of the noble spreads far and wide.
Nothing does me harm but my belly,
    And that thing dangles on its underside.

And another poet says in a *mawāliyā*:

Ah wretched world—all my life hard pressed,
    By the woes of this belly that lets none rest!
All day I build, then sup, go lie me down;
    Mornings I rise, find what I built knocked down![321]

For the same reason, the poet is not content just to look, because he cannot satisfy his desire that way, and he is not of the species of the ant that he should live by smell alone;[322] on the contrary, he belongs to the human species and, moreover, to that of the people of the country hamlets, any of whom would consume a crock, or two crocks, of wheat groats or *bīsār* or stewed beans for breakfast, as we shall see—so he is not to be blamed if his strength collapsed.

11.10.16 In the same vein, I am reminded that it happened that a doctor was sitting in a market examining people's ailments when a young man of refined physique, a child of the wealthy and well-to-do, came to him and sitting down before him stretched out his hand to him and said, "See what ails me!" The doctor felt his pulse and asked him, "What have you eaten today?" "A few beans with linseed oil for breakfast," he said. The doctor told him, "Get a few raisins and senna pods plus a little sugar and take these, for therein lies your cure." So the young man rose and left him. Then up came a countryman, a real hulk, like a mast on a mountain in bulk, and to the doctor his proximity he increased, puffing like some crawling beast, and said to him, "Gently see what sickness ails me, for I feel my belly fails me!"—holding out a hand like a clog, with a forearm like a log. The doctor took his pulse and asked, "What delivered you such a punch, and what did you eat for breakfast and for lunch?" The other said to him, "I'll tell you now, by the truth of the Prophet, to whom we salaam, and by the grave of Abū Muʿaykah, son of Abū Juʿrām! When I got up from sleeping, I found my wife, Umm Muʿaykah, had put out a big pot of *bīsār*, and I pulled out the bread and tossed down a crock or two . . . say three." "And what else?" said the doctor. The man said, "I went to our neighbor, Umm Daʿmūm, and found stewed beans at her place. I ate a crock or two of them . . . say three." "Indeed," said the doctor, "and what else?" "I went off to our field of beans, and ate a bundle or two of them . . . say three. And I left the field and, at the house of the bailiff of the hamlet, I saw some *kishk* and tossed down a crock or two of it . . . say three. And I saw there was a wedding in our alley, and they invited me over, so I went into their house. They cooked lots, and I ate a crock or two of that food . . . say three. And I saw someone selling yellow cucumbers by our house, so I ate a heap or two . . . say three. Then I came to you to see what's wrong with me, because I feel my appetite is failing me." The doctor told him, "Take of raisins a hundredweight or two . . . say three, and of senna pods a hundredweight or two . . . say three." The man said to him, "I heard you prescribe a little senna, sugar, and raisins for the man who came to you before me, and you want to prescribe them for me by the hundredweight?!" The doctor replied, "Vilest of peasants! Could anything deal with such meals as those but hundredweights of purges such as these?" Then he slung his bag over his shoulder and swore that he would not sit in the market anymore that day because of that peasant. Now the record's straight as regards the import of such a state, and the explanation's plain as regards such tales inane.

Next the poet, having done with talk of that particular food, felt a desire for something coarser that is used by the people of the countryside in most of their dishes. So he said: 11.10.17

TEXT

wa-lā shāqanī illā l-mudammas wa-rīḥatū 11.11
ʿalā man jatū jafnah wa-nuṣṣu raghīf

And nothing has made me yearn like stewed beans and their smell!
Happy is he to whom comes a bowl with half a loaf!

COMMENTARY

wa-lā shāqanī ("And nothing has made me yearn"): from *shawq* ("yearning, desire"), which is the softening of the heart and its inclination towards the beloved. ʿUmar ibn al-Fāriḍ, God benefit us through him, says, "Were it not for you, the mention of my home would not make me yearn (*mā shāqanī*) . . . ."[323] *Shāqa* ("it caused yearning") is of the measure of *qāqa* ("it honked"), which is the sound a goose makes. The paradigm is *shāqa, yashūqu, shawqan*, like *qāqa, yaqūqu, qawqan*, and what he means to say is, "My yearning has not grown and my thirst has not increased for any dish . . ." 11.11.1

11.11.2 *illā l-mudammas* ("like stewed beans"):[324] *mudammas* being taken from *dims* ("bedding straw for cattle") because the beans are cooked in a fire fueled with *dims*, as will be explained. The paradigm is *dammasa, yudammisu, tadmīsan,* active participle *dāmis,* passive participle *madmūs.*[325] There are two kinds, the rural and the urban, even though the origin is the same, namely, fava beans, the difference being due to the fact that things are ennobled at times by virtue of place and at others by virtue of excellence of manufacture.

11.11.3 To make the urban kind, which is that sold in Cairo and other cities, they take clean white beans, discard any bad ones, and put them in large broad-bellied kettles with narrow mouths just wide enough for a man to insert his hand into when he serves from them. Then they pour enough sweet, pure water over them to cover them and they plug the mouth of the kettle tightly with some clean palm fiber or a clean vessel and they cook them in a strong, clean fire of threshings that makes no smoke or unpleasant odors, such as that of a baker's pit or the like. For a whole night they watch over them, adding water whenever they dry out, until the taste is good, the consistency just right, the aroma enticing, and they taste wonderful and are beautifully cooked. At this point the beans take on a golden color and the consistency of, for example, pressed dates, so that any who sees them wants to eat them. When they want to eat some, a man, or a woman if she so desires, will buy enough for him or herself, and add clarified cow's butter or olive oil or clotted cream, and bring clean white bread. They may also be eaten accompanied by green leeks and limes or vinegar. All this makes them excellent nourishment, sustaining for the limbs and filling for the stomach. A little thyme balances them,[326] especially if coffee is drunk immediately afterward. A man can go from morning to night on this alone.

11.11.4 As for the second kind, namely, the *mudammas* of the country people—which is what the poet craves—God spare you such a disgusting sight! If you've never tasted shit, try this! They take the beans, be they good or bad, as is. The peasant's wife may well take them from the cow's or the ox's feeding trough and blow the remnants of straw off them, and put them in a vessel called a *bawshah* ("earthenware pot") and cover them with dirty, foul-smelling water drawn from the ponds or from the cut-off stretches of Nile water that remain in their villages after the flood recedes, or from the wells. She plugs the mouth of the pot with flax straw mixed with dung or with a filthy rag and puts it into the fire chamber of the oven, which is filled with bedding straw and dung cakes, which may also be heaped on top of it, and she closes the door of the fire chamber on it tightly till the morning. Then she takes it out, by which time the beans will have mixed with the odors of the droppings and the dung cakes and that foul-smelling water and turned black and become like goat droppings and developed a foul smell. Next she gets the crock, shakes the pot, and empties the beans into it. The countryman then sits down, like a snarling dog, and she brings him dry sorghum or barley bread, and he cuts and swallows till his belly is filled. If you were to eat it, you would think you were eating sheep droppings or something of the sort. Some of them eat it with leeks or onions, and sometimes they add some wheat or chickpeas, and their great men put a little linseed oil on it. Some of them have no bread, and such a one gulps it down in lumps in the morning without saying a prayer or washing his face, until he has had enough. Then he washes it down with water until he is like a swollen waterskin, and takes his cudgel and sets off like a . . . .[327] Such is their *mudammas* and the nature of their food, God preserve you from it!

wa-rīḥatū ("and their smell"): originally *wa-rāʾiḥatuhu*, the glottal stop being omitted for the meter, or in accordance with rural usage;[328] that is, "its smell, mixed with the aforementioned odors, caused me to yearn for it, because I think it so delicious when my appetite yearns for it; consequently I crave it, and beans, but I find none of these things because I am so poor." *Rīḥah* is derived from *rīḥ* ("wind") or from *rawāḥ* ("going") or from the *abū riyāḥ* ("windmill toy") that boys play with or from *rāḥ*, which is one of the words for wine. The poet says: 11.11.5

Wine (*rāḥ*) is like the wind (*rīḥ*): if it passes a perfume
It turns sweet, and it turns bad if it passes a corpse.

Or it, *rīḥah*, may be from the words of the poet:

The ferryboat's going and coming (*rāyiḥah jayyah*),[329]
By a thread[330] it's jerked along.
You in the open-fronted cloak,
See where my foot stepped wrong!

And with the same meaning a poet says in a *mawāliyā*, as a riddle:[331]

What make you, my friend, of something going and coming
From beneath a wall, both dead and living,
On the ground thrown down, yet standing and sitting,
Moving, well-built, yet atop a wall reclining?

11.11.6 Next, the poet, having mentioned his craving for *mudammas* and its smell, and the eating thereof that follows naturally from that—for seeing and smelling cannot take the place of eating and chewing—desires to do just that, and says:

11.11.7 *'alā* ("happy is he"): this is a preposition, though used here as a verb,[332] the meaning being "May the standing of him to whom comes a bowlful be exalted (*'alā*) and raised up!" or "May his body be exalted (*'alā*), his soul invigorated and his belly satisfied, and may he become renowned for strength after hunger!"—as the poet says:

Our Zayd rose high above (*'alā*) your Zayd's head, on the day of battle,
With a white sword of Yemen, sharp on both edges!

—or perhaps the preposition is used in its original function, the meaning being "in any case (*'alā kulli ḥāl*), verily . . ."

11.11.8 *man jatū* ("he to whom comes"): that is, he who acquires . . .

jafna(h) ("a bowl"): full of the aforementioned stewed beans, even if it be a gift, or alms, *wa-* ("and") who acquires along with it . . . 11.11.9

nuṣṣu raghīf ("half a loaf"): (the *f* of *niṣf* having been elided in accordance with the rural language,[333] as when they say *nuṣṣ fiḍḍah* for *niṣf fiḍḍah*), or as an example of "restraint,"[334] or by way of apocopation, as when the poet says, "Gently now, Fāṭim! A little less disdainful . . . ,"[335] should such a thing befall him, then it would be the most blessed and happiest of days. The fact that he asks for half a loaf and not a whole one is an allusion to the fact that stewed beans are Hot and do not call for a lot of bread; thus half a loaf will be enough for him, when combined with all the beans he is going to eat without bread, for example. Or it may be a case of just asking for any little thing to satisfy his hunger temporarily. 11.11.10

The *jafnah* is a large vessel made to hold food. The Almighty has said, «*wa-jifānin ka-l-jawābī* ("and basins like reservoirs"),»[336] the latter being plural of *jābiyah*, which means a large tank. Describing a people as being much given to eating and as having capacious bellies, a poet says: 11.11.11

> Every lout has a belly like a vat (*jābiyah*),
> Which, if you change the dots, comes out as "twat" (*khāyibah*).

In another copy, the word occurs with *h*, that is, as a *ḥafnah* ("handful"), of stewed beans. A *ḥafnah* is what fills a man's two cupped hands, when the fingers are brought close together. However, it is more appropriate with *j*. Between *jafnah* and *ḥafnah* there is "orthographic paronomasia." *Jafnah* is derived from the *jafn* ("lid") of the eye, because the former protects the food just as the *jafn* provides a protective covering for the eye and whatever kohl or anything else may be put on it, such things suffusing the lids, which close over them and preserve them, allowing them to affect the eyesight[337] and perfect the charm of the face. As the poet[338] says: 11.11.12

> I say to his eyes when closed in sleep,
> The lids with kohl suffused,
> "Blessed be He who grants you rest at night,
> When He knows how cruelly by day you're used!"

The paradigm is *jaffana, yujaffinu, jafnatan* ("to hollow out (a bowl)").

11.11.13 Next the poet desires another dish, one of those most often eaten in his village and coarser in nature than stewed beans. He says:

TEXT

11.12 *ʿalā man raʾā l-bīsāra fī l-jurni jā-lū*
wa-yadʿas wa-law kān bi-l-qulinji ḍaʿīf

> Happy is he who sees *bīsār* come to him on the threshing floor
> and bolts it, though he be by colic enfeebled!

COMMENTARY

11.12.1 *ʿalā* ("Happy is he"): the meaning of *ʿalā* is explained in the preceding verse.

11.12.2 *man raʾā* ("who sees"): visually.

11.12.3 *(a)l-bīsāra*: *bīsār* is of two kinds, rural and urban, as was previously seen to be the case with regard to other dishes. The rural is composed of two things—dry Jew's mallow and pounded beans, nothing more. The way the people of the countryside cook it is to put the dry mallow and a small quantity of pounded beans in the pot, cover with water, and put the pot in the oven until it is almost done. Then they take it out and break up the lumps with a wooden whisk until it reaches the right consistency and the beans have crumbled and their smell permeates the air. After this they return it, if necessary, to the oven, adding water, if required, until it is done. Next they make it a garnish by frying onion in a little sesame oil and ladle it out into a crock or a milk pot and crumble some barley bread or flaky sorghum pastry into it until it turns into something like slabs of dung mixed with straw, and they eat it with green or dry onions. One of them will eat a crock or two, mixed with crumbled bread or pastry, for lunch, and a crock for dinner, and pick up his stick, with his leather sandals slung behind his neck, and set off with the animals, or to reap or plow; and this is the greater part of their food, especially in Ramadan at the time of the breaking of the fast or just before dawn, so that the peasant ends up looking like a swollen waterskin, as previously noted. Then he lies down on top of the oven with the dung and the daub on his legs, he and his wife, without a prayer or any other act of worship, and the flatulence goes around and around in their bellies and erupts like a hurricane, and this serves as their incense all night long. None of them gets up in the morning but the stink of his *jubbah* wafts about from the quantity of farts, audible and inaudible, therein. Should he have intercourse that same night with his wife their fate will be farting and fracas, and gas and tintamarre. Such is their condition with regard to eating and coition—we seek shelter with God from the peasant's disposition!

As for the urban kind, how delicious it is, and how toothsome, good, and wholesome! What happens is that, should one of the great men of Cairo or one of the other cities to which Jew's mallow is brought for sale or in which it is grown have an appetite to make it, he may do so in a variety of fashions. One of them will take it dry and cleaned of stems, shortly after it has been dried, or perhaps dry it in his own house and entrust it to whoever, wife or servant, will see to the cooking of it. The latter then places it in a tinned copper basin or Anatolian-style casserole with a tight-fitting lid and adds pure, cold, sweet water and heats it over wood[339] until it reaches the right consistency. Then she gently breaks up the lumps and makes it a garnish of Syrian or local garlic mixed with clarified cow's butter and adds the fat from the tail of a sheep and throws in some seasonings such as pepper and so on, plus a little cumin to get rid of its harmful attributes. Another may add to this a few crushed beans but also increase the fat or clarified butter until the latter absorbs 11.12.4

the taste of the beans and the taste of the fat, butter, seasonings, and so on predominates. Yet others use small mutton kebabs in place of the beans, this form being called "the Gathering of Loved Ones."[340] Another way is to take it, that is, the mallow, when green and fresh, gathered that day, and chop it well (though some Turks do it without chopping), then heat it as before and make a garnish for it with fats, clarified butter, and seasonings, as described above; it is then very delicious. Some stuff it with meat, and this kind is called "the Softener of Constitutions" for its Coldness, the ease with which it is eaten, the speed with which it is digested, and the lightness that results in the body. Another kind is yet more delicious and appetizing than the preceding and more beneficial and makes a more delicious dish. This consists of taking the mallow when small, when it is starting to sprout, chopping it well, and cooking it with chicken or goose, with a lot of fats and seasonings, or with mutton. The people of Cairo are very fond of this type and make it often, so much so that one of them may spend large amounts of money on mallow when it first appears and invite his closest friends over to eat it. They consider it more delicious than the feast-day foods, and talk of this treat, and the guest will say, "Tonight So-and-so fed me mallow, the first of the year!" Sometimes they eat it with clean toasted bread made of finely sieved flour and baked with fennel-flower seed or fennel, which they crumble into it, so that it absorbs those wonderful fats and the flavors of the fatty meats.

11.12.5 This follows from their excellent judgment, intelligence, and love of things when they first appear, as exemplified by the proverb that says, "Everything new is delicious and everything old distasteful" and, in the same vein, the words of Ibn ʿArūs, God have mercy upon him and benefit us through him:

They hold you high on your debut—
  Something dear for a dear hand to hold.
But Muslin, when you fade, they toss you out—
  And so it was for me, when I grew old.

—for everything, when it first appears, holds an appeal of a special kind, and, for children, joy unconfined. There is also a kind called *būrānī*[341] made by tearing up the mallow leaves and making a garnish for them with clarified butter; then they prepare it as previously described.

This is why Master ʿAbd al-Wahhāb al-Shaʿrānī, God benefit us through him, mentions that it is desirable to eat things such as vegetables and fruit and the like at their first appearance, for their health benefits when new are greater than when old. The people of Cairo are of this school and think it auspicious to obtain things when they are still new, and care nothing for them when they are old—may God reward them for their doughtiness, granting them everlasting pleasure in their womenfolk and seasoning to perfection their togetherness, and God protect us from the countryside and its stupidities, the coarseness of its food and of its people's proclivities! 11.12.6

Question: What is the wisdom in calling mallow with fava beans *bīsār*, and what is the wisdom in calling mallow *mulūkhiyyā*, and what are the etymology and the meaning of the latter? The Facetious Answer may take two forms. The first is that the father of the man who originally invented *bīsār* was a peasant who used to grow *mulūkhiyyā*. However, there was bad blood between him and his son, and the latter went to the field of his aforementioned father and stole some of the aforementioned *mulūkhiyyā* and took it to his wife, who said to him, "What do you want with this?" He replied, "I intend to have it made into food," and he took its leaves and placed them in a pot and put it on the fire. Then along came his young son, who threw into the pot a few stewed fava beans that he had taken from the donkey's trough, and the *mulūkhiyyā* mixed with the beans. Next, after what was in the pot had cooked, he took it and ladled it into a crock and sat down and ate from it. Then his father came in and said, "What's that green stuff?" and the man spoke deceitful words to him and said, "It's grass we brought from the field." Later it came out that he had stolen the *mulūkhiyyā* from 11.12.7

his father's field, and the two of them fought, and his father swore that he would stay no longer in the village and mounted his donkey and went off to another village, with the result that the son took to crying out, "*Abī sār! Abī sār!*" ("My father has gone off! My father has gone off!"). Finally, they dropped the *a* from *abī* ("My father") and constructed this compound term out of a noun and a verb as a name for that dish, calling it *bīsār*. And one of my refined brethren, God have mercy upon him, informed me of another possible answer, which is that when the beans were placed in the pot they called out, "*Biya sār*," using their "natural tongue," that is, "through me (*biya*) it has become (*sār*)," meaning "through these beans my taste has become"[342] good. A third possibility is that the word is formed from *busr* ("fresh, juicy plants"), or from *bīsārah*,[343] on the basis of the verse on the same topic:

> Happy was Mizārah—
> She loved to cook *bīsārah*!

11.12.8 As for *mulūkhiyyā*, Ibn Sūdūn, may the Almighty have mercy on his soul, defines it by means of the following term coined for it in his *Works*, when he says on the topic:[344]

> Abū Qurdān[345]
> Sowed a feddan
> Of *mulūkhiyyā*
> And *bādinjān*.[346]

This is a name for a green tender plant. It was originally *yā mulūkhī*. Then they put the vocative particle *yā* at the end. Abū Qurdān was the first to call it so, or so they say. It came about as follows: when he sowed it in his feddan and it became ready for cooking, he tore some of it out and left it where it was and went off on some other business. Then one of his children came along and took it. When Abū Qurdān came back he could not find it, and he called out for it, omitting the vocative particle because he thought it must be somewhere close to him, and he said, "*Mulūkhī*!" ("My tearings!"). However, it answered not a word. Then he introduced the vocative particle, but before he could say *mulūkhī* a second time, his son came to him and informed him that he was the one who had taken them, so the net result was *mulūkhī yā*,[347] and then the second *yā'* was joined to the first and the word became *mulūkhiyyā*.[348] End of answer.

It is nicknamed Little Greeny and given the *kunyah*s "Mother of Fats" and "Mother of Joys." There is no food more refined or more beneficial to the health. A certain scholar has composed a wonderful book on its virtues. As for al-Ḥākim bi-Amri-llāh's having banned it, this was because Our Master Muʿāwiyah, may the Almighty be pleased with him, was greatly attached to it, it being his favorite food, especially at the start of the season.[349] 11.12.9

fī l-jurni ("on the threshing floor"): this is the place prepared for threshing fava beans and wheat, and the word is also applied to the hollowed-out stone in which coffee beans are pounded. One says, "Today So-and-so brought his crop to the threshing floor (*jarrana zarʿahu*)," meaning that he transported it from the field and put it there, one bit on top of another, in the form of a pile, and started taking it little by little from the edges and threshing it with the threshing sledge, the quantity so taken being what the peasants call a *ramyah*. It is said the origin of *jurn* is *jarm*, with *m* instead of *n*, taken from *jarm al-laḥm*, namely, "the removal of the meat from the bone with a knife"; the *m* got changed into an *n* because of the closeness of the points of articulation. The appositeness of this sense comes from the fact that the threshing sledge "bones" (*yajrimu*) the wheat, or the beans, or whatever grains are thrown to it, from the ears, and frees it, just as the knife frees the meat from the bone. The same term (*jurn*) is also applied to the *jarm* that is made out of palm fronds.[350] 11.12.10

jā-lū ("come to him"): with suppression of the glottal stop, that is, *jā'a ilayh*.[351] The subject pronoun refers to the *bīsār*, that is, happy is he to whom *bīsār* comes while he is on the threshing floor threshing 11.12.11

wheat and riding the threshing sledge, or while he is turning the wheat so that it passes under the blades of the sledge, or standing guard, for example, because when so engaged he will be weary and hungry. For this reason he says . . .

11.12.12 *wa-yadʿas* ("and bolts it"): that is, gulps it down at agonizing speed without taking any time to chew and swallow. *Daʿs*[352] is a rural expression used in this sense,[353] and the paradigm is *daʿasa, yadʿasu, daʿsan*, active participle *dāʿis*. This way of eating is unacceptable, because the proper way to eat is to make the size of the mouthful as small as possible and take a long time chewing. As the proverb says, "Make your mouthfuls small and take time over your chewing, and God will bless you in your eating."

11.12.13 A Fatuous Problem. The poet attributes the coming to the *bīsār*, which is a food, and it is inconceivable that a food should come on its own, so what is the wisdom in that? The Facetious Answer is that this should be taken as an example of "the omission of the first element of a genitive construction,"[354] that is, *a man* came with it, carrying it until he handed it over, in the same way that one says for example, "The ship came," that is, the navigator brought it, and in the same way that one says, for example, "Tonight a dish full of lentils or *bīsār* came to me." On this basis there is nothing problematic in the poet's words.

11.12.14 *wa-law kān* ("though he be"): that is, though the one who desires this food, namely, the poet, be, by the sickness called . . .

11.12.15 *al-qulinji ḍaʿīf* ("colic enfeebled"): that is, though he be indisposed. Colic is a dry flatulence that prevents vapor[355] from circulating through the limbs. It prostrates the sufferer when it breaks out and prevents him from inhaling, to the point that he almost gives up the ghost. It has Hot and Cold forms. The sign of the Hot is that the sickness breaks out on exposure to heat and hot winds and on sudden waking from sleep. The treatment is to eat green aloes, always on an empty stomach, for this denies the sickness access to the stomach cavity, and dissolves it. The sign of the Cold form is the eruption of the sickness on exposure to extreme cold, clouds, rain, cold winds, and so on. The treatment is to take aloes of Socotra, seeds of garden cress, pepper, and dry ginger in equal parts, and pound all these with an equal quantity of white sugar till smooth. This is made into a powder, which is taken at breakfast on an empty stomach, when the sickness breaks out. It is effective. The sufferer from the Hot form of this sickness should avoid eating hot things and the sufferer from the Cold form should avoid eating cold things, especially when the sickness first breaks out. This is effective, if the Almighty wills.

The meaning is that the poet was so poor and hungry and so lacking in the wherewithal to prepare this food that he wished that it would come to him and that he might eat his fill of it, even if he were to be stricken with the colic and even if eating it should cause him further harm, for it is a crude, vile food, especially if used by someone suffering from this sickness, to whom it will do great injury. If it be asked why the poet mentions this particular illness and not others, and how come he is acquainted with it when he is from the countryside and what is the etymology of its name,[356] the Facetious Answer would be that he only mentions this illness because it consists of complex gases, this thus falling under the rubric of hyperbole. *Bīsār* does immense harm to the sufferer from flatulence, especially if he eats green or dry onions with it, for it causes his belly to fill with wind and farts, silent and audible, and these multiply in it, so that the latter becomes a second illness on top of the first. Nevertheless, he is so hungry that he longs for it even though he should fall victim to these things or die on the spot. As for how he came to be acquainted with the sickness, it may be that he heard of it from a doctor who was describing it, or from anyone else. As for the etymology of the name, it may be from *qawq* ("screeching") or from the *quwayqah*, which is a bird the size of a dove with a large head, also called the *būmah* ("owl"), which inhabits ruined places. The proverb says, "Follow the owl, and it will lead you to the ruin." White hairs are sometimes likened to it, just as black hair may be 11.12.16

likened to the black crow. Imam al-Shāfiʿī, may the Almighty be pleased with him, said on this topic:[357]

O owl, who made your nest above my crown,
Atop my head, after the crow had taken flight—
Seeing my life depart, you came a-visiting,
For the ruin, above all abodes, is where you love to light.

11.12.17 Apropos of the owl and its preference for inhabiting ruins, I am reminded that once a certain king oppressed his subjects outrageously. Now, he had a minister who was sagacious and wise, and to him the people brought their troubles and complained of the king's tyranny. The minister then decided to play a trick on the king to turn him aside from his oppressive ways and guide him to justice. One day he and the king went out to relax outside the city. They proceeded until they passed by some ruins, and the king heard a male owl calling to a female. He said to the minister, "How lovely is the call of this bird to the female owl!" and the minister replied, "Sire, do you know what he is saying to her?" "No," said the king, "but do you, minister, know the language of the birds?" "I do," he replied. So the king asked, "What was he saying to her?" The minister responded, "This bird, sire, is in love with her and is smitten with desire for her, and he was saying to her, 'Mistress of Birds and Lovers' Delight, I wish to be one with you and be joined with you in holy matrimony.' And she replied, 'You will never be able to afford my dowry, even though love and yearning for me exercise you.' 'And what is your dowry?' he said to her. Said she, 'Ten ruined cities.' 'What joyful news,' said he, 'for if this king of ours continues to treat his subjects until the end of the year as he is treating them now, you may have a hundred ruined cities!'" The king took in the meaning of the minister's words and realized that he had been neglectful of his subjects and that they were living in parlous injustice and that the minister had given him advice and guided him towards justice through the language of the birds. "God reward you well!" he said to him, and from then on he manifested justice towards his subjects and relieved them of the abuses and catastrophes from which they had been suffering, and from that day and hour he behaved with righteousness and the people found comfort in his change of state. Our words are now clear, the answer to the problem has appeared.

Next the poet longed for another dish that is made in the countryside and elsewhere, and said: 11.12.18

TEXT

ʿalā man qashaʿ jafnat balīlah malānah 11.13
wa-law kānat[358] *bi-lā qulqāsi yā dandīf*

Happy is he who sees a bowl with *balīlah* filled,
though it be without taro, you good-for-nothing!

COMMENTARY

ʿalā man qashaʿ ("Happy is he who sees"): that is, *qashaʿ* means "to see" in the language of the country people: one says *qashaʿtak*, that is, "I beheld you" and *qashaʿtu l-maḥalla l-fulānī* ("I saw such and such a place"), that is, "I beheld it."[359] The same word is used in the sense of something's "turning away": one says *inqashaʿa l-saḥāb* ("the clouds were scattered"), that is, they turned aside and were borne away to another place.[360] 11.13.1

An Amazing Thing: one day a man heard a bird say the same word in an orchard of Damascus. What happened is that he entered an orchard one day to look around and eat some of the fruit that had fallen from the trees and he heard someone say, "I see you (*shuftak*)! I spy you (*qashaʿtak*)! Go!" so the man fled, thinking that the owner of the orchard was shouting at him. As he was leaving the orchard, a man met him and asked him, "Why are you running?" so he said, "In the orchard I heard a person say such and such to me." The man laughed and said, "Go back and eat what you like and fear no one! It is a bird, not a man, and that is its language, with which it frightens those who enter the orchard." The man was amazed and ate until he had had enough, and went his way. And I myself, while 11.13.2

heading for the port of al-Quṣayr on my way to make the pilgrimage by sea from Upper Egypt in 1075,[361] heard a bird in a wheat field say, "The flour has ripened in the ear, glory to the Ancient, the Eternal!" and everyone on board the ship heard it. Al-Ḥalabī, in his biography of the Prophet, mentions a raven that memorized the Chapter of the Prostration,[362] and when he prostrated himself would say, "To You my blackness has bowed down, in You my heart has placed its faith."

11.13.3 Another Amazing Thing: A certain king once received a gift of a bird with four wings, pleasingly formed. When the time came for the dawn prayer, it would utter the name of the Almighty with clear tongue and then stand by the king's head and say, "Prayer is better than sleep"[363] twice, then pronounce blessings on the Prophet, God bless him and grant him peace, and fall silent. Such things are numerous, so glory be to God who is capable of anything—«and there is not a thing but glorifies His praise.»[364]

11.13.4 *jafna(t)* ("a bowl"): defined above.[365]

11.13.5 *balīlah* ("with *balīlah*"): a name for boiled wheat with some chickpeas added. This is sold in the cities too and is delicious, its tastiness lying in the addition of salt and chickpeas, for the latter adjusts its humors. Chickpeas are the purest food there is, according to a commentator writing on the Chapter of the Cave.[366] As for the *balīlah* that is mentioned here in the verse, the country people make it into a dish, the method being to put the wheat in an earthenware pot, to which they may add a few chickpeas, and then cover it with water and place it on the fire till done. Then they take it and eat it with sorghum or barley bread, or break off bits and swallow them without bread, for they make it dry, and one just breaks off a piece with his hand and swallows it. They garnish it with fried onions and a little sesame oil, and their great men put in a little taro. It is called *balīlah* because of the wetting (*ball*) in water it receives when it is boiled, or because of its sloppiness and moistness, which is why any futile, slack-twisted,[367] slothful man is referred to as a *balīlah* for his inability to earn a living and his failure as a breadwinner. *Balīlah* is of the measure of *habīlah* ("stupid") or *ʿawīlah* ("parasitic, sponging"), and the paradigm is *balla, yabullu, balīlatan* ("to wet").[368]

malānah ("filled"): referring to the bowl 11.13.6

wa-law kānat ("though it be"): as though the *balīla* which is in the bowl be . . . 11.13.7

bi-lā qulqāsi ("without taro"): that is, he has no need of the latter, and all he desires is anything that can be called food, to satisfy his hunger. Taro is a winter food, the most delicious thing eaten in that season, since it is Hot and Dry, which fits the coldness of the period, especially when it first appears on the market. If eaten with mutton and the addition of clarified butter with greens and so on, its nature is tempered and it acquires a most delicious flavor, its Hotness being dissipated and its nature tempered. The best parts of it are the female heads and the "fingers"—which are the thin bits that look like human fingers—because these all cook quickly. The worst is the red part because it is slow to digest and slow to cook. If taro is eaten grilled, it stops liver pains and relieves throbbing piles. There is no value or benefit to eating it raw. 11.13.8

A Useful Note: Four things beginning with *q* are used in winter: the above, *qushṭah* ("clotted cream"), *qaṣab* ("sugarcane"), and the *qasṭal* ("water pipe"). 11.13.9

It is called *qulqās* because it derives from *qalqasah* ("colocassation"),[369] since it resembles "colocassated," that is, dry, mud, because when it is pulled out of the ground it is like lumps of "colocassated," dry, mud. It is formed of two verbs, one in the perfect tense, the other imperative. A poet says: 11.13.10

> If they ask you of my heart and what it suffered,
> Say, "It suffered tarobly, tarobly, tarobly!"[370]

Another Useful Note: It is said that, when Pharaoh claimed divine status, they reprehended him, telling him, "A god neither urinates 11.13.11

nor defecates!" So Pharaoh invented the banana and started eating it and reached a point at which he defecated only rarely. He did this by taking some taro plants from the ground when small, splitting each tuber in half, filling it with sugar, and putting it back in the soil by a method he devised, so that the sweetness mixed with the taro, and the banana grew from it and took on its form. This is why you will notice that its leaves are close in shape to those of the taro in terms of breadth, though the banana's are longer than the taro's. So it is written in one of the books of wisdom.

11.13.12 *yā dandīf* ("you good-for-nothing"): originally this is *yā dandūf*, of the measure of *yā buʿbūṣ* ("you little bump"), the *ū* having been turned into an *ī* for the sake of the rhyme. A *dandūf* is a person who comes and goes and achieves nothing. One says, "So-and-so *yudandifu*,"[371] that is, there is no benefit in his comings and goings or blessing in his efforts and earnings. Or it may be that it is the proper name of someone from the poet's village, seeing that it is counted among their names.[372] It is derived from *dandafah* ("acting ineffectually"),[373] or from Aḥmad al-Danaf, or from the *nadf* ("carding") of cotton.[374]

11.13.13 The poet then goes on to long for a basin full of any food whatsoever and says:

TEXT

11.14 *ʿalā man jatū qaṣʿah wa-huwwa bi-yaḥrit*
wa-yaqʿud yujarrif li-l-ḥanak tajrīf

Happy is he to whom comes a basin while he's plowing
and sits and shovels away into his gob!

COMMENTARY

11.14.1 *ʿalā man jatū* ("Happy is he to whom comes"): the origin of the second word is *jāʾathu*.[375]

11.14.2 *qaṣʿah* ("a basin"): that is, someone brought it to him; it did not come of its own accord, as previously explained,[376] the subject pronoun of the preceding verb referring to the omitted agent. The *qaṣʿah* is a wooden vessel, round in shape and made for food and other things.[377] The vessel that is made in the form of a watering trough, on the other hand, is called a *mansaf*.[378] In the Tradition it says, "We taught Adam all the names, even the *qaṣʿah* and the *quṣayʿah* and the *faswah* ('silent fart') and the *fusaywah*."[379] It is called a *qaṣʿah* because, when one sits and eats from it, he bows his back (*yaqṣaʿu ẓahrahu*), that is, he bends over and eats. Thus it falls into the category of "naming a thing after the properties of the one who eats from it."[380] Or it may be from *qaṣaʿa l-qamla wa-l-barāghīth* ("he squashed the lice and fleas between his fingernails").

wa-huwwa ("while he"): with *u* after the *h* and double *w*, for the sake of the meter, or according to the language of the countryside.[381] 11.14.3

bi-yaḥrit ("is plowing"): of the measure of *bi-yaḍriṭ* ("is farting audibly"), which is something that happens in plowing, for sure; that is, at the time of plowing, happy is he to whom comes any food whatsoever, be it lentils or *bīsār* or anything else. 11.14.4

wa-yaqʿud ("and sits"): as one sits who is hungry and tired out from the labor of plowing and so on that he has endured. 11.14.5

and *yujarrif* ("shovels"): of the measure of *yukharrif* ("he talks twaddle") or *yugharrif* ("he ladles"), that is, his hand would perform the function of the shovel that shovels things . . . 11.14.6

li-l-ḥanak ("into his gob"): from *taḥnīk* ("to make worldly-wise"), of the measure of *taḥkīk* ("to rub") or *tadkīk* ("to pass a drawstring through a waistband"). The word is applied to the upper and lower jaws of a human being, and it is reported that the Prophet, God bless him and grant him peace, "stuffed the jaws of" (*ḥannaka*) a child with dates, in which case it would fall into the category of "naming a thing after what drops into it." It is also applied to the mouth (*al-fam* and *al-fāh*);[382] one says either *fataḥa famahu* or *fataḥa fāhu* ("He opened his mouth").[383] The author of the *Badīʿiyyah*,[384] may the Almighty have mercy on his soul, says: 11.14.7

My mouth (*famī*) speaks of my secrets, and naught reveals
The secrets of my heart but the speech of my mouth (*famī*).

11.14.8 *tajrīf* ("*away*, used as an intensifier"): properly *tajrīfan* because it is a verbal noun, but the *an* has been dropped for the sake of the rhyme.[385] That is, because of the pangs of hunger, the severe exhaustion, and the great hardship he has suffered, he shovels food into his "gob" (that is to say, "his mouth") with an intemperate, continuous shoveling, conducted at speed and with haste, until he is satisfied and stuffed to the limit. By so doing, he achieves his desire, his good humor is restored, and he acquires renewed vigor for plowing and what have you.

11.14.9 Next he longs for another of the dishes of the country people, but this time one that is uncooked. He says:

TEXT

11.15 *ʿalā man daʿas bi-l-ʿazmi fī l-mishshi bi-l-baṣal*
wa-law kāna bi-l-kurrāti kāna ḍarīf

Happy is he who gobbles energetically at *mishsh* with onions—
and were it with leeks, that would be nice!

COMMENTARY

11.15.1 *ʿala man daʿas* ("Happy is he who gobbles"): defined above.[386]

11.15.2 *bi-l-ʿazmi* ("energetically"): that is, with strength and vigor, for to approach something with *ʿazm* ("determination, resolution, energy") is to approach it with boldness and vigor. One says, "So-and-oso has great *ʿazm*," that is, abnormal strength.

11.15.3 *fī l-mishshi* ("at *mishsh*"): that is, the *mishsh* of blue skimmed-milk cheese that has been left to age till it has become sharp and salty enough to cut the tail off a mouse, for this is the thing the country people most often eat for lunch and sometimes for dinner, too.[387] One of them will get the *mishsh* crock and dry barley bread and green or dry onions and eat until his eyes weep from the sharpness of the *mishsh* and the smell of the onions, and wash it down with water and set off for the fields or to plow or thresh. The great ones among them put a little linseed oil on it and squeeze lime over it, especially . . .

bi-l-baṣal ("with onions"): that is to say, with chopped onions, for it is tastier to eat it thus than to eat it on its own. Some of them eat it with leeks, which makes it more likely to generate flatulence, especially if it is eaten in a confined space, in which case the farts will accumulate there until they fill it from top to bottom. 11.15.4

Mishsh is of various kinds. There is strained *mishsh*, which has been defined above,[388] and full-fat *mishsh*, which is the kind used in the cities and is lighthearted and delicious. One speaks of *ḥālūm*-cheese *mishsh* and of cottage-cheese *mishsh*, which is the *mishsh* of the country people referred to previously. One also speaks of oven-cheese *mishsh*. *Mishsh* is of the measure of *wishsh* ("face") as that word is pronounced in the language of the country people.[389] When one of them insults another, he says, "*Damm ihdim wishshak*" ("Blood destroy your face")![390] for example. It is derived from *mashash* ("splint"), a disease of horses and donkeys. One says, "*Jāk mashash* ('Get splint')!" that is, may God afflict you with it. The first kind, that is "strained *mishsh*," is good against mange, if drunk; the second is good against blockages and strengthens the stomach; and the third is good for nothing—on the contrary, it is pure harm, no more, no less! Or it may be derived from *mashy* ("walking"), because, if poured on the ground, it will "walk" on, that is, spread over, it. 11.15.5

Onions are Hot and Dry (and, some say, Moist). They inhibit phlegm but provoke migraines and headaches, cause wind, and weaken the eyesight. Overconsumption results in forgetfulness and disorders the mind. As for their good qualities, they drive away pestilence, for it is related concerning God's Messenger, God bless him and grant him peace, that he said, "If you enter a land where there is pestilence, and are afraid of catching the disease, eat of its onions!" They are good against foul waters, release the carnal appetite, 11.15.6

provoke sexual excitement, increase the semen, and improve the complexion. They get rid of coarse freckles, tetters, and black vitiligo when powdered, kneaded with honey, and applied to these. Pounded smooth and applied to the roots of the hair they are good against "fox disease," which is hair loss. The juice, used as an ointment, revives one who has fainted, and vinegar and milk balance its humors if it is eaten with either.

11.15.7 *wa-law kāna bi-l-kurrāṭi kāna ḍarīf* ("and were it with leeks, that would be nice!"): that is, because they are Hot and Soft, and stir up the stomach and the blood, though, like onions, they weaken the eyesight and cause wind, as previously noted. However, they tighten the phallus and are good for piles. They are best eaten with sesame oil. Eating raw onions, garlic, and leeks is disapproved of for one entering a mosque unless he take something to rid his mouth of the smell, in accordance with the words of the Prophet, God bless him and grant him peace, "The eater of garlic, onions, and leeks, let him not approach our mosque; for the angels suffer from those things from which men suffer"—by analogy, this extends to all mosques, for the wording is specific but the intention is general. A Useful Note: I have seen in a book that all edible green plants found their way onto the table of Master Jesus, peace be upon him, except leeks.[391] As for the squill, it has excellent properties that are mentioned in works on medicine. It is a remarkable fact that, if a wolf steps on one, it dies instantly. This why if a fox is in fear for his life from a wolf, it gets a squill tuber and puts it at the entrance to its hole; when the wolf sees it and smells it, it runs away and never comes back, and it thus acts as a protection for the fox, glory be to Him who inspired it with this wisdom!

11.15.8 *ḍarīf* ("nice"): originally, *ẓarif*, with *ẓ* and not with *ḍ*; his use of the first form is in accordance with rural usage. That is, it would be a pleasant thing, meaning that they would be less injurious than onions (albeit more likely to cause flatulence), for leeks are far more appetizing and tasty; there would be no harm therefore if they were present, and this, indeed, is what he wants.

Next the poet desires some milk product to drink. He says: 11.15.9

TEXT

ʿalā man sharib matrad malāna muṭanbir 11.16
mina l-labani l-ḥāmiḍ yariffu rafīf

Happy is he who drinks a crock, full to the brim
of sour milk that flutters!

COMMENTARY

ʿalā man sharib ("Happy is he who drinks"): drinking is the passing of water and other fluids via the mouth into the belly. The Almighty says, «Eat and drink»[392] and He says, «But they drank thereof, all but a few of them.»[393] It does not cover what a man puts in his mouth and then expels, like the tobacco that is used nowadays: when people refer to this as "drinking," they do so not in a real but in a figurative sense.[394] 11.16.1

matrad ("a crock"): this is a vessel of red pottery, smaller than the *shāliyah*. It is the vessel most in use among the country people, especially at their weddings. The word was originally composed of two verbs, *māt* ("it died") and *radd* ("it returned") because, when it was first made and broke, they made another one instead, and said, "It returned (*radd*) after it died (*māt*)." Then they omitted the *alif* and made it a proper name and said *matrad*.[395] It is of the measure of *maqʿad* ("seat") or *masnad* ("cushion"). What the poet wants is the milk that is within it, not the crock itself, for it is just a container for what it holds, and the idea of drinking the crock itself is not to be entertained. Some say that it was given this name because bread is frequently found in it (*li-taraddud al-khubzi fīh*) and food is placed upon it, in which case it would belong to the category of "naming the container after the thing contained"; or that it was named after a 11.16.2

city called Māturīd from which Shaykh al-Māturīdī, God benefit us through him, took his name.

11.16.3 *malāna* ("full"): that is, not lacking, so that it be satisfying to both the stomach and the eye, for a person may well reckon something that is less than full to be too little, and not be satisfied when he sees it. This is why he wants it to be full . . .

11.16.4 *muṭanbir* ("to the brim"): of the measure of *muzanbir*[396] or *muṭarṭir* ("raised"); one speaks of a *kuss muzanbir* ("an engorged cunt") and a *zubb muṭarṭir* ("a stiff prick"); that is, one that is high above its surroundings, referring here to the extreme sourness and stiffness of the milk. One says, "So-and-so's belly is 'brimful' (*miṭṭanbar*)" that is, inflated (*manfūkh*), or "He died and became brimful (*iṭṭanbar*)," [397] that is, "became inflated" (*intafakh*), and one says, "Blood fill your belly to the brim! (*damm yiṭanbar baṭnak*)" for example, that is, "May you die and inflate!"; and similarly one speaks of the Hijazi turban made of white and yellow silk, on which the local turban is modeled, as "brimming over" (*miṭṭanbar*), this description being used perhaps because, when one wraps it around his head, it becomes large, high, and "brimming over" (*miṭṭanbar*) in the same way that sour milk rises above the edges of the crock. It is derived from *ṭanbarah*,[398] which is frottage with young boys. The poet says:

> If you're into your "instrument" and your nature's
> "tamborine-ish,"
> Rub away gently and remember the one they hung![399]

—the background to these words being that a certain reprobate took a young boy intending to practice frottage with him, but he "misfired" and rammed it home. The boy died, the man was hung, and a lot of verse was composed, of which I recall only this opening line. Or it may be from *ṭunbūrah* ("tambourine"), of the measure of *ʿuṣfūrah* ("sparrow"). The poet says:

Garden sparrow, how you scratch around
With hand and foot, when nothing's on the ground!

Next he reveals what this thing that is "brimming over" is by saying 11.16.5

mina l-labani l-ḥāmiḍ ("with sour milk"): he specifies that it is sour because he is unable to obtain fresh milk, which is why it is as though he were saying, "I desire it even though it be sour, anything else being beyond my reach." This would be especially true if it were the hot season, for, if he were to drink it then, it would quench his thirst and refresh his heart, as long as it were only moderately sour, for it is Cold and Moist. However, it is harmful if excessively sour, and, in fact, the poet's words indicate that he wants precisely the milk that has gone excessively sour, as evidenced by the following words: "that flutters." The finest milk is cow's milk because it is good for all medicines and all diseases. In the Tradition it says, "Its flesh is a disease,[400] a medicine its milk and cheese."

yariffu rafīf ("that flutters"): that is, it is so sour that it has started 11.16.6
to flutter, just as a bird's wing does, meaning that it makes boiling and bubbling sounds like those of a wing fluttering. *Yariffu* is of the measure of *yasiffu* ("he gulps") or *yaluffu* ("he bolts").[401] *Rafīf* is the verbal noun, with the *-an* dropped, as in similar cases.[402] It is derived from the wooden *raff* ("shelf") that is put up in houses, or from the *rafrāfah*[403] that they make of chicken, goose, and other ingredients before Ramadan or at the end of Shaʿbān.

Next the poet wants something else, which the people of the vil- 11.16.7
lages close to the sea or the saltwater lakes and such-like areas make use of. He says:

TEXT

ʿalā man jatū ʾummu l-khulūli li-dārū 11.17
wa-yaʿzim ʿalā ʾahli l-balad wa-yaḍīf

Happy is he to whom mussels come, to his house
and who invites the people of the village and plays host!)

COMMENTARY

11.17.1 *ʿalā man jatū* ("Happy is he to whom (mussels) come"): that is, come to him by the agency of another,[404] and reach him.

11.17.2 *ummu l-khulūli* ("mussels"): a creature that forms inside the small shells resembling almonds that are found on the shore of the sea and the saltwater lakes. It moves quickly, but if one touches it, it goes still and does not move, remaining like a stone until he leaves it. This creature is enclosed within two small shells and has a thick white color, like semen or mucus. They take it and extract it from these shells and put salt and vinegar and lime on it and eat it. Sometimes they take it out while still alive and knead it with salt and eat it, this making the most disgusting, vile, and revolting dish—we seek shelter from it with God and give praise and thanks to Him that we have never eaten it, for sound natures spit it out and refuse it, and the appetite turns from it in disgust! As for the natures of the people of the countryside, on the other hand, do not ask us to speak of them, for they are revolting and seek only what is revolting, and they find this dish most delicious and their miserable souls hold it in high esteem. No one who has a sound nature will eat it or even look at it, for the very sight of it, not to mention its consumption, gives rise to revulsion. They are given the nickname *umm al-khulūl* ("mother of vinegars") because salt and vinegar and lime are put on them continually while they are being eaten.

11.17.3 *li-dārū* ("to his house"): that is, the poet's house, meaning that he would not have to exert himself to get them by hunting for them or buying them; on the contrary, he would look and find them in his house, someone having brought them as charity or a gift.

wa-ya'zim 'alā ahli l-balad ("and who invites the people of the village"): that is, gathers them to eat of this precious dish that resembles dog's vomit and hosts them in his house, that is, honors them there. One says, "So-and-so invited (*'azama 'alā*) So-and-so," that is, he determined (*'azama*) inwardly[405] and resolved with certainty that he would take him and honor him, or "invited him" (*'azamahu*),[406] meaning, give him permission to come to his house, and honor him with food and so forth. 11.17.4

wa-yaḍīf ("and plays host"): *yaḍīf* is joined to *ya'zim* by the coordinating conjunction *wa-*, in which case the questions becomes, "Does the former contrast with the latter, or is the meaning the same?" for "the determination to invite (*'azm*)" is different from "(the actual provision of) hospitality (*ḍiyāfah*)." In the former case, the meaning would be "he first determined inwardly that this person must come to him," it being understood that he would then be "annexed to him" (*yanḍāfu ilayh*), that is, follow him to the place in which he wished to provide him with hospitality. Thus understood, it would be a matter of "annexing a thing (*iḍāfat al-shay'*) to something other than itself."[407] The paradigm is *ḍāfa, yaḍīfu, ḍiyāfatan*, or *ḍuyūfan*.[408] A guest is called a *ḍayf* because he is "annexed to" (*yanḍāfu ilā*) the one who hosts him, meaning that he and the other are in a relationship analogous to a possessive annexation—the one cannot be detached from the other until a nunation comes between them, in which case it separates it from the relationship of annexation.[409] The poet says: 11.17.5

> It seems to me that I'm a nunation, you an annexation:
> Whenever we meet, you leave no place for me to be!

Through this fatuous investigation, the facetious meaning has now been revealed.

Next, the poet moves on from this desire to something else almost as revolting as mussels. He says: 11.17.6

TEXT

11.18 *anā-n shuftu ʿindī yawma ṭājin mushakshikin*
fa-hādāka yawmu l-basṭi wa-l-taqṣīf

If I see next to me one day a casserole of fish skins
then that is a day of happiness and one on which of one's
clothes to make boast!

COMMENTARY

11.18.1 *anā* ("I"): meaning Abū Shādūf and no one else.

11.18.2 *in shuftu* ("if I see"): seeing (*al-shawf*) is the opposite of blindness (*al-ʿamā*), or it may be from *shiyāfah* ("eye medicine"). The meaning is, if I behold it . . .

11.18.3 *ʿindī* ("next to me"): at home, or in the place in which I happen to be, or in the field and on the threshing floor, for example.

11.18.4 *yawma* ("one day"): that is, one day when Fate has bungled and the Almighty is looking kindly on me

11.18.5 *ṭājin* ("a casserole"): name for a round earthenware vessel with a wide belly, in which fish, rice, meat, fowl, and other things are cooked, which is used throughout the country, though food can only be cooked in it in the oven. It is derived from *tatjīn* ("speaking harshly") or from *ṭijānah* ("the art of cooking in a casserole") or from *waṭ' al-jinn* ("treading on the jinn"), for *ṭājin* is a puzzle word,[410] deriving its hidden meaning from the fact that some person *waṭi'a jinnan*, that is, "'stepped on' (*dāsa*) a company of jinn," the word being constructed, from this perspective, from the combination of a verb, a subject, and an object, the subject (which is omitted) being "you"; thus the meaning is "(You there,) tread on some jinn! (*ṭa' anta jinnan*)"[411] A similar word is *ṭāfiyah*, that is, a *ṭā'ifah* ("group, company") of people.[412]

There is further category of such puzzle words, different from the preceding, exemplified by someone's saying that the name Ḥammād means "Take something empty and fill it with water";[413] and, for verse, my own lines on the name Shaḥātah: 11.18.6

He wreaked havoc on folk with his cute ways,
Making nice (*wālif*) after being tightfisted (*shuḥḥ*).
Long ago said I, to be done, "Get lost (*tih*)!—
My commentary's got your meaning untwisted."[414]

But the most exquisite word puzzle I have seen is a poet's words on the name Aḥmad, which go:

How many a one bends in prayer in the ban tree's shade,
Joined to a pearl in a bird's beak displayed![415]

mushakshikin ("of fish skins"): of the measure of *muḥakkik* ("rubbing"), the name of the food that he wants to see and of which he wants to eat. It consists of the skins of salt-cured fish: they eat the flesh and take and wash the skins in water and put them in a casserole with sliced onions and a little linseed oil, then put it in the oven until it is done and eat it with bread. Sometimes they put some cotton-seed cake dissolved in water on top of it as a substitute for sesame paste. This is highly regarded by them, and especially by their womenfolk, as much as if it were grilled mutton, which is why he says . . . 11.18.7

fa-hādāka ("then that"): with *d*, in accordance with rural usage,[416] as the poet says in a *mawāliyā*: 11.18.8

You there (*yā hādāk*), on your cheeks you've roses twain,
And would you could feel your lover's pain!
By Him to whom the angels in Heaven raise their paean,
Though I lose two brothers a day, your memory will forever remain!

11.18.9 *yawmu* ("is a day"): that is, then that day on which this casserole of fish skins comes to me is a day of . . .

11.18.10 *al-basti* ("happiness"): the opposite of *qabḍ* ("being unhappy"; literally "constriction"); that is, the *basṭ* ("unfolding") of the soul and the relaxing of the heart consequent on the acquisition of the object of desire, the easing of access to what is sought, the presence of what is wanted, the satisfaction of hunger, and the pleasure of the members of my household and all those who are with me when it comes to me. The poet says:

> Verily, among the best of my days are those when I'm happy
> (*mabsūṭ*) in myself!

11.18.11 *wa-taqṣīf* ("and one on which of one's clothes to make boast"): connected to *basṭ* by the coordinating conjunction *wa-*; derived from *qaṣṣāfah* ("clippers"). One says, "Today So-and-so is *qaṣṣīf*," with double *ṣ*, that is, happy, joyful, and walking proudly, belt and knife at his waist, letting the fringes of his mantle trail along the ground; or that today he is wearing a new shift and has draped his mantle over it; and one says, "Today he's the *qaṣṣīf* of the hamlet," meaning that there is no one more elegantly dressed or more dashing. Or it may be derived from the *qaṣf* ("snapping") of a stick, that is, the breaking of it, or from their expression *qaṣfah tajīk* ("May a snapping afflict you!") or *qaṣfah naqāwah* ("a snapping 'with your name on it!'") or *fulān jatū qaṣfah* ("So-and-so got snapped!"), for example.

11.18.12 A Fatuous Discussion. Why is this food called *mushakshik*, what is the meaning of this word, and why is it appropriate for the skins of salt-cured fish? The Facetious Answer: it is said that in view of its similarity of taste to *mishsh* and *kishk* mixed together, they made its name by combining those two names, with different vowels, and said *mishakshik*. Or it may be taken from a woman's pricking (*shakshakah*) of it with a stick or a spoon when it is almost done, to test it, or from the expression *shakshakahu* ("he pricked it") with a needle. Or it may be from *shamma kishk* ("he smelled *kishk*") backward, in which case its inventor, when he cooked it, smelled it, and they said, "What has this man smelled?" and one of them said *shamma kishk* ("he smelled *kishk*"), that is, he smelled some food whose smell is as sour as *kishk*; then they put the *m* in front of the *sh* and made it a proper name and said *mishakshik*, with an *a* after the first *sh*, an *i* after the second, and no vowels after the *k*s. The contention's now straightened out, the silliness exposed for what it's about.

Next the poet longs for another vegetable that is cooked and eaten in its season and which is the country people's most delicious dish. He says: 11.18.13

TEXT

matā ʾanḍuru l-khubbayza fī l-dāri ʿindanā 11.19
wa-ʾandifu minhā bi-l-ʿuwayshi nadīf

When shall I see mallow in the house at home
and cram it down with a little piece of bread?

COMMENTARY

matā ("when"): that is, I resolve and intend that when I . . . 11.19.1

ʾanḍuru ("see"): with *ḍ*, in accordance with rural usage, its pronunciation with *ẓ* belonging to the classical language;[417] that is, (when) I see with my eye, and not with my ear or my mouth, for seeing is specific to the eye (the poet says: 11.19.2

The eye did see and my sickness is from my eye) . . .

al-khubbayza ("mallow"): with *u* after the *kh* and double *b*: plural *khabāʾiz* . The plural of *khubbayz* may be *khabbūz*, or *khabāyiz* or *khabbāzīn*, or what have you, to choose from among the possible facetious plurals.[418] In the feminine, it is *khubbayzah*, which is what is intended in the poet's verse, since the pronoun refers to it, as we shall see in the discussion of his words *wa-ʾandifu minhā*.[419] The word is derived from *khubz* ("bread") because the leaves, in their roundness, resemble rounds of bread. It sprouts on the edges of the 11.19.3

cultivated land following heavy rains, and in low-lying and other lands. The best sort is that with a long stalk and broad, dark-green leaves, which is the kind that sprouts next to cultivated plants, or sprouts from seed. The worst sort is that with a short stalk, whose leaves are bluish in color, which is the kind that is far from cultivated crops and water. This kind is plentiful and sprouts in graveyards and in the low-lying parts of salt-logged land. It is Cold and Moist, eases the bowels, opens obstructions, and reduces fevers. It is as easy to digest as Jew's mallow, providing it is prepared according to the instructions given below. The people of the countryside take the leaves, chop them like Jew's mallow, put fresh coriander on them, garnish them with fried onions and sesame oil, crumble barley bread onto them, and eat them. This is the thing they eat most of for as long as it is available, because it costs them nothing but the onions, the sesame oil, and a little coriander, as mentioned. It is the thing they eat most of during the winter. The people of the villages on the river cook it with goose and chicken and so on, and the people of the cities cook it with fatty meats such as mutton or the like, and chicken, and they add fats, clarified cow's butter, greens, spices, and similar things, and this is the only way it should be eaten, for this way it is light and tasty. The way the country people do it, however, as described above, is worthless, and the same goes for the people of the villages on the river, for these, even if they do make it with chicken, add no clarified butter or fat, just rice and sesame oil, without greens or anything else; on the contrary, they eat it on its own. The latter is, nevertheless, more refined than the recipe of the country people referred to above. The best place to eat it, however, is in the cities, because they go to some trouble over it, which makes it light to eat and very tasty. They say, "Food is an expense: you get what you pay for."

11.19.4 It is said that, when Sultan Qāyitbāy stayed in Dimyāṭ and met with al-ʿAynī, who built the ʿAyniyyah,[420] which is a mosque built in the style of a royal mosque, al-ʿAynī prepared for him a great banquet and prepared him his own plate of gold, containing two chickens, and placed these before him. The sultan ate some and had never in all his life tasted anything more delicious. "Who prepared you these chickens?" he asked al-ʿAynī. "A slave girl of mine," he responded. "Could you spare her?" asked the sultan. "She and her master," returned al-ʿAynī, "are the sultan's to command," and he made him a gift of her. When the sultan brought her back to Cairo, he commanded her to prepare him two chickens, and she did so, but they did not turn out as before, and he did not find them as tasty as the two he had eaten in Dimyāṭ. When the sultan reproached her for this, she said to him, "My Lord, you get what you pay for. My master who prepared you those two chickens cooked them in a vessel made of gold, and the water he used was rosewater and such like, and the firewood was aloe wood, and he stuffed them with many spices as well as musk and ambergris, and ladled them into a dish made of gold. That exquisite taste was from this costly preparation." The sultan marveled at what al-ʿAynī, may the Almighty have mercy on his soul, had done.

fī l-dāri ʿindanā ("in the house at home"): that is, in the poet's house, not someone else's, because he is the one who desires it; and for the same reason he says "at home," that is, at our place and no one else's, so that the children can eat some of it and rejoice that it is there. A house is called a *dār* because of its being encircled (*li-tadwīrihā*) with baked brick, limestone, and so on, this being the way that city houses are. The houses of the countryside, on the other hand, are built of slabs of dung mixed with straw, sometimes including daub and dung cakes. Or the *dār* is so called because one goes about (*yadūru*) and then returns to it. Or it is derived from the game of *dārah* that the children of the country people play after sunset: one boy squats on his haunches and another boy does the same with his back to him and the rest circle round them and hit them; if one of the first two catches one of the others, he sits him in his place, and so on. From this they learn dexterity and how to strike and move quickly, and so forth. 11.19.5

11.19.6 *wa-ʾandifu minhā* ("and cram it down"): that is, cram down the mallow, the meaning being that he takes a little of it quickly and stuffs it into his belly, thus resembling the cotton teaser (*naddāf al-quṭn*), when he works the cotton with his bow and stuffs it into the mattress.[421] This gives rise to such statements as, "Last night So-and-so 'crammed down' (*nadaf*) two crocks of lentils, or of *bīsār*," that is, he ate them fast. Or it may be derived from Aḥmad al-Danaf, one of the clever rogues of Cairo of former times, whose life is well known to storytellers.

11.19.7 *bi-l-ʿuwayshi* ("with a little piece of bread"): diminutive of *ʿaysh* ("bread"), so called because it is on this that livelihood (*maʿīshah*) depends. The poet says:

Put not your faith in fine clothes
But think of your bones when bored by the worm;
On seeing the fripperies of this world, declare
"Dear God, the true life is the life the world to come!"[422]

—or it may be derived from the *ʿushsh* ("nest") of a bird because the latter has the same round shape as bread. As for why bread is also called *khubz*, this comes from *takhbīz* ("baking"), which is the process of bringing something to a state of maturation by fire. One says, "So-and-so beat So-and-so until he 'baked (*khabbaza*)' his ribs," that is, until the beating on them produced an effect similar to the thorough cooking of bread, or he broke them, for example, bread being easily broken. Or it may be that "he baked his ribs" means that he separated them one from another.

11.19.8 *nadīf* (used as an intensifier):[423] of the measure of *natīf* (literally "plucked"), which is someone who plucks his beard in order to make himself effeminate or who has a morbid craving for passive sodomy—God protect us from it, for it is an affliction that squirms hotly in the anus as worms squirm in carrion. The poet says:

Indeed, it is a sickness like a fire ignited
In the anus, squirming as worms in carrion squirm.

The surest cure for it is that mentioned by al-Shaʿrānī, God benefit us through him, namely, the repeated administration of an enema made from the liquid from salt-cured fish.[424] The sufferer will then recover, the Almighty willing. The word was originally *nadfan*, but the final *an* was dropped and it was turned into a diminutive for the sake of the rhyme;[425] that is, "I will stuff myself so full with mallow that I am utterly sated and feel no more hunger for the rest of the day, or the rest of the night."

Next the poet moves on from food to the green pulses, and says: 11.19.9

TEXT

matā ʾanḍuru l-fūla l-mushaywī bi-furninā 11.20
wa-luffū bi-qishrū wa-l-ʿurūqi lafīf

When shall I see grilled beans in our oven
and bolt them down with their skins and stalks in a manner
uninhibited?

COMMENTARY

matā ʾanḍuru ("when shall I see"): with my eye, as in the preceding line . . . 11.20.1

al-fūla ("beans"): meaning green fava beans brought from the field and put in the oven and grilled. What he wants is that these beans should be . . . 11.20.2

al-mushaywī ("grilled"): diminutive of *mashwī* of the measure of *ʿuṭaywī* ("little gift") or *khuraywī* ("little turd"), the latter containing both diminution and weight, for sure. 11.20.3

bi-furninā ("in our oven"): not in someone else's oven. 11.20.4

wa-luffū ("and bolt them down"): originally *wa-ʾaluffuhu* with a glottal stop, which he omitted for the sake of the meter;[426] from *laff* (verbal noun), which is cramming the mouth and swallowing and chewing fast without looking at or examining the food, which is why he says . . . 11.20.5

11.20.6 *bi-qishrū* ("with their skins"): that is, I will eat them without removing the skins, out of joy at having them and because I am so hungry.

11.20.7 *wa-l-ʿurūqi* ("and stalks"): joined to the *qishr* ("skins") by the coordinating conjunction, that is, and I bolt their stalks down too

11.20.8 *lafīf* ("'in a manner uninhibited,' used as an intensifier"[427]): that is, in an intemperate way, with great agony and bestial lust until I have had enough of them, and I will give no thought to the roughness of the swallowing that follows from their being as is, with skins and stalks, and I will not do as others do, that is to say, take them from the oven, put salt on them, leave them until they cool, and then skin some and eat them, for I have such a longing for them and am in such a hungry, poor, and wretched state that I will bolt them down with all that is on them.

11.20.9 A Useful Note: Green fava beans before grilling are Cold and Moist (or, according to others, Cold and Dry). They are prepared for eating by adding salt and thyme. The benefit to the health of eating them hot or grilled lies in completely removing the skins and eating them with sugar. In one of the books of medicine it says, "Whoever eats pulses for forty days and then contracts leprosy has only himself to blame, and if a woman eats pulses for forty days, she will never get pregnant." They considered them a contraceptive.

11.20.10 Next, the poet desires something baked and longs to obtain it. He says:

TEXT

11.21 *matā ʾanḍuru-n ṭaḥana l-ṭaḥīna wa-jibtū*
wa-baṭṭiṭu minnū faṭīrah rahīf

When shall I see that he's ground the flour, and I've brought it
and pat myself out from it a pastry that's crumbly?

COMMENTARY

11.21.1 *matā ʾanḍuru* ("when shall I see"): explained above . . .

an ṭaḥana ("that he's ground"): referring to one of the millers . . . 11.21.2

(a)l-ṭaḥīna ("the flour"): which I put in the mill, and which I subsequently have gone to and seen . . . 11.21.3

wa-jibtū ("and I've brought it"): that is, and after giving the miller his fee, I have brought it to my house . . . 11.21.4

wa-baṭṭiṭu ("and pat myself out"): on the pattern of *wa-ḍarriṭu* ("and I fart repeatedly or loudly") and *wa-barbiṭu* ("and I splash"),[428] both of which are certainly appropriate; derived from *baṭṭ* ("ducks"), which are fowl raised in the houses that resemble geese but are smaller and have very short legs, or from *baṭbaṭah* ("flattening" or "splashing"), or from the *biṭaṭ* ("vessels") in which clarified butter and other things are put, or, quite possibly, from sheer stuff and nonsense. 11.21.5

A Fatuous Point for Discussion: Why is wheat en masse called *ṭaḥīn*,[429] and is the latter term an adjective or a proper noun belonging to the former? We declare the Facetious Answer to be that in its original form it was wheat, without a doubt; then, all of a sudden, the process of milling descended unexpectedly upon it, which converted it from one state to another. Thus it is a question of "the naming of a thing after what fate may bring" via the attribute that comes to exist in it and converts it from one state to another. Similarly, a man, when he dies, and after death unexpectedly descends upon him, is referred to as "dead." This being the case, this substance, enjoying its strength to the full before the milling, was then analogous to a man while alive, and was therefore known as "wheat," but when the mill turned upon it and ground it up, its first name was obliterated, and it became *ṭaḥīn*. Likewise, when mortal fate turns upon a man, his name disappears and he becomes "dead" and the ground grinds him up and he is no more, until he is resurrected. Thus we conclude with the right answer to these fatuous investigations. 11.21.6

In some copies of the text we read *an ṭaḥantu l-ṭaḥīn* ("that I have ground"), with the *t* clearly written, in which case he would be the 11.21.7

one who milled it, by himself, which is the more appropriate, for the people of the countryside make a common mill in the house or in the hamlet, and when one of their men has wheat to mill, he takes his ox and hitches it up and grinds it. In the villages by the river, however, they pay a fee for milling, and all their mills are operated by horsepower, as in the cities. The previously described process takes place only in the hamlets and small villages, to which the poet, without doubt, belongs, as was made clear earlier, when his own village was mentioned. He says, "When shall I see that I've ground the flour and I've brought it, and pat myself out, that is, knead it with water or a little milk and take each piece of dough and place it on a rag or some bran or a dung cake, for example, and strike it with the palm until it is thin, and then take another, by which means I will obtain" . . .

11.21.8 *minnū* ("from it"): that is, from this dough . . .

11.21.9 *faṭīra* ("a pastry"): from *faṭūr* ("breakfast"), because they eat it for breakfast, or from *fuṭrah* ("fungus"), or from ʿĪd al-Fiṭr ("The Feast of the Breaking of the Fast").[430]

11.21.10 *rahīf* ("(that's) crumbly"): an adjective modifying "pastry," that is, moist and thin. His words contain "restraint," since he mentions the pastry and how to make it without mentioning eating it; it is thus to be inferred from his words that, after patting out the pastry, he baked it in the oven or in the pit that they make in the barn and on top of which they put droppings and sometimes dung cakes too, and ate of it till he had had enough.

11.21.11 Then the poet says:

TEXT

11.22 *a-yā maṭyaba l-julbāna wa-l-ʿadsa-dhā-stawā*
wa-shirshu baṣal ḥawlū wa-miyyat raghīf

Ah, how good is vetch and lentils when cooked
with a bunch of onions around it and a hundred loaves!

a-yā ("Ah"): [431] meaning "Ah, you people" . . . 11.22.1

maṭyaba ("how good"): in taste and scrumptiousness . . . 11.22.2

(a)l-julbānah ("is vetch"): of the pattern of *jidyān* ("young goats") or *khirfān* ("sheep"), derived from the *jilbah* ("ferrule") of a staff, or from the fact that the person who sowed it watered it originally with a draft ox (*thawr jalab*), or from *jalabat al-ʿabīd* ("traders in slaves"). *Julbān* is a plant that is grown from seed, the latter resembling that of Jew's mallow, and it has small pods resembling the pods of Jew's mallow and grows intertwined with itself like clover. The country people grow it and eat it as they do green fava beans, and sometimes they cook it with lentils and eat it, as described by the poet. They grow it in large quantities, and the animals eat it too. 11.22.3

wa-l-ʿadsa ("and lentils"): joined to the preceding by the coordinating conjunction, that is, and how good lentils are with it! Lentils are too well known to require comment. 11.22.4

(i)dhā-stawā ("when cooked"): since lentils, unlike vetch, cannot be eaten raw but indeed must be eaten cooked. They are Cold, Dry, and Heavy, resembling millet in their effect and impeding the release of the bowels. The broth is more beneficial than the grain, and eating it softens the heart. In *The Flowers in the Calyces*,[432] it says that one of the prophets complained to the Almighty of the hard hearts of his people and God inspired him to "command them to eat lentils, for that will soften their hearts!" And in the Tradition it says, "You are enjoined to eat lentils, for they soften the heart and cause copious tears!" and seventy prophets have given them their blessings. At the same time, it is to be feared that excessive consumption thereof will cause harm: in *The Canon*,[433] it says that excessive consumption thereof leads to leprosy and damages the nerves and engenders melancholic humors. According to one physician, it should be taken with fresh chard. It may be prepared in two ways: husked, 11.22.5

which is the easier to digest, and unhusked, which is called "lentils in their jackets." The country people put them in an earthenware pot and put that in the stokehole of the oven or in the oven itself, covered with water, until they are cooked. Then they whisk them with the wooden whisk and make a fried garnish for them with a little sesame oil and onions, like *bīsār*. The city people, on the other hand, and especially those of Turkish descent, cook them well and put fat from a sheep's tail, clarified butter, and spices on them, for they like to eat them with a lot of fat. Sometimes they make them with mutton, which is why they give them the place of honor on the dining cloth, for they hold them in the greatest esteem. Sometimes they are done with taro, if they are husked, and this is the most delicious and tasty way. The villages on the river cook them with rice, making them thick; they husk them and add rice and call it *baghliyyah* (with *a* after the *b*, no vowel after the *gh*, *i* after the *l*, double *y*, and nothing after the final *ah*).[434] This kind is very heavy, a feature in which it resembles peas. Sometimes they eat them with onions without bread, and peas likewise they prepare with rice.

11.22.6 All these cause flatulence and do harm to the stomach, especially peas, for they are the most harmful. One person built on the letter *b* in the noun *bisillah* and used it to form two appropriate adjectives: *bisillah bāridah bāyitah* ("postprandial perishing peas"), then went on to build on the letter *t* to describe the harm they do, saying *tuʿshī tufsī tunsī* ("turn me blind at night, turn into farts, and turn my memory into a blank!"), which constitutes a display of "sequential rolling and unrolling,"[435] the meaning being, "peas turn me blind at night, being perishingly cold enough to turn into farts, and postprandially turn my memory into a blank!" Then he says . . .

11.22.7 *wa-shirshu baṣal* ("with a bunch of onions"): *shirsh* is a name for a tied bundle of onions; it is called a *shirsh*. The word is also applied to the beginning of the emergence of a silent fart. Thus it is a term common to both farts and bunches of onions, which is why one says *fī liḥyitak shirsh* ("A *shirsh* in your beard!"), for instance. It is one of those words that read the same forward and backward, the beginning being the same as the end.[436]

ḥawlū ("around it"): that is, the bunch of onions will be arranged around the lentils, after they have been ladled into the small or medium-sized milk crock, because it is the custom in the country villages and elsewhere to place the onions around the lentils or the *bīsār* or the *mishsh* or whatever else there may be and for a man to take an onion and break pieces off it as though it were a cucumber. City people, on the other hand, peel it first and chop the onion into four segments and place them around the dining tray, and consistency is maintained. If the juice is squeezed out of the onion, it loses its piquancy and makes a balanced food. 11.22.8

wa-miyyat raghīf ("and a hundred loaves"): the origin is *wa-mi'ah*, but he drops the glottal stop for the sake of the meter; that is, a hundred loaves of barley bread. He specifies this number as being sufficient to satisfy his craving for food, or because he might invite someone to eat with him, for example, or a guest might turn up unexpectedly. A hundred, under such circumstances, would be enough to eat from and to hand around. Similarly, the bunch of onions, which is a bundle large enough to fill the hand, as explained above,[437] would also be enough for him to eat from and to hand around, if anyone should join him. 11.22.9

Next he proceeds to another thing and longs to obtain it. He says: 11.22.10

TEXT

a-yā maḥsan al-khubza l-muqammar ʿala l-nadah 11.23
wa-fawqū mina l-sarsūbi ḥalbū naḍīf

Ah, how fine is toasted bread first thing
and on top of it, of milk-and-beestings, one milking's-worth
that's clean!

11.23.1 *a-yā* ("Ah"): that is, Ah, you people . . .

11.23.2 *maḥsana* ("how fine is"): that is, how delightful and refined and delicious is the food called . . .

11.23.3 *(a)l-khubza* ("bread"): that is, clean white bread . . .

11.23.4 *al-muqammar* ("toasted, crisped"): by fire, not by the sun . . .

11.23.5 *ʿalā l-nadah* ("first thing"):[438] at breakfast, at the descent of the dew, which is the fine moisture that descends in the morning until the sun rises, so called because it "bedews" (*yunaddī*) the ground, that is, it wets it lightly. It has many beneficial properties for crops and other things. It contains general blessing and is used figuratively to stand for liberality and generosity. One says, "So-and-so's hand is 'like dew'" and "So-and-so 'has no dew,'" for example, and "dew is the companion of excellence."[439] A poet said in praise of Sultan Zayd, governor of Mecca the Ennobled, may the Almighty have mercy on his soul:

> I asked of Generosity (*al-nadā*) and Munificence, "From Adam's time
> Have you not lived long years, and many a time have you not died?"
> Said they, "Indeed, for long we were quite dead, but when
> Zayd came to rule God's House, we were revived!"

11.23.6 Thus to break one's fast, at that time of day, with toasted bread has many benefits. In the words of the doctors, "A dry crust is the body's balm." In a book of medicine I saw that the stomach is coated with something resembling hair. When a person breaks his fast with a dry crust, it comes down on the hair like a razor and shaves it off. However that may be, the healthiest way to break one's fast is with dry, toasted bread.

11.23.7 *wa-* ("and"): especially if there be . . .

fawqū ("on top of it"): that is, on top of the toasted bread, after it has been broken into pieces and put in the vessel . . . 11.23.8

mina l-sarsūbi ("of milk-and-beestings"): *sarsūb* being of the measure of *juʿbūb* ("black part of a wick"). It is milk into which a little of the milk that descends immediately after an animal is born and which they call *musmār* ("beestings") has been put. They take this and put it in a red earthenware casserole, with a little salt to season it and make it last till they need it. When they want *sarsūb*, they put milk in a basin and pour into it some of that milk that they call *musmār* and boil it over the fire. It is called both *mufawwar* ("boiled") and *sarsūb*. They crumble toasted bread into it, along with pressed dates, and eat it, and it is extremely delicious. They also make it in a casserole and put it in the oven after adding the beestings. This makes it solidify and they then call it *libbih*, with *i* after the *l* and after the *b*,[440] and they eat it, and it is extremely delicious. 11.23.9

The most beneficial milk is that of ewes, and the finest is cow's milk, on the basis of the words of the Prophet, God bless him and give him peace, "You are enjoined to drink the milk of the cow, for its milk is a cure, its butter is a remedy, and its flesh is a disease"; and the finest of that is what is drunk straight from the udder or as it is milked. When mixed with sugar, it brings color to the body, purifies the complexion, eases the bowels, and increases sexual potency. *Libbih* is so called because it is derived from *lubb* ("intelligence"), or from *labwah* ("lioness; sexually voracious woman"). Or it may be from the expression "Someone *labbaka* ('struck you hard on the chest') with a drover's whip," for example, or from "The young kid *labba* ('butted') its mother" when it wanted to drink from her. The poet says: 11.23.10

You're like the kid when it nuzzles and like
The collared puppy in their haste for the milk.

ḥalbū ("one milking's-worth"): that is, the amount of a *ḥalb* ("a milking"), which is as much milk as it takes to fill a *miḥlāb* or a *maḥlabah* 11.23.11

("earthenware milk pitcher"), or it is derived from "the man milked (*ḥalaba*) with his hand"—being, in either case, a name for what is milked from an animal. The meaning is that there should be, on top of the aforementioned bread, enough milk, mixed with beestings and extracted by milking, to cover it with a portion of milk . . .

11.23.12 *naḍīf* ("that's clean"): the word is originally *naẓīfan*, but he gives it with *ḍ* in accordance with rural usage[441] and drops the *an* for the rhyme; that is, containing nothing in the way of traces of dung or adherent dust or the like that might sully it, since they feel no shame about touching dung and similar impurities while they are handling milk—on the contrary, sometimes they smear the cow or buffalo's udder with dung so that it gives milk faster. The poet therefore requests that this *sarsub* be good and clean and free of such things, even though he might be excused if it were not.

11.23.13 Next he explains how he will eat it. He says:

TEXT

11.24 *wa-ʾaqʿud ʿalā rukbah wa-nuṣṣin wa-shammir*
ʿani l-kaffi b-īdī mā ʾakhāfu mukhīf

And I'll sit with one knee crooked and roll up my sleeves
from my hand, with my hand, and fear no frightener.

COMMENTARY

11.24.1 *wa-ʾaqʿud* ("And I'll sit"): in preparation for the consumption of this bread with *sarsūb*, as does one who is hungry and seized by great appetite for the dish.

11.24.2 *ʿalā rukbah wa-nuṣṣin* ("with one knee crooked"):[442] this being the sitting posture of a strong, vigorous person who intends to eat a lot or who is ravenous for food, for example. The polite way of sitting, on the other hand, is quite different and consists of the person sitting with both his knees tucked beneath him, not looking to the right or the left, eating what is in front of him, and not stretching out his hand roughly to food that is far from him. As once it happened that one man said to another, as they were eating at a banquet, "So-and-so, may I move this dish closer to you?" and the other replied, "My hand can fetch from Mecca!" and he stretched his hand out roughly and let out an audible fart. The first man said to him, "And how much does a grab bag of catfish fetch in Mecca?" at which the other was overcome by embarrassment and got up and left without eating. It is a fact that eating has its own etiquette, which is described in a number of books.

wa-shammir ("and roll up my sleeves"): from *tashmīr*, which is the act of pulling the sleeve back. 11.24.3

ʿani l-kaffi ("from my hand"): that is, from his hand. One says, "He raised (*shammara*) the skirts of his robe," meaning he raised them out of the way of something filthy, and "He lifted his skirts to expose (*shammara ʿan*) his member," that is, he wanted to find a back alley in which to make water; used figuratively, *tashmīr* means "holding back" from sinful acts.[443] The poet[444] says: 11.24.4

> Tuck up your robe, for you are resolute and bold,
> And changing times and trouble cannot affright you!

What our poet has in mind, however, is a physical raising, namely, the lifting up of the sleeves, which involves the use of the *shimār*,[445] which the boys of the countryside make from wool; they place it round their shoulders and raise their sleeves with it, and it has a fringe that hangs down to the buttocks of the beardless boy and has a kind of beauty. It is a matter of great importance to them, to the degree that some boys attach yellow, red, green, and black silk-wool and silk to it to make themselves attractive to their lovers. Most drummers' boys make them in imitation of women's braids, with little knots on the ends of the fringes to decorate them.

b-īdī ("with my hand"): originally *bi-yadī*;[446] with *my* hand and not with anyone else's, for I do not need anyone else to roll up my sleeves for me—on the contrary, I will take care of rolling them up myself in order to free my other hand of anything that might prevent it from 11.24.5

taking food. This indicates that his sleeve was long, or he would not have needed to roll it up, and that what he wanted to achieve by rolling up his sleeves was the rapid and vigorous upward and downward motion of his hand while eating and paying attention to no one. This is why he says . . .

11.24.6 *mā ʾakhāfu* ("and fear no"): that is, and eat of these beestings, having no fear that anyone will come to me or hold me back from it.

11.24.7 *mukhīf* ("frightener"): originally *mukhīfan,* that is, no scarer will get between me and my appetite—on the contrary, I will have no cares at all if it reaches me and I manage to acquire it from anyone, and no fear or terror will seize me until I have had enough and sated myself with it to excess, nor will I fear indigestion or anything of that sort.

11.24.8 Then he felt a yearning for another dish, one of the most delicious of those made by the people of the countryside. He says:

TEXT

11.25 *ʿalā man qashaʿ rūḥū ḥidā l-ruzzi bi-l-laban*
wa-yaqṭaʿ wa-yablaʿ min taqīl wa-khafīf

Happy is he who finds himself next to rice pudding
and cuts off pieces and swallows them, heavy and light!

COMMENTARY

11.25.1 *ʿalā man qashaʿ* ("Happy is he who finds himself"): that is, sees himself, that is, his own person, not some other person's person . . .

11.25.2 *ḥidā l-ruzzi bi-l-laban* ("next to rice pudding"): that is, *hidā* is equivalent to *ḥidhāʾahu,* with *dh,*[447] that is, *muḥādhiyahu* ("adjacent to"), meaning that he is sitting next to it. This rice pudding is a delicious dish and is what they eat most of in the villages on the river, because there is so much milk and rice there. It is Hot and Moist and good for heartburn, and how delicious and tasty it is if clarified cow's butter is put on it as it is taken off the fire! It is eaten with pitted pressed dates, too, but is tastier and more appetizing with clarified butter. The more milk it has the better, and the less rice the better still. The worst sort is when a lot of water has been mixed with the rice, which is how the people of the countryside make it: they make it very thick and cut pieces off it as one would chunks of hard mud. People of Turkish descent make it with milk alone, without water, and add just a little rice, so that it is like a drink, which is why they eat it with spoons. This makes it sweet and delicious, and this kind is the best tasting and most appetizing. In general, milk dishes are more appetizing than lentils, *bīsār*, and the like. The poet says:

> Dishes cooked with milk beat those with coriander,
> And lentils and *bīsār* cause dropsy.

The kind the poet desires to be next to, however, is that mentioned above, namely, the thick sort that is as hard as a rock, for this is what is known to them and in his village. The villages on the river, on the other hand, make it halfway, neither thick nor runny, though they do usually add a little water. The poet, of course, knows only what is to be found in his village, which is why he says . . . 11.25.3

wa-yaqṭaʿ ("and cuts off pieces"): cutting can apply only to dry food; that is, he cuts off pieces with his hand 11.25.4

wa-yablaʿ ("and swallows"): from *balʿ*, meaning "swallowing," which is the passing of food down the throat; one says, "So-and-so was swallowed by the whale," meaning that he entered its insides and reached its belly. From the same one also gets *ballāʿah* ("drain"), because the latter "swallows" water inside itself. *Qaṭʿ* ("cutting") means the severing and separating of one thing from another; one says, "So-and-so 'cut' So-and-so" for a while, meaning that he shunned him and kept his distance from him. 11.25.5

min taqīl ("heavy"): that is, pieces larger than the normal mouthful, meaning that this would be a major cutting, meaning that the mouthful would fill the hand and be big enough to make the eyes water. I made reference to this in a sermon on different dishes I composed a while ago, which goes as follows:[448] 11.25.6

11.25.7 Praise be to God, to whom for sure all praise is owed, who hands out ease and care in measured load, who has adjured us to be pilgrims to His Ancient House,[449] and who has made honey companion to the ghee of cows! Him I praise as one by hunger waylaid, whom God with a basin of *basīsah* (made with fine pastry) saved, one who thereon ate his fill, and thought of Him with no ill will but slept in God-given ease and reconciliation. And Him I thank as a mortal slave who has made renunciation of all things sour plus cheese well aged after fermentation, bearing witness that there is no god but God alone, companionless—testimony that spares its maker deprivation! And I bear witness that our Master and Prophet Muḥammad, God bless him and grant him peace, is His slave and messenger, speaker of sooth, endowed with truth and approbation! God, bless and grant peace and benison to Our Master Muḥammad, his Kith and Companions, the people of disclosure and confirmation, and make this blessing abundant!

11.25.8 Good people, why do I behold you of sweet rice with honey all unaware? Showing for fluffy rice with mutton never a care? Baklava on its platters shunning? From fat geese and roasted chickens running? What are these, my brethren, but the doings of the indigent and the deeds of the financially incontinent? Apply yourselves then, God have mercy upon you, to acquiring cash that you may carry off dishes precious and victuals delicious! Our Master, the Imam ʿAlī, master of knowledge and understanding, God honor his visage, has said[450] that the joys of this world are three: the eating of flesh, the riding of flesh, and the insertion of flesh into flesh. So he to whom God has given much, let him be thankful, and he to whom God has given little, let him be stoical.

11.25.9 To eat rice pudding you are commanded, for it is a dish both excellent and commended, and the day that starts with it is the most blessed day, to the peasant especially—when he goes to his cow and milks it, and his wife brings the basin and hangs it, and pours the milk in and lights a fire beneath and stirs it with white rice, and cooks it, and into dishes spoons it, and the aged shaykh comes and crooks one leg and sits upon it—at this, my brother, the vessels are set out next to one another, and each man draws close to the other, and nothing can be seen but hands tearing and tongues at work, epiglottises jumping and throats a-jerk. Eyes water at the size of the bite, and the belly from excess of passion grows ever less tight; nay, it gets ever more flighty, exclaiming, "Glory to Our Lord, the Almighty!" If your brother Muslim beats you to a munch, knock his head off with a punch! And seize, God have mercy on you, upon this edifying discourse, and have nothing to do with foods that are coarse, such as lentils and *bīsār* (which is beans with mallow brought to a boil), or stewed beans and beans with linseed oil, or groats with beans and peas, and stuffed oven-cheese—all these cause gas, and eating them is truly crass.

Next, to the use of sumptuous foods, such as Mutton, you are bidden, for he is Lord of Foods[451] in This World and the Hidden, and to drinks that are sweet and cold, for of these a Tradition from the Prophet (God bless him and give him peace) is told, and praise God, you who are rich and blessed, and be patient, you who are poor and hard-pressed! We beseech God to bestow upon us all such sumptuous foods and provide us all with ease both before and after our decease, and to number us all among the blessed, and save us all from the haunts of the ravenous hard-pressed, and forgive our sins and yours and those of all who Islam have professed. Amen. «Seek forgiveness of Him»[452] and He will grant you forgiveness, and how great is the triumph of those who seek forgiveness! 11.25.10

11.25.11 It is related on the authority of Sahlab, who had it from Mahlab, who had it from Zinṭāḥ, son of Naṭṭāḥ, son of Qalīl al-Afrāḥ,[453] that he said, "A certain Bedouin arose from his slumbers and sweet dreams and ate a two-year-old camel for breakfast, then endured till the middle of the day, ate forty chickens stuffed with mutton and roasted in clarified ghee, drank two skins of wine, went to sleep in the sun, and died, thus meeting his Maker sated, intoxicated, and irrigated!"

11.25.12 Praise be to God, embellisher of rice with milk and dispeller of grief! I bear witness that Mutton is Lord of Foods and the body's relief! And know that clotted cream is not something to shun or of which to be suspicious, and that blancmange is better still and even more auspicious! Prepare yourselves, then, to eat and drink, knowing that soon in God's sight you'll stand and that by your works you'll be saved or damned, and that the Lord of Might will soon review what you have earned, and that those who went hungry will come to know «by what a great reverse they have been overturned.»[454] Be pleased, O God, with the four leaders great,[455] by the Almighty in the Qur'an designate—the fig, the olive, the peach, and the pomegranate![456] And be pleased, O God, with those that remain of the ten,[457] in number six, of foods deluxe, namely, blancmange and rosewater jelly, and fattened squabs with vermicelli, and fluffy rice stuffed with mutton and fried, and bee's honey, almonds, sugar, and *kunāfah* drenched in butter clarified, and little pancakes that in syrup and butter swim, and squash that's stuffed with meat and onions to the brim, as well as the baklava earlier described, and stall-fed sheep, and hot-pot and *qirmiziyyah*[458] with fatty meat—may God bestow them on us all to eat!

O God, bring us, after dispersal, all together, and grant victory, support, and safety to Sultan Sugar-Candy, may he rule for ever—son of Flagon, Mallawī sugar's noble scion! Aid him, O God, with sugarcane spears and thrusters, and sticky dates and grapes in clusters! And unite us with him at day's beginning, middle, and end, and to him and to his soldiers victory send, that we may benefit from him in This World, O Lord of All. And destroy, O God, the reprobates three, namely, *bīsār*, lentils, and the pea! Slaves of God, whoever wishes to wrap himself in the robes of God's pleasance, let him eat bananas in his parents' presence! Before eating, unwind, and follow the example of the Best of Mankind.[459] Neither fight one another nor fall to blows, O Slaves of God, but brethren be! God commands you to eat of what your minds desire only what His religion declares to be good and forbids you to eat what is forbidden, though it be the tastiest of food, and forbids you «wickedness. He exhorteth you that you may reflect!»[460] 11.25.13

wa-khafīf ("and light"): that is, and he will eat light mouthfuls as well as large ones, to achieve a just balance and not be misled by the words of the poet[461] who said: 11.25.14

Eat hearty! If you survive, you can tell your folks,
And if you die, you'll meet your God with your stomach full!

One should divide his stomach into three equal parts: one third for food, one third for drink, and one third for appetite; on this basis he will neither eat excessively, nor hunger excessively. As the author of *The Mantle*,[462] God have mercy on his soul, says:[463] 11.25.15

And fear hunger's traps as those of satiety,
For an empty stomach may be worse than dyspepsia!

Next, the poet moves on to a kind of condiment that he felt a longing for. He says: 11.25.16

TEXT

11.26 *ʿalā man malā qaḥfū jubaynah ṭariyyah*
wa-rāḥa warā l-jāmūsi yarʿā l-nīf

Happy is he who fills his cap with a moist little cheese
and goes behind the buffaloes to graze on *nīf*!

COMMENTARY

11.26.1 *ʿalā man malā qaḥfū* ("Happy is he who fills his cap"): the *qaḥf* ("cap") is a tall thing made of wool or hair that is worn on the head and lacks both elegance and style. Some dervishes and most buffoons use it. They also wear another thing that resembles it, called the *ṭurṭūr*,[464] from which the *qaḥf* differs in being wide where it meets the head and narrow at the top,[465] and in being shorter than the *ṭurṭūr*. The *ṭurṭūr* was much used in the past. Felt caps (*libdah*, plural *libad*) are used in a number of ways: some resemble the *qaḥf*, and some the European hat; nowadays there is a sect that wears the *libdah*s that resemble European hats—they are righteous people, Sufis. Subsequently the velvet *qāwūq*[466] made its appearance, and came to be seen as chic and glamorous, appealing and sophisticated, and the wearing of the *libdah* and other similar hats was abandoned, the only people continuing to wear them being certain shabbily ascetic Sufi dervishes. This is why they say, "Hey you, go to hell like the *libad*!" Much has been said about their fall from favor, including the saying, "*Libdah*, if to market you come, all you'll get is a spike up your bum!"[467] It is called a *qaḥf* because of its coarseness (*qaḥāfah*) and stiffness, which is why a man of bad character is likened to it, and one says, "He's a *qaḥf*," that is, evil-natured. The poet says on this topic:

Refinement is ever among the great diffused,
But did you ever see a *qaḥf* of polished views?

11.26.2 The word is derived from the *qaḥf* ("head") of a fish or from the fact that the man who first fashioned such caps was from Quḥāfah, which is a well-known village held as an endowment for the benefit of Master Aḥmad al-Badawī, God benefit us through him.

jubaynah ("with a moist little cheese"): *jubaynah* is the diminutive of *jubnah* ("piece of cheese"), of the measure of *ubnah* ("passive sodomy"), and is the unit noun from *jubn* ("cheese"). 11.26.3

ṭariyyah ("moist"): that is, as it was made and before it got hard, that is, at the moment of its removal from the reed strainer in which they make the cheese. He fantasizes that God will bestow on him enough moist cheese to fill his cap, even if he acquire it as a gift, or as alms given him by someone else, or by theft—for one's God-given means of subsistence are whatever one is sustained by, even if it be ill-gotten. The author of *The Most Pleasing Portions*,[468] God have mercy on his soul, says, "One's God-given means of subsistence is whatever provides sustenance, even if it be something forbidden," etc., and Abū Nuwās,[469] God have mercy on his soul, says: 11.26.4

"Leave ill-gotten gain and pull your belt still tighter!"
So my critics (but what do they know?) said,
But if I find no gains well-gotten,
And eat nothing forbidden, I'll just drop dead!

If it be said, "Why does the poet want to fill his cap with cheese, when a cap is not designed for carrying cheese; especially given that he says 'moist cheese,' which means that, were he to put it in his cap, the latter would suffer in two ways, the first being that the cheese would soil the cap, the second that the liquid from the cheese would soak, and thus spoil, it?" we respond that a facetious answer may be given from various angles. On the one hand it may be that he wants enough cheese that, were it to be placed in his cap, it would fill it, his cap being large and tall, so as to provide him with something to eat with his bread for the rest of the week, or of the month, because he lacks any such and is in need of it; while in contrast if he got only a little, it would not suffice him or take care of his children. Or it may be that what he says should be taken literally, because, if one 11.26.5

gives country people food or anything else, they take it in the skirts of their cloaks or robes, and in their sleeves, and in the turban cloths that are on their heads, and in the past they used to place it in their caps, for they would generally wear these on their heads without anything wrapped around them; so if one of them got something from the market and had no basket or plate, for example, he would put it in his cap. As for the soiling and dirtying of his cap, the poet would pay no heed to such a thing, for his cap would have cost at most one or two *nuṣṣ*, and with his constant use of it and the passage of time and its getting soaked in sweat and its general condition, it would have turned as hard as wood, and neither the moisture of the cheese nor anything else could make any difference to it. Thus his words turn out to be literally true, and the problem's now revealed, its silliness no more concealed.

11.26.6 *wa-rāḥa* ("and goes"): that is, and proceeds, *rāḥa* being derived from *al-Rawḥā'*, a place in the Hijaz, or from *rāḥah* ("rest, ease; palm of the hand"), or from *rīḥ* ("wind"), or from the *abū riyāḥ* (literally "father of winds, wind thing") that is made on a long cane and which consists of four blades stuck onto four pieces of cane; small children play with it and it is well known in the cities and elsewhere.

11.26.7 *warā* ("behind"): that is, following . . .

11.26.8 *(a)l-jāmūsi* ("the buffaloes"): a sort of cattle, for the word "cattle" (*baqar*) encompasses the buffalo and other sorts; it is enormously large and has a thick black hide. Cattle are called *baqar* because they "cut open" (*yabquru*), that is, furrow,[470] the earth; the unit noun is *baqarah* ("cow"). The country people use the word as a term of abuse for a beardless boy, saying, for example, "You're a cow!" meaning "How effeminate you are!"

11.26.9 A Silly Topic for Debate. "Why don't they say to a beardless boy, 'You she-buffalo! (*yā jāmūsah*)' for example, when the latter is analogous to the ordinary cow in that the bull buffalo mounts her and serves her, the she-buffalo thus resembling the cow in this respect, with nothing to distinguish her?" We respond that the facetious answer may be from any of various points of view. The first is that the buffalo is covered under the name "cattle," as explained above, so that the same name embraces both species. The second point of view is that the term *jāmūsah* is a compound formed of a proper name and a verb. Thus, should someone say to a beardless boy *anta yā jāmūsah* ("Hey there, you buffalo-cow!"), it might be understood, for example, as "Hey there, boy! Has a man called Mūsā come (*jā(')* . . . *Mūsā*)?" as though he were questioning him about him, in which case the calumny would be deflected from the boy, and he would have no idea what was meant. Similarly, there is a riddle that says *imra'atun waladat jāmūsah* ("A woman gave birth to a buffalo"), that is, at the time of her giving birth came a man called Mūsā (*jā(')* . . . *Mūsā*). The third point of view is that the name *jāmūs* is derived from *tajmīs*, which means "groping around, feeling with the hand, etc." (*taḥsīs*). One says, "So-and-so is groping around (*yujammisu*) in the dark," meaning that he is feeling about (*yuḥassisu*) for something to take hold of. The name *baqar* ("cattle") is derived from *baqara* ("to cut open") the earth, that is, to furrow it with the plow, from which perspective it resembles the placing of the penis in the cunt, for example, since the former "furrows," that is, enters, the latter, and the same is true of the beardless boy, for the prick is inserted into his anus, for example. Thus, it is as though an analogy were drawn between the verb *baqara* and the associated term of abuse to a boy and the act itself, while *tajmīs* ("groping") would be analogous to the preliminaries. The verb, of course, is stronger than the noun, as witness the fact that groping and kissing are like sowing, while fucking is reaping, implying that fucking is stronger than groping, which is why they abuse the beardless boy with the former and say to him, "You cow (*yā baqarah*)!"[471] The problem's now revealed, its silliness no more concealed.

yarʿā l-nīf ("to graze on *nīf*"): that is, he drives the buffaloes so that 11.26.10
they may graze, not so that he may graze, the verb "to graze" referring to the buffaloes; that is, he drives the buffaloes to the place

where the plant called *nīf* grows, and they graze, that is, eat. One says "The buffaloes or the cattle are grazing (*bi-yarʿā*) in such and such a place," meaning they are eating there. The word they use for the person who drives them and takes care of their needs by way of milking, driving, tethering in the field, tending, guarding, and so on, is *rāʿī* ("herder") because he stays with them all the time and they are under his wing; he must therefore look after them (*yurāʿīhim*) with kindness and compassion. In the Tradition it says, "Every one of you is a shepherd, and every shepherd shall be questioned about his flock," that is, on the Day of Resurrection everyone will be asked concerning those under his charge, be they animals or anything else. *Nīf* is a plant that sprouts on its own in the earth, a consequence of the descent of waters thereon, and is found mostly in uncultivated lands. It is derived from the *nīfah* that is made in the cities, which consists of meat grilled in a clay oven and eaten, and is very delicious, or from the *nūf* ("yoke") that is placed on the necks of oxen when they are being used for the waterwheel or the plow. He mentions cheese but not bread, and it appears that he had some with him, which he had been eating for a while with nothing to go with it. Consequently, he fantasizes about filling his cap with enough cheese to last him a good while.

11.26.11 Next, he proceeds to yearn for another dish that the country people, and others, love to eat. He says:

TEXT

11.27 *ʿalā man qashaʿ laqqānata-mmū malānah*
mina l-hayṭaliyya-llī lahā tarṣīf

Happy is he who sees his mother's bowl full
of *hayṭaliyyah* that gleams

COMMENTARY

11.27.1 *ʿalā man qashaʿ* ("Happy is he who sees"): that is, sees in reality and not figuratively . . .

laqqānata-mmū ("his mother's bowl"): or, equally, that of his father's wife; *laqqānah*[472] is the feminine form of *laqqān*,[473] of the measure of *khirfān* ("sheep"), and is also called *qaṣriyyah*. It is a vessel made of earthenware that holds less than a kneading bowl and more than a middle-sized milk crock. It is called a *laqqānah* because, if one wants to drink from it, he has to lap up (*yaluqqu*) the water with his tongue or his mouth, because it is too heavy for him to lift;[474] or because the first person to make one was from Laqqānah, a famous village from which God has produced outstanding scholars who are celebrated for their virtues and from whose learning the people will continue to derive benefit to the Day of Resurrection, may God benefit us through their blessings! He designates the *laqqānah* as belonging to his mother because it was hers and the only one he knew and he had nothing else. Then he desired to see it . . . 11.27.2

malānah ("full"): not short-measured. He drops the glottal stop for the meter.[475] Then he specifies the thing that he desires, and says . . . 11.27.3

min al-hayṭaliyyah ("of *hayṭaliyyah*"): which is a dish that is made out of wheat starch and milk and is extremely good to eat.[476] It is lighter than rice pudding, especially if honey is added, for starch is Cold and Dry and sweet things moderate these qualities. Milk is Moist, as explained earlier (though some say that it is Moderately Hot and Moist) while rice is Hot and Dry, making the starch a degree less heavy, though it is also true that rice goes with all foods; as someone said, "If rice were a man, he would be tolerant and clement," because it accepts whatever is done to it. It gets its name, *hayṭaliyyah*, from the *haṭl* ("downpouring"), namely, the raining, of clouds, because it resembles their whiteness, or from the *haṭl* of clothes, which is their being long, and dragging on the ground, and being shiny. This is why the poet says . . . 11.27.4

(i)llī ("that"): with double *l*, meaning *allatī*;[477] a rural form. 11.27.5

lahā tarṣīf ("gleams"): that is, because of its beauty and intense whiteness and shininess, it gleams, that is, radiates light, and one 11.27.6

longs to eat it and savor it. One says, "So-and-so is wearing a white overgown that gleams (*turaṣṣif*)," that is, shines and radiates light. The word is derived from al-Ruṣāfah, a well-known village in Iraq. An amusing story has it[478] that a man was going between al-Jisr and al-Ruṣāfah when he saw a lovely slave girl, outstandingly comely and beautiful, walking along. Said he, "Abū l-ʿAtāhiyah spoke the truth!" without specifying what the latter had said, at which she shook her head and said, "Not so! It was Abū l-ʿAlāʾ al-Maʿarrī who spoke the truth!" and did not specify what he had said either. The man was overcome with embarrassment, let her be, and went his way. Nearby was another man, who overheard what they said, and he chased after the woman and said to her, "Tell me what you meant and what he meant, or I'll report the two of you to the caliph!" She answered, "When he said, 'Abū l-ʿAtāhiyah spoke the truth,' he had in mind his verse:

> The eyes of the wild antelope between al-Ruṣāfah and al-Jisr
> Summoned love from places I know and know not!

"—while by the words of Abū l-ʿAlāʾ al-Maʿarrī I meant,

> Ah, her abode in al-Khayf! Within easy reach,
> But before it lie terrors!"

In other words, she had communicated to him that her abode lay nearby but was close to that of the Commander of the Faithful, "so you will not be able to attain your desire." Observe the slave girl's quickness of wit in grasping what was meant, and the man's command of the language and his understanding likewise of what was meant!

11.27.7 Next he explains how he will eat of the *hayṭaliyyah*, saying:

TEXT

11.28 *wa-ʾaqʿud lahā bi-l-ʿazmi fī rāyiqi l-ḍuḥā*
wa-ʾasḥab lahā maṣbūbata-mmi Waṭīf

And I'll sit down to it with ardor in the clear forenoon
and keep snatching away at the pancakes of Umm Waṭīf

COMMENTARY

wa-ʾaqʿud ("and I'll sit down"): that is, I will seat myself unhurriedly, nay, I will adopt a firm posture without fear or alarm, and none will do me harm. 11.28.1

lahā ("to it"): the pronominal suffix refers either to the bowl that contains the *hayṭaliyyah*, in which case his words "and I'll sit down to it" mean I will eat of it while it is in it, the thing that he eats thus being the *hayṭaliyyah*, not the bowl itself, or the suffix refers to the *hayṭaliyyah* itself, in which case there is no problem (the latter being the preferred referent). The outcome of these facetious investigations now is clear. 11.28.2

bi-l-ʿazmi ("with ardor"): that is, forcefully and vehemently, or it means that he will sit down to it determined (*ʿāzim*) to eat of it, for example... 11.28.3

fī rāyiqi l-ḍuḥā ("in the clear forenoon"): that is, when the sun is high, at the time at which the forenoon prayer is permitted.[479] This time of the morning is called *ḍaḥwat al-nahār* and is the right time for lunch, when the belly is empty and hunger extreme. 11.28.4

wa-ʾasḥab ("and keep snatching away at"): he will take them quickly and repeatedly, for *saḥb* means pulling a thing quickly with a rope or anything else. The poet says: 11.28.5

The ferryboat's going and coming
By a thread it's pulled back and forth (*yansaḥib*).

Thus, *saḥb* may be applied to taking a thing over and over again.

lahā maṣbūbata-mmi Waṭīf ("the pancakes of Umm Waṭīf"): that is, snatch from the pancakes that Umm Waṭīf makes, Waṭīf being her son, so called because he used to make dung cakes into *aṭwāf*,[480] 11.28.6

some saying that he had a little enclosure in which he would place the dung cakes, course upon course, while others claim that the name comes from his circumambulating (*ṭawāf*) of the cow when he was little. The name that he was given when he was born was Daʿmūm, but he became known by the former, and that is the one that stuck to him and was turned into a proper name, and it was by that that his mother became known, people referring to her as Umm Waṭīf ("Mother of Waṭīf").

11.28.7 Pancakes (*maṣbūbah*) are made in two kinds, one from wheat flour, the other from rice flour. The people of hamlets and villages that have not planted rice make them of wheat, and the people of the rice villages make them of hulled rice. Those made from wheat are called *qaṭāyif*. Sometimes they make them from rice alone, while the poor make them from the barnyard grass that appears among the rice plants when they turn white, adding to it a quantity of hulled rice. It is called *maṣbūbah* ("poured") because they make a runny dough like that for *kunāfah*, heat the oven, take half a dried gourd or empty coconut, make holes in it, attach it to a long stick, scoop up some of the dough, and pour it out inside the oven in floppy soft disks the size of loaves of bread; in other words, it is so called because it is "poured out" (*tuṣabbu*) in this way. *Qaṭāyif* are made in the cities of special finely sieved white flour and poured out onto small iron or copper sheets called "patches," but they are small, the size of the disk-shaped loaf of bread called a *qurṣah*. They are the most delicious of all the different types and the tastiest, especially when fried in clarified butter and drenched in honey. Praise God, we have eaten them many a time and enjoyed them thoroughly, and we beseech the Almighty to feed them to our brethren the dervishes and grant them the luxury of tasting them! These, however, are a far cry from what the poet has in mind and are, indeed, totally unknown to him. What was known in his village were the pancakes of Umm Waṭīf, who is said to have been the poet's wife, as mentioned earlier,[481] though others claim she was another woman in his village who was well known for making them. *Qaṭāyif* are so called because the flour of which they are made is *muqaṭṭaf*, that is, bolted with a fine sieve, in which case it would be an example of "naming a thing by the name of the attribute that fate may bring."

In essence, what he is saying is that, when he snatches at the pancakes and beholds the *hayṭaliyyah*, he will sit down and eat of them until he has had enough, lest anyone should think that all he wants to do is to look at them, which would be an absurdity. As the poet says: 11.28.8

Looking alone no blame involves—
  Only sucking saliva and kissing moles.
Looking alone will not put out your fire—
  Only consummation at home with the one you desire.
Let silver then as messenger to your beloved race,
  Then enter the dome and the shaykh will show you his
    grace[482]

—and so on to the end of the poem, the same stipulation holding for all verses in which he speaks of "seeing," for his sole object is to see while eating and not just to look at the food, as this would never satisfy him, especially in view of his enormous appetite and huge hunger.

Next he turns to another dish, and says: 11.28.9

TEXT

alā yā tarā-shḥālu l-laban baʿda ghalwihī 11.29
  wa-law kāna bi-l-khubzi l-sukhayni radīf

Now I wonder, how is milk after it's boiled
  (and were it with bread, nice and hot, riding pillion, that
    would be better still)?

COMMENTARY

ʿalā yā tarā ("Now I wonder"): he seeks to inquire, test, query, and ascertain the truth concerning something far distant from himself, 11.29.1

which he has not seen or witnessed, as though he were someone asking after a friend who has been away from him for a long time, which is why he says . . .

11.29.2 *(i)shḥālu* ("how is"): meaning, "What is the state of this absent thing?" just as a man says, on meeting his friend after a period during which he has missed him, "How are you (*aysh ḥālak* and *mā ḥāluka*) today?" for example.

11.29.3 *(a)l-laban* ("milk"): is the same as *ḥalīb.*[483]

11.29.4 *baʿda* ("after"): putting it in the basin and . . .

11.29.5 *ghalwihī* ("it's boiled"): the word is originally *ghalyihi*, the *y* being changed to a *w* in accordance with rural usage;[484] that is, its being boiled with fire. In other words, "Is it delicious to eat and sweet to taste?"

11.29.6 *wa-* ("and"): especially . . .

11.29.7 *law kāna* ("were it"): referring to this boiled fresh milk . . .

11.29.8 *bi-l-khubzi* ("with bread"): explained above[485]

11.29.9 *(a)l-sukhayni* ("nice and hot"): diminutive of *sukhn* ("hot"), used for the sweetness of the form,[486] in the spirit of the verse of the poet who says:

> I didn't say my "little" darling in deprecation—
> Rather, a cute thing's name grows sweeter with diminuation.

This is why he said *sukhayn*, of the measure of *ṭunayn* ("little sheaf of sugarcane"); that is, "heated (*musakhkhan*) with fire."

11.29.10 *radīf* ("riding pillion"): of the measure of *kanīf* ("latrine"); derived from *radf*, which is the riding of one person behind another on the same mount. *Sukhayn* is derived from *sukhūnah*, which is "fever," because fever is hot and very dangerous, and bread when heated is like fever in its hotness and the way it heats the body when it afflicts it, God preserve us from it! He makes the bread the "pillion rider" of the milk in the sense that it is inseparable from it and not to be detached from it, in order that it may be eaten with it; thus, it is like the man who is mounted behind another—he never leaves him nor parts company with the back of his mount: the two of them are on its back and never separate or dismount unless together and neither ever parts from his companion.

The line in question is an example of the pleasuring of one of the five senses, namely, the hearing, for it is as though he were saying to them, "Inform me as to how milk is, and what it is like to eat it with bread, and whether it is tasty eaten in this fashion, and pleasure my ears by saying its name, for then perhaps I will see it in reality and eat of it truly!" As Abū Nuwās, God have mercy on him, says:[487] 11.29.11

> Come fill my cup, and tell me, "This is wine!"
> And serve it to me openly that all may so divine!

—the probative authority lying in the words "and tell me, 'This is wine!'"; that is, "Tell me this is wine, so that I may feel pleasure at hearing its name and my ears may feel pleasure at hearing it spoken," for the other four senses have had their pleasure and now it is the turn of the hearing—as Ibn al-Fāriḍ, God benefit us through him, says:

> Pass my beloved's name around, though it be with blame:
> My wine is hearing tales that contain his name

—"That my hearing may witness" and so on, to the end of the poem.[488]

Next, after wanting to indulge his hearing with mention of boiled milk with heated bread, he wants to indulge it further with "flaky-pastry-in-milk," in the hope that God might perhaps grant his wish and allow him to eat of all of these things, which would not be something difficult for God, for "God Almighty is with the meek." So he says: 11.29.12

TEXT

11.30 *alā yā tarā ʾishḥālu mafrūkatu l-laban*
ʿalā zalṭihā qalbī yariffu rafīf

Now I wonder, how is flaky-pastry-in-milk?
At the thought of its gulping my heart beats violently!

COMMENTARY

11.30.1 The meaning of this verse is similar to the one before.

alā yā tarā ("Now I wonder"): that is, I wonder if anyone can give me a satisfying report on . . .

11.30.2 *ʾishḥālu* ("how"): that is, I am asking about the state of . . .

11.30.3 *mafrūkatu l-laban* ("flaky-pastry-in-milk"): that is, flaky pastry that is crumbled (*yufraku*) with milk, or, in other words, made with fine white flour and baked in the oven or the cooking pit and crumbled, that is, broken up with the hands while hot, and put into a butter pot or crock. Then fresh milk is poured over it until it covers it and is absorbed by it and it turns into something like *tharīd* ("crumbled bread moistened with broth"), that is to say, something soft and smooth to swallow and gulp down, for *tharīd* is delicious and the best of foods:[489] in the Noble Tradition it says, "The superiority of ʿĀʾishah over all other women is as that of *tharīd* over all other foods," and a further Tradition is cited that says, "Eat *tharīd*, for in *tharīd* is blessing."

11.30.4 Next he says:

ʿalā zalṭihā ("at the thought of its gulping"): and at the height of my desire for it and my agony at its inaccessibility . . .

11.30.5 *qalbī yariffu rafīf* ("my heart beats violently"): the last word is originally *rafīfan* because it is a verbal noun, the *an* being dropped for the meter;[490] that is, it palpitates very hard, its palpitation resembling the fluttering motion of a bird's wings, because it so desperately wants to gulp down this flaky-pastry-in-milk.

The word *zalṭ* ("swallowing without chewing, gulping") derives from *zalaṭ* ("pebbles"), with *a* after the *l*, plural of *zalaṭah*, meaning small smooth stones that are formed in sand and on the seashore. The *zalṭ* ("gulping") of food is named after the latter because of the smoothness and quickness of the action, which occurs without chewing; or because the piece of food that is gulped down resembles a large pebble, for a pebble, when thrown from the hand, gains force and speed, as witness the expression "A pebble in your head!" for example, meaning, "May a blow from a pebble strike your head at speed so that the striking impacts upon it!" The action is thus likened to the throwing of a pebble because he takes a piece of food quickly, tosses it down his throat, and gulps it down in just the same way that a man throws a pebble—hard and with force. In addition, flaky pastry is soft and milk is moist, so they do not need to be chewed with the teeth. This is why he expresses his sorrow at his separation from this dish and why his heart, being so overwhelmed by desire for it, takes to fluttering and palpitating like a branch on which sits a bird that is moving and fluttering its wings. All of this is due to the enormity of his longing, the promptings of his appetite, and the delay in attaining the object of his longing and desire—for you will find that the lover's heart is always palpitating at its separation from its beloved and only quiets down when he meets with him and talks to him, whispering sweet nothings to him and delighting him with nocturnal discourse. When this happens, what ails him disappears and his senses are lulled by the comfort that the presence of the beloved and being united with him bring him. Master 'Umar ibn al-Fāriḍ, God benefit us through him, says:[491] 11.30.6

And a boy like a bough
　On which my heart forever is descending.
Sweet his speech but
　With a sweetness heartrending.
I both protest and praise its work—
　Marvel, then, at one complaining and commending!

—albeit the words of the Master, God benefit us through him, and his ilk have nothing in common with the matter at hand.

11.30.7 Next he promises himself that, when he sees the bowl of his cousin (of whom more later) full of bread-in-broth,[492] he will eat it all up, so great is his appetite, so enormous his hunger, and so long his wait for it. He says:

TEXT

11.31 *anā-n shuftu laqqānata-bni ʿammī Mukhaymirin*
malānah mina l-taftīti malwa ṭafīf
qashartū jamīʿū mā taraktu baqiyyatū
li-ghayrī wa-lā ʿindī bi-dā tawqīf

Should I see the bowl of the son of my uncle Mukhaymir
full of bread-in-soup brimming over,
I would polish it off completely and leave nothing over
for others, and would not pause!

COMMENTARY

11.31.1 *Anā* ("(Should) I"): meaning Abū Shādūf and no one else . . .

11.31.2 *(i)n shuftu* ("see"): that is, should I perceive with my eye, not with my ear, as previously explained . . .[493]

11.31.3 *laqqānata* ("the bowl of"): previously described, etymologized, and explained . . .[494]

11.31.4 *(i)bni ʿammī* ("the son of my uncle"): the latter being the brother of my father . . .

11.31.5 *Mukhaymirin*: so called because he had a large hole in which he would ferment (*yukhammiru*) dung and in which perhaps he would also urinate, or because he used to bring the yeast (*khamīrah*) for the bread to his mother before it was baked, or because he used to eat the leavened (*mukhammar*) dough before it was shaped into loaves, or because his face was so ugly it looked like cracked yeast, for they use this as a term of abuse and one says, "You with the face like cracked yeast" (*yā wajh al-khamīrah al-mushaqqaqah*)! . . .

malānah ("full"): that is, referring to the bowl in question . . . 11.31.6

mina l-taftīti ("of bread-in-broth"): *taftīt* is the plural of *fatt*, which is the crumbling of bread into small or large morsels, the small being better; on this lentils or *bīsār* are poured and it is then left until it dries and comes to resemble rocks. 11.31.7

malwa ṭafīf ("brimming over"): that is, completely full and brimming over, meaning that it is too much to be contained within the rims of the vessel; derived from *taṭfīf al-kayl* ("the scanting of the measure")—the Almighty says, «*waylun li-l-muṭaffifīna* ("Woe to the defrauders")!»[495]—or from *ṭaffa l-mā' 'alā l-jurūf* ("the water overflowed the dikes") when it rises above them, or from al-Ṭaff, a place in Iraq in the area of Karbalā', where Our Master and Our Lord the Imam al-Ḥusayn, God be pleased with him, was martyred. 11.31.8

The brief version of his story[496] is that, when Mu'āwiyah died, Yazīd dispatched someone to al-Ḥusayn to take his oath of allegiance, but he refused and left for Mecca. Then letters came from Iraq saying that they had sworn allegiance to him there after Mu'āwiyah's death. Ibn al-Zubayr advised him to leave and return to Iraq while Ibn 'Abbās, Ibn 'Umar, and several Companions advised him not to, but to no avail, and he sent his cousin Muslim ibn 'Aqīl to the people of Iraq to obtain their oath of allegiance. This Muslim did, and he sent word to al-Ḥusayn to join him. Our Master al-Ḥusayn then left Mecca, making for Iraq. Yazīd learned of his departure and sent word to his governor of al-Kūfah, 'Ubayd Allāh ibn Ziyād, ordering him to seek out Muslim and kill him, but news of this did not reach al-Ḥusayn until he was three miles from al-Qādisiyyah. There al-Ḥurr ibn Yazīd al-Tamīmī met him and said to him, "Go back, for what I left behind me does not bode well for you," and he told him the news. He also met al-Farazdaq and questioned him, and al-Farazdaq told him, "The hearts of the people are with you 11.31.9

but their swords are with the Umayyads, and the decision will come from Heaven." At this, al-Ḥusayn made ready to turn back, but the brother of Muslim was with him and said to him, "We shall not go back until we have taken our revenge for him or been killed!" Ibn Ziyād had mustered four thousand, or, as some say, twenty thousand, to oppose him, and caught up with him at Karbalāʾ. So al-Ḥusayn set up camp, and there were with him forty-five horsemen and about one hundred infantry, and the army met him under the command of ʿUmar ibn Saʿd ibn Abī Waqqāṣ, whom Ibn Ziyād had made governor of Ray with a letter of appointment executable upon his return from fighting al-Ḥusayn.

11.31.10 When they met in battle, al-Ḥusayn, exhausted by the fight, said to him, "Allow me one of three choices. Let me either reach a border town, or return to Medina, or turn myself in to the son of Muʿāwiyah." ʿUmar accepted his conditions and sent word to Ibn Ziyād, who wrote to him, "I will accept nothing of what he asks for until he turns himself in to me." Al-Ḥusayn refused and they prepared to do battle with him, and most of those ranged against him were men who had pledged him their allegiance and been his followers. When he was certain that they were going to fight him, he rose among his companions to address them. He praised God and lauded Him and then said, "You have seen how the matter stands, how the world has turned and become fickle and withdrawn its favor, and it has come to a point at which all that is left is to drink the dregs of the cup or live a life of abasement—like tainted grazing. Do you not see that the truth is not acted upon and that falsity is not refrained from? Let the Muslim then desire to meet the Almighty, for in death I see only happiness and in life among the wrongdoers only sin." Then they fought him, and the end of the matter was that he was martyred and seventeen youths of his house were martyred with him. This was at Karbalāʾ, as related by al-Ṭabarānī.[497]

11.31.11 The eminent scholar Master ʿAbd al-Raʾūf al-Munāwī, God benefit us through him, says in his *Biographical Dictionary*:[498]

If you say this is contradicted by what is reported on the authority of al-Ṭabarānī also, on the authority of ʿĀʾishah, that the Prophet, blessings and peace be upon him, said, "Jibrīl informed me that al-Ḥusayn would be killed in the land of al-Ṭaff, and Jibrīl brought me this earth and told me that in it would be his resting place,"[499] and by what Ibn Saʿd relates on the authority of ʿAlī, Commander of the Believers, God be pleased with him, who said, "I went in one day to the Chosen One, blessings and peace be upon him, and his eyes were brimming with tears, and I asked him why and he said, 'Jibrīl has informed me that al-Ḥusayn will be killed on the bank of the Euphrates,'"[500] I would say that there is no discrepancy, because the Euphrates debouches from the farthest borders of al-Rūm, then passes through the land of al-Ṭaff, which is a dependency of Karbalāʾ. Thus the discrepancy we repel; the reports agree and hang together well.

These are his words, God benefit us through him.

After they had killed him, they severed his head and carried it to Ibn Ziyād, who sent it to Yazīd, along with the members of his family who were with him. Among these were ʿAlī, the son al-Ḥusayn, who was sick, and his paternal aunt, Zaynab. When they were presented to Yazīd, he was overjoyed and stood them like prisoners at the door of the mosque and insulted them viciously; and when they placed the noble head before him, he started knocking at its front teeth with a rod he had in his hand, saying, "So, Ḥusayn, I meet you face to face!" and gave his joy free rein. Later, when the Muslims detested him for that and everyone hated him, he repented. Abū Yaʿlā has published, on the authority of Abū ʿUbaydah, a Tradition attributed to the Prophet: "The affairs of my nation will be maintained in justice until they are spoiled for the first time by a man of the Banū Umayyah called Yazīd."[501] And it is reliably reported on the authority of Ibrāhīm al-Nakhaʿī that he said, "Were I one 11.31.12

of those who fought al-Ḥusayn, then entered Heaven, I would be ashamed to look into the face of the Chosen One, God bless him and grant him peace." The jinn were heard to lament for him, according to reports published by Abū Nuʿaym[502] and others.

11.31.13 He was killed on ʿAshūrā',[503] a Friday, of the year 61. At the moment of his killing, the sun was eclipsed entirely so that the stars appeared at midday, and for six months the horizons of the heavens were red and blood was seen in them, and the earth stayed seven days like a clot of blood, while the rays of the sun appeared on the walls as though they were draperies dyed with safflower beating against one another. It is said that not a stone was overturned in Jerusalem that day but fresh blood was found beneath it, and the turmeric that was with their soldiers turned to ashes; and they slaughtered a she-camel among the soldiers and beheld fires in her flesh, and they cooked it and it tasted bitter as colocynth. Then they set off with his head, making for the son of Muʿāwiyah,[504] and they made camp at the end of the first day's march and drank wine, and a pen of iron came out towards them from a wall and wrote in blood:

Can a nation that killed al-Ḥusayn expect
his grandsire's intercession on the Day of Account?

11.31.14 Then Yazīd the son of Muʿāwiyah ordered that his family be returned to Medina and that his Noble Head be paraded from town to town. Ibn Khālawayh recounts, on the authority of al-Aʿmash, on the authority of Minhāl ibn ʿAmr al-Asadī, that the latter said, "By God, I saw the head of al-Ḥusayn as it was being carried, when I was in Damascus, and before it was a man reciting from *Sūrat al-kahf*, and when he came to «Or deemest thou that the people of the Cave and the Inscription are a wonder among our portents?»[505] the head uttered words in faultless Arabic and cried out loud, 'More wonderful than the people of the Cave are my killing and my carrying!'" Ibn Ḥajar, giving a chain of authority that goes back to ʿAlī, says that the Chosen One, God's blessings be upon him, said, "The killer of al-Ḥusayn lies in a sarcophagus of fire and bears half the torment of mortal man." People differ over where the head of al-Ḥusayn ended up after it went to Syria, and where it came to rest. One group tends to the belief that it was paraded until it ended up at ʿAsqalān, where the commander received it and buried it, and that when the Franks conquered ʿAsqalān, al-Ṣāliḥ Ṭalāʾiʿ, the Fatimid minister, ransomed it from them for a huge sum and went out many days' march to meet it, then built over it the famous shrine in Cairo.[506] Others state that it was borne to Medina along with his family and buried in al-Baqīʿ. The view endorsed by a certain party among the Sufis, may God be pleased with all of them, is that it is in the Cairo tomb.

Next the poet draws attention to the insufficiency of seeing the bread-in-broth and to the fact that only eating it all will satisfy him. He says: 11.31.15

qashartū jamīʿū ("I would polish it off completely"): with regard to eating and other things, *qashara* means "to take the whole of a thing" or "to devour it entirely." The word is also used in connection with luck: one says, "So-and-so has a jinxing ankle" (*kaʿbun aqshar*) and "Your ankle brings jinxes" (*kaʿbuka aqshar*), and in the same vein one speaks of "ankles and thresholds and horses' forelocks"; and one speaks of "a jinxing woman" (*imraʾah qashrāʾ*) and "a jinxing man" (*rajulun aqshar*), meaning that he is ill-fortuned and poor and brings ill fortune and poverty with him when he stays with or calls upon a person, and so on. In our village there was a butcher, called Sukaykar ("Little Sugar"), who fell in love with a beautiful woman, called Kaʿb al-Khayr ("Ankle of Good Fortune"). When he was in the midst of his throes of love for her she died and a man of letters said of him: 11.31.16

Sukaykar's thing with the Ankle was doomed—
His ankle was a jinx, polished her off at one go.
Had Death asked me, "Shall I wait?" or had I seen him,
I'd have said, "By all means take him. Just leave the Ankle in the shoe!"

The story of Ṭuways that is told in the books belongs in the same category. All these things are, however, merely occasions that the Almighty brings about through the agency of whomever He pleases, for good or evil; were it not so, it would not say in the Noble Tradition, "No contagious disease, no evil omens, and no good augurs!"[507] Once a crow cawed and a man said, "May it be well, God willing!" One of God's initiates heard him and rebuked him, saying, "Do not say that! Are good and ill in any hands but the Almighty's?"

11.31.17 *qashartū jamīʿū* ("I would polish it off completely"):[508] that is, I would eat it all and leave none of it for anyone else, because I crave it and I am extremely hungry; consequently, when I see it, I will leave none of it. This is a typical sign of bootlessness, for if one is greedy and indulges his appetite for food and eats a more than normal amount, it will harm him and do him injury, and illnesses will arise therefrom, which is why it has been said, "Most people die of overeating." The poet says:

If you want to live healthy and be at ease,
Eat sparingly of your favorite victual.
As Dr. Hippocrates and others have said,
He lives long who eats but little.

11.31.18 It is said that three physicians met at the court of the king of India: an Indian, a Greek, and an Egyptian. The king said to them, "Let each of you prescribe for me a medicine that prevents all disease!" The Indian said, "The medicine that prevents all disease is to breakfast every day on a few wild chicory seeds." The Greek said, "The medicine that prevents all disease is to breakfast every day on three sips of hot water." The Egyptian said, "The medicine that prevents all disease is to eat only when you feel hungry and to get up in the morning with an appetite; do this, and you will suffer no sickness but the sickness of death." All of them said, "The Egyptian is right!" And when al-Muqawqis, king of Egypt, sent the Prophet, may God bless him and give him peace, the two slave girls, Māriyah and Sīrīn (who were from the city of Anṣinā, which is now a ruin on the banks of the river Nile in the region of Upper Egypt), and the mule called al-Duldul and honey from Banhā (a village in the region of Cairo, belonging to al-Qalyūbiyyah), and with them a physician, he said, "If he accepts the gift and sends the physician back, he is a prophet." When the gift and the physician reached the Prophet, may God bless him and give him peace, he accepted the gift and sent back the physician, and said, "We are a people that eats only when hungry, and when we eat, we do not eat until we are full. Thus we have no need of a physician." When the words of the Prophet, may God bless him and give him peace, reached al-Muqawqis, he said, "How mighty a prophet he is! He has put all wisdom into a couple of words!" And in the Noble Tradition it says, "Go hungry and be healthy!" for hunger is the source of vigor in worship and produces a healthy, disease-free body. This is especially true of those who perform spiritual exercises and practice seclusion, for the outcome of this for them is hunger. As the Initiate of the Almighty the Imam al-Būnī[509] states in one of his books, "No one can perform a spiritual exercise correctly so long as there is so much as a grain's weight of satiety within him."

Overeating may spring from several causes. It may be from excessive greed for food or from habit. We have seen people eat a crock of food and not be satisfied, and we have seen people eat a hundred roasted eggs with bread and not be satisfied. A certain tyrant used to eat a ewe, roasted, for lunch. One day he ate and then wanted to have intercourse with his wife, but she refused. When he reproached her, she said, "How can you reach me when there is so much of ewe between us?"[510] And Master Muḥyī l-Dīn ibn al-ʿArabī, God benefit us through him, states in *The Positions of the Stars*[511] that ʿAbd al-Malik[512] was a glutton who one day passed a man who had with him two baskets, of roasted eggs and of figs. ʿAbd al-Malik ate everything that was in them and got sick and died as a result. Al-Walīd,[513] one of the kings of the Banū Umayyah, was 11.31.19

a stubborn tyrant who would drink a skin of wine and eat a young camel. One day he opened a copy of the Qur'an and saw, «And they sought help from their Lord and every stubborn tyrant was brought to naught!»[514] and he ripped up the book and recited:

Threatenest thou me with "stubborn tyrant"?
Well, that I am indeed!
When thou seest thy Lord on Doomsday say,
"The one who ripped me was Walīd!"

—all of which was due to his obduracy and excessively tyrannical ways. Al-Ma'mūn used to eat a lot, and a certain physician concocted for him the dish called *ma'mūniyyah*.[515] He tried eating it and found that his stomach was filled and his consumption of food decreased, for a little of it is enough to nourish a person. This is why it was named after him. On the other hand, the case of the *walī* who used to eat large amounts of food, enough to satisfy a great multitude, is an example of divinely granted freedom of action and a demonstration of God's miraculous grace.

11.31.20 It is said that a glutton once passed by a village on a journey and a man invited him in and sat him down. At the time, his wife was at the oven baking bread, so the man brought his guest a quantity of bread and went off to get something to go with it. When he returned, he found that the man had eaten all the bread, so he put the condiments in front of him and went to get him more bread, and returned, and found that he had eaten the condiments, and so it went on until the guest had eaten all the bread the host's wife had baked and the condiments too. When he saw this, the host asked, in an attempt at cordiality, "Where are you on your way to?" "Cairo," said the man. "Do you have business there?" asked the host. "Indeed," said the man. "And what is that?" asked the host. "A clever doctor was recommended to me there," said the man, "so I decided to go to him." "Why?" asked the host. "I am a man," said the guest, "who eats little, and my bowels are obstructed. I want him to prescribe me something, lest I give up eating altogether." Then the host said to him, "I have a favor to request of you: I beseech you in God's name, if you complete your business with the doctor and come back, don't pass by my house! If this is how you behave when your bowels are obstructed, what will you do when they've been opened up?" Then he expelled the man from his house and he went his way.

mā taraktu baqiyyatū li-ghayrī ("and leave nothing over for others"): that is, for anyone other than myself, be they near or far. 11.31.21

wa-lā ʿindī bi-dā tawqīf ("and I would not pause"): that is, I would not pause in my eating or feel ashamed before anyone who might pass by, or invite him, or feed from it anyone other than myself; nor would I look at it to see whether it was cold or hot, or tasty or only so-so, or permitted or forbidden. In no case would I bother with such questions or pay any heed to such things. 11.31.22

Next he felt a desire to eat a dish made of salt fish, called *fisīkh*, and hoped and yearned for it. He says: 11.31.23

TEXT

anā khāṭirī ʾaklat fisīkhin ʿalā l-nadah 11.32
ʾaḍālu ʿalayhā bākiyan wa-ʾasīf

Me, my wish is for a meal of *fisīkh* first thing.
I shall ever weep for it and grieve!

COMMENTARY

anā ("Me"): meaning me, Abū Shādūf, and no one else, as previously explained in relation to other verses. 11.32.1

khāṭirī ("my wish"): that is, my desire, and what constantly occurs (*yakhṭiru*) to my mind, and what I am longing and waiting for, is . . . 11.32.2

ʾaklat fisīkhin ("a meal of *fisīkh*"):[516] an *aklah* ("meal") is a single instance of *akl* ("eating"), and *fisīkh* is a kind of fish called *būrī*, and another kind called *ṭūbār*; they take these and stack them one on top of one another, having first put salt on each layer. The salt is 11.32.3

absorbed, water leaches out, the fish shrinks, and the salt preserves and hardens it. Then they take them and sell them. The country people and others eat them: they take a fish and slit its belly and then the man or the woman takes the fish in his left hand, or in both hands, and squeezes lime over it and picks at it, morsel by morsel, taking a bit of the flesh in his mouth and then a morsel of the bread, like a dog worrying at a piece of carrion, the filth and vile stench all over his mouth and hands. They eat it even in the marketplaces and, stranger still, I was told by someone I trust from Samannūd that he entered the ablutions area of a riverside mosque dedicated to a saint called al-ʿAdawī, God benefit us through him, and saw an individual from the countryside sitting in the latrine with a piece of *fisīkh* and a loaf from which he was eating. My friend went up to him and said, "Would you eat in the latrine?" and the man replied, "And would you drive me from the House of God?" The man laughed at him and let him be.

11.32.4 Amazingly, it is highly prized among the women of the countryside, who find it delicious beyond all comparison, especially those of the hamlets and the villages of the swamplands, for they set eyes on it only when the Nile is high, when it is brought to them in boats from Dimyāṭ and Rashīd and sold by the grain and the gram. They have an enormous liking for it, and it is taken for sale to Upper Egypt and elsewhere and is famous throughout Egypt. Roe-bearing gray mullet (*fisīkh al-baṭārikh*), on the other hand, they leave out in the air until it hardens and turns drier than *fisīkh*, and this is a dish of the great. It is called *baṭārikh* because its belly is full of *baṭrūkh* ("roe"), unlike ordinary *fisīkh*, which has none. They eat the flesh with vinegar and oil, sometimes adding chopped garlic and onions, and spices. It is considered a great delicacy in the cities and elsewhere, and they go to great lengths to eat it. They also eat it on its own, calling it *ṣirṣ*, with *i* after the first *ṣ*, after setting aside the roe from its internal cavity in another container, with sesame oil. All of this is extremely tasty but is Hot and Dry, and the proper time to eat it is in the winter.

Fisīkh is so called either because of its disintegration (*tafassukh*) when eaten, or because the first person to make it broke wind while he was eating and someone smelled it and said, "He farted! Yeccch!" (*Fisī! Ikhkh!*) and they put these two words together and made them into a name, saying *fisīkh*. It is said that a countryman heard a reciter of the Qur'an say the words of the Almighty, «And therein is all that souls desire and eyes find sweet»[517] and he said to him, "And is there *fisīkh* too, Shaykh?" to which the man replied, "Indeed, and everything else that your disgusting appetite desires!" 11.32.5

ʿalā l-nadah ("first thing," literally "at the dew"): that is, when the dew descends, for it is cool then, and, *fisīkh* being Hot and Dry, eating it at the beginning of the day may moderate its effect, if it be summer, though in the winter it may be eaten at any time whatsoever. It is preferable that one drink something sweet afterward or eat some dates, for this eliminates any harmful side effects. 11.32.6

ʾaḍālu ("I shall ever"): explained above . . .[518] 11.32.7

ʿalayhā ("(weep) for it"): that is, for this meal of *fisīkh* because of my disgusting soul's excessive longing for it. 11.32.8

bākiyan ("weep"): that is, I shall go on weeping over the nonappearance of this meal. Weeping consists of the shedding of tears and their falling onto the cheeks; one also says "the heavens wept" when it rains, and "the clouds wept"; the Almighty says, «And the heaven and the earth wept not for them.»[519] The poet[520] says: 11.32.9

I wept, for her tears made me weep for love
Of her; and the credit goes to the one who wept first!

The word *bukāʾ* ("weeping") is derived from *bakka l-jarḥ* ("the wound oozed"), when blood comes out of it.[521]

wa-ʾasīf ("and grieve"): the word is shortened for the meter, the original form being *aḍālu asīfan* ("and I shall ever . . . grieve") for this meal until I get it, and sorrow will not leave me until I eat my 11.32.10

fill of it. Grief is the extreme passion experienced at the loss of a beloved and separation from a friend. The poet says:

I grieve for none but the one I love,
And he whom I do not love need bear no blame.

11.32.11 Next he moved from a desire for something disgusting to a desire for something wholesome. He says:

TEXT

11.33 *ʿalā man naḍar fī furni dārū ṭawājin*
zaghālīla min burji-bn-Abū Shaʿnīf

Happy is he who has seen in the oven of his house casseroles
of squabs from the dovecote of the son of Abū Shaʿnīf!

COMMENTARY

11.33.1 *ʿalā man naḍar* ("happy is he who has seen"): with the eye . . .

11.33.2 *fī furni* ("in the oven of"): the oven is the thing in which fire is kindled and bread is baked and has been described in Part One of this book . . .[522]

11.33.3 *dārū* ("his house"): that is, the house of the poet, the pronominal suffix of *dār* referring to him, meaning that he would not see them in anyone's house but his, and that the casseroles are not to be found in anyone's oven but his, so that, should this indeed befall him, he might be easy in his mind and of good cheer.

11.33.4 *ṭawājin* ("casseroles"): plural of *ṭājin*, described above,[523] full of . . .

11.33.5 *zaghālīla* ("squabs"): these are the chicks, taken from the dovecotes, of the free-ranging pigeons, which are also called "field pigeons" because they feed in the fields and where crops are sown and on the threshing floors. They are nutritious and act as an aphrodisiac if spices and clarified cow's butter are added. They are too delicious for words. *Ḥamām* ("pigeons, doves") is a generic term for everything that sips[524] and coos. Then he specifies that the squabs to which he is referring must be . . .

min burji ("from the dovecote of"): and not from squabs born to house-raised pigeons. *Burj* (literally "tower") is the singular of *burūj* and is also used of the Citadel (Burj al-Qalʿah)[525] and of a "mansion" of the zodiac (*burj al-kawākib*). Here the reference is to the dovecote (*burj al-ḥamām*),[526] which is a round building in which waterwheel jars[527] are set, the pigeons coming to these jars and laying their eggs and raising their chicks in them and dunging in them too. The peasants call their manure "capital" and use it for sowing watermelons and palm trees, which they feed with it; it is something with which they are extremely familiar. They also take the chicks and sell and slaughter them; so it is in all villages. The name *zaghālīl* is derived from *zaghalantah* ("ranunculus"), which is a plant, bluish in color, to which squabs are likened because their feathers are blue, or it may be derived from the *zughaliyyah,* a class of people who make counterfeit silver coins, which they call "sparrows"; they call the piaster coin a *faras* ("mare"), the charcoal that they use *zabīb* ("raisins"), the bellows that they blow with *al-shaykh* ("the old man"), and they have a whole jargon for their craft, but they appear to live in constant terror of the police and great poverty and from hand to mouth. The Imam al-Shāfiʿī, God be pleased with him, was asked about alchemy and said, "I know people who have been impoverished by it but none who have been enriched." Pigeons are in a similar state, at frequent intervals the peasants enter their houses, take their chicks, slaughter them, and sell some of them, so that they are in constant fear, like the *zughaliyyah.* The singular of *zaghālīl* is *zughlūl,* just as the singular of *habābīl* ("idiots") is *hibbawl. Burj* is derived from *tabarruj,* which means "showing off one's finery"; the Almighty used the term when He said, without «displaying their finery (*mutabarrijātin bi-zīnah*).»[528] 11.33.6

A Silly Topic for Debate: Is there any connection between the bird called *ḥamām* ("pigeon") and the *ḥammām* ("bathhouse") that 11.33.7

is well known in cities and is designed for ablutions and personal cleanliness, bearing in mind that the word is the same, except for the doubling of the *m*, or what is the situation? We reply, the Facetious Answer is as follows: a connection may be discerned from two perspectives, one analogical, the other medical. The first is that, in a bathhouse, people are crowded together and throng around the basins and tanks, mingling intimately with one another and indulging in pleasant converse and so forth.[529] Similarly, in a dovecote the pigeons crowd together and mingle intimately and go into the jars to see their chicks and twitter and coo and so forth. From this perspective, the jars are the basins and tanks and the going in to the chicks is reminiscent of the private booths and of meeting with beardless boys for massage and scrubbing with a rough cloth and so on;[530] and the ascent of the pigeons afterward to the top of the dovecote, whence they go off to find their food, is similar to the people leaving the bathhouse to gain their daily bread and their livelihood. As it says in the Tradition, "If you were to put your trust in God as you should, He would provide for you as He provides for the birds, which set out in the morning with their stomachs empty and return in the evening with their stomachs full." This is the gastronomical-analogical perspective. The other perspective is that the bathhouse is Hot and Moist and does good to every member, so long as the temperature is moderate. The best bathhouses are those of ancient construction, with spacious halls and sweet water; they have so many beneficial qualities that they are called "the silent doctor." The flesh of pigeons is the same, in that it is heating and stimulates the sexual appetite—even though the chicks are both Moist and Coarse—especially if spices are added, as noted earlier; when this is done, the benefit they confer is complete. The best of their meat is from wild pigeons. Long-term consumption of those raised indoors causes fever and excess of blood. The connection with bathhouses would be along these lines. Our response is now transparent, the silliness apparent.

11.33.8 The name *ḥamām* for the birds is derived from *ḥawm* ("hovering"),[531] which is "hesitating in flight"; one says, "The bird hovers (*yaḥūmu*)" when it does the preceding, the paradigm being *ḥāma, yaḥūmu, ḥawman*. As for the building *ḥammām*, it is derived from *ḥummā*, meaning "fever", since, when a person enters it, the heating and the sweating that overcome him make him appear as though he were suffering from a fever; or from *ḥumūm* ("bathing"), which is plunging into water, from the expression *fulānun istaḥammā fī l-baḥr* ("So-and-so bathed in the river"), meaning he swam in it and immersed himself in it; or from *ḥamīm*, which is "extremely hot water," whence the words of the Almighty, «Boiling water (*ḥamīm*) will be poured down on their heads.»[532] The same word is applied to a loving friend, because of the great heat and desire that love contains, whence the words of the Almighty, «There will be no friend (*ḥamīm*) for the evildoers, nor any intercessor,»[533] that is, no friend to intercede for them. The first *m* of *ḥammām* is double because the thing itself is so hot and has such a strong effect. *Ḥimām*, with *i* after the *ḥ*, on the other hand, is "death." It gets the *i* after the *ḥ* because when a man is alive he enjoys vigor and strength, but when he dies he is diminished,[534] his wisdom is gone, and nothing is left but his remains. As the poet says:

> These are our remains that bear witness to us;
> So look, when we are gone, to our remains.

It is derived from the notion of "extremity, crisis" (*shiddah*). One says *ḥumma l-amr* ("things reached a critical point") when things get tough—and there can be no doubt that death is a major crisis in terms of its effect on the escape of the vital spirit and its release from the body, etc. This concludes our facetious investigations and silly references.

(i)bn- ("son of"): also called "boy" (*walad*) and "scion" (*najl*). One 11.33.9
may say either "So-and-so's boy" or "So-and-so's scion."

Abū Shaʿnīf: the first word is, in genitive construct,[535] properly *abī*, 11.33.10
but his tongue was too awkward to allow him to say that. Abū Shaʿnīf is his *kunyah*. His original name was ʿAflaq, or, according to some

reports, Baḥlaq, and the name of his son mentioned in the verse was Falḥas, which is a dog's name. He became known by this *kunyah* because he used to steal the grass called *nīf* (mentioned above)[536] and put it down for his animals; thus stories of his thievery became widespread, and people in the village took to saying *shāʿa bi-l-nīfi* ("he became well known for the *nīf*"), that is, for stealing the *nīf*. Then they dropped the preposition and the gentive case,[537] retained the verb and the noun, put them together as a compound, and made it *Shaʿnīf*. The word *shaʿnīf* derives from *shaʿnafah*,[538] of the measure of *qalḥafah* ("dessication"), and the meaning may be one and the same. The paradigm is *shaʿnafa, yushaʿnifu, shaʿnafatan*.

11.33.11 Next he explains how he eats squabs, and that they are eaten with flaky pastry.

TEXT

11.34 *wa-faṭṭar faṭāyir min ṭaḥīni-bni ʿammū*
wa-yaqʿud lahā qaʿdat ghulāmin ḥasīf

And made *faṭāyir* cakes from the flour of his cousin
and sits down to them like a lovelorn adolescent!

COMMENTARY

11.34.1 *wa-faṭṭar* ("and made"): of the measure of *wa-shammar* ("and hitched up his skirts"). The poet says:

And he hitched up his skirts to reveal a prick, and pissed down on her
Quite deliberately, till she was drowning in piss.

His words mean that "if these squab casseroles fall to my lot and God fulfills my wish through their arrival where I am, eating them will bring me no pleasure unless they are accompanied by flaky pastry," which is why he says . . .

11.34.2 *wa-faṭṭar faṭāyir* ("and has made *faṭāyir* cakes"): a verbal noun[539] like *ʿamal ʿamāyil* ("he did (terrible) deeds"), or like *qashshar qashāyir* ("he peeled peelings"); the meaning is "he patted out, or manufactured, *faṭīr*." *Faṭāyir* is the plural of *faṭīrah*, though this may also take the plural *faṭīr*,[540] like *khamīrah* ("yeast cake") and *khamīr* ("yeast"), or *ḥimārah* ("she-donkey") and *ḥamīr* ("donkeys"). *Faṭīr* is said to be Heavy and Coarse and unsuitable for human consumption because it generates flatulence; however, this is only true if it is eaten alone. When eaten with other things it does no harm. The preceding refers exclusively to the *faṭīr* of the countryside, which the poet wants. They take plain flour and knead it with water without any yeast and put it in the oven or stew it in the cooking pit, this latter type being called "slow-cooked *faṭīr*" (*faṭīr dammāsī*). Then they take it and eat it, and this is the Heavy type that is discommended. The *faṭīr* that is made by the great, on the other hand, is prepared with the finest flour, into which they work clarified butter and honey, and this type does no harm. Or there is the type to which they add clarified butter while kneading and bake for breakfast and so on; this is the desirable kind.

min ṭaḥīni-bni ʿammū ("from the flour of his cousin"): whose name was Ghindāf; that is, his cousin would have donated it to him for nothing, or lent him the flour till such time as his circumstances should improve and he could give it back to him, or given it to him as a present, or the poet was able to steal it and bake it in the oven or the cooking pit. He would then remove the squab casseroles from the oven and crumble the aforesaid *faṭāyir* into the broth and prepare himself to eat of it. 11.34.3

wa-yaqʿud lahā ("and sits down to them"): that is, to the squabs, or to the thing as a whole . . . 11.34.4

qaʿdat ("like"): with the demeanor of one sitting like . . . 11.34.5

ghulāmin ("an adolescent"): a *ghulām* is one whose moustache has started to sprout. The poet[541] says: 11.34.6

Among us are the lad whose lip has just begun to sprout,
The spinster, and beardless boys, and white-haired men.

Some define a *ghulām* as anyone who has lived nine years since being weaned, others as one who has reached maturity and strength.

11.34.7 *ḥasīf* ("lovelorn"): an adjective qualifying *ghulām*, that is, afflicted with *ḥusāfah*, that is, worries and gloom and great hunger and sorrow. The poet is saying, "I too, like him, will be afflicted with worries and great hunger, for I cannot believe that I shall ever behold this dish and this *faṭīr*, and eat of it till I have had enough and my hunger disappears and my appetite is satisfied, like an adolescent boy who, afflicted with sorrow and grief, sits absorbed in thought till God drives away his sorrow and reunites him with his loved ones and he is overjoyed and filled with happiness at finding himself once more with them—for 'the lovers' meeting is a feast.'"

11.34.8 Apropos of which, an Initiate of God once passed two men eating during Ramadan and asked them, "What do you think you are doing?" to which they replied, "We are two true lovers whom fate had separated for many a year. Then we met today, and 'the lovers' meeting is a feast' and to fast on a feast is a sin!" "And what," said the other, "is the mark of your love?" One of the two replied by saying, "Cut my arm!" and held it out to him, and the man cut it and the blood came out of the other's arm, without a wound, for their two souls and two bodies had become as one soul in one body. As the poet[542] says:

We are two bodies as one body.
We are two souls that have become a single form.

And Ibn al-ʿArabī,[543] God benefit us through his blessings, says:

When we met to say good-bye, and hugged and hung,
I reckoned us one single, doubled, sign;
And though as selves we may be twain,
To outside eyes we must appear as one.[544]

There is much in the same vein on the inclination of lovers and the quest of Initiates, God benefit us through them every one!

Next, the poet moves on to another tasty dish for which he longed. He says: 11.34.9

TEXT

ʿalā man naḍar ṭājin samak fī furaynihī 11.35
wa-law kāna yā-khwānī bi-lā tanḍīf

Happy is he who sees a casserole of fish in his little oven
though it be, my brothers, uncleaned!

COMMENTARY

ʿalā man naḍar ("Happy is he who sees"): with his eye, not hears with his ear . . . 11.35.1

ṭājin ("a casserole"): full of . . . 11.35.2

samak ("fish"): a name for a whole category, consisting of many different sorts, which the Almighty has permitted to be consumed, along with locusts, both dead and alive.[545] The Prophet, God bless him and grant him peace, said, "Two dead things and two things containing blood have been permitted to us: fish and locusts, and the spleen and the liver." Large fish are Cold, Moist, and Coarse, and small fish are Cold, Moist, and Subtle. The best is fresh fish, whose humors may be adjusted by cooking with clarified butter, onions, and hot spices; they also increase sexual appetite. Salted fish are Hotter than fresh, and Drier. Large fish are most nutritious when eaten with old wine and raisins, and small fish when eaten with old wine and *fālūdhaj*, especially if taken from sweet running water. Those with scales are to be preferred to those without; a doctor says, "Eat of them what is scaly and leave of them what is slimy." The scaly ones are those such as the mullet, the bream, and the barb, each of which is very delicious and has its own particular taste and tastiness. Mullet, for example, is stuffed with onions and 11.35.3

spices and prepared with fluffy rice and is also used in casseroles to make a broth and in other ways and is very delicious. It may also be made with groats, and I have eaten it this way many times in Dimyāṭ. It may be made with rice, but this has to be slightly sticky. To this they add lime juice and call it *fuqāʿiyyah*; I have eaten it, and it is very delicious and has a subtle flavor. Bream is considered more of a delicacy and better tasting than mullet and resembles a large perch; in the proverb it says, "If there's no chicken to be seen, eat bream!" It is prepared in various ways, like mullet. As for the barb, it is the best tasting of all, and is found only on the riverbed. They have special tricks for catching it, and they get it and present it to great men, emirs, and viceroys as a gift. Its taste is outstanding, and it is more nutritious than any other kind, especially if fried and stuffed, in which case words cannot describe how tasty it is—you want to eat your fingers, it's so good! The proverb says, putting the words into the mouth of the barb, "If you find better than me, don't eat me!" There is also a kind of fish called perch, whose taste is slightly bitter but makes delicious eating, and is said to feed on the plants of Paradise.

11.35.4 All of this, however, is far from what the poet has in mind. What he means is the fish that he catches from his village when the water of the Nile retreats and the ponds and holes are left full of water; black catfish are generated therein, and little perch and small fry and the like, and their children go down and fish in them, then bring the fish, clean them, and put them in casseroles with a little linseed oil and some chopped onion and put them in the oven until they are done, and eat them with maize or barley bread, the whole thing having a cloying stench and a foul smell, though to them it is the most delicious of foods. The small black catfish they take and bury in the cooking pit until they are a little ripe, and then they eat them while the blood is still running, God protect us from such things!

11.35.5 Speaking of fish, I am reminded that a man once loved a woman of surpassing comeliness and beauty, whose husband, God bless him, was one of our more dim-witted and credulous brethren.

One day her lover passed her and said, "It's ages since we met!" and she replied, "Come to me tomorrow at the end of the day!" On the morrow she said to her husband, "I feel like cooking fish today for us to eat," so he went to the market and brought some. She cleaned it and prepared it and put it in a big casserole, and told him, "Take this, go with it to the baker, and spare me the effort of cooking it. And tell the baker to send it with his boy at the time of the afternoon call to prayer." So her husband took it and went with it to the baker and gave him his wife's instructions, and the baker said, "To hear is to obey!" The baker cooked the fish and sent it to her at the agreed time, and while she was sitting and eating, her friend with whom she had made the tryst knocked on the door. She opened it and he went up and ate some of the fish and made free with her comeliness and beauty and had from her what he desired. While he was talking with her, her husband suddenly knocked on the door. The man was terrified but she told him, "Fear nothing but stay silent and do not say a word." Then she opened the door to her husband and made a show of sorrow and tears, so that he asked her, "What has befallen you?" to which she replied, "The baker's boy brought me the fish casserole, and when I took the cover off and started to eat, a man jumped out at me, so I sat down in fear and trembling, and he's still sitting in the house." The husband ran quickly upstairs, where he found the man sitting, and said to him, "Who put you inside the casserole? Was it the baker or his boy?" His wife told him, "Take him and go to the baker, and he'll tell you the truth of the matter! And tell him, 'From this day on, don't ever put anyone in our casserole again to scare us and put us through hell!'" So he took the man by the hand and went with him to the baker and told him what had happened. The baker realized what was going on and how things really stood, so he got up and struck the man, and told him, "I put you into the meat casserole, and you disobeyed me and got into the fish! If you go on disobeying me, I'll give you hell!" at which the man replied to the baker, "Master, I'll never disobey you again! The casserole you put me into I'll never get out of!" Then the baker said to the husband, "Tell your wife that I gave him hell and she'll never find him in a casserole again." The husband then went off and reported to her what had happened, and the woman was delighted and said, "If he puts anyone in our casserole after this, it'll be the last time we ever have anything cooked at his place!" Then the husband left her and went about his business. Observe this Ḥaydarian[546] trickery and that amazing credulity!

11.35.6 An Amazing Thing: Someone caught a fish and found written on its side, with the pen of God's omnipotence, "There is no god but God, Muḥammad is the Messenger of God!" He let it go, out of respect for the testament of faith. And more amazing than this, one of God's Friends was in a ship, and the wind rose and the ship was about to sink, and that holy man said, "Be still, Ocean, for on your back is an ocean like you!" meaning an "ocean of knowledge," and the ocean grew still and the wind dropped, by the will of the Almighty. Then a great fish emerged from the waters and addressed the Initiate and said to him, "You claim that you are a Friend of God and an ocean of knowledge and understanding, but should I ask you a question, would you know the answer?" "Speak!" said the man. Then the fish spoke in accents clear, saying, "If a man is transformed into some other shape, is the period that his wife must wait before remarriage that set for a dead man or that for a living?"[547] The shaykh was confounded and at a loss to answer, so the fish said to him, "Where now is your claim?" The man said, "I seek God's forgiveness for what I said! Guide me to the truth!" and the fish told him, "If he be transformed into something inanimate, the period to be observed is that for a dead man, and if he be transformed into an animal, the period is that for a living."[548] Then it disappeared into the waters. At this the holy man repented of his claim and turned back to God, Glorious and Mighty, who, in His magnanimity, accepts the repentance of His slaves—glory to Him who is capable of all things! The wonders of the ocean are beyond counting.

Apropos of the story of the baker and the fish, I am reminded that devotion is a rare thing among men. I find admirable the words of the poet who said: 11.35.7

I had a bosom friend, whose love I'd learned to trust,
Sincere in all he said, a lover true,
But he betrayed my love, then spurned my company—
Now how I wish his love I never knew!

And a poet[549] said:

Many brothers I had whom I thought shirts of mail—
And so they were, but for my foes.
I thought them shafts shot straight—
And so they were—'twas at my heart they bent their bows.
They said, "Our hearts are pure!"
And they spoke true—but of all love for me, I must suppose.
They said, "We've tried so hard!"
And so they had—but only to increase my woes.

And another said:

Let me flog my hopes in punishment
And nail my longings to a cross
For being friends with those who have no worth—
White are their garments, but inside all is dross.

And Imam al-Shāfiʿī,[550] may God be pleased with him, said: 11.35.8

Stay far from men
If by them no respect to you is paid,
And do not say, "I did them many a favor
In the good old days!"
People will treat a man like Little Dog
If they see his tail's Frayed.

And he also said,[551] may God be pleased with him:

Meeting men will gain you nothing
But drivel and gossip
So make your meetings few, unless
To acquire knowledge or bestow profit.

11.35.9 And another said:[552]

None there is these days whose love you would desire,
No friend whose heart, when time is unjust, proves true.
So live alone and visit none,
And a word to the wise will do!

And Ibn ʿArūs, Pole of the Maghrib, has it that:

Men are a deep, deep sea,
Distance from them an ark—
So look to your pitiful soul
And these words of mine do mark!

11.35.10 *fī furaynihī* ("in his little oven"): that is, in the poet's oven, using the diminutive for the meter, the meaning being that he should come from the field or the threshing floor and find it in his oven ready and cooked, so that he should not have to concern himself with catching it and flavoring it with linseed oil and onions and so on.

11.35.11 *wa-law kāna* ("though it be"): that is, though this fish that I long for be . . .

11.35.12 *yā-khwānī* ("my brothers"): he uses this word to address his companions and friends. One's "brothers" are one's friends and loved ones, and all believers are brothers in the Almighty. The Almighty has said, «The believers are indeed brothers,»[553] and in the Tradition it says, "The believers are to one another like a building whose parts hold each another up." And someone said, "He who loses his brothers has lost his manhood."

11.35.13 It is said that a man went to al-Maʾmūn and said to him, "I am your brother, so give me enough from the treasury to support me!"

"By what logic are you my brother?" asked al-Ma'mūn. "By the logic of the words of the Almighty, «The believers are indeed brothers»," said the man. "You speak truly," said al-Ma'mūn. "Give him one penny!" "This is not the gift of a king!" said the man. Al-Ma'mūn responded, "Were I to divide up the treasury among your brothers, you might well get less!" Then the man left and got nothing but the one penny (though some say he gave him more and the man retired giving thanks). Al-Ma'mūn, God have mercy on his soul, loved clemency and forbearance so much that he used to say, "Clemency has been made so dear to me that I am afraid that I shall not be rewarded for it!" As an example of his clemency, one of his slave girls once was serving him grilled meat on iron skewers when one of the skewers fell from her hand onto his robe, burning it and ruining it. When he looked at her, she said, «Those who control their wrath!» "I have controlled my wrath," he replied. «And are forgiving of mankind!» she said. "I forgive you," he said. «And God loves those who do good works!» she said. "I set you free, for the sake of the Almighty," he replied.[554] His was an outstanding capacity for clemency and forbearance that no one else could be capable of, God have mercy on his soul.

bi-lā tanḍīf ("uncleaned"): that is, if he were to find this fish in a casserole in his oven unwashed and uncleaned with water—and, truth to tell, they stack them in the casserole bones, heads, and all, just like grilled beans in the cooking pit—he would want to eat it even in that state, because he is so poor, so indigent, and so keen to see and eat it. The proverb says "The drowning man rests his weight on straw," and another says "Better with its own mud than washed in a pond!" In any case, it would stop his hunger and satisfy his craving, for if anyone finds something for which he has a craving, however vile, he holds it dear and eats an excessive amount of it, for an animal appetite will drive men to the most disgusting of foods, and all who obey their carnal appetites and cravings suffer. Master Jesus, blessings and peace upon him, said, "You will never attain what you 11.35.14

want until you abandon what you crave."[555] And the author of *The Mantle*, may the Almighty have mercy on his soul, says:[556]

Oppose your appetite and Satan! Defy them both!
No honest counselors are they, so hold them in suspicion!

Denying the appetites brings salvation and ease, and reward on the Day of Judgment. It is said that Master ʿUmar ibn al-Fāriḍ, God benefit us through him, long craved *harīsah*, refusing to give in to his appetite and persevering until one day some appeared before him in his cell. But when he stretched out his hand to eat of it, the wall of the cell was rent, and a figure emerged from it and said to him, "Faugh on you, ʿUmar!" "I have not eaten of it," he said, and thereafter he gave it up and went the rest of his life without touching it, denying his appetite.[557]

11.35.15 An amusing joke is told, to the effect that a certain dervish had a disciple to whom he was forever saying, "Deny your inclinations! Should they say to you, eat this, then deny them and eat something else, and never give in to them!"[558] One day a luxurious dish came to the shaykh, while a bowl of lentils was placed in front of the disciple (what was placed in front of the shaykh was fluffy rice with fried mutton). The disciple stretched out his hand and took the dish from in front of the shaykh and put it in place of the bowl of lentils. His shaykh said to him, "Have I not told you, 'Deny your inclinations?'" but the disciple responded, "Master, my inclinations told me to eat from the bowl of lentils, so I denied them and took this mutton with fluffy rice!" Now the shaykh had a beautiful serving boy, and, coming in one day to the place of retreat, he found the disciple sodomizing him, so he said to the disciple, "What monstrous acts are these?" The disciple replied, "Master, my inclinations told me, 'Fuck the shaykh!' so I denied them and did this boy instead!" The shaykh told him, "Get out, God strike you dead! How wicked and vile you are!" So he left and never went back.

11.35.16 Next the poet craved something that is only seen in his village on the Feast of the Slaughtering.[559] He says:

TEXT

ʿalā man raʾā fī l-talli kirsha mulaqqaḥ 11.36
wa-min fawqihi l-dibbān yiʿiffu ʿafīf
d-anā-n shuftuhū khadtū bi-ḥālū salaqtū
wa-kaltū bi-tiflū mā arā taqnīf

Happy is he who sees in the refuse dump tripes tossed away
even if the flies have settled on them in swarms!
If I saw them, I would take them all, boil them and eat them
with the undigested matter that's on them, and feel no
revulsion.

COMMENTARY

ʿalā man raʾā ("happy is he who sees"): that is, sees visually, as explained above with reference to other verses . . . 11.36.1

fī l-talli ("on the refuse dump"): that is, the refuse dump of his village, which is a high mound that generally forms around the village, for anyone who has dust or ashes dumps them outside his dwelling on the outside of the village in front of his house and his neighbor does likewise, and so it continues until the mounds join and rise and grow larger from the quantities of garbage and so on that are thrown on top of them and turn into one tall mound that can be seen from far away. Next to it are deserted places where they all piss, men, women, and children, and where most of them shit too. The men and the women climb up to it when they piss and engage in friendly chats and conversations about the field, the crops, and the harvest, the calves and the buffaloes, and so forth. Sometimes quarrels break out while they are pissing and one of them attacks his opponent, the piss all over his jubba or running down his outer garment till it—that is, his *jubbah*—is soaked, and trades blows with his comrade with the shit on his clothes, and so on, until the matter turns either to reconciliation or killing. Their women are the same when defecating: they feel no embarrassment at talking about spinning 11.36.2

wool or jute and so on, for they are ignorant of latrines, which are not built in their houses and which they cannot afford, unless it be in the house of the bailiff in the hamlet, for him and his people to piss in. The poet says:

I asked the countrymen, "No latrines have your houses?"
Said they, "Not one!"
"What do you, then," I asked, "with your spouses?"
Said they, "All of us shit on the dump as one!"

11.36.3 Thus the refuse dump (*tall*) and the mound (*kawm*) to them are the same thing, which they call also the *ʿilliyyah*, with *i* after the ʿ, double *l*, and *i* after it. Says the poet:

I came to the hamlet of a forenoon
And found it of people free—
They'd all gone up an *ʿilliyyah*,
And there they'd taken a pee.

—that is, they had all gone up on top of it and then collectively—women, men, and children—had pissed.

11.36.4 They also use the word *ʿilliyyah* of a room built of mud, as distinct from brick, which is why they say, "So-and-so today is *fī l-ʿalālī*," that is, he now sits higher than other people and has acquired higher status and value than the rest.[560] On the same topic, their poet says:

Two gazelles—what could be cuter!
How the henna on their feet stirs my desire!
When, O Time, will you unite us,
That to the upper rooms we may retire?

The refuse heap or mound is not used by them exclusively to relieve themselves. It may be used for conversation, friendly chats, and evening talk among themselves, as well as for spinning jute and wool and so forth.

11.36.5 If it be said, "The poet's use of the preposition *fī* in the phrase *fī l-tall* might lead one to understand that he saw the tripes *inside* the refuse dump, where they ought to be hidden from him, even though he confirms that he actually saw them by saying 'on which the flies' (for flies settle only on exposed things and not on things that are covered over and protected)—just as one uses the same preposition in the phrase *fulānun fī l-dār* ('So-and-so is in the house') that is, 'inside it'—how answer you?" we would reply that the Facetious Answer is that *fī* ("in") here is used in the sense of *ʿalā* ("on"), that is, he saw tripes discarded on the refuse dump or mound (*ʿalā l-tall awi l-kawm*), just as one says *fulānun fī l-jabal* ("So-and-so is on the mountain"), that is, on top of it, not inside it, since it would be impossible for him to penetrate the mountain and go inside it.[561] Or that the preposition is to be taken in its literal sense, and the words *fī l-tall* mean that there was indeed inside the refuse dump a hole into which they would piss and into which they would throw tripes, for example—in which case his claim that the tripes were *inside* the refuse dump would be correct, even though they might be exposed and visible to people. Thus the problem's now revealed, this silliness no more concealed.

kirsha mulaqqaḥ ("tripes tossed away"): that is, the tripes of the animal that they slaughter on the day of the Feast of the Slaughtering, for that is the only day on which they see meat, and in fact they would never throw the tripes on the dump. On the contrary, normally they would take them and remove the remaining food particles from them and wash them and cook them with the animal's offal; this they call *jaghl maghl* and hold in the highest esteem. In the cities, on the other hand, the tripes would be sheep's and they would add the head and the trotters, and this they call *saqaṭ*; they make it with spices, clarified butter, and coriander and pour vinegar over it, all of which makes it extremely tasty. Sometimes they sell it with the head, which they roll up in the clean, washed tripes, and sometimes without. They also sell the heads on their own, grilled. The trotters are made into a dish of broth and bread, which they sell with vinegar, fat, and garlic poured over them, which makes them 11.36.6

very tasty, as is well known in the cities. The country people, however, put all of these things into a basin or an earthenware casserole and add coriander and a little sesame oil, garnish it with a little fried onion or garlic, and eat it, and they know nothing of clarified butter or spices or anything of that sort. Sometimes they boil the tripes in water and eat them as a broth.

11.36.7 *Kirsh* is derived from *takarrush* ("buckling, warping"), which means being protuberant and conspicuous; that is, the stomach (*kirsh*) is protuberant and conspicuous in the same way that one says of a wall whose stones project beyond the true and which is on the verge of collapse that it is *mukarrash* ("buckling"), that is, about to fall, or "So-and-so is *ṣāḥib kirsh* ('a big-bellied man')," that is, his stomach is conspicuously large, especially if he be a fat, big-bodied man, in which case his stomach will appear large and protruding. In the Tradition it says "God detests the fat scholar," though fatness is a desirable quality in sheep and cattle. One speaks of a "fat ram, bursting with fat and flesh." When it is slaughtered in this condition and its head is rolled up in its tripes, the *saqaṭ* made from it is tastier than anything else, because of the butter and the fat.

11.36.8 Apropos of which, Sultan Qizilbāsh once sent a message to Sultan al-Ghawrī, threatening him in the following verses:[562]

Sword and dagger are sweet basil to us—
  With narcissus and myrtle we have no truck!
Our drink is the blood of our foes
  And the skulls of our foes are our cup!

—to which Sultan al-Ghawrī responded:[563]

God has a ring for His creatures,
  By whose inscription their fortunes are sealed:
"Let sleeping dogs lie lest they bite,
  And beware what you yourself may reveal!"
The battlegrounds of injustice are tyrants
  That may drive a sultan from throne and from field.

When the ram's kidneys' fat overflows
 Its head's rolled up in its tripes and concealed.
And, like it or not, we're like a dead man
 When he's borne on his bier from the field!

However, Sultan Qizilbāsh was not deterred by Sultan Qānṣawh al-Ghawrī's message; on the contrary, he marched against him with his horses and his foot soldiers. Al-Ghawrī's deputy did battle with him and drove him back discomfited, and God brought the consequences of his deceitfulness down upon his own head, and the advice that Sultan Qānṣawh al-Ghawrī gave him in the words "When the ram's kidneys' fat overflows," etc., did him no good. These are examples of what happens to the unjust man when he goes too far and behaves tyrannically: God will sometimes take him off all of a sudden. In the Tradition it says, "God grants the tyrant time but does not forget him, and when He takes him, He does not let him escape." 11.36.9

Thus the poet begs the Almighty and beseeches Him of His bounty and His graciousness that he might see some tripes tossed away on the refuse dump, meaning the mound, that his companions, out of forgetfulness, had overlooked and left behind, or that the bailiff of the hamlet might have slaughtered a ram and thrown his tripes on the refuse dump, for if the country people themselves slaughter an animal on the day of the feast, they leave nothing of it behind, and they take its tripes and all its offal and cook and eat them. The poet therefore prays that Fate will one day slip up and he will see these tripes that he longs, asks, and lusts for, because he is unable to join the people of the hamlet in the price of an animal.[564] 11.36.10

wa- ("even if"): even if it be that . . . 11.36.11

min fawqihi l-dibbān ("the flies (have settled) on them"): *dibbān* being the same as *dhibbān*,[565] the common people using it in the form *dibbān* because *dhibbān* is too heavy for their tongues; the singular is *dibbānah* and *dibbūn* is a single male.[566] *Dibbān* is of the 11.36.12

measure of *khirfān* ("sheep") or *jidyān* ("kids") and *dibbūn* is of the measure of *mamḥūn* ("sluttish") or *ma'būn* ("passive sodomite"). One of the poets of the country people says in a *mawāliyā*:

How I wish, sweet thing, I were a fly—
I'd settle on your lip,
You'd swat at me, and I'd say, "Hi!"
And "Hey there, good looking, you with the drowsy eye!
How come you give others favors,
But when I come, you tell me 'Fie!'?"

11.36.13 Flies have numerous peculiarities and useful qualities that are mentioned in certain books. These include the fact that, if a fly is taken and tied alive inside a piece of cloth large enough to keep it from dying and is hung on one suffering from inflammation of the eyes, he will recover. And a virtuous man was once asked why God created flies, and he said, "To humiliate tyrants, for a fly may settle on a king's crown, and there is nothing he can do to prevent it." The polytheists used to anoint their idols with saffron and so on, and the flies would settle on them, so the Almighty sent down the following verses as a rebuke to them and to their idols: «Lo! Those on whom ye call besides God will never create a fly though they combine together for the purpose. And if the fly took something from them, they could not rescue it from him. So weak are the seeker and the sought!»[567] Flies have many enemies, among them a small animal called the "hyena of the flies" that resembles a small spider except that its mouth is wide and its legs are shorter than those of a spider. It takes the fly quickly in its mouth and casts it into something that it extrudes from its mouth like a spider's web, where the fly remains caught until it dies. The Initiate of the Almighty, Master 'Abd al-Wahhāb al-Sha'rānī, mentions in his *Blessings*[568] that his wife, Umm 'Abd al-Raḥmān, was afflicted by a severe illness that had brought her to the point of death. One day, he went into the lavatory and he heard a voice say to him, "Release the fly from the hyena of the flies, and We will release your wife from her illness!"

So the Shaykh turned to the wall and heard the sound of the fly and carefully released it, and his wife was released from her illness immediately and the Almighty cured her.

yiʿiffu ʿafīf ("have settled in swarms"): that is, the flies pile up one on top of another from the sheer quantity that descend on the tripes to suck the moisture from them and so on. *Yiʿiffu* is with *i* after the *y* and after the ʿ.[569] One says, "The flies settled (*ʿaffa*) on a thing in swarms" when they descend on it in large numbers and pile up on top of one another. When it is with *a* after the *y* and *u* after the ʿ, it is from *ʿiffah* ("abstinence").[570] One says, "The man abstained from the thing" (*ʿaffa ʿan al-shayʾ*), meaning he drew back from it. 11.36.14

d-anā-n shuftuhū ("If I saw them"): that is, if God granted me the sight of some tripes tossed away on the refuse pile . . . 11.36.15

khadtū[571] ("I would take them"): that is, *akhadhtuhu*,[572] with omission of the initial *a* and change of *dh* to *d*, in keeping with rural usage. 11.36.16

salaqtū ("boil them"): meaning "I would throw them in the basin or the cooking pot and throw water on them and nothing else and boil them without garnish or sesame oil and so on," he is that poor and indigent. 11.36.17

wa-kaltū bi-tiflū ("and eat them with the undigested matter"): that is, with the fodder that is in the stomach, even though it be defiling, as a way to emphasize his longing and great need. This is something that gluttons are reproached for among them: one says, for example, "So-and-so eats tripes with the shit on!"—apropos of which, it happened that a man from the countryside went up to Cairo to sell a quantity of eggs so as to pay off the taxes that he owed, and he sold them and set off back for his village. When he was in Bayn al-Qaṣrayn, he saw tripes for sale and said to himself, "Buy a copper's-worth for Umm Muʿaykah and eat a copper's-worth yourself, even if you have to go into debt on your taxes!" So he gave the tripe seller two copper 11.36.18

pieces, and the man cut him off the bits they sell for cats, which he ate without salt, and for another copper he took a large hunk to which he added liver and lights, and wrapped everything up in his headcloth that was on his head and tied it up, and the money that he had made by selling the eggs was tied to the headcloth too. Then he journeyed until he passed by a village on the road and noticed a tree, beneath which he sat down to rest, and the breeze caressed him, and he lay down. Along came a dog, which smelled the meat that was on his head and grabbed the headcloth with the meat and climbed up onto the roofs of the village. The peasant got up and ran after it shouting, and entered the house onto whose roof the dog had climbed. When the women saw him, bare headed and in this state, they said, "A thief, in the act!" and they seized him and handed him over to the bailiff in the village, who beat him and imprisoned him for two days, till men of goodwill interceded on his behalf and they let him go. Thus, as a consequence of his lack of manners and his ignorance, he lost the headcloth and the money and took a beating and returned to the hamlet a hopeless case.

11.36.19 *mā arā taqnīf* ("and feel no revulsion"): meaning "I would not abstain from eating it because it had the undigested matter on it, or because it had filth around the edges, for example, for my carnal appetite relishes the eating of it and does not hold back." In *The Blue Ocean and Piebald Canon* it says that *taqnīf* is derived from *qanf*, which is refraining from something: one says, "You are 'finicky' (*qinif*)" or "So-and-so 'recoils' (*yataqannafu*) in disgust." Or it may be from *qunnāfah* with *u* after the *q*, which is the thing that is inserted in the hole in the yoke on an ox's neck. A mental lightweight may be chided with the same word: one says to him, "You yoke peg!" The poet says:

> My mind has grown so silly, I trow,
> I've started behaving like the yoke peg of a cow!

Next, finding no easy access to tripes tossed away on the dump or mound, he beseeches the Almighty to grant him his desire and that, after a while, should he live so long, he might go to the city and eat his fill of tripes and other things such as lupine and *muqaylī*. He says: 11.36.20

TEXT

anā-n ʿishtu lā-rūḥu l-madīnah wa-ʾashbaʿū 11.37
kurūsha wa-law annī amūtu kafīf
wa-ʾākhudh maʿī ghazla l-ʿajūzi wa-bīʿū
wa-ʾākul bi-ḥaqqū yā-bna binti ʿarīf

If I live I shall go to the city and eat my fill
of tripes, though I should die "impaired"
And I'll take with me the old woman's yarn and sell it
and eat with the proceeds, O son of the daughter of *ʿarīf*

COMMENTARY

anā-n ʿishtu ("if I live"): *ʿishtu* being from *maʿīshah* ("living"), which is the sustaining of the body and its refreshment with food and drink. That is, "if I live long and if the Almighty has ordained sufficient days for me" . . . 11.37.1

la-rūḥu l-madīnah ("I shall go to the city"): by which he means Cairo—may the Almighty protect it and grant its people eternal pleasure, let its inhabitants continue in the enjoyment of its luxuries forever, and protect its eminent scholars and noble commanders, for it is the city of conviviality and amusement, of pleasure and fulfillment, whose women God has distinguished by making them comely and handsome, full of loveliness and perfection, sweet in their social relations, refined in their conversations. How many a lover by their charms has been beguiled, and he who does not marry a Cairene cannot hope to keep his reputation undefiled! And its cute young boys, like gazelles, whose grace the ben tree's branch excels—they have no like in Iraq or on Anatolia's ground, 11.37.2

and none more refined in company and compliance may be found! As I said on this subject:

11.37.3 You who the love of beauties would know,
Break camp and off to Cairo go!
How many a beauty with perfection aglow
In Cairo puts his charms on show!
Its cute young boys are nowhere else to be found,
Not in Anatolia, nor in Iraq,
Nor in the cities of the Persian lands—
No, by him who climbed the seven heavens' arc![573]
By nature with refinement they're graced
And their saliva is sweet to the taste.

11.37.4 Whoever turns aside from them in disinclination
Let him forever forgo the joy of consummation!
How many a beauty with perfection aglow
In Cairo puts his charms on show!
How comely they are and how refined!
How elegant! How many you see!
With every stripling swaggering by
You say, "This one's the apogee,"
Then see another better still—
Glory to the Maker of Humanity!

11.37.5 So live with them as long as nights shall last
For love of them, I think, is no trespass!
How many a beauty with perfection aglow
In Cairo puts his charms on show!
Wonder, then wonder yet again—
On the days of feasts and fun,
Everywhere gazelles in gorgeous garments strut,
While aslant each cheek a mole doth run.
Truly, you'd think the garden of Riḍwān[574]
Had op'ed and out they'd come!

11.37.6 Some of them desire to bring men low
With beauty of form and curves on show.

How many a beauty with perfection aglow
In Cairo puts his charms on show!
By Mighty God I swear, and swear again
By him for whom the moon was split in twain,[575]
From love of them my patience has worn out,
While passion's put all hope of sleep to rout!
I'm left without a penny to spend
And looking alone will not make my longing end.
In any case, what can I do 11.37.7
But pray, and even that's no go—
How many a beauty with perfection aglow
In Cairo puts his charms on show!
Yūsuf I'm called—I pray God
To forgive my every sin.
Shirbīn's my town, mighty
Among cities is its standing!
A town of pride in rank
And brains, whose fame all men do hymn![576]
So now let constant blessings flow
And to the prophet of dazzling beauty go—
How many a beauty with perfection aglow
In Cairo puts his charms on show!

Glory then to Him who gave them figures chic and ruddiness of cheek, Who made their way of talking delicate and their behavior immaculate, and Who endowed them with dispositions kind, rarely to demurral inclined. Their speech is gentler than the breeze, in sweetness their saliva heaven's nectar exceeds. As the poet has it: 11.37.8

There's no city in the world like Cairo—
Its people revel in its life of ease.
Its breeze is the gentlest thing in the world,
Its people yet gentler than its breeze.

wa-ʾashbaʿ ("and eat my fill"): *shibaʿ* ("satiation") is the filling of the stomach with food and drink. Excessive satiation is harmful. The 11.37.9

word may be used concretely, that is, in the sense just given, and abstractly, in which case it means wealth after poverty. One says, "Today So-and-so is 'full' (*shab'ān*)," that is, has become rich after he was poor and filled his stomach after he was hungry, especially if he tasted hardship and sickness at the start of his career and God was generous to him later—in which case he will be extremely tight in worldly matters and very stingy. Such people are known as "newly blessed" as they have no comprehension of the value of such wealth and do not use it for its appointed purposes,[577] Fate merely having gone mad enough to allow them to acquire it. The poet says:

One newly blessed with wealth is a sinkhole for it—
His eyes with want still burn.
Fate went mad, and he got rich—
Woe to him, should Fate to its senses return!

On the other hand, should the individual acknowledge God's blessings and thank Him for that wealth and be diligent in doing good works and giving charity and alms, then that is recommended and commended.

11.37.10 *kurūsha* ("of tripes"): plural of *kirsh* ("stomach, craw"); that is, "if I reach the city, I will indubitably eat my fill of the tripes that are boiled and sold there and achieve my goal and my desire with respect to them . . ."

11.37.11 *wa-law annī* ("though I"): after eating my fill of the aforementioned tripes and satisfying my appetite . . .

11.37.12 *amūtu kafīf* ("should die 'impaired'"): that is, blind: one says of someone, "His sight was 'impaired'" if he was afflicted with blindness. In a Divine Tradition[578] the Almighty says, "If I take the eyes of My slave in this world, and he is patient, his reward with Me shall certainly be Paradise." The great man of letters al-Būṣīrī[579] says:

When my eyes are inflamed, night companions disappear,
And friends of hearth and home no longer pay me mind.

They say, "If he gets better, we'll be nice to him then.
If he's 'impaired,' we'll wish him well for going blind!"

—because a person with inflamed eyes is an invalid who is not to be visited, and if he goes blind they tell him, "Now you are one of the people of Paradise!" and "Good fortune is yours!" and so on, as one observes people doing nowadays. But in truth, the blind man is to be pitied, and kindness to him brings great remuneration, and solid compensation, especially if he be poor, for then he's as good as dead for sure. It is said that the following words were found written on the crown of Chosroes: "Justice, If It Lasts, Brings Prosperity," "Injustice, If It Lasts, Brings Ruin," "Poverty Is the Red Death," "The Blind Man Is As Dead Though He Be Not Buried," and "He Who Leaves No Sons Will Not Be Remembered." God has afflicted his slaves with nothing more injurious than blindness, and the one-eyed man is half as badly off as the blind man; as the proverb says, "A blind man complained to a man with one eye, 'How bitter the cup of blindness!' The one-eyed man replied, 'My story is half of yours!'" And, in another proverb, it says, "A one-eyed man hated by his family is still better off than a blind man."

kafīf ("impaired," that is, "blind") is of the measure of *natīf* 11.37.13
("plucked"), a word used to describe a young boy if his beard has grown and he wants to play the role of a girl or has a morbid craving for passive sodomy (God Almighty save us from such things!) for such always shave their beards and doll themselves up for the profligate and pluck out the roots of their hairs with their fingernails or pull them out with tweezers—for when a young boy has no down on his cheeks he is found attractive but with the growth of his beard his charms evaporate, and his face turns ugly as his nape.[580] As the poet says:[581]

Bearded now is the lad who once
With himself was so smitten.
"Comely" once was his face,
But soon it got rewritten.

How my sight was gladdened
When it saw him thus and was cured!
Thanks be to God for a beard
That nape from face procured!

And another said:

He plundered us all with his charms, till
God put his beauty to sack.
His beard appeared and that was it—
"God spared the Believers attack."

11.37.14 Some brazen lovers prefer men with beards. The poet says:

A fornicator they call the one who loves cute girls
While the lover of smooth boys they call a bugger,
So chastely to bearded men I turned,
For I'd rather be neither one nor t'other!

To others' fancies old men have appealed, these holding that censure of such things is repealed. As the poet says:

I love him as a babe in swaddling clothes and as a beardless boy,
And with a beard, and covered in gray hairs.

And another[582] says:

I came to love him as an aged man whose white hairs
On his cheeks were like jasmine over roses.
Censurer, it's known what boys are wanted for—
With him I'm safe from any who envies or opposes.

11.37.15 Degrees in love may be discerned, and one man's meat in love is by another spurned. As a poet[583] said:

I loved her as a gray-haired hag, whose own son's hair had turned—
For one man's meat, in love, is by another spurned!

—all of which comes of delivering oneself over to lust and wallowing in passion and affection. The sophisticated lover, on the other hand, is attracted only to the more refined brand that's fit to kiss and embrace—though it'll cost you money in either case.

wa-ākhudh maʿī ghazla l-ʿajūzi wa-bīʿū ("And I'll take with me the old woman's yarn and sell it"): by which he means his wife's yarn, her name being Qaṭīʿah, or, as others claim, Baʿrah bint Qallūṭ ("Dropping, daughter of Big Turd"); and if her name were indeed Baʿrah bint Qallūṭ it would be appropriate, because the dropping is related to the big turd, being its daughter. Baʿrah certainly must contain the true meaning, with Big Turd being the latter's father, as it always sticks to her. The word *ʿajūz* ("old woman") may be applied both to an aged woman and to wine, which may be called "old woman" but also "virgin" and many other names. In a description he gives of it among a number of verses the Initiate of the Almighty al-Ḥakkāk[584] says: 11.37.16

> Crone and virgin both! Wonder at her!
> By two names she's known by all who give her names.

The words constitute "advancement and deferment."[585] The meaning is "If I live long enough, I will go to the city and take with me some of the old woman's yarn and sell it there . . . .

"*wa-ākul bi-ḥaqqū* ('and eat with the proceeds'): tripes and other things, even if later I should die 'impaired,' because, if I realize my dream, I will not care if I live the rest of my life blind, so long as I have satisfied my appetite and obtained what I wanted from the Almighty." 11.37.17

yā-bna binti ʿArīf ("O son of the daughter of ʿArīf"): he addresses one of the male inhabitants of the hamlet, said by some to have been a relation and by others a friend. The meaning is that he directs to this man his complaint against what afflicts him and says to him, "You must share my joy if I live long enough and go to the city and 11.37.18

eat my fill of tripes there, and then come back to you!"—which indicates that he was a friend, a fact confirmed by his addressing him rather than any of the other inhabitants of the hamlet; for one complains of his case only to a friend, who feels joy at his joy and sorrow at his sorrow and takes on the burden of his anxieties or helps him materially if he be well off, and distracts him by talking to him and so on. As the poet[586] says:

> Complaints must be to a stalwart man
> Who can help you, distract you, or share your pain.

And Ibn ʿArūs says:

> When trouble strikes, I do advise you,
> Make your complaint to those who love you.
> A burden shared is easily borne,
> But if left lying around will surely trip you!

11.37.19 This "son of the daughter of ʿArīf" had the name Kharā Ilḥas ("Lick-Shit"), according to report, and his father's name was Fisā l-Tīrān ("Ox-Fart"), a name he acquired because, whenever they tethered the oxen to the feeding trough, he would stand in their midst and fart, a thing he was much given to doing; then those close by would smell the farts and ask him, "Did you fart?" and he would reply, "It's ox farts!" so they named him "Ox-Fart." As for his maternal grandfather being called ʿArīf, this could be for any of several reasons. Some say that he used to teach (*yuʿarrifu*) the children the way to the places at the foot of the refuse dump where they could piss and shit, while others say that he used to teach "The Westward Migration of the Banū Hilāl"[587] and their doings; others again say that he possessed knowledge (*maʿrifah*) and understanding in cracking drover's whips, beating drums, and tootling on pennywhistles and so on, and yet others that he used to instruct (*yuʿarrifu*) the bailiff in matters of extortion, telling him, "Take so much from this one and so much from that," like an unpaid servant, and that this is why he came to be called ʿArīf.[588] The word is also used of the person whom the schoolmaster at the *kuttāb* puts in charge of teaching (*yuʿarrifu*) the children to read and the instruction and also to inform (*yuʿarrifu*) the teacher of how they behave in his absence, as is common in the cities and elsewhere—for every *kuttāb*, by custom, must have an *ʿarīf*.

Next the poet says: 11.37.20

TEXT

wa-ʾasriq mina l-jāmiʿ zarābīna ʿiddah 11.38
wa-ʾākul bi-him min shahwatī fi l-rīf
wa-ʾashbaʿ mina l-turmus wa-ʾākul muqaylī
wa-luffū bi-qishrū mā arā tawqīf

And I'll steal from the mosque slippers in great number
and eat of them, such an appetite I have, in the countryside,
And eat my fill of lupine, and eat *muqaylī*
and eat it with the skin, and never stop

COMMENTARY

All the preceding is the continuation of what he said to the aforementioned "son of the daughter of ʿArīf." That is, he says, "If I go to the city and sell the 'old woman's' yarn and, with the proceeds, eat tripes and thus satisfy my appetite for the aforementioned tripes, and see the lupine and *muqaylī* that I long for but have no money on me, then I will go into one of the mosques that are on the outskirts of the city quarters, where the people from the countryside pray," for *zarābīn* are found only on the feet of country people, the meaning being the same as *marākīb* ("slippers"). The singular is *zarbūn*, on the measure of *mamḥūn* ("sluttish") or *maʾbūn* ("passive sodomite"); they are the slippers that the peasants walk in, and they also call them *jawād* and *tarjīl*. 11.38.1

wa-ʾasriq ("and I'll steal"): theft is a sin and prohibited. The Almighty has said, «As for the thief, both male and female, cut off their hands,»[589] meaning, do so if the thief has stolen at least the minimum 11.38.2

amount necessary to incur this punishment, which is a quarter of a dinar, and so long as there is no doubt as to his guilt; if there is doubt, amputation is not practiced, as the books of jurisprudence state.[590] The Almighty has allowed the amputation of the hand of the thief as a warning to him and because he has broken faith and betrayed its high worth and committed treachery and dishonored it. A man once wrote to a scholar in verse as follows:[591]

> A hand may be ransomed for five hundred gold pieces—
> How come it's severed for a quarter dinar?

The scholar replied by saying:

> The dearness of trust makes the hand itself dear,
> While the baseness of treachery makes it cheap—see how wise the Creator!

—that is, when this hand trespassed on others' property and took it and betrayed its trust, God reduced its value, and its base treachery made its amputation permissible; and this is an instance of the wise ways of the Creator, Glorious and Sublime, and an example of the rules that He has made incumbent on His creation,[592] in terms of obligations and prohibitions and so forth.

11.38.3 *min al-jāmiʿ* ("from the mosque"): meaning the place of prostration (*masjid*); it is called a *jāmiʿ* because it gathers (*yajmaʿu*) the people for prayer and worship and so on, while the *masjid* is so called because of the prostration (*sujūd*) that takes place there.[593]

11.38.4 *zarābīna* ("slippers"): it has been explained above that what is meant by this is "slippers" (*marākīb*) or *tarājīl.*

11.38.5 *ʿiddah* ("in great number"): meaning "many" because the slipper thief needs to be possessed of great expertise in stealing and a total lack of religion. The expertise lies in his getting close to the slippers' owner and making him think that he just wants to pray; indeed, the thief may stand next to the man and wait until he bends over in prostration to the Knower of Secrets, then make off with his slippers.[594] The lack of religion lies in his not knowing how to pray and entering the mosque for no reason other than to steal. He may even be in a state of major ritual impurity,[595] and his clothes may be befouled, since it is usual for most peasants to know no shame in such matters, and they know nothing of prayer or worship, and the only reason most of them go into the mosque is to spin wool and jute or to calculate their taxes or take refuge in its shade when the weather is hot. Sometimes they tie up their calves or cows inside it, and usually they turn it into a place where they talk about the field and the wall and the sowing and the reaping, and they make a rumpus and a ruckus there and as much fuss, bother, and disturbance as though they were in the cattle barn, and our poet was one of this sort and implicated in their doings. This explains why he calls himself a thief and why he says to the aforementioned "son of the daughter of ʿArīf," "If I go to the city and eat tripes out of the proceeds of the yarn and run out of money, I will play sneak thief and snoop around and ask about some of the mosques that are on the outskirts of Cairo's quarters and steal slippers from them."

wa-ʾākul bi-him ("and eat of them"): this contains a pun: it may 11.38.6
mean either that he will sell them and eat from the proceeds, or that people will come across him red-handed in the act of snatching them and seize him and make him "eat" a drubbing with the slippers that he stole, the latter constituting a figurative eating. In fact, it is generally the case that if a slipper thief falls into their hands, they thrash him on the back of his neck with the slippers till they fall to pieces. One says, "Today So-and-so 'ate' a drubbing with slippers" and "So-and-so stole a pair of slippers and they caught him and thrashed them to pieces on the back of his neck." In short, stealing slippers requires a deft hand and savoir faire, even though it is the lowest form of theft.

It is said that a sharp-witted thief passed a merchant sitting in 11.38.7
his shop with a pair of shoes by his side, which the thief decided to

take. Quietly sidling up to the man, he placed his right foot in one of the shoes and was about to put his left foot in the other when the merchant turned around, so the thief, having gotten just one of the pair, ran off and hid himself at a distance where the merchant could not see him. Then the merchant wanted to leave and, failing to find one of his shoes, he asked his servant, "Where's the other one?" and the servant told him, "I don't know." So the merchant said, "It must have been stolen. Take this one and go to So-and-so and tell him to make me another like it." The servant took the shoe and went off, and the thief went ahead of him so that he could see to whom he gave it. Then, when the servant went back to his master, the thief brought the shoe he had taken and told the man, "Don't make anything for the merchant. He has found the missing shoe," and he showed it to him and told him, "Give me the other one." The man gave it to him, and that way he got the first shoe by thievery and the second by trickery. When the merchant's servant came back to ask for the shoe, the man told him what had happened, and he informed his master, who marveled at the thief's quick wits.

11.38.8 The tale is told too that the great man of letters al-Būṣīrī[596] once visited Cairo and went to the slipper market at Taḥt al-Rukn[597] to buy himself a pair of red slippers. He stopped at a shop and the slipper seller said to him, "I have a pair of slippers as red as your face,[598] Shaykh of the Arabs!" and the next shopkeeper said to him, "By the life of your head, Shaykh of the Arabs, I have a lovely pair of slippers!" and they started making jokes at his expense. He waited patiently until they were done and then said to them, "Shaykhs of the market, I am a stranger, and you have to give me a special deal on a pair, for people have told me that 'slippers are a glut on the market today and so cheap they're "on their makers' necks"!'"[599] They said, "He's taken his revenge on us all with his polite words!" and they asked him, "Pray tell, are you al-Būṣīrī?" "I am," he said. Then they honored him and gave him a pair of nice red slippers free of charge, and he took them and went to visit al-Badrī, the lutenist, who was Cairo's leading musician, may the Almighty have mercy on him. When al-Badrī saw him coming towards him wearing his new slippers, he said to him, "How come your face is so red, Būṣīrī?" to which the latter replied, "I fucked early (*badrī*) and went to the baths!"—a response that was wittier than the question. The following, by the same aforementioned al-Būṣīrī, is one of his pieces written in praise of al-Badrī:[600]

Al-Badrī got perfect at singing
   And learned it inside out.
His doorman swears on his wife
   That after he first "went in," he never again "went out"![601]

The Arabs compare a shoe to a riding camel, and this occurs in the poetry of both the ancients and the moderns, and al-Mutanabbī uses it in various places in his verse. Ibn Khallikān, may the Almighty have mercy on his soul, once said:[602] 11.38.9

> Our friend Jamāl al-Dīn al-Irdabīlī,[603] that great man of letters and wonderful composer of tunes and so on, came to me while I was in the government offices in Divinely Protected Cairo and sat with me for a while at a time when there were people with business to conduct crowding around me. Then he got up and went out. Before I knew it, his servant arrived with a piece of parchment in his hand on which were written the following verses:[604]
>
> Master, through whose presence
>   The days have made their virtues manifest,
> My pilgrimage to your abode I made as one by passion drawn,
>   Not one who carries out the rite at God's behest,
> And there I caused my mount to kneel within the sacred space—
>   Thus was she ennobled and men desired of her to be possessed;

And as I sought for her I tried to find a verse
For him whose prosody leads the rest:
"And if the mounts to Muḥammad bring us,
Their backs thenceforth to no man's service may be pressed."

I studied it and asked the servant, "What's the story?" He told me that when al-Irdabīlī left me he found his slippers had been stolen. I thought the way he worked in the line from another poem was very clever.

11.38.10 Here ends the quotation from Ibn Khallikān.

The final lines, which the poet quotes, are from a eulogy by Abū Nuwās dedicated to al-Amīn Muḥammad, son of Hārūn al-Rashīd, and were written when the former was caliph. The first line goes:

Campsite, what has time wrought upon you?
No smiling face remains to draw me to your rest!

Elsewhere in the same poem, describing his she-camel, he says:

She braved every desert terror with me,
Reckless, of dash and daring much possessed,
The others running behind her as though
She an imam were, they in line behind her dressed—
And if the mounts to Muḥammad bring us,
Their backs thenceforth to no man's service may be pressed.

11.38.11 The story is told that a man stole a pair of slippers and gave them to his son to sell, but they were stolen in turn from the boy. The latter went back to his father, who asked him, "Did you sell the slippers?" "Yes," he said. "How much did you get for them?" The son replied, "The same as you paid." "But they were stolen!" said the father. "And they were stolen from me," said the boy, "so you lost nothing and you gained nothing." The father laughed at his son's joke and let him go.

And the story is told that the door of Judge Abū Sālim's house was stolen, so he went to the mosque and had its door removed. When they asked him, "What are you doing?" he replied, "I'm taking this door because its owner knows who took mine!" And the story is told that Juḥā's father had two wives, Juḥā's own mother having died. One day his father left to set off on a journey, but as he went out the door he remembered that he had forgotten his slippers, so he shouted to his son, "Juḥā, fetch my slippers!" Now his wives heard him shouting but didn't know what about, so they said to Juḥā, "What's your father saying?" He replied, "He says, 'Fuck your father's wives while I'm away!'" The wives cursed him out and said, "Nonsense!" "Listen for yourselves," he said, "and you'll see that it's true!" Then he said to his father, "One of them, father, or both?" meaning, "Shall I bring one of the slippers or the pair?" "Both, of course!" answered his father. "Now do you believe me?" said Juḥā. The wives thought that he had told him, "Fuck them both," though all his father meant was "both slippers." So Juḥā fucked them to his heart's content until his father returned. 11.38.12

And the story is told that al-ʿAynī was sitting with a grandee of Damascus in a place that overlooked the highway. "Sir," said the latter, "they say that the people of Cairo are distinguished from those of our city by their quick-wittedness and sophistication, but I would like to see this for myself." While he was talking, a seller of beans in linseed oil went past, crying his wares. Al-ʿAynī said to his friend, "Is there any viler wretch in Cairo than this?" "No," said the Damascene. "Wait, then," said al-ʿAynī, "while I show you how quick-witted he is." Then al-ʿAynī called to the man, who came over to him bringing his beans and bread. "I want some beans," said al-ʿAynī, "but I have no money. All I have is a single slipper—can I get some with that?" "My dear sir," said the man, "I'll feed you with whatever you give me!" Al-ʿAynī laughed and the Damascene marveled at the man's quick wit, and they rewarded him well, and he went his way. 11.38.13

11.38.14 And there is a riddling rhyme by a poet that makes fun of a man called ʿIwaḍ that goes:

My slippers were stolen from me
  And everything seemed bad.
I went to al-Sirw of a morning
  And from there I took ʿIwaḍ![605]

11.38.15 *min shahwatī fī l-rīf* ("out of my appetite in the countryside"): that is, "out of the appetite that I experience, namely, for eating tripes and filling my belly with them, for I find none in the countryside; but if I go to the city and do as mentioned above, I will satisfy my appetite and attain my goal."

11.38.16 *wa-ʾashbaʿ mina l-turmus* ("and eat my fill of lupine"): by which he means lupine that has been salted after being steeped in water for several days. This is something the people of the countryside have a liking for because it is their equivalent of nuts, that is, it is something they nibble on on feast days and make presents of to one another. It has high status among them, is always on sale in the cities, and is the equivalent of fruit to the country people: they take pride in eating it if they go to the city, along with *muqaylī*. Lupine has an important property, mentioned by the learned scholar Shihāb al-Dīn al-Qalyūbī, may the Almighty have mercy him, which is that, if one eats a handful of lupine with the skin regularly every day for breakfast, his eyesight will grow stronger.

11.38.17 *wa-ʾākul muqaylī* ("and eat *muqaylī*"): that is, "and I'll eat my fill of *muqaylī*," which is sprouted beans fried on the fire, which is how it gets its name.[606] It is too well known to require description.

11.38.18 *wa-luffū bi-qishrū* ("and eat it with the skins"): that is, "that and the lupine together because I am so hungry for them, since, were I to peel the lupine and the *muqaylī*, it would seem to me to take forever, because I would need to peel them one by one and that would not assuage my desire." The poet, after all, is a countryman, and in the country they take them by the handful and toss them down without swallowing and know nothing of peeling or anything of that sort.

Apropos of which, a man once sat with his servant in a dark place eating raisins. The master said to the man, "Eat them one by one, and I shall do the same." When they had done eating, the master said, "My good man, I was too greedy to bother with you and started eating them two by two!" to which the servant replied, "Sir, you may have been eating them two by two, but I was tossing them down my throat by the handful!" It is the custom of the Arabs to eat raisins by the handful and dates in fives, and they find this the tastiest, pleasantest, and most relaxing way to eat. The poet says: 11.38.19

May the tents bring good health to their masters,
And the dates to those who eat them five by five!

Some people peel lupine and *muqaylī* one by one, but the country people do the opposite. Thus he says . . .

mā arā tawqīf ("and never stop"): meaning "I'll not stop eating them with the skins on." By *laff* he means "eat."[607] One says "So-and-so ate up (*laffa*) a crock of lentils," meaning that he ate them all. The same verb is also used for things other than food, such as the turban, and wrapping a cloak, and one also says *dāhiyah taluffak* ("May a disaster consume you!"), etc. 11.38.20

Next he says: 11.38.21

TEXT

wa-ʾākhudhu lī libdah wa-karra mushanyar 11.39
wa-ʾanzil ka-mā kalbi-bn-Abū Jaghnīf

And I'll get me a felt cap and a *mushanyar* headcloth
and go back like the dog of the son of Abū Jaghnīf

COMMENTARY

wa-ʾākhudhu lī libdah ("And I'll get me a felt cap"): this too is a continuation of what he said to the aforementioned son of the 11.39.1

daughter of ʿArīf. The meaning of his words is, "If luck is on my side, when I steal the slippers, and I sell them and eat with the proceeds, either literally or figuratively, as explained above, and I have anything left over, even five *nuṣṣ*, I'll get myself a new felt cap with one of the five."

11.39.2 *wa-* ("and"): "with the remaining four I'll get" . . .

11.39.3 *karra mushanyar* ("a *mushanyar* headcloth"): that is, a head wrapper with fringes of red yarn, for this is what the country people call *mushanyar*, and it is worn only by their great men. One says, "So-and-so is wearing a felt cap and a *mushanyar* head cloth today," meaning that he has become one of the great men of the hamlet. Consequently, the poet longs for the same, meaning that, if he goes to the city and God is merciful to him in the matter of stealing slippers, he will get what he wants and go back to the hamlet with a felt cap and a *mushanyar* headcloth, in power and glory, like the dog mentioned below. He therefore says . . .

11.39.4 *wa-anzil ka-mā kalbi-bn-Abū Jaghnīf* ("and go back like the dog of the son of Abū Jaghnīf"): this dog belonging to Abū Jaghnīf 's son was well known in the hamlet for strength and courage and for jumping on the other dogs and snatching loaves of bread and eating eggs, so that, if one of the people of the hamlet was blessed by God with a felt cap and a *mushanyar* headcloth, they would say, "Today So-and-so is like Abū Jaghnīf's son's dog," that is, strong, audacious, and larcenous, to the point that he has gained enough to dress himself decently and clothe himself respectably and become one of the great, just as one might compare a person in terms of baseness with a dog or a pig and say, "You're a dog!" for example. The father of the dog's owner was given the *kunyah* Abū Jaghnīf (or Jaghnāf or Jaghnūf) according to report, because of his obnoxiousness and loquacity. One says, "So-and-so is a *jaghnāf*," meaning that he is an obnoxious prattler of useless words, or so I find in *The Blue Ocean and Piebald Canon.*

The famous story from *The Thousand and One Nights* provides a pointed example of obnoxiousness and loquacity.[608] It tells how one of the great men of Damascus once prepared a banquet and went out to invite people and came across a youth who was charming in appearance, refined in person, and outstandingly comely, but lame. The man invited the youth to the banquet, and the youth accepted and went into the house where the guests were seated, and these all rose to greet him out of respect and regard for their host. As the youth was about to seat himself, however, he caught sight of one among the guests whose profession was that of barber, and thereupon he refused to sit down and attempted to leave the gathering. The host, however, took hold of him, abjured him with oaths, and said to him, "What makes you come with me and enter my house and then leave before my hospitality is complete?" "By God, My Master," said the youth, "do not stand in my way! The cause of it all is that I caught sight of that ill-omened wretch of a barber, may the Almighty strike him dead! He is a man of despicable vices and hateful devices, of stumbling gait and unlucky fate!" When the host and the guests heard the youth's words against the barber, they were revolted to be sitting in the same gathering with the man and said to the youth, "By God, we will not eat another bite till you have told us what this barber did to you, for we have come to hate him just from hearing you describe him!" 11.39.5

"My friends," said the youth, "I suffered with this wretched old man in my home city of Baghdad a story so amazing that it should be written with needles on the pupils of men's eyes, there to serve as admonition for the wise. He is the cause of my lameness and my broken leg, and I have sworn that I will never sit with him in the same place, or live with him in the same city. I left Baghdad because of him and came to live in this, the farthest of cities from there, and now that I see him among you, I shall not stay here this night but be on my way!" "Tell us what you suffered from him!" they said, and he demurred, but they insisted, while the barber's face turned pale and he hung his head low. 11.39.6

The youth, however, said, "Listen, my friends! My father was a rich man of Baghdad, and he was given no son but me. When I grew up and reached the years of discretion, my father passed into the mercy of God, leaving me great wealth and servants and followers. I started dressing well and indulging myself and was living in great felicity, when one day I was walking in one of the alleys of Baghdad and I saw a bench and sat down to rest. Suddenly a young girl like the radiant sun, more beautiful than any I had ever set eyes on, put her head out of a casement to water her flowers. When I looked at her, she smiled. Then she closed the casement and disappeared. Fire burned in my heart, and I was overcome with love for her, and I remained sitting on the bench in a daze till sunset. At this point, the judge of the city appeared riding on a mule with slaves and servants before him and came to the girl's house and went in. Thus I discovered that he was her father, and I returned to my house sad at heart, and my passion and lovesickness increased and I started to pine away and grow sick for love of her. I continued in this state for several days, my relatives weeping over me and understanding nothing of my state, till one day an old woman came to see me to whom my case was no mystery. 'My son,' she said to me, 'Tell me your story and I will get you what you want!' Her words stirred my heart, and she sat down and I told her what had happened. 'Describe to me the place where you saw her,' she said, so I did so, and I told her, 'Her father is the judge of Baghdad.' 'My son,' said she, 'I know her and I know her father, and I visit her often. Her mother and father keep a close eye on her. Nevertheless I will try and arrange for you to meet her, which is something no one else can do for you; so recover your spirits and be happy!'

11.39.7 "When I heard her words, my appetite for food and drink returned, and I told her, 'Go to work, and whatever you need from me, take!' So she left me and went off to her and came back to me grim-faced, telling me, 'I spoke to her, but she insulted me and gave me harsh words.' When I heard this, my illness grew worse than ever. The old woman would come to visit me every day, and one day she came to me smiling and said, 'Give me a tip for my news! The girl's heart softened towards you when I told her that you had grown sick with love of her and for her sake, and she told me, "Give him my greetings, and offer him comfort and tell him I suffer a thousand times more than he! Let him come to the house on Friday before the evening prayer and I will come down and open the door for him and take him to my rooms in the private apartments where we can be alone together for an hour, and he can leave before my father comes back."' When I heard the old woman's words, the pain I had been feeling disappeared and my family rejoiced and I was left waiting until Friday should finally come. On that day the old woman came to me and said, 'Get yourself ready, shave your head, put on your finest clothes, and be on your way to your tryst. And get cleaned up at the baths, for you have plenty of time!' and she left me.

"I told one of my servants, 'Go to the market and get me a 11.39.8
barber—one who is intelligent, skilled, and lacking in curiosity!' He absented himself for a while and then brought me this wretched old man, may God not help him! When the latter entered, he greeted me and I returned his greeting. Then he said, 'Sir, your body looks wasted.' 'I was sick,' I told him. 'God chase harm, grief, and every ill away,' he replied, 'and keep every sickness at bay, and let your feet never give way; and may God heal you and anneal you, and please you in all He gives you!' to which I replied, 'May God accept your prayers!' Then he said to me, 'Rejoice, my dear sir, for surely good health is yours, if God wills!' Then he asked me, 'Do you wish me, my dear sir, to cut your hair or to let your blood? For it is reported on the authority of Ibn 'Abbās, God be pleased with them both,[609] that the Prophet said, "God relieves him of seventy calamitous ills who cuts his hair on a Friday," and it is reported on the same authority, too, that he said, "He who is cupped on a Friday may not be spared the loss of his sight."' 'Get on with it, you,' I said. 'Shave my head and leave this much ado and all this claptrap too, for I am still sick from my illness.' So he put his hand into his barber's sack and pulled out a cloth and opened it to reveal an astrolabe of seven sheets, all

inlaid. This he took and, going to the center of the house, raised his head towards the sun's rays, observed for a while, thought long and hard, and then said, 'Know, my dear sir—may God grant you every success, and heal you and cure you and guard you from bad cess, and ever guide you and never let you digress!—that there has elapsed of this day[610] (it being Friday the eighteenth day of Ṣafar[611] of the year seven hundred and fifty-three after the Migration of Our Lord Muḥammad,[612] God bless him and grant him peace, which took place seven thousand years after the era of Our Lord Adam,[613] peace be upon him, three hundred and twenty years after the era of Alexander the Greek, and four hundred years from the start of the Persian reckoning) with the ascendant on this aforementioned day of ours being eight degrees and six minutes from Mars, according to the calculation, the lord of the ascendant, as it happens, being Saturn, which is in the third of the astrolabe, Mars being with it in the ascendant and entering with it into its sextile . . . all of which indicates that it is excellent for the removal of hair and also, my master, that you intend to meet some soul, though the ascendant in that respect is bad and the undertaking not recommended.'

11.39.9 "'By God,' I said to him, 'you've vexed me, suffocated me, depressed me, and jinxed me with these nasty prognostications! I didn't summon you to read the stars or to talk a lot of nonsense to me about things that are none of your business. I summoned you to cut my hair, so do what I summoned you to do and leave well alone what I haven't asked you to do, or go your way and let me get another barber!' 'My dear sir,' he replied, 'you should thank God that you called for a barber and He sent you someone who is barber, astrologer, and physician, knowledgeable in alchemy and magic, grammar and philology, logic, motifs and imagery, jurisprudence and history, arithmetic and the science of Traditions! I have read books and studied them, and had experience of affairs and understand them, and managed all manner of things and mastered them. You ought rather to praise God for what he has given you and thank Him for the favor He has done you, for the Almighty has said, «Ask those who are acquainted with the Scriptures if you know not!»[614] and the Prophet, God bless him and grant him peace, has said, "The scholars are the heirs of the prophets." Praise the Almighty, I am not some incompetent that you should talk to me that way! I am telling you that today you should take into account what I say about the planets, for I am offering you good advice out of compassion. If only I might be in your service for just one year, for it is my duty to serve you, just as it was my duty to serve your father before you. I seek no reward—just to be of service to you would be the dearest thing to my heart, for the sake of the high esteem in which I hold you and to honor your father, God rest his soul, for he did me many kind deeds in the old days and showed me generosity beyond calculation, because he loved the way I served him. He would allow no one but me to serve him because he found me so well-mannered and sparing of words, such a good worker and so dexterous. For these reasons he liked me well, and he loved me too for my lack of curiosity. It is, therefore, my sacred duty to serve you!' When I heard him speak thus, I told him, 'Today you will surely kill me with your prattling and rambling about things that do not concern you!' 'My dear sir,' he replied, 'are such as I to be accused of rambling and prattling? By God, your father, God rest his soul, when I attended him, would have wished that I could talk in front of him for a whole year that he might borrow from my knowledge, sample the pearls of my verse and my wisdom, and observe the excellence of my art! Now, we are seven brothers, the first called Burbler, the second Bellower, the third Burbelino, the fourth the Aswan Mug,[615] the fifth Braggart, and the sixth Screecher. Me they call the Silent because I speak so little. If you want me to tell you all about who I am and where I'm from, and everything that happened to my six brothers, from beginning to end, listen well!'

"As he kept on talking and stretching everything out to no pur- 11.39.10
pose, my heart sickened and I felt as though my spleen had burst, so

I said to my servant, 'Boy, give him four dinars and let him leave me and go to perdition, for I shall not shave my head today.' But when he heard what I said to my servant, the miserable wretch said to me, 'What words are these, my dear sir? I simply cannot allow myself, as a Muslim, to take a penny from you till I have shaved you. It is my duty to serve you and my obligation to make you presentable. Once I have done so, I care not whether I am paid or not. You, my dear sir, may know nothing of my worth and merit, but I know yours, because of the high esteem in which I held your father, may the Almighty rest his soul, and grant you long life! How people missed him! God only knows, he was generous and great, openhanded and wise, liberal and loving to his friends! Once on a Friday just like this blessed day he sent for me, so I went in to where he was and found that he had a party of guests with him. "Let my blood!" he said. So I got out my astrolabe and took the elevation and found that the ascendant was inauspicious for the letting of blood. I informed him of this and told him, "Let my lord be patient for an hour until this ascendant changes and I may relieve him!" He was delighted and said, "By God, what a competent fellow you are! Anyone else would just have let my blood!" and he praised me to his guests and I told them all sorts of marvelous stories and he was very impressed and his guests were ecstatic. I recited the following:

I came to my lord to let his blood,
  But couldn't find a good time for phlebotomization.
So I sat down and told them of marvels galore
  And scattered before him pearls of learning, fruits of my very own lucubration.
He listened, amazed, and said to me,
  "You pass all understanding, you mine of information!"
Said I to him, "Lord of all men and mankind,
  You've flooded me with kindness, may you never discontinue your consideration!

For you are lord of kindness, generosity, and giving,
You sublime treasure of toleration, magnanimation, and education!"

"'Your father, God rest his soul, hearing my narration and versification, was greatly moved and shouted to his servant, "Give him a hundred dinars and a robe of honor!" and he gave them to me. Then I took the ascendant and found it to be excellent, so I let his blood.'

"After this the wretch kept up his talking and his raving till I said, 'May God divest my father of His mercy for having known one such as you!' but the wretch laughed at my words and said, 'There is no god but God! Glory be to Him who changes but is not changed! I can only suppose that your illness has affected you, for I see that your brain is deficient. Nevertheless, one grows wiser as one grows older. It must be the sickness that is making you talk nonsense. The Almighty has said, «Those who control their wrath and are forgiving of mankind,»[616] and the Almighty has said, «We have enjoined men to be kind to their parents,»[617] and it is reported on the authority of Anas ibn Mālik that the Prophet said, "Whoever pleases his parents pleases God and whoever displeases his parents displeases God," and the poet says: 11.39.11

Give to the poor when Fate treats you well,
And seize every chance to give alms.
Poverty's a hidden ill without cure,
Wealth an adornment that to ugly fronts adds charms.
Pass greetings around when you're out in society
And help your parents out of filial piety!

"'You are to be excused, however, my dear sir. The Almighty says, «There is no blame upon the blind or upon the lame or upon the sick.»[618] Your father and your grandfather would do nothing without consulting me, and, as the proverb has it, "He who has no older relative, let him take a counselor!" The poet[619] says:

> If you resolve upon a thing
>
> Consult one who is older, and do not disobey him!

"'You will find no one more experienced in affairs than me, and yet I stand before you ready to do you service and I have not lost my temper with you, even though you lost yours with me!'

11.39.12 "'Fellow!' I said to him, 'You have held me up and given me a headache with your endless talk. For God's sake, leave me!' and I made a show of ignoring him, and I wished to leave, for the moment I was waiting for and the hour that I sought had drawn close, while I was in a state of misery because of this wretch and his loquaciousness. Then he said, 'My dear sir, I don't blame you at all. I am delighted to see you today with this beard when just yesterday I used to carry you upon my shoulder and take you to the *kuttāb*!' 'By God's truth,' I exclaimed, 'Just shave my head and leave me!' At this, seeing that I had lost my temper, he took the razor, stropped it, approached my head, and shaved off some hair. Then he lifted his hand and said, 'My dear sir, "Haste is the Devil's and patience the Merciful's." The poet says:

> Proceed with care, haste not in matters that concern you.
>
> Be merciful to men, and you will meet with mercy.
>
> There is no hand but God's is above it,
>
> No tyrant but shall meet with God's tyranny.

"'The best things are those that are undertaken with caution; yet I see that you are in a hurry and have something in mind, and I am afraid lest it be something unbefitting or improper, so tell me what it is, for the time of the prayer is close,' and he threw down his razor and took up the astrolabes and went into the sun and said, 'Three hours, no less and no more, remain until the prayer time.'

11.39.13 "I said, 'I beseech you by God, man, stop plaguing me with your words, for you have vexed me and depressed me!' So he approached and took the razor in his hand and shaved a little more. Then he threw it down again and went on blathering at me until two hours had passed and one hour was left and I was afraid that, were I late for the tryst, I would be unable to get in to see her, so I told him, 'Shave my head quickly and stop talking so much, for I want to be on my way to a party at a friend's house to which I am invited!' When the wretch heard mention of a party, he said, 'We are God's and to God we shall return! By God, Sir, you have reminded me that I have a company staying with me as guests. I want to make them food, but I have nothing. Just get me everything I ask for, and then you and I will go home, and you will honor me today with your presence at my place, and my banquet will be better than your friend's!' 'Take whatever you want, shave the rest of my head, and leave me be!' I said to him. 'Time is running out, and there is no need for me to go to your house,' and I had everything he asked for brought, even incense of aloes, all in the hope that God would rid me of him so that I could go to where I wanted to be.

"Then he said, 'Sir, mine too is a charming company:[620] there's 11.39.14
Zaytūn the Bathhouse Keeper, Big-Mouth, Salawṭaḥ the Bean Seller, 'Ikrishah the Grocer, Saʿīd the Porter, Suwayd the Ropemaker, Ḥāmid the Trashman, and Abū 'Ukāshah the Bath Attendant, plus Sheep-Larks, and each of them has a story that I, should you desire, will tell you. Now, Ḥāmid the Trashman dances to the tambourine and sings to the pipes, and I've composed to describe him:

My life I'd give for a trashman o'er whom I've gone crazy,
With the sweetest disposition, graceful as branches a-sway!
When Fate granted him to me one night I told him
(For I waste with longing whene'er he's away),
"You've fired up your love in my heart!" Said he,
"No wonder, when it's a trashman who's stoking the blaze!"

"'So, my dear sir, come with me to my friends and forget yours, for you may find yourself going to see people who talk too much and upset you, or one of them may be inquisitive and try your patience, given that your illness has made you so quick to fly off the handle.'

11.39.15 "'Some other day,' I said, 'for I intend to go to my friends and you must go to yours.' 'God forbid, my lord,' this wretch then said, 'that I should abandon you and let you go on your own!' 'Fellow,' I replied, 'no one but me can get into the place I'm going to.' 'I think, my lord,' he said, 'that you have a tryst today with some girl, otherwise you would want to take me with you, but who is better suited than me to help you obtain what you desire? I fear, however, she may be some foreign woman who will get you into trouble, for no one can get away with anything in the city of Baghdad, and its governor is an ogre. He may catch you with her, in which case he will cut off your head.' I told him, 'You wretched old man, what nonsense is this you're throwing at me?' and I was filled with rage, and the prayer time had arrived, and he had finished shaving my head, so I told him, 'Take this food to your friends now, and I will wait for you to come back and then you can go with me,' and I kept on buttering him up and trying to fool him, while he kept saying, 'I won't go without you!' and 'I won't let you go on your own!' until I swore to him that I would wait until he came back and that then we would go together. At this he took everything I had given him and left, and then sent the stuff on with a porter to his house and hid himself in an alleyway.

11.39.16 "I arose immediately. The call to prayer had been given and time was running out, so I dressed and rushed off, on my own, till I came to the alley and stopped at the house in which I had seen the girl, with this wretched barber, unbeknownst to me, following behind. I found the door open and I went in and found the old woman waiting for me behind the door, and she took me upstairs to the girl's quarters, but, before I knew it, the master of the house had returned from the prayer and entered the main hall and closed the door of the house behind him. I looked out of the window and saw this wretched barber, God strike him dead, sitting outside the door, and said to myself, 'To God we belong and to God we shall return! How did this wretch discover my whereabouts so that the Almighty could send him to expose me?' At this point, the master of the house struck one of his slave girls, and his slave came to intervene on her behalf, and he struck the slave too and the slave cried out, and this miserable barber thought the man was hitting me, and he shrieked and rent his clothes and threw dust on his head and started saying, 'My master has been murdered in the judge's house! Alas for my master, alas for my master!' so that people came from all sides in answer to his cries. Then he proceeded to my house, the people behind him, and informed my family and my servants, telling them, 'My master has been murdered in the house of the Judge of Baghdad!' and they came after me, screaming and with their hair untied, the barber in front of them yelling, 'God aid the sultan against the judge! He has murdered my master!'

"Hearing the noise of the crowd and the screaming and shouting and the people saying, 'Would you murder young gentlemen in your house?' and the barber saying, 'Alas for the slain! Alas for my master!' the master of the house came out and opened the door and the people yelled at him, while this wretch said, 'God aid the sultan against you!' 'What is the matter, good people?' he asked. The barber said to him, 'Would you murder our master in your house?' 'And where is your master,' said the judge, 'that I should murder him?' This miserable barber then said to him, 'You beat him with cudgels and he cried out, but now his voice has ceased, which means you murdered him!' 'And who put your master in my house without my permission?' asked the judge. He replied, 'He's your daughter's lover and he went to visit her, and when you came you found him and beat him and murdered him, and now either the sultan settles things between us, or you bring him out of the house right away!' The judge, who was covered with embarrassment and shame before the people, said to him, 'If you are telling the truth, go in yourself and bring him out,' so this rascal went up and entered the house. 11.39.17

"When I saw him, I looked for a way of escape or a place in which I could take refuge, but all I could find was a large chest, so I got into that, pulled the lid down on top of me, and held my breath. This vile 11.39.18

wretch looked around and seeing nothing but the chest in the room I was in, went to it and lifted it onto his head, while I was going crazy, and he exited with me in a hurry. When I realized that he was not going to let me go, I braced myself and threw myself from the chest onto the ground, breaking my leg in the escape. I saw that people were clustered around the door as thick as flies, so I started throwing gold coins over their heads, which distracted them, and I took off running through the alleys of Baghdad, this vile wretch running behind me saying, 'Praise God, my master, for saving you from being killed! I'm right behind you; don't be afraid! You had no call to make passes at the judge's daughter! Wooing women is a tricky business!' and he continued pursuing me with accusations of foul deeds through the markets and disgracing me with his words until I escaped from him into a caravansary, and I said to the doorkeeper, 'I beseech you in God's name, keep him away from me!' and the doorkeeper attacked him and stopped him from coming in. By this time, I was sick at heart and on the verge of expiring, and I summoned a jurist and wrote my will and sent it to my family. Then I took some money and traveled, and I swore that I would never live in the same town as this abominable barber.

11.39.19 "When I came to this city of yours, Damascus, the host of this banquet invited me and I saw this rascal seated here, so I could not bring myself to sit or to eat. Such, good people, is my story." Then they turned to the barber and said, "Is this true?" and he lifted his head and said, "Certainly! And he should praise God that I saved him, and that he only broke his leg and didn't get his head chopped off, and that I did him this favor!" "God strike you dead, you unspeakable wretch!" they said. "You disgraced this young man, exiled him from his family, and disgraced the Judge of Baghdad!" Then they expelled him from their company and did honor to the youth, marveling at what the barber had done to him, and each then went his way. Generally speaking, loquacity is a common trait among those who practice this profession, but this wretch went too far in his obnoxiousness and bad manners.

Next the poet says: 11.39.20

TEXT

11.40

wa-yajlis bi-janbī ʾIbnu Jarwin wa-Kul Kharah
wa-ʾIbnu Kuli l-Ṣakka l-Naḍīfa wa-ḍīf
wa-Ibnu Fisā l-Tīrān wa-Ibnu Kharā-Lḥas[621]
wa-Qallūṭu wa-l-Ziblah wa-Ibnu kanīf

And by me will sit Son-of-Puppy and Eat-Shit
and Son-of-Take-a-Good-Slapping-on-the-Back-of-the-Neck, and so on and so forth,
And Son-of-Ox-Fart and Son-of-Lick-Shit
and Big-Turd and Dropping and Son-of-Latrine

COMMENTARY

These are the shaykhs of the poet's village, whose names he takes pride in repeating and running off his tongue. The meaning is that he is saying: If I come back from the city wearing a felt cap and a turban with red fringes and I am like the aforementioned dog, the aforementioned shaykhs of the village will come to me and sit next to me, they being eight men altogether: 11.40.1

The first is *ʾIbnu Jarwin wa-* ("Son-of-Puppy and") the second is the son of . . . 11.40.2

Kul Kharah wa- ("Eat-Shit and") the third is . . . 11.40.3

ʾIbnu Kuli l-Ṣakka l-Naḍīfa ("Son-of-Take-a-Good-Slapping-on-the-Back-of-the-Neck"): that is, a slapping in which the blows follow one another in rapid succession, so that they leave the nape of the neck looking like the flag of Master Aḥmad al-Badawī, for example.[622] It is said that the requirements for a good slapping on the back of the neck are that it be administered by a strong man, that the recipient's neck be properly prepared, with nothing to impede the impact of the slaps, and that the slaps follow one another rapidly and with alacrity, so that they make the nape turn 11.40.4

red, for the sign of a good slapping on the neck is the redness and swelling of the nape.

11.40.5 The tale is told that Abū Nuwās was keeping company one night with the Commander of the Faithful Hārūn al-Rashīd when the latter gave him a slave girl as a gift and told him to take her home with him. However, Hārūn al-Rashīd told her, "When he asks you to do it with him, give him a good slapping on the back of the neck, and the more he asks, the more you slap him." When Abū Nuwās reached his house and wanted to do it with her, she rained slaps on the back of his neck, etc. The next day he went to the caliph in the greatest of pain, unable to turn his head to the right or the left. "What sort of a night did you have with the slave girl, Abū Nuwās?" asked the caliph. "She was great," the latter replied, "but you've taught her a very bad habit!" The caliph laughed and gave him gifts of money and other things.

11.40.6 *wa-ḍīf* ("and so on and so forth"): inserted in order to fill up the line. The fourth of those named is . . .

11.40.7 *ʾIbnu Fisā l-Tīrān* ("and Son-of-Ox-Fart"): so called because his father was confined to his house for a period by a sickness that afflicted him, to wit, constant farting. He made a place for himself among the oxen in the thing that is called the *ṭuwālah* ("feeding trough") and farted there day and night, with the result that when anyone smelled the smell they would say to him, "What's that?" and he would reply, "ox farts," and that is how he got his name. And the fifth is . . .

11.40.8 *ʾIbnu Kharā-Lḥas* ("Son-of-Lick-Shit"): his father was so called because he used to lick dung a lot when he was little. It is reported that he used to take off his skullcap and place it on the ground and shit in it till it was full, and then lick it out, and that is how he got his name. And the sixth is . . .

11.40.9 *Qallūṭu* ("Big-Turd"): derived from *qalṭ* ("to produce a large, firm turd"), on the measure of *ḍarṭ* ("to fart audibly") and of *halṭ* ("to be flaccid and large (of the belly)"). One says, "So-and-so's turds have grown fat," meaning that he has become rich and acquired high status in the hamlet. And the seventh of the village shaykhs is . . .

al-Ziblah ("Dropping"): so called because when he was young he used to busy himself picking up the droppings from the flocks and selling them, and this was the basis of his good fortune. A friendship existed in the village between him and Big-Turd. Big-Turd was always there and never left, but Dropping would sometimes leave and sometimes stay. This Big-Turd lived in the very heart of the village, while Dropping lived on the edge. They would send one another presents too, and there was both an affective and a familial relationship between them, for droppings are closely related to turds. Despite all this, Lick-Shit was the mightiest in the village, and the most senior of them all. 11.40.10

An Amusing Story: a certain dull-witted governor told his secretary, "Write to so-and-so in harsh terms and say to him, 'You shit, do such and such!'" But the secretary said, "My Lord, that is not appropriate!" so the ruler told him, "In that case, lick the 'shit' off with your tongue!" And the eighth is . . . 11.40.11

'Ibnu kanīf ("Son-of-Latrine"): he always took care of the needs of the village, and he was a crony of Big-Turd and Lick-Shit, though Lick-Shit had been Son-of-Latrine's bosom buddy when they were young. When he grew up, however, Son-of-Latrine became his crony. As a certain poet put it in a *mawāliyā*: 11.40.12

A bat fell in love with a beetle and woke the next day possessed,
And he built her then a palace inside a privy made of brick,
And he brought her nuts and food and drink—
What better boon companion could such a shitty friend possess?

Next the poet says: 11.40.13

TEXT

11.41 *wa-ʾafraḥu bi-l-lammah wa-yansarru khāṭirī*
wa-hādhā murādī ya-bna binti ʿarīf

And I'll rejoice in the throng and my heart will be happy
and this is my hope, O son of the daughter of ʿArīf!

COMMENTARY

11.41.1 All this is addressed to the aforementioned son of the daughter of ʿArīf. That is, he prays God to allow him to achieve his goal of stealing the aforementioned slippers and to grant him that he might leave the city with a felt cap and a turban with red fringes and have status and esteem, and that the shaykhs of the village listed above—and whose names there is no need to repeat, since repetition serves no function, and I have already given both the substance and the taste of their names—would meet with him. The poet says, in sum, "If I attain this, it will be all I could ask for or desire of this world, and the fulfillment of every pleasure I have longed for, for I have grown old and my wife has turned into a barren old woman, and if the Almighty grants me what I have asked for, provision for my wife will be up to Him, for He is Generous, the Provider for the Old, while I am as the one described by the poet who said:

You who asked for bread, got it,
Then said, 'Now what about my wife?'
Get up early and primp your beard—
Serendipity's a condition of life!" [623]

—or it may be that he intends his request to apply only to himself, thinking "a wife can eat shit" and "a thousand beards rather than my own."

11.41.2 Next he concludes his verses with blessings on the Prophet, God bless him and grant him peace, saying:

TEXT

wa-ʾakhtim qaṣīdī bi-l-ṣalāti ʿalā l-nabī 11.42
nabī ʿarabī makkī sharīfin ʿafīf

And I close my ode with blessings on the Prophet,
an Arab prophet, of Mecca, noble, sinless.

COMMENTARY

Here the poet is guided by the Noble Tradition in which the Prophet, God bless him and grant him peace, says, "The angels will never cease to ask for forgiveness for anyone who calls for blessings upon me in a book as long as my name shall remain in that book" (poetry, etc., counting as a book). In the *Cure* (*Shifāʾ*) of Ibn Sabuʿ[624] it says, on the authority of the Prophet, God bless him and grant him peace, "Call often for blessings upon me, for they quench the anger of the Merciful and undermine the wiles of Satan." The Traditions cited on the virtue of calling for blessings on the Prophet, God bless him and grant him peace, are numerous. 11.42.1

Some Miscellaneous Anecdotes with Which We Conclude the Book[625]

12.1 It is said that a man married a woman who had been widowed five times before. When the sixth got sick, she started to weep and say, "To whom will you entrust me after you die?" The husband said, "To the wretched seventh!"

12.2 And the tale is told that a certain wit was a great drinker in secret, though he had been strictly enjoined by his father not to behave so. News reached his father of what was going on, and he followed reports of him until he came across him with a flagon of wine. When, however, he grabbed him and said to him, "What's this?" the son replied, "Milk!" "Give over!" said the father. "Milk is white, and this is red!" Said the boy, "I spoke the truth. It was white but when it saw you, it got embarrassed and felt bashful and blushed, and God curse those who have no modesty!" His father was abashed and left him and went his way.

12.3 And the tale is told that, whenever the wife of a certain man got angry with him, he would whip up her legs and set about pleasuring her. One day she said to him, "Whenever I lose my temper with you, you bring me an intercessor of yours to whom I cannot say no!"

12.4 And it is said that a madman went in to see a judge, holding on to his penis, and said to him, "Peace be upon you, and God's mercy!" The judge stood up, bared his backside, turned it towards the madman, and said, "And upon you be peace! The Almighty has said, «When greeted, return the greeting with one better or the same!»"[626]

And the tale is told that al-Aṣmaʿī[627] said, "I was with Hārūn al-Rashīd, and he said to me, 'Whom do you have at home to keep you company?' I replied, 'I have no one.' When I went back to my house, he sent me a slave girl of surpassing beauty and comeliness, who charmed me with her conversation and took off her clothes and mine. Then we ate and drank and made merry, and I wanted to do it with her, but I couldn't get it up and was completely overcome by lassitude. She tried moving my penis in her hand, but it still wouldn't go stiff, and my chagrin and embarrassment before her grew. When she despaired of it, she said, 'Forget your penis, mister! It's a write-off!' Then she got up and said to me, 'Lie on your back so I can wash it and put it in its shroud!' I was too embarrassed to disobey her so she washed it and wrapped it in a handkerchief and said to me, 'Get up and pray for it!' So I got up, in an agony of embarrassment, and made my ablutions and prayed the morning prayer and went straight to see al-Rashīd. 'What's up?' he asked me, and I said to him, 'Commander of the Faithful, my case is bizarre!' and told him what had happened to me with her. He laughed until he fell flat on his back and said, 'We need her more than you, for her youth,' and he sent me another slave girl instead, plus ten thousand dinars". 12.5

And a Magian died with an outstanding debt. Some of the father's creditors said to his son, "Why don't you sell your house and pay off some of your father's debt?" The son said to them, "If I sell my house and pay off my father's debt, will he go to Heaven?" They said, "No." "Then leave him in Hell and me in the house!" said he. 12.6

And it is said that there was a grammarian whose name was Zayd,[628] and he saw a youth whose name was Bakr. When he found himself alone with him he said to him, "My boy, inflect my penis with the correct 'movements'[629] for it is an indubitably 'active' participle,[630] and extend it to your backside as one would a long open vowel between two words and glottalize it so that it does not break off in the middle,"[631] and went on at great length in this vein until a man called ʿAmr came in and slapped Zayd on the back of the neck 12.7

and said, "And put the correct inflections on "Amr struck Zayd!'—at which the boy got up and ran off saying, 'And put the correct inflections on "And Bakr got out and ran away!"'"

12.8 And it is said that a grammarian got sick far from home, and he saw a youth whom he knew to be a son of the neighbors, so he told him, "Proceed to my family and tell them that So-and-so has been afflicted by a malady that has pained his knees and hurt his testes, ruined his complexion and aggravated his infection, denied sleep to his eye and made him cry," and went on at great length to the youth in the same vein. The youth said, "Sir, why don't I keep it short and tell your family, 'He's dead!'? Then we can drop the rest."

12.9 And it is said that a miser was on the point of death and his son said to him, "Give me your last will and testament!" The man said, "If you are at table and someone addresses you, just say, 'Yes,' and say it once only, for if you say it a second time, the moving of your jaws will make you miss a second chew!"

12.10 And a lazy freeloader once said, "If the sun rises on a poor man and he has not yet eaten, a voice will call the prayer for the funeral of a stranger out of the heaven of the roof of his mouth!"[632]

12.11 And it is said that a man brought his wife some meat and told her, "Boil some, for that is good for the belly, and fry some, for that is good for the back, and grill some, for that is good for intercourse." She said to him, "Husband, we have neither pots nor fuel. Let's just grill the lot!"

12.12 And a grammarian stood before a butcher's shop and said, "Is this the meat of the juvenile sheep or the mature goat?" The butcher replied, "It's the best mutton." The grammarian asked, "Did you slaughter it to be eaten or because it was ailing?"[633] "I slaughtered it," said the butcher, "so that I and my children might keep body and soul together." "Was it a male, possessed of testes twain, or a female, possessed of an equal complement of nipples?" asked the grammarian. "It was a male," said the butcher. "If it butted a wall, it knocked it down!" "Did it sip water through the sides of its mouth, or suck it up with its lips?" asked the grammarian. The butcher said,

"It dangled its snout in the water and drank till it was full!" "Did it graze on wormwood and artemisia, or cornstalks and sweet basil?" asked the grammarian. "It grazed on any plants it could find!" said the butcher. "Did you whet your whittle and hone your hacker?" asked the grammarian. "I made it so sharp that, if it fell on your miserable neck, it'd cut it in two!" said the butcher. "Did you start with the *basmalah*[634] and pronounce the *ḥayʿalah*,[635] which some take to be of the measure *fayʿalah* while others take it to be of the measure *faʿlalah* (the former being correct)?" asked the grammarian. At this the butcher told his servant, "Get the skin so I can split it over the shoulders of this wretch who has wasted our time and brought my business today to a standstill!" On hearing this, the grammarian uttered an insult and ran off.

And the tale is told of a certain wit who eulogized a great man in an ode, for which the latter rewarded him with a donkey saddle and girth. The poet took these on his shoulder and left. One of his friends passed by him and said, "What are those?" The wit replied, "I praised our master the emir with my best verse, and he rewarded me with some of his best clothes!" Word of this reached the emir and he laughed and sent after him with a good reward. 12.13

And the tale is told of al-Aṣmaʿī that he said, "In the desert I saw a lovely slave girl with a black mole on her cheek. 'What's your name?' I asked her. 'Mecca,' she said. Then I said, 'What is this black spot?' 'The Black Stone,' she said. I said to her, 'I would like to circumambulate the House[636] and kiss the Black Stone.' 'Dream on!' said she. 'It is a land «ye could not reach save with great trouble to yourselves.»'[637] Then I pulled out a purse containing a few dinars and gave it to her and she said, '«Go into them in peace, secure!»[638] if you want, and kiss the Black Stone, and, if you wish, you may enter the Sanctuary.' I was amazed at her beauty and good looks." 12.14

And it is said that a man was traveling with a party that included a beautiful woman who was accompanied by a beautiful boy, and the man committed adultery with the woman and buggered the boy. Later the woman said to the boy, "I know him. Perhaps when we 12.15

return we can get the better of him and expose him to the authorities." The boy said, "As far as I'm concerned, I had my back to his face but you had your face to his, so your evidence should be more telling than mine!"

12.16 And a simpleton once sent the following verses to a friend:

When I think of you whom I adore
    The snot my beard flows o'er!
Would you were with me when I empty my gut—
    You'd stick your tongue right up my butt!
Your breeze the rain in the skies does stem
    And has filled my knees with a kind of phlegm!
If you don't visit me, I'm bound to die,
    For love has set my stomach awry!

12.17 Al-Ma'mūn said to Yaḥyā ibn Aktham, as an indirect jibe, "Who was it that composed the verse that goes:

A judge who supports the severest punishment for adultery
    But sees nothing wrong with those who commit sodomy?"

and Judge Yaḥyā answered, "Doesn't the Commander of the Faithful know the author?" "No, I don't," responded al-Ma'mūn. "It's by that profligate Aḥmad ibn Abī Nuʿaym," said Yaḥyā. "He's the one who also said:

Our Prince takes bribes, our Ruler
    Stuffs boys, and the Boss is the worst kind of boss.
I don't see how such largesse can end
    When the nation's ruled by the Banū l-ʿAbbās!"

Al-Ma'mūn was too nonplussed and embarrassed to speak.[639]

12.18 And among the poetry attributed to al-Ḥarīrī,[640] may the Almighty rest his soul, we find:

In these times, your friend's a snake,
    Your buddy tastes bitter—avoid him and his evil beware!

Play hypocrite, for hypocrisy's the rage
And hypocrites do well—your wares will find a buyer, never fear!
Pimp and pander, oppress and vaunt your vile doings,
For your world has produced no man noble or fair.
The only fault you can have is religion, for if you look round
Heretics and atheists are all you'll find here!

Similar are the words of that eminent man of letters al-Būṣīrī,[641] God excuse his sins: 12.19

Six things in love you ought to do
For which after death to be remembered:
Play faggot, pimp, and fornicate,
Sing, make bets, and be a drunkard!

Let Us Conclude This Book with Verses from the Sea of Inanities

13.1 We declare:

Done is the book of bosh and drivel,
With its description of the country people.
I made it, concisely, in two parts;
It came out like a pipsqueak that from the beaten path departs.[642]
Yet, for all its obnoxious topics
And blind stumblings, you gnostics,
Its language in expression unrefined,
And all the silly arguments that therein you'll find,
And its inquiries that resemble the licking of shit,
O best of friends, for sure and no doubt about it,
13.2 Taken as a whole it's not completely without merit
By way of a joke or a story apposite.
And the prime mover that drove me to it,
And to explain it, copy it, and duplicate it,
Was the Initiated Sage unique in his time,
The Scholar of Islam of fame sublime,
He who was the leader to whom students would go,
Of sciences and letters the very meadow,
Of excellence and fulfillment the source,
Meaning the Imam Aḥmad al-Sandūbī, of course—

May the Lord of the Throne with gardens of ease reward him
    And with the sight of our Most Generous Lord award him!
And God have mercy on those who read 13.3
    This book of mine, and to the truth them lead,
And on him who finds therein some faults or flaws
    And mends them—for instinct to error all men draws;
And blame me not, but tolerance prefer,
    And excuse, good fellow, your brother, who could not demur,
And praise be to God that it is ended.
    And may God's blessings and peace be extended
To the Prophet Aḥmad,[643] Hāshim's offspring,
    And to those stars of guidance, his Companions and kin,
As long as dove shall coo
    Or lightning in dawn's darkness glow.

Notes

1 Elsewhere (§11.33.10), al-Shirbīnī mentions that Falḥas is a dog's name, as does al-Jāḥiẓ (*Al-Ḥayawān*, 1:257); dogs are so called because Falḥas was the name of a proverbially greedy man (see, e.g., al-Maydānī, *Majmaʿ*: 1:234). The name may also be understood as Fa-lḥas ("Go lick!").

2 *Father* of ʿAmrah (Abū ʿAmrah) is "an idiom meaning pennilessness and hunger, and also a man who, every time he camped with a group, brought disaster with him, in the form of fighting and war" (al-Fīrūzābādhī, *Qāmūs*).

3 Neither place exists.

4 Literally "Hitch up your skirts for me and bend over."

5 According to a later reference (§11.4.5), Fasāqil was Abū Shādūf's paternal first cousin.

6 The words may be read two ways, depending on how they are divided: as above, in which case the literal meaning is "its length grew less," or as *qallaṭū lahā*, meaning "they excreted large, firm turds at it." Similarly, below, the words "(its width) rendered its length odious" translate *(ʿarḍuhā) ḍarra ṭūlahā*, which mean literally "(its width) harmed its length," may also be read *ḍarraṭū lahā* "they farted audibly at it."

7 See vol. 1, §5.2.7 on the proverbial stupidity of schoolmasters.

8 "O Umm ʿAmr . . . may be!": these lines are taken from a poem by Jarīr ibn ʿAṭiyyah (ca. 33–111/653–729) (*Dīwān*, 161); the remaining lines are anonymous.

9 Meaning, perhaps, the Bard of Shammirṭāṭī and Tall Fandarūk.

10 "This . . .": the referent is unclear.

11 Umm Faswah: "She-of-the-Silent-Fart."

12 Dating to before the fifteenth century: cf. al-Ibshīhī, *Al-Mustaṭraf*, 1:43.

13 I.e., his wife.

14 Literally "Puppy, Son of Shit-Go-Lick."

15 "God . . . moisten his head-brick" (*Allāh . . . bashbish ṭūbatū*): a conventional expression, referring to the brick on which the head of a corpse rests in the grave.

16 The sense of *shirāʿah* is unclear.

17 "every Zayd and ʿAmr": i.e., "every Tom, Dick, and Harry."

18 Like a bard reciting the *Sīrat Banī Hilāl*, the poet opens with an address to the hero of the latter epic, Abū Zayd al-Hilālī Salāmah, though in al-Shirbīnī's version the poet's donkey and staff substitute for the steed and sword of the original.

19 Literally in the Arabic "and were not my father in his grave," which contradicts the context.

20 Literally "The one with the little spout."

21 Literally "The one with the turban."

22 I.e., Easter, when Copts traditionally color and eat eggs.

23 The poet, whom al-Shirbīnī quotes further below (§11.1.14), is unidentified; however, see also "al-Buhlūl" below (§11.10.6).

24 The attribution is dubious.

25 Ibn al-Rūmī (221–283/836–896) (*Dīwān*, 4:1592).

26 "patience fair" (*al-ṣabr al-jamīl*): reminscent of Q Yūsuf 12:18 and 12:83 «(My course is) a comely patience (*fa-ṣabrun jamīl*)» and Maʿārij 70:5.

27 The verses are unlikely to be by Ibn Muqlah. Ibn Ḥajar attributes them to Taqī al-Dīn ibn Razīn, i.e., Muḥammad ibn al-Ḥusayn ibn Razīn (d. 680/1281–82) (Ibn Ḥajar, *Al-Durar* 3/330).

28 The exemplars of awfulness named here are not to be found in the standard works on this topic and are probably invented for the occasion, mimicking, to some extent, the patterns of the names of the preceding four and having appropriately contrary meanings: Uṭrūsh, "Deaf"; Ibn Qaynah, "Son of a Slave Girl"; Qarnān, "Cuckold" (see

al-Muḥibbī, *Qaṣd*, 2:160); Ibn Ayham, "Son of a Madman." The moral is that, in this hypocritical world, the worthy are neglected and the unworthy adulated.

29 Q Ṭāhā 20:106.

30 The lines "But when aroused ... too far to keep" are attributed by Ibn Ḥamdūn to ʿAmr ibn Mālik al-Jaʿdī (Ibn Ḥamdūn, *Al-Tadhkirah*, 6:85).

31 Abū Shādūfi: i.e., Abū Shādūfin, with a meaningless short vowel supplied for the meter as throughout these texts.

32 "These words are metered ..." (*hādhā l-kalām lahu baḥr ...*): al-Shirbīnī kicks off the commentary with a display of verbal virtuosity that evokes, through multiple puns and allusions, a range of literary and grammatical terms and conventions, along with comically irrelevant associations. One element is the pun on the dual meaning of *baḥr* (pl. *buḥūr*) as both "(poetic) meter" and "ocean, sea, large river," which is probably extended by reference to *madd* (see n. 34, at end), which in turn, and in another sense, may contrast with *qadd* (see n. 33).

33 "and tuned" (*wa-qadd*): in normal usage "shape." However, Dozy defines *qadd*, on the authority of a nineteenth-century source, as "*des paroles, qui ont les désinences grammaticales, adaptées à un air populaire*" (Dozy, *Supplément*). Similarly, Hava defines it as "musical tune" and, in Syrian colloquial Arabic, "popular tune, song."

34 "crooned" (*madd*): literally "stretching, protraction." Al-Shirbīnī may be using it here as a technical term under the rules governing Qurʾanic (but *not* poetic) recitation (*tajwīd*), where it means "duration" in the sense of the number of beats assigned to each syllable (Nelson, *Art*, 24–27), or, more impressionistically, the "drawing out of the voice over long vowels (in Koran recitation)" (Wehr, *Dictionary*). Another interpretation would contrast *madd* with *qadd*, using the latter in its basic function as a verbal noun meaning "cutting (short)." This would imply that the words of the ode contain both pausal forms (*qadd*) and full forms (*madd*), which might in turn be

interpreted to mean that they contain both colloquial forms (superficially similar to the pausal forms of formal Arabic in their lack of desinential endings) and formal forms, which is in fact the case. The association of *madd* in the sense of "tide" with *baḥr* "ocean/meter" is evoked, as is, further on in the same passage, yet another sense of *baḥr*, namely, "span (of a chain)."

35 In the following, al-Shirbīnī plays with the names of five of the sixteen normative poetic meters (see W. Stoetzer, "Prosody," in *EAL*, and van Gelder, *Sound*, 341–60): *al-ṭawīl* ("the Long"), *al-madīd* ("the Extended"), *al-kāmil* ("the Perfect"), *al-wāfir* ("the Exuberant"), and *al-basīṭ* ("the Extended," or "the Outspread," here translated "the Diffused"). The actual meter is *al-ṭawīl*, and there is no such meter as the "Long *and* Extended" (*al-ṭawīl al-madīd*).

36 *mutahābilun mutahābilun*: i.e., the meter *al-kāmil* (literally "the Perfect"), as stated, though the actual meter is *al-ṭawīl* (see preceding note). The Arabic spelling (متهابل) is unusual, in that prosodic mnemonics are normally written with the implicit nunation realized as a final letter *nūn* (i.e., متاهابلن) to allow complete representation of the syllable count; in the manuscripts of *Brains Confounded*, the nunation is suppressed throughout, as it is in the manuscript of *Risible Rhymes*, but has been realized in the translation. The mnemonic uses the root *h-b-l*, associated with "foolishness" and "doltishness" (see also vol. 1, p. lxi).

37 "the Meter of the Chain" (*baḥr al-silsilah*): in addition to the "meter/sea" ambiguity, al-Shirbīnī evokes both the nonstandard meter called *silsilah*, related to the Persian *dūbayt* meter (see van Gelder, *Sound*, 126–27) (even though the latter bears no relation to that of the verses quoted here) and the East Port of Alexandria, known as "the Sea of the Chain." Finally, the meaning of *baḥr* as "span (of a chain)" is part of the wordplay.

38 *halhalah halhalah*: i.e., LSL LSL, perhaps implying the rare meter *al-mutadārik*; the mnemonic is based on the root *h-l-h-l*, which includes the sense of "weaving (both cloth and verses) finely or flimsily."

39 Possibly a popular comic air or ditty, or a parody of some well-known song.

40 In works on prosody, verses representative of a particular meter may be presented in this "articulated" form, to demonstrate more clearly the division of the feet; cf. *Risible Rhymes*. The above division of the feet does not, however, conform to that of *al-ṭawīl,* or any other meter. The correct division is: *yaqūlu | abū shādū | fi min ʿuẓ | mi mā shakā*.

41 From the root *q-l-l* and unrelated to *qawl* (root *q-w-l*).

42 From the root *q-y-l* and unrelated to *qawl* (root *q-w-l*).

43 The last three forms all derive from the root in question, namely, *q-w-l,* and the last two are, indeed, forms of the verb itself; it is thus a specious and circular argument to speak of them as being etymons of *qāla* "to speak."

44 I.e., the Kaaba at Mecca.

45 The first day of Dhū l-Ḥijjah (the month of pilgrimage), 1074 fell on June 25, AD 1664.

46 That the author should apply such uncomplimentary terms to himself is, of course, surprising. One interpretation is that he held his listeners, as ignorant laymen, in such contempt that he regarded any attempt to bring true knowledge down to their level as no better than buffoonery, etc.

47 *The Thousand Lines on Grammar*: the *Alfiyyat al-naḥw* of Muḥammad ibn Mālik (ca. 600–72/1203–74), a very popular textbook of grammar in the form of a poem of about a thousand lines.

48 "Muḥammad, Malik's son, *has said*...": the opening line of the *Alfiyyah*; in Arabic, the past tense may denote "an act which is just completed at the moment, and by the very act, of speaking" (Wright, *Grammar*, 2:1); thus, either the present ("he says") or the past ("he has said") is acceptable in such a context.

49 A piece of misdirection by al-Shirbīnī, for the poet seems to have been punning, and the first hemistich can also be read (with one metrically valid amendment) as meaning "Then he said, 'It is a keen sword (*māḍī*) in similar words (*bi-qawlin muḍāriʿin*)'/Though that

keen sword is in reality his" (without context, the exact sense of the second hemistich must remain obscure). This interpretation is supported by a verse by Yaḥyā ibn Aḥmad ibn Hudhayl al-Tujībī, where the same double entendre is found in a *nasīb*: the loved one's figure is described as . . . *sayfan ka-sayfi liḥāẓihī / fa-hādhā huwa l-māḍī wa-dhāka muḍāriʿuh* ("a sword like the sword of his glance/For the latter is a keen sword, the former its like" (al-Maqqarī, *Nafḥ al-ṭīb*, 5:489).

50 The following line is taken from one of the poet's famous panegyrics addressed to the Hamdanid ruler of Aleppo, Sayf al-Dawlah (al-Mutanabbī, *Dīwān*, 4:98).

51 "and silence the vowels of his verb": this may be understood both literally, i.e., "and silence (i.e., dissuade) him from moving to perform the action in question" and, taking the words in their specialized grammatical senses, "and put *sukūn*s (the signs written above consonants to show that they are not followed by a vowel) on the verb instead of vowels," referring to the use of jussive forms of the imperfect verb to form negative imperatives; in other words, the hero of the panegyric completes his action before any can tell him "Don't!"

52 On such compound proper nouns, see vol. 1, n. 383.

53 Though *shādūf* is used today to describe the whole device (which works on the same principle as a well sweep), al-Shirbīnī's statement implies that it was, in his day, *abū shādūf* (literally "the thing with the cantilevered arm") that had that sense; thus the poet's *kunyah* would refer to the device itself, making the appellation more derogatory than if it were to mean simply "the person with the *shādūf*." The raising of water manually was among the most physically demanding, lowest paid, and least regarded of agricultural tasks in Egypt before mechanization. Pictures of the *shādūf* may be found in Lane (*Manners*, 327) and Hinds and Badawi (*Dictionary*, 975).

54 "scoop" (*qaṭwah*): "A vessel . . . with four cords attached to it . . . . Two men, each holding two of the cords, throw up the water by means of this vessel" (Lane, *Manners*, 328); the *qaṭwah* is made of leather.

55 I.e., they added the letters of prolongation ا (*alif*) and و (*waw*) to the original word شدف, making it شادوف; and, indeed, *fāʿūl* is an intensive pattern (cf., e.g., *jāsūs* "spy"), so that *shādūf* would be a logical formation from the root, in the sense of "that which constantly scoops."

56 This is misinformation, because the root of *ab* is *ʾ-b-w*, that of *āba* is *ʾ-w-b*.

57 I.e., Ibn Zurayq al-Baghdādī (d. ca. 420/1029) (*GAS*, 2:700–1); the line is from his famous *ʿayniyyah* called *Al-Qaṣīdah al-Andalusiyyah* (see, e.g., al-Ṣafadī, *Al-Wāfī*, 11:112).

58 *ābin*: sic, for *āʾib*.

59 See Vrolijk, *Bringing a Laugh*, 134 (Arabic).

60 "a perfect tense . . . verb" (*fiʿl māḍī*): in reality, the verb is imperfect. The word *māḍī* ("perfect") does not occur in Ibn Sūdūn's original.

61 *abū* . . .: an example of the rhetorical figure called "restraint," which will be referred to explicitly at §11.9.8 and §11.10.17.

62 See vol. 1, n. 430, on the use of letters to represent numbers.

63 Cf. Q Āl ʿImrān 3:12 *wa-yunshiʾu l-saḥāb*.

64 The verses are very similar to others written by Ibn Nubātah (686–768/1287–1366) about an Abyssinian youth, and the last hemistich is identical to Ibn Nubātah's (al-Ibshīhī, *Al-Mustaṭraf*, 2:230).

65 These verses occur in varying forms in disparate contexts; see, e.g., Ibn Khallikān, *Wafayāt*, 6:152ff., where they are described as having being addressed to a youthful Ḥasan ibn Wahb (later an important official in the Abbasid bureaucracy), after the latter objected to the judge's own advances.

66 These verses are quoted, with different frame stories and differences in wording, by, e.g., al-Masʿūdī (*Murūj*, 4:23) and Ibn Khallikān (*Wafayāt*, 6:152ff.), who attribute them to Rashīd ibn Isḥāq (b. 240/854, d. ?), and by al-Iṣfahānī (al-Iṣfahānī, *Al-Aghānī*, 18:91), who attributes them to Ibrāhīm ibn Abī Muḥammad al-Yazīdī.

67 Q Baqarah 2:155.

68 Q Sharḥ 94:5, 6.

69 See n. 304.

70 Q Sharḥ 94:1 «Have we not dilated thy bosom [with joy]?»

71 In Q Sharḥ 94:5 and 6, the word *ʿusr* ("hardship") occurs between two occurrences of the word *yusr* ("ease").

72 In fact, the meter requires an *i* after the *l*; by claiming that the word has no desinential inflection al-Shirbīnī may be pointing to the essentially colloquial character of the word when used in this sense, with *i*, versus literary *qull.*

73 Al-Shirbīnī later contradicts this by attributing the form without *ah* to the colloquial; both forms are, however, cited in the classical dictionaries (e.g., al-Fīrūzābādhī, *Qāmūs*, 3:40, s.vv. *qillah* and *qull*).

74 "the Red Death" (*al-mawt al-aḥmar*): i.e., "violent death" (Lane, *Lexicon*, 642).

75 This word occurs in the colloquial glossary of Yūsuf al-Maghribī (d. 1019/1610), who vocalizes it *ʿatr* and connects it to literary Arabic *ʿitrīf* (al-Maghribī: *ʿatrīf*), which he defines as "one who is base, licentious, daring, energetic, tyrannical, and overbearing" (al-Maghribī, *Dafʿ*, 30b). In modern Egyptian, *ʿitrah* means "strong, of outstanding personality" and is used, for example, of neighborhood heroes.

76 The poet is Ibn Sūdūn, to be found in Dār al-Kutub MS Adab 329 and related mansucripts of his *dīwān* (on which, see Vrolijk, *Bringing a Laugh*, 75, 104–5 English). I am indebted to Arnoud Vrolijk for this information.

77 Perhaps from Turkish *kulak* "ear, ear-shaped appendage, flap" and, in any case, without etymological connection to *qill*, etc.

78 The *qullah* is made of earthenware, the neck is narrower than the body, and it has an earthenware membrane pierced with holes that acts as a filter between the body and the neck (Hinds and Badawi, *Dictionary*, 971, illus.).

79 ʿAlī ibn al-Ḥasan, called Ṣurra Durr (d. 465/1073).

80 Al-Maydānī, *Majmaʿ*, 1:155.

81 These verses appear, with differences, in al-Shāfiʿī's collected works, where they are described as being of dubious attribution (al-Shāfiʿī, *Shiʿr*, 265).

82 "incarnation and corporealization" (*al-ḥulūl wa-l-tajsīm*): "After a long fight among the theological schools, the incorporeality of

God was recognized by Islam . . . ." (Tj. de Boer, "Djism," in *EI2*). Al-Shirbīnī may be obfuscating here: al-Mujassimah is a word used by their opponents to attack the Hanbalis and other theological conservatives, who, however, have no connection with the Ahl al-Ḥulūl, who were mystics whose belief in incarnation of the divine in the human was widely considered heretical; the celebrated mystic al-Ḥusayn ibn Manṣūr al-Ḥallāj (244–309/857–922) was executed in Baghdad for such beliefs.

83 See vol. 1, §4.2.2.

84 "Properly" in the sense that an *alif* would be attached to the word in the literary language as the sign of the accusative (making it نحيفا). The disappearance of most such inflections from colloquial Arabic is one of the features that most clearly separate it from the literary idiom.

85 Ibn al-Wardī (681–749/1292–1349) (al-Ghuzūlī, *Maṭāliʿ*, 1:81). For a discussion of the use made by fourteenth-century poets of the fact that *qamar* ("moon; beautiful person/face") and *qimār* ("gambling") share the same root in Arabic, see Rosenthal, *Gambling*, 143, where these verses are quoted in translation, with a difference in the two last words, al-Ghuzūlī reading *fa-hwa qamar* ("He is a moon") which, according to Rosenthal, may be taken as a pun meaning "He has won." Al-Shirbīnī reads *anti qamar* ("You (fem.) are the moon"), which should then mean "You have won!"

86 Q Ṣāfāt 87:88; the reference is to Ibrāhīm (Abraham) and his rejection of star worship.

87 *qaṭīm*: derived, according to Dozy, *Supplément*, from Latin *catamitus*.

88 Q Aʿrāf 7:133: "So we sent them the flood and the locusts and the *qummal* and the frogs and the blood"—al-Shirbīnī probably treats *qaml* and *qummal* as the same because of their identical consonantal skeletons; al-Bayḍāwī in his commentary glosses *qummal* as "full-grown ticks or, according to some, the young of the locust, before their wings sprout" (al-Bayḍāwī, *Anwār*, 1:356).

89 I.e., *Ḥayāt al-ḥayawān al-kubrā* by Kamāl al-Dīn Muḥammad ibn Mūsā al-Damīrī (742–808/1341–1405).

90 Al-Damīrī himself attributes this claim to "the Arabs" and dismisses it as "one of their lies" (al-Damīrī, *Ḥayawān*, 2:200).

91 Unit nouns typically are formed from collective nouns by the addition of the "feminine" ending *ah*; thus, *qamlah* really means simply "a louse," though al-Shirbīnī insists on creating a matching masculine form *qāmil* from the active participle.

92 Al-Shirbīnī's implication that *ʿuqrubān* and *thuʿlubān* are dual forms is spurious: even though they end in *ān*, formally identical to the nominative dual ending, they are singular nouns denoting the male of the species (though according to some authorities, *ʿuqrubān* may denote, rather than the male scorpion, the earwig or some other creature); nor could *ʿuqrubān* be dual in the verse—which is presumably of al-Shirbīnī's own composition—since its position in the sentence would require the genitive dual ending *ayn*. Consequently, his contention on the basis of these forms that the dual may be used as a form of address to a single person, while not necessarily incorrect (see n. 93), is irrelevant.

93 Q Qāf 50:24 *alqiyā fī jahannama kulla kaffārin ʿanīd* "Throw into Hell every stubborn ingrate!" According to al-Bayḍāwī, the verb is either addressed by God to two persons (e.g., the two angels who guard Hell Fire) and is thus dual, or to one person but using the dual form for extra force (as al-Shirbīnī seems to imply here), or not dual at all but of the "energetic" form, i.e., *alqiyan*.

94 Al-Shirbīnī's quotation apparently conflates two sayings of al-Ḥajjāj's, namely, *yā Ḥarsiyyu-ḍrib ʿunuqahu* ("Strike his neck" (singular)) (al-Mubarrad, *Al-Kāmil*, 2:96)—a passage in which the words *yā ghulām* "Boy!" also occur—and *yā Ḥarsiyyu-ḍriban ʿunuqahu* ("O Ḥarsī, strike his neck") (al-Mubarrad, *Al-Kāmil*, 1:383), the latter using the energetic form (see n. 93); i.e., the quotation does not in fact support al-Shirbīnī's contention.

95 Neither word is etymologically related to *burghūth*, but the consonantal skeletons of the first two words, when joined, yield the consonantal skeleton of the latter (i.e., برغوث = بر + غوث).

96 These lines have not been located in al-Suyūṭī's works and are not quoted by al-Damīrī; they may be from the former's unpublished *Al-Ṭurthūth fī fawā'id al-burghūth* (*The Ṭurthūth [a medicinal plant] on the Benefits of Fleas* (*GAL*, 2:154 and *Suppl.*, 2:192, no. 218); elsewhere, they are described as anonymous.

97 Al-Shirbīnī contends that all lice are female because the word for a single louse (*qamlah*) is grammatically feminine.

98 An introductory formula for riddles.

99 The diminutive is restricted in modern Egyptian to a closed list of words. However, the use of diminutives here and elsewhere by al-Shirbīnī imply that this class was productive in his day.

100 I.e., the words vary only in the absence or presence of a dot below the first letter, حمير (*himmayr*) versus جمير (*jimmayr*).

101 *The Book of the Physick of the Poor* (*Kitāb ṭibb al-fuqarā'*): probably the *Kitāb al-fuqarā' wa-l-masākīn* (*The Book of the Poor and the Pitiful*) (*GAL*, 1:271) of Abū Bakr Muḥammad ibn Zakariyyā al-Rāzī ("Rhazes") (ca. 251–313/865–925).

102 Though metathesis may generate new forms in Arabic, al-Shirbīnī's proposed etymology is unlikely, because *ṣībān* derives from the root *ṣ-'-b*, while *ṣubyān* is from *ṣ-b-y*.

103 The verb means "to soap"; the true verbal noun is *ṣabyanah*; *ṣībyān* ("boys") is for comic effect.

104 *Al-Qāmūs al-muḥīṭ* defines *nimnim*/*numnum* as "whiteness that appears in the fingernails of young people" (al-Fīrūzābādhī, *Qāmūs*, 4:183).

105 A variety of mint.

106 Cf. *nam*, sg. imperative verb: "Sleep!"

107 Al-Ḥarīrī: *Al-Maqāmah al-ḥalabiyyah* (no. 46) (*Maqāmāt*, 372).

108 Word puzzles are an ancient genre in Arabic literature (see further *EAL*, s.v. "lughz"); for other similar examples, see, e.g., al-Ibshīhī, *Al-Mustaṭraf*, 2:233–37.

109 Al-Shirbīnī explains later on (§11.18.5) that *ṭājin* ("casserole") may be deconstructed as *ṭa'* + *jinn*, i.e., "tread on (or screw) some jinn!" while *ṭāfiyah* (a metaphasis of *ṭā'ifah* ("company, group of people, etc.")) equals *ṭa'* + *fiyya*, i.e., "tread on (or screw) me!"; *yāsamīn*

("jasmine") is to be understood as equivalent to *ya's* ("despair") plus *mayn* ("lying").

110 "An old man and a maiden in the belly of a bird" (*shaykh wa-jāriyah fī baṭn 'uṣfūr*): the sentence may also be read *shaykhun wajā ri'ah* ("an old man stabbed a lung" (while cutting up the bird)).

111 I.e., عُنّاب ("jujube fruit") since the first letter of the word is ع, called *'ayn*, which also means "eye," leaving ناب "fang" as the rest of the word.

112 The word is unvoweled in al-Shirbīnī's text but is given here as in the autograph manuscript of Ibn Sūdūn's elegy on his mother's death quoted below (see Vrolijk, *Bringing a Laugh*, 57–58 Arabic).

113 Many of the children's words cited by al-Shirbīnī in the following passage are current in modern Egyptian Arabic. Those unattested today or used with a different meaning are: *namnam*—unattested (but cf. *namnim* "to nibble" and "to make tiny" (Hinds and Badawi, *Dictionary*, 887), in which latter sense the example given concerns food (al-Shirbīnī's sense is confirmed in the verses of Ibn Sūdūn's that follow); *buff*—used today to warn a child that food is hot (informants); *aḥḥ*—used today, inter alia, as "an exclamation expressing reaction to extreme heat or cold ~ ouch!" (Hinds and Badawi, *Dictionary*, 8); *wāwah*—today "a hurt place" (on a child's body) (Hinds and Badawi, *Dictionary*, 921), but see n. 117, below.

114 Compare the modern proverb *illi 'āyiz id-daḥḥ ma-yqul-shi aḥḥ* "he who wants something nice shouldn't say 'Ouch!'" (where *daḥḥ* is understood by some to mean "eggs," so that the proverb implies that if you want eggs, you must put up with having your hand pecked by the hen).

115 Dozy, *Supplément*, 1:98 : "en parlant d'un chameau, rendre un son qui ressemble au glouglou de la bouteille."

116 I.e., the words are identical, except for the initial letter (أح، دح، بح).

117 In modern Egyptian, *wāwah* means "a hurt place, bruise, scratch," etc. on a child's body; this sense fits better in the verse that follows (see next note) and has been translated as such there.

118 "You who stole . . . 'Yumyum'": al-Shirbīnī fails to comment on the word *ninnā*, which is still current, as a "word used to lull a child to sleep" (Hinds and Badawi, *Dictionary*, 887).

119 The poem from which these lines are taken occurs in Vrolijk's edition (Vrolijk, *Bringing a Laugh*, 57–58 Arabic); see also ibid., 44–46 (English) for comments on this poem.

120 Literally "bend me, twist me."

121 I.e., the two words are identical in form (allowing for the conventional lengthening of the final vowel of *taḥnīnī* at the end of a verse) but different in meaning.

122 Al-Shirbīnī's formulation is unclear, but he probably means that there exists another type of body vermin in addition to those already named and it is called either *liḥḥays* or *liqqays* (probably diminutive forms, cf. *ḥimmayr*, etc., above). Neither word seems to be known today. Even al-Shirbīnī's equation of (the classical) forms *laḥisa* and *laqisa* is problematic, as the latter is not recorded in the lexica as meaning "lick," but rather, in the expression *laqisat nafsuhu*, "to be bad-tempered . . . to want to vomit" and in the expression *laqisat nafsuhu ilā* "to be greedy for a thing" (*WKAS*, 1084).

123 "according to the analogy of Fuṭays": see vol. 1, n. 366.

124 The word is no longer attested in these senses, but note modern Egyptian *malḥūs* "soft in the head, cuckoo" (Hinds and Badawi, *Dictionary*, 781).

125 Implying that the creature itself is rendered more harmful by virtue of the unpleasantness of its synonyms and associated words.

126 For no apparent reason, al-Shirbīnī here switches to Form II of the verb, which means "to give to lick."

127 Arab grammarians traditionally recognize three parts of speech, namely, the verb (*fiʿl*), the noun (*ism*), and the particle (*ḥarf* or *adāh*, which includes prepositions, adverbs, conjunctions, and interjections). Some grammarians, however, regard the interjections (*aṣwāṭ*) as "hav[ing], by either origin or use, a certain verbal force," because they are "either originally Imperatives . . . or equivalent to Imperatives." They therefore call them *asmāʾ al-afʿāl* ("verbal substantives") (Wright, *Grammar*, 1:296B), thus creating a "fourth part of speech," although the authority for al-Shirbīnī's naming this category "residual" (*khālifah*) is not clear.

128 Thus, in its more general sense, the word denotes "ring," though in relation to a garment it means the yoke or neck band.

129 Q Āl ʿImrān 3:180.

130 The verb means "to surround with a ring."

131 I.e., with the rearrangement of the dots, جبتك حمره becomes ختنك حمزه.

132 Though, in fact, *jāba* (root *j-w-b*) has no etymological relationship to *jabba* (root *j-b-b*).

133 The meaning of the verb is as given; *jubbatan* is for the argument.

134 At the beginning of the Ottoman period, Khāyir Bey, the Mamluk general turned Ottoman governor, "reportedly cut off half of every Mamluke's beard, handed it to him and said, 'You must abide by the Ottoman law, shave your beards, wear tight sleeves, and do everything like the Ottomans'" (Winter, *Egyptian Society*, 9).

135 Cf. al-Ibshīhī, *Al-Mustaṭraf*, 1:38.

136 I.e., tears and blushes.

137 *nakhīl*: "palms."

138 *minkhāl*: a variant of *munkhal* ("sieve").

139 The literary construction in which a verb is followed by a verbal noun of the same root (*mafʿūl muṭlaq*) gives an intensive sense; thus "which they shovel a shoveling" = "which they shovel intensively (or in great quantities)." In correct literary usage, the verbal noun would take the accusative ending *an*, but in the semi-colloquial, semi-literary poetic idiom employed here, this ending is dropped. The poet also plays with the internal form of the word (*jarf* is the standard verbal noun, *jarīf* an unattested form), a technique that is in fact typical of *sīrah* (epic) poetry, though in the latter such changes constitute a complex form of wordplay and provide much of the aesthetic pleasure, which does not seem to be the case here.

140 Because the pronominal suffix *hū* of *yajrufūhū* is masculine, while *nukhālah* is feminine; i.e., he should have said *yajrufūhā*.

141 Because the feminine pronominal suffix *hā* is a long syllable.

142 "truncation" (*tarkhīm*): "the rejection of one or more of [the] final letters [of a word]" (Wright, *Grammar*, 2:88A), though this applies primarily to vocatives, as in the example that follows.

143 The verse is by the pre-Islamic poet Imru' al-Qays; the translation is adapted from Arberry's *Seven Odes*, 62.

144 Fāṭim (in the Arabic Fāṭima or Fāṭimu) is the truncated form of Fāṭimatu.

145 I.e., one should understand the phrase as *shabīhu qishr al-nukālah yajrufūhu* "like *the husks* of bran that they shovel."

146 See al-Damīrī, *Ḥayawān*, 2:374.

147 Bashshār ibn Burd (ca. 98–167/714–84) (*Dīwān*, 2:189).

148 "They spared not one and let not one remain" (*mā khallā wa-lā baqqah*): al-Shirbīnī puns on two meanings of *wa-lā baqqah* in this colloquial verse: according to the first (as in the translation), *baqqah* is to be understood as a Form II verb, "it caused to remain"; according to the second, as a unit noun ("a bedbug"), thus "[and left] not one single bedbug."

149 See n. 6.

150 Q An'ām 6:74.

151 For an illustration of a present-day *maḥlabah*, see Hinds and Badawi, *Dictionary*, pl. A3.

152 For an illustration of a *qādūs*, see Hinds and Badawi, *Dictionary*, pl. E11.

153 The final *ih* is of special interest to the linguist, because it provides rare evidence for the behavior of a short vowel in a pre-modern colloquial dialect (the values of such vowels normally being hidden by the orthography). In this case, the ending *i(h)* of *qarrūfih* may be taken as evidence of an alternation between *i(h)* after consonants that are neither emphatic nor back, and *a(h)* in other environments in reflexes of the old Arabic "feminine" ending *a(h)* (see Blanc, *Perte*, and Davies, *Profile*, 81–85). Al-Shirbīnī provides another example below: *libbi(h)* for *libba(h)* (§11.23.9).

154 In fact, *kūz* is from the root *k-w-z*, *kazz* from the root *k-z-z*.

155 "the analogy of Fuṭays": see vol. 1, n. 366.

156 "Large handle-less earthenware jar used for storing and filtering water" (Hinds and Badawi, *Dictionary*, 389; pl. A7).

157 *qirr* (cited in the lexica as *qurr*): by stating that the word has "no vowel after the *r*," the author emphasizes that he is thinking of it in its colloquial form.

158 This fanciful etymology depends, for any semblance of plausibility, on the consonantal outline in Arabic script of the two putative etymons; thus, قر (*qirr*) + وفي (*wafiya*) = قروفي, which is equivalent in sound to *qarrūfi(h)*.

159 The letter *wāw* functions as both a consonant (*w*) and as the marker of the long vowel *ū*.

160 Using the *nisbah* ("relative") ending *ī* to form an adjective from the place name, as is conventional.

161 Q Naḥl 16:66.

162 I.e., she added *-ah*.

163 Literally "with nunation (*tanwīn*) and the vowel *i* after the *m*." Nunation is the addition of *n* to a short vowel at the end of a substantive and serves various grammatical functions in literary Arabic (see Wright, *Grammar*, 1:12) but is generally absent from the colloquial dialects. In this case, the form *yawmin* (which occurs twice more in the Ode) probably represents a conflation of *yawm* and conjunctionalizing *an* (*an al-maṣdariyyah*), meaning "on the day when."

164 Muslim fasts, such as that of the month of Ramadan, are restricted to the hours between sunrise and sunset.

165 The point echoes a wider position taken by the pious of the day, namely, that "the principle of *wara*ʿ ('scrupulousness') . . . prohibits a man of religion from accepting favors from a ruler. Any material benefit which came from the rulers was *ḥarām* (morally tainted), because the rulers oppressed the people. Since the high officials could not maintain an extravagant standard of living on their salaries, they must obviously have accepted presents from fellahs and other simple people" (Winter, *Society and Religion*, 263).

166 The ascription of partners to God (*shirk*), or polytheism, contradicts the fundamental tenet of the Muslim faith, that "There is no god but God."

167 See al-Ḥillī, *Al-Badīʿiyyah*, 262.

168 I.e., *fuq lī* and *fa-qlī* are identical in skeleton except that the second is augmented by the additional *alif* (which al-Shirbīnī counts as a consonant); on *al-jinās al-mazīd* see vol. 1, n. 242 and on *al-jinās al-muḥarraf* see Cachia, *Rhetorician*, 25.

169 I.e., the poet adds a dot above the letter ع so that عم ("paternal uncle") becomes غم ("grief") (paronomasia) and puns on the identicality of form of *khāl* ("maternal uncle"), which, in the inflected form in which it occurs in the verse, reads *khālī*, and of *khālī* ("devoid (of), empty (of)") in line-final "pausal" form.

170 I.e., ʿAlī ibn Abī Ṭālib.

171 I.e., Cain's murdering Abel; see Q Māʾidah 5:27–31.

172 "may the envious not prevail" (*al-ḥasūd lā yasūd*): a formula against envy and the evil eye.

173 The word is unattested but glossed below.

174 Al-Shirbīnī correctly identifies the colloquial form *aysham* (and the related *tayshimah* and *mayshūm* below) with the classical root *sh-ʾ-m*; however, this particular colloquial metathesis is no longer attested in Egyptian Arabic. On the other hand, *shūm* (brought in further on) is probably unrelated to this root.

175 As the story of Ṭuways (see Glossary) makes clear, the *mashʾūm* is not personally responsible for the dire events that become associated with his name; rather, he carries an aura of ill fortune.

176 Not the name of a tree but, apparently, of a quality of wood, cf. modern Egyptian *shūmah* "quarterstaff, cudgel."

177 Meaning, perhaps, that the poet would be happy to be in a situation in which condolences are required but would make even that gesture under protest.

178 The male sandgrouse flies long distances in the desert to fill its breast feathers with water, which its young then suck.

179 As usual, al-Shirbīnī disingenuously explains away a colloquial form (*minnū* versus literary *minhu*) as due to the constraints of meter (see vol. 1, p. liv).

180 As above, *akhūhu* follows colloquial morphology (albeit with the addition of the pronominal suffix in literary form), while *akhīhi* conforms to literary grammar; the meter would not, however, be changed.

181 *khanfūr* is not considered an active participle form.

182 *Sic*, but should read "paternal uncle's"; see what follows.

183 I.e., Muḥaylibah.

184 I.e., Khanāfir son of Fasāqil.

185 Al-Shirbīnī insists on the literary voweling for these two forms (versus colloquial *yiqarraṭ/yiḍarraṭ*), thus turning them into pseudo-learned forms, presumably to emphasize their ludicrousness as objects of scholarly discussion.

186 The word has not, in fact, been mentioned before, unless al-Shirbīnī is referring to the immediately preceding sentence, in which case the "two forms" would be the formal and the colloquial vowelings.

187 The lines do not appear in Abū Nuwās's collected works, and the attribution is dubious.

188 "Earringed" (*muqarṭaq*): al-Shirbīnī's interpretation of the word in this sense is at odds with its generally accepted meaning, namely, "dressed in a close-fitting tunic," and also stretches the rules of the consonantal root system, by which *qurṭ* belongs to the root *q-r-ṭ*, while *muqarṭaq* belongs to *q-r-ṭ-q*.

189 Al-Shirbīnī plays on the double meaning of *bayḍ* as "eggs" and "testicles."

190 Perhaps the wolf spider, which carries its eggs conspicuously on its back.

191 The latter is a more formal term than *bayḍ*.

192 *Khiṣy* may also be read as *khaṣī* "eunuch," and, in the following, al-Shirbīnī appears to be making a joke along the lines of "it takes two eunuchs to make a whole man."

193 Al-Shirbīnī repeats the assertion regarding the related form *khiṣā* below, but there is no authority in the lexica for the use of either in this latter sense, and his following argument that the two words

derive from one another is meaningless, in that they are (according to al-Shirbīnī) one and the same.

194 "and additionally they are in the position of annexation while it is in the position of the elevated and erected vowels": in grammar, *iḍāfah* ("annexation") is the genitive relationship between two nouns such as *ḥikmat allāh* "the wisdom of God" or *bayḍatu fiḍḍah* "an egg of silver," in which only the first noun may take the nominative (*rafʿ*, meaning, in nongrammatical usage, "elevatedness") or accusative (*naṣb*, meaning in nongrammatical usage "erection, construction") cases (see Wright, *Grammar*, 2:198–234). Al-Shirbīnī is saying that the testicles are equivalent to the second term in such a construction, while the penis, with its "elevatedness" and "erection," is equivalent to the first.

195 The lines have been attributed to Abū l-Ḥusayn al-Jazzār (601/1204–5 to 679/1280–81) (see Ibn Ḥijjah, *Thamarāt*, 48).

196 A further dig at the king, since the poet is saying that he is like both penis and testicles, while the king is like an anus that is large enough to accommodate both.

197 "No, may I be divorced—times three" (*lā ʿalayya al-ṭalāq thalāthah*): which may be read without a pause between *al-ṭalāq* and *thalāthah*, in which case it means "No, may I be triply divorced!" (the standard formula of irrevocable divorce, frequently used in oaths) or with a pause in the same place, in which case it means "No, may I be divorced! Three [thousand]!"

198 *duldūl*: by analogy to modern Egyptian *daldil* "to dangle" but in the classical lexica "hedgehog."

199 *zubb*: in its reflex *zibb*, a standard, coarse, modern colloquial term.

200 *ayr*: a literary but still obscene term.

201 *ghurmūl*: "The penis . . . (in an absolute sense) . . . or a large and flaccid penis before its prepuce is cut off . . . or [the penis] of a solid-hoofed animal" (Lane, *Lexicon*, 2253).

202 *duldul*: presumably a by-form of *duldūl* above.

203 *dhakar*: another formal and not obscene term, occuring (as *zakar*) in modern colloquial Arabic.

204 *khuṣā* with *u*: albeit al-Shirbīnī does not, in fact, cite this form above.

205 I.e., *khiṣw* and, presumably, *khuṣw*.

206 I.e., *khuṣā* and *khiṣā*.

207 Ramzī mentions three villages of this name, of which the most important appears to be that on the northern edge of Cairo and which is also known as Khuṣūṣ ʿAyn Shams (Ramzī, *Qāmūs*, 2/1:33).

208 There is no such verb, though *khaṣā*, *yakhṣī* ("to geld") exists.

209 al-Ṭunayn: the reference is obscure; elsewhere (§11.29.9) *ṭunayn* is defined as "little sheaf of sugarcane."

210 In fact, the two words derive from separate roots, *līf* from *l-y-f* and *multaff* from *l-f-f*.

211 A favorite image of the classical poets, in the sense of a promise that is not kept or a person who fails to fulfil his promises.

212 The base form from which the "construct" form *nazlat* derives.

213 Ramzī lists four villages whose names appear in this form, with the definite article, and several dozen in which the word is the first part of a genitive construction (*nazlat*...; "the settlement of..."); the word appears to survive in modern Egyptian in this sense in place names only.

214 The verse that follows is taken from the *muʿallaqah* of Imruʾ al-Qays (*Dīwān*, 19), but the verse contains neither of the roots under discussion.

215 "As for those [peasants] who have plundered and burned villages and killed their inhabitants, they [the Inspectors] search for them and hunt them down using the best of means, wherever they may be on the face of the earth, be it even 'on the red bull's horn' [?], and apply against them the most severe and cruelest punishments slowly, so that they reveal the names of their partners, and then they seize these. [Having seized them] they flay them alive and break their hands and legs and recover from them the stolen wealth. Thus they put an end to them all for the betterment of the world" (Shalabī, *Siyāḥatnāmah*, 434).

216 "However that may be" (*fa-ʿalā kull ḥāl*): this discreet disclaimer, and the framing of the whole passage in terms of "former times," appear

to hint that the situation at the time of writing differed from that just described; the rest of the account focuses on injustices committed by Inspectors. In 1599, almost a century before al-Shirbīnī, the Turkish visitor ʿĀlī Muṣṭafā denigrated the Inspectors (*kushshāf*, sg. *kāshif*: "District Directors"), writing "Strange is also the despotry of the district directors (*kashif*) over the poor people, the tyranny and onslaught of a band of revenue farmers (*mültezim*) on the subjects (*raʿaya*) on the basis of the Circassian law. Some good-for-nothing, some roistering rough of the *jundis* of Egypt, who does not possess five aspers, pledges the revenues of a province and becomes a *kashif*" (Tietze, *Description*, 56).

217 "the suppression of the first term of a genitive annexation" (*ḥadhf muḍāf*): on "annexation" (*iḍāfah*), see **n. 194**.

218 "Ibrāhīm the Beloved" (Ibrāhīm al-Khalīl): i.e., "the Beloved of God," cf. Q Nisāʾ 4:125 «and God took Ibrahim as His beloved» (and similarly Isrāʾ 17:73); for the commentators' anecdotal explanation of the circumstances in which the epithet was first used, see Sale, *Koran*, 75 note f.

219 Ibn Nubātah (686–768/1287–1366) according to al-Ibshīhī (*Al-Mustaṭraf*, 2:34).

220 "juxtaposed contrasts in the wording" (*al-ṭibāq al-lafẓī*): i.e., "smile" and "tears," "weep" and "laugh."

221 The pre-Islamic poet ʿAlqamah (see *Al-Mufaḍḍaliyyāt*, nos. 119, 392).

222 These verses do not appear in al-Qāḍī l-Fāḍil's published works.

223 Al-Kumayt ibn Zayd (60/679–80 to 126/743–44) (*Dīwān*, 236).

224 Unlike other vultures, the Egyptian vulture (*rakhamah*; *Neophron percnopterus*) has largely white plumage.

225 "its two nests": perhaps meaning "on the head and in the beard."

226 A slightly different version of the above is to be found in his collected works (Ibn Durayd, 308).

227 Al-ʿAqīq and al-Liwā: literally, "the channel worn by a torrent" and "the winding sands," names inherited from and evocative of pre-Islamic poetry.

228 "they saw impurity," etc.: the point is unclear.

229 I.e., the poet says *shābat ʿawāriḍī*, with a nonanimate plural noun (*ʿawāriḍī*) following a feminine singular verb (*shābat*); this is, however, correct according to formal Arabic grammar, and al-Shirbīnī's insinuation that it represents a special rural usage is (presumably deliberately) misleading; moreover, the second of his two proposed alternatives (*shābū ʿawāriḍī*) is itself incorrect in that the non-animate plural noun should not be preceded by a plural verb.

230 I.e., why does he use the form that is homophonic with the other sense mentioned rather than the less ambiguous verbal noun *nuzūl* ("descending")?

231 *Nazlah* is grammatically feminine, *nuzūl* masculine.

232 "the words of Abū Nuwās": not in his collected works.

233 See vol. 1, §5.3.14.

234 Cf. G. J. H. van Gelder, "Shiʿr," in *EI2*: "If traditions are to be believed, the great bards of the Dj̲āhiliyya considered that the poem was the speech of a god or of a dj̲innī (demon)."

235 Ibn al-Fāriḍ is buried in Cairo's Southern Cemetery, close to the Muqaṭṭam Hills, at the foot of al-ʿĀriḍ, the rocky outcrop on which stand the early Ottoman *khānaqāh* (lodge) and tomb of the Sufi Shāhīn al-Khalwatī.

236 Neither *ṣārī* (root *ṣ-r-y*) nor *ṣurr* (root *ṣ-r-r*) is related to *ṣāra* (root *ṣ-y-r*). The *ṣurr* (in other sources usually *ṣurrah*) was the annual cash allocation in support of the wages, pensions, and alms for various categories of servitors, guards, and beneficiaries attached to the Two Sanctuaries (al-Ḥaramayn) of Mecca and Medina, which had been administered from Egypt since the time of the Mamluks (see Shaw, *Financial*, 254ff.).

237 See n. 163.

238 "And ask the village" (*wa-s'al al-qaryah*): Q Yūsuf 12:82; the verse is used in textbooks on rhetoric as an example of "ellipsis" (*ījāz*) achieved through "curtailment" (*ḥadhf*).

239 The innuendo is either sexual or implies that he goes off with his crowbar to make holes in the mud walls of houses or animal pens and so enter and burgle them.

240 *shahlāṭ*: the word is unattested elsewhere.

241 The conquest of Egypt began in 18/639.

242 "The Muslim jurists disagree whether Egypt was taken by force... or by treaty.... Behind the theoretical dispute... lay the practical problem of how to legitimise any Muslim demands for increasing taxes without violating Islamic law" (J.-L. Arnaud and J. Jankowski, "Miṣr," in *EI2*).

243 See Ibn ʿAbd al-Ḥakam, *Futūḥ*, 87.

244 The two words are unrelated, *dīn* belonging to the root *d-y-n*, while *dīwān* is a Persian loanword, assimilable to the root *d-w-n*.

245 Meaning, perhaps, "different nations" (i.e., brings together Turks, Circassians, and others, with Egyptians).

246 The attribution is dubious; elsewhere, these verses are described as anonymous.

247 Al-Shirbīnī plays with the colloquial use of *rūḥ* as a reflexive pronoun ("I void my loose bowels all over *myself*") and its basic meaning of "spirit, breath of life," as though the poet had said, "I void my loose bowels on my Self."

248 Al-Shirbīnī's intent is not clear: it is a verb, *harra*, with which the commentary should be concerned, and not a noun; and the plural of *hirr* (if this is what is intended) is normally given as *hirarah*.

249 I.e., either "you will observe the kind of *hurār* just described" or, punningly, "you will observe that people have voided their loose bowels there."

250 The meaning of the verb is as given above.

251 I.e., *ḥidhāʾ*, its literary reflex.

252 *nisāʾ*... *niswah*: literary forms, in contrast to colloquial *niswān*.

253 Q Baqarah 2:195.

254 See §11.3.1.

255 I.e., Ḥassān ibn Thābit; on the accusations of cowardice against him, see Ḥassān ibn Thābit, *Dīwān*, 15.

256 River travel was faster and cheaper than travel by land. Gonzales, who traveled in Egypt in 1665–66, notes that the journey from Damietta

to Cairo took five days and that there were daily sailings in both directions (Gonzales, *Voyage*, 71–72).

257 Presumably Masjid al-Khiḍr, a village on the west bank of the eastern branch of the Nile, near Quwisnā (Ramzī, *Qāmūs*, 2/2:202).

258 At this point, al-Shirbīnī substitutes the more colloquial form *ʿabāʾah* (equivalent to modern colloquial *ʿabāyah*) for the literary form *ʿabā(ʾ)* used in the verse.

259 Thus the *ʿabāyah* of Shirbīnī's day differed from that of today, which is usually plain black or brown (cf. Hinds and Badawi, *Dictionary*, 561, illus. 976; see also Lane, *Manners*, 30, 32).

260 Perhaps meaning the Prophet, his daughter Fāṭimah, his son-in-law ʿAlī, and their sons, al-Ḥasan and al-Ḥusayn.

261 In fact, the roots are unrelated: *ʿabāʾ*/*ʿabāʾah* are from *ʿ-b-ʾ*, while *ʿabba*, etc., are from *ʿ-b-b*.

262 Several treatises dealing with the permissibility of listening to music (*samāʿ*) exist, the consensus of the polemicists being that "stringed instruments, the *kūbah* drum, and the *mizmār* [a reed instrument] are forbidden" because of their potential to distract the listener from his religious duties or because of their "salacious associations," the interdiction of the *kūbah* being attributed to its use by *mukhannathūn* ("effeminates") (Nelson, *Art*, 46). The exemption of the *nafīr*, though not mentioned in the best-known treatises, may be attributed to its use in war.

263 I.e., the adjective is being applied metonymically, and it is not the drum that is violent but the beating of it.

264 al-Ṣaghīrī: the name appears here and in the verses that follow in this form in all the witnesses, but no such person existed. Rather, the name is a misreading of the word *al-ṣafīrī,* as found in verses that form part of an account of an apocryphal exchange between the Buyid chief minister and man of letters al-Ṣāḥib ibn ʿAbbād (326–85/938–95) and the celebrated author of *maqāmāt,* Badīʿ al-Zamān al-Hamadhānī (358–98/968–1008), as recounted by al-Ṣafadī (*Al-Ghayth*, 2:105). According to al-Ṣafadī (d. 764/1363), al-Hamadhānī farted in the

presence of al-Ṣāḥib ibn ʿAbbād. Al-Hamadhānī explained the unfortunate noise as *ṣarīr al-takht* ("the creaking of the chair"), to which al-Ṣāḥib responded *bal ṣafīr al-taḥt* ("rather, the whistle of the fundament"). Thus the verses begin, according to al-Ṣafadī, *qul li-l-ṣafīriyyi*, meaning "Tell the ass-whistler . . . ." In addition to this, it should be noted that al-Ṣafadī was himself mistaken, for the verses first occur in the anthology *Yatīmat al-dahr* by al-Thaʿālibī (350–429/961–1038), where they refer not to Badīʿ al-Zamān al-Hamadhānī but to an otherwise unknown jurisprudent called al-Khuḍayrī who committed the same faux pas before al-Ṣāḥib ibn ʿAbbād, whose lines thus properly begin *yā-bna l-Khuḍayrīyyi* ("O Ibn al-Khuḍayrī . . .") (*Yatīmat al-dahr*, 3:198).

265 Cf., e.g., Q Anbiyāʾ 21:81 «And unto Solomon (We subdued) the wind and its raging.» *ʿūd*: "lute."

266 Abū ʿAbd al-Raḥmān Ḥātim ibn ʿUnwān (d. 237/851), known as "the Deaf" (al-Aṣamm), was an ascetic of Balkh, sometimes referred to, for his wise sayings, as "the Luqmān of this nation."

267 The following passage, in rhymed prose, is reminiscent in setting and tone of the *Agony of the Love-Sick Plaintiff and the Teardrop of the Weeper* (*Lawʿat al-shākī wa-damʿat al-bākī*) of Ṣalāḥ al-Dīn Khalīl ibn Aybak al-Ṣafadī (d. 764/1363) and may be intended as an *homage* to—or parody of—the latter.

268 Cf. Q Anʿām 6:95 «Lo! God (it is) who splitteth the grain of corn and the date pit (for sprouting)!»

269 I.e., "until he died."

270 Al-Ghawrī does have preserved works, mostly of poetry, but there is no record of treatises on fake farting.

271 Begins on D and has E flat, B half-flat, and F sharp.

272 "their transitions" (*nahazātuhum*): the meaning is unclear.

273 Al-Ḥillī, *Al-Badīʿiyyah*, 153.

274 The word occurs only in colloquial (modern Egyptian *yadōb*), and its etymology is not obvious; Fischer suggests that it comes from *yā duʾūb "O cares! O pain!" with semantic and phonological

contamination from *dōb/dhōb* "now, immediately," originating in **idhā huwa bi-* (Fischer, *Bildungen*, 156); al-Shirbīnī's connection of the word to *da'b*, of which *du'ūb* must be a plural, is consistent with this, though the reference to the different root *d-b-b* (*dabb*, *dubb*, and *dabīb*, see below) is simply playful.

275 This practice, more often called *dabīb*, is referred to frequently in classical literature, as in the verses by Abū Nuwās cited earlier by al-Shirbīnī (vol. 1, §5.3.8); see further Bosworth, *Underworld*, 119–24 and, for its continuing prominence in the twentieth century, Dunne, "Sexuality," 187.

276 "calculating the money that I owe in tax and weighing out the tax in kind" (*ḥisāb al-māl wa-wazn al-kharāj*): here, and only here, al-Shirbīnī seems to make a distinction between *māl* and *kharāj* as taxes in specie and in kind; elsewhere (§11.8.3) he equates the two.

277 Bahā' al-Dīn Zuhayr (581-656/1186-1258) (*Poetical Works*, 92).

278 The terms that follow (*maẓālim, ziyādāt al-kharāj, 'awā'id, maghārim, kulaf, gharāmat al-baṭṭālīn*) refer mostly to illegal levies that grew up during the seventeenth century and lasted through the eighteenth (for further instances and a discussion, see 'Abd al-Raḥīm, *Al-Rīf*, 135–38); see, further, Glossary, s.v. *maẓālim*.

279 Al-Ma'mūn visited Egypt in 214–15/829–30 to crush a series of Coptic revolts. The following paragraph is found, with differences of detail, in al-Maqrīzī (*Al-Khiṭaṭ*, 1:81).

280 Ramzī identifies the village with Tunnāmil al-Sharqī in the province of al-Sharqiyyah (Ramzī, *Qāmūs*, 2/1:174).

281 An error for Aḥmad ibn Abī Du'ād (see Ibn al-Zubayr, *Al-Dhakhā'ir*, 104), chief judge under the caliph al-Mu'taṣim (r. 218–27/833–42).

282 I.e., by refusing the gift.

283 This paragraph is an abridged quotation from al-Maqrīzī, *Al-Khiṭaṭ*, 1:103 infra.

284 In his *al-Khiṭaṭ*, al-Maqrīzī explains that the term "land-based" (*kharājī*) applied to taxes on agricultural land, collected annually, and any "gifts" taken in kind from the peasants (al-Maqrīzī, *Al-Khiṭaṭ*,

1:103), while "lunar" (*hilālī*) applied to those that were levied on property and commercial enterprises and were collected monthly (ibid., 107). The fact that the latter fell on the urban classes may explain why they are condemned so vehemently in scholarly sources; the former affected only the peasants, and their legitimacy went unchallenged. Al-Maqrīzī goes on to mention that, after being abolished by Aḥmad ibn Ṭūlūn, the lunar taxes were reintroduced by the Fatimids, under the name of *mukūs* (ibid., 104).

285 "with or without the nunation in this verse" (*bi-l-tanwīn wa-ʿadamihi fī hādhā l-bayt*): any of the forms *wa-yawmin* (with nunation) or *wa-yawma* and *wa-yawmi* (without nunation) is metrically and syntactically defensible, the first possibility being the *wāw rubba* construction, the second and third being construable as the first terms of an *iḍāfah*; however, the first alternative, with nunation, has already occurred in the Ode (§11.6.1).

286 "The corvée" (*al-ʿawnah*): as al-Shirbīnī emphasizes in what follows, this form of compulsory labor was used exclusively on the tax farmer's private plot. Another term, *al-sukhrah*, was used of forced labor on public works, especially the maintenance of the irrigation system. The first sort of corvée was abolished in the early nineteenth century, the second in the period before and just after the British occupation in 1882, by which time year-round cotton cultivation had reduced the availability of labor during the summer.

287 Umm Waṭīf is a *kunyah* meaning literally "the mother of the man with the bushy eyebrows." Though the exact point of al-Shirbīnī's remark is obscure, there may be an allusion to the phrase *yā waṭfa* "You (feminine) with the bushy eyebrows" mentioned by al-Maghribī (*Dafʿ*, fol. 35a, 16; Zack, *Egyptian Arabic*, 314) as a term of abuse used by peasants.

288 These are beehive-like domes made by building up courses of dung cakes; a fire is then lit in the hollow interior to dry the dung to prepare it for use as fuel.

289 In traditional Egyptian society, women are rarely referred to by their given names.

290 "the big storage jar" (*al-zal'ah al-kabīrah*): the *zal'ah* is a "large storage jar with handles (usually for water)" (Hinds and Badawi, *Dictionary*, 377, pl. A10).

291 The meaning of both verbs is "to help," the form *'ān* being a colloquialization of the literary Form IV *a'āna*.

292 The roots *h-d-d* and *h-d-m* are not, in fact, related.

293 I.e., «Lo! Kings, when they enter a township, ruin it» (Q Naml 27:34).

294 I.e., the consonantal skeleton of the verb *hadd* (هد), repeated, is identical to that of the noun *hudhud* (هدهد).

295 Q Naml 27:20; see also vol. 1, n. 250.

296 In fact there is no relationship, *hudhud* belongs to the root *h-d-h-d* and *hadiyyah* to the root *h-d-y*.

297 "The gift of friends is on leaves of rue": see al-Ibshīhī, *Al-Mustaṭraf*, 1:37 (without explanation of the meaning).

298 Cf. Q Naml 27:17 «And there were gathered unto Solomon his armies of the jinn and humankind, and of the birds, and they were set in battle order.»

299 "nature's tongue": see vol. 1, n. 348.

300 An even less plausible etymology, as *hadhayān* belongs to the root *h-dh-y*, which shares only one consonant with *h-d-d*.

301 Al-Shirbīnī spells out the word in detail, perhaps because it constitutes an unusual colloquialized poetic, or pseudo-poetic, form of the literary Arabic *hādhā* ("this").

302 I.e., it is a (near) palindrome; though al-Shirbīnī uses the singular, the comment applies to both forms of the demonstrative (masculine, then feminine) used in the verse, because *hādah* and *hādihī* have the same consonantal skeleton, the difference in the voweling being indicated by the meter.

303 I.e., the caliph 'Umar ibn al-Khaṭṭāb (r. 13–23/634–44).

304 Perhaps Abū Wuhayb Buhlūl ibn 'Amr, a "wise fool" who was a contemporary of Hārūn al-Rashīd (d. 193/809) (see al-Nīsābūrī, *'Uqalā'*, 69–77, who does not, however, mention these lines) and who is "usually pictured as a cunning vagrant, wielding a staff or riding it

as a hobby-horse" (Dols, *Majnūn*, 358)—to which "my reedling" (*quṣaybatī*) in the verse below refers. Or this "al-Buhlūl" may be identical with the Yaḥyā al-Buhlūl quoted by al-Shirbīnī earlier (§§10.14, 11.1.14). Verses attributed by al-Shaʿrānī to Buhlūl al-Majnūn ("Crazy Buhlul") (al-Shaʿrānī, *Lawāqiḥ*, 1:58) are closer in style and sentiment to those of al-Shirbīnī's "Yaḥyā al-Buhlūl" than they are to the verse quoted above.

305 Al-Shirbīnī takes terms such as "Coarse," "Moderate," "Hot," and "Moist" (see, e.g., §11.10.9 and passim) from Galenic medicine, which dominated the theory and practice of medicine in the pre-modern Arab world. The keystone of the Galenic system was the maintenance or restoration of *eukrasia* ("proper balance"), by practicing moderation in general and, especially, by maintaining a balance among foods consumed, according to their different humors; by including other qualities such as Coarse and Heavy, however, al-Shirbīnī's goes beyond the classical set of Hot, Cold, Dry, and Moist (see further Dols, *Majnūn*, especially 10–14).

306 Van Gelder (*Dishes*, 99 n. 123) notes that a similar statement, "Noble parents, low offspring," is attributed to Galen by ʿAlī ibn ʿAbd Allāh al-Ghuzūlī (d. 815/1412) in his *Maṭāliʿ al-Budūr* (2:55); this explains why al-Shirbīnī refers below to these words as a quotation.

307 On the evolution of this dish, which is found in Iran, Turkey, and parts of the Arab world in a wide variety of forms, see Aubaile-Sallenave (though the description there of Egyptian *kishk* as a "sweetmeat made from milk . . . flour and sugar" (Aubaile-Sallenave, "Al-Kishk", 127) appears to be based on Mehren's misreading of the above passage) and, for nineteenth-century Egypt, Lane's description (*Manners*, 488 n. 3).

308 *hirāsh* is usually defined as "quarreling, wrangling," but the author, seriously or not, asserts below (§11.10.13) that it is used here in the meaning given.

309 See vol. 1, §§2.5 and 2.26.

310 *Sic*: al-Shirbīnī seems to have forgotten that the second sort does not contain any beans and is presumably thinking of the first only.

311 Presumably al-Shirbīnī means "these three."

312 I.e., كعك (*kaʿk*), شاش (*shāsh*), and باب (*bāb*), and the longer examples that follow read the same forward and backward when only the consonantal skeleton is taken into consideration and short and quiescent vowels (as in *kaʿk*) and inflectional endings (as in the Qurʾanic verses and the lines by al-Ḥarīrī below) are ignored.

313 Q Muddaththir 74:3.

314 Q Anbiyāʾ 21:33 and Ṣāffāt 37:40.

315 These verses are from *maqāmah* XVI ("al-Maghribiyyah") (al-Ḥarīrī, *Maqāmāt*, 113). The original contains a further three lines, each of them a palindrome.

316 I.e., they turned س into ش, etc., so that كس (*kuss*) became كش, implying that كشك (*kishk*) has some relation to كسك (*kussik* "your cunt").

317 The verbal patterns *mufāʿalah* (as in *muḥāraqah*) and *fiʿāl* (as in *niqār* and *hirāsh*) are often interchangeable.

318 *nayrūb* . . . *daylūb*: both words are unattested elsewhere.

319 Literally "a mischievous, or a slanderous, man" or "a strong man." The passage contains many confusing and seemingly circular statements, which may be deliberate, in view of the references to "confusion" and getting "mixed up."

320 Both *gharf* and *gharīf* are valid verbal-noun forms; al-Shirbīnī's comment complicates the issue for the sake, perhaps, of a dig at grammatical overanalysis.

321 I.e., "though I eat at night, I am hungry again the next morning," meaning that I cannot escape the belly's demands.

322 See §11.2.21.

323 Ibn al-Fāriḍ, *Dīwān*, 377.

324 Stewed fava (broad) beans, today called *fūl midammis*, remain perhaps the most important staple, after bread, of the Egyptian diet.

325 In reality, the last two forms belong to verbal Form I, whereas the first three belong to verbal Form II.

326 I.e., balances their humors, see n. 305.

327 "like a . . . ." (*mithl al-nuʿūt*): the word is unattested in the lexica in an appropriate meaning.

328 While *rīḥah* is indeed the colloquial word for "smell" and *rāʾiḥah* one of its literary equivalents, the former is, just as likely, a reflex of literary *rīḥah*, with the same meaning.

329 Here, *rāyiḥah* is the colloquial active participle from *rāḥ* "to go" and identical, except for the substitution of *y* for the glottal stop, with literary *rāʾiḥah* "smell."

330 "a cord" (*khayṭ*): i.e., the suspended rope using which small ferryboats are pulled from one side of a canal to the other.

331 I.e., the answer to the riddle that follows is "a ferryboat": the explanation may be that the ferryboat is "going and coming" across the canal; it comes from beneath the bank (the "wall"); it is "dead and living" because it is both inanimate and constantly moving; it is flat on the "ground," i.e., the water, but could equally be described as sitting on it or standing in it; the sense of "atop a wall reclining" is unclear.

332 The formula *ʿalā (man)* is unattested elsewhere but is plausible as a genuine colloquial form, if *ʿalā* is taken as an optative verb (from *ʿalā* "to become high, elevated" etc.), in which case the use of the perfect tense rather than the more colloquial imperfect may be attributed to the specialized poetic diction of the epic style. Al-Shirbīnī describes this verb as a preposition simply because it is identical in pronunciation, and in his spelling, to the preposition *ʿalā* ("on"); the former, however, is more correctly spelled with *alif* (i.e., علا vs. على).

333 I.e., *nuṣṣ* is the colloquial (but not specifically rural) reflex of literary Arabic *niṣf* "half"; a *nuṣṣ/niṣf fiḍḍah* is a silver piece.

334 Al-Shirbīnī presumably means that the word *nuṣṣ* (نص) is orthographically a fragment of *niṣf* (نصف) and that it is up to the reader to supply the rest of the word.

335 Where "Fāṭim" is a conventionally shortened form of "Fāṭimu" or "Fātima"; the translation is Arberry's (*Seven Odes*, 62).

336 Q Sabaʾ 34:13 (of Sulaymān) "They made for him what he willed: synagogues and statues, and basins like reservoirs, and boilers built into the ground."

337 Kohl has been believed to strengthen the eyesight (see Lane, *Manners*, 36).

338 Shihāb al-Dīn Aḥmad ibn ʿUthmān al-Amshāṭī (d. 725/1325) (al-Ṣafadī *Aʿyān*, 1:288).

339 "wood" (*ḥaṭab rūmī*): literally "Anatolian fuel"—the standard Egyptian non-dung-based cooking fuel (*ḥaṭab*) of the time consisted of vegetable debris from the fields, such as sugarcane stalks; after the Ottoman conquest, however, real firewood was imported as a luxury item from the forests of Anatolia (*al-Rūm*) (Raymond, *Artisans*, 1:187).

340 Al-Shirbīnī paraphrases Ibn Sūdūn (Vrolijk, *Bringing a Laugh*, 136 Arabic, lines 11–12), who gives the name of the dish as "Gatherer of Loved Ones" (*mujammiʿat al-aḥbāb*); see further n. 344.

341 In present-day usage, "made of dry (as opposed to fresh or green) ingredients" (Hinds-Badawi, 111); see also Perry, "Būrān."

342 Accidentally or not, al-Shirbīnī here confuses *sāra* "to proceed" with *ṣāra* "to become," providing indirect evidence that the two had by his time come to be realized as homophones (*ṣāra*) as a result of regressive assimilation to emphatic *r*, as in modern Egyptian pronunciation.

343 This is the form in which the word occurs today.

344 Cf. Vrolijk, *Bringing a Laugh*, 134–36 Arabic. Ibn Sūdūn attributes these verses to "some person" and builds around them a commentary (a part of which al-Shirbīnī quotes below; see also vol. 1, p. xxxv). They may have been a popular ditty: Ibn Sūdūn refers to them as belonging to "what has become well known, spread far and near, and filled the ear" (ibid., 134 Arabic).

345 In modern Egyptian, "Abū Qirdān" is the name of the cattle egret, a common bird of the fields. Ibn Sūdūn specifies the voweling as given above (Vrolijk, *Bringing a Laugh*, 134 Arabic).

346 Eggplant.

347 I.e., the man said *mulūkhī yā* . . . ("My tearings! O . . .") and never completed the call.

348 I.e., ملوخي + يا = ملوخيّا.

349 Al-Ḥākim bi-Amri-llāh was famed for his eccentric ordinances, some of which—including perhaps that mentioned here—may be understood in the context of tensions between Shiites and Sunnis in Egypt at the time (see M. Canard, "Al-Ḥākim Bi-Amr Allāh," in *EI2*).

350 The lexica include neither term in an appropriate sense.

351 I.e., with suppression of the glottal stop of *jāʾa*, formal reflex of colloquial *ja* ("he came"), plus substitution of enclitic *li* for *ilā*, also as in the colloquial.

352 The verbal noun.

353 The intransitive senses recorded for modern usage are "to force one's way; to step, stamp" (Hinds and Badawi, *Dictionary*, 290).

354 See n. 194; here however, al-Shirbīnī uses the term *muḍāf* loosely or by analogy, since what is omitted (in fact, replaced) is the logical subject of a verb.

355 "vapor" (*bukhār*): meaning perhaps the *pneuma* of Galenic medicine (see Dols, *Majnūn*, 2–22).

356 Al-Shirbīnī seems to imply that a peasant is unlikely to know so technical a term as *qulinj*, whose true etymon (as distinct from the facetious ones suggested by the author below) is the Greek *kolikos*, unless (as he points out below) he hears it from "a doctor or someone else."

357 These lines occur, with variations, as part of a longer piece attributed to him, uncertainly, in his collected works (al-Shāfiʿī, *Shiʿr*, 236).

358 *kānat*: the hemistich scans only if this word is read, as is possible in modern Egyptian, as *kāt*.

359 *qashaʿ* appears to have disappeared from modern Egyptian dialects except for those of the oases of the Western Desert (Behnstedt and Woidich, *Glossar*, 379).

360 This is the meaning in literary Arabic.

361 The first day of Dhū l-Ḥijjah, the pilgrimage month, of 1075 was AD 14 June 1665; al-Shirbīnī had also made the pilgrimage the previous year (see §11.1.3).

362 I.e., the thirty-second chapter of the Qurʾan, called *The Prostration* (*al-Sajdah*) because believers prostrate themselves at the following verse: «Only those believe in Our revelations who, when they are reminded of them, fall down prostate and hymn the praise of their Lord, and they are not scornful» (Q Sajdah 32:15).

363 Part of the call to the dawn prayer.

364 Q Isrāʾ 17:44.

365 See §11.11.11.

366 Cf. Q Kahf 18:19 «Now send one of you with this your silver coin unto the city, and see what food is purest there and bring you a supply thereof.»

367 Literally "of loosely hanging sleeves"; the translation is tentative.

368 The correct verbal nouns are *ball* and *billah.*

369 Since the sole realization of the root *q-l-q-s* attested in the lexica is the noun *qulqās*, *qalqasah* and its derivatives are probably nonce words. *Qulqās* derives from Greek *kolokasia*, whence the Latin.

370 I.e., *qulqās* is formed of *qul* ("speak!") plus *qāsā* ("it suffered"), the final *ā* of the second word being explicable as the pausal form of the accusative *qulqāsan*, explainable as the "accusative of admiration or blame" (*manṣūb ʿalā l-madḥ aw al-dhamm*).

371 Using the denominal verb.

372 See vol. 1, §3.43, where it occurs as the name of one of the village shaykhs.

373 A meaningless statement, as *dandūf* and *dandafah* (a verbal noun form) are of equal status in the same root.

374 From root *n-d-f* as against *dandūf*'s *d-n-d-f*, and hence, in reality, unrelated.

375 I.e., *jā'athu* is the literary reflex of colloquial *jatū.*

376 As in the case of "the *bīsār* came," see §11.12.7.

377 Cf. Hinds and Badawi, *Dictionary*, 704: *qaṣʿah* "bowl or basin without a base."

378 The word is attested in Egypt today only in the sense of "lid of a *mājūr*" ("earthenware kneading bowl") (Behnstedt and Woidich, *Glossar*, 469).

379 *qaṣʿah . . . quṣayʿah . . . faswah . . . fusaywah*: *quṣayʿah* and *fusawyah* are diminutives.

380 On such categories of figurative speech, see vol. 1, n. 236; here, however, al-Shirbīnī is clearly parodying this kind of terminology.

381 In modern Egyptian, *huwwa* is the standard third-person singular personal pronoun for both rural and urban dialects, versus literary *huwa.*

382 *Ḥanak* has the basic sense of "jaw" but is also used in derisive or vulgar speech to refer to the mouth itself.

383 A red herring, because it is not *fam* (and its irregular declension) that is at issue here.

384 See al-Ḥillī, *Al-Badīʿiyyah*, 82, where the verse is used to illustrate the device called *radd al-ʿajz ʿalā al-ṣadr*, i.e., using the same word at both the beginning and the end of a line of verse.

385 I.e., *tajrīf*, verbal noun of *yujarrifu*, is used here as an intensifier ("he shovels a shoveling" = "he shovels repeatedly or in great quantities, he shovels away") in the construction called *mafʿūl muṭlaq* ("objective complement," see Wright, *Grammar*, 2:54C ff.), which would require, under the rules of formal Arabic, an indefinite accusative, i.e., *tajrīfan*. One may also deduce from al-Shirbīnī's comment that the rhyme letter of the Ode is quiescent, even though many lines can be correctly construed, both metrically and syntactically, with final vowel.

386 See §11.12.12.

387 Jacques Berque, speaking of the first half of the twentieth century, remarks, "Les fromages, frais ou conservés . . . ou même fermentés, *meššš*, constituaient . . . le mets 'qui fait passer le pain'" (Berque, *Histoire*, 32).

388 Mentioned, if not defined, in the discussion of wheat groats (*kishk*) above, see §11.9.8.

389 Again, *wishsh* is the standard colloquial reflex of literary Arabic *wajh*, rather than a specifically rural form (see vol. 1, pp. liii–liv).

390 On this unusual curse form, see vol. 1, n. 29.

391 The table is that referred to in Q Māʾidah 5:114: «Jesus, son of Mary, said, "O God, Our Lord! Send down for us a table spread with food from heaven, that it may be a feast for us, for the first of us and the last of us, and a sign from Thee!"»

392 Q Baqarah 2:187.

393 Q Baqarah 2:249.

394 "Smoking" is expressed as "drinking smoke (or tobacco)" (*shurb al-dukhān*).

395 I.e., the letter *alif*, indicating the long *ā* in *māta* (مات), was omitted, so that رد + مات became مترد.

396 Presumably from *zunbūr* ("wasp; clitoris").

397 In the second of these forms, the spelling reflects the colloquial rather than the literary morphology (اطنبر versus تطنبر); thus, for consistency, one should read *miṭṭanbar* rather than *mutaṭanbir*, etc., in this sentence and the rest of the passage.

398 Of which the literal meaning may be "to play the tambourine" (*ṭunbūrah*) (see the author's reference to this instrument below).

399 "If you're . . . hung" (*idhā kunta ālātī wa-ṭabʿuka riqqī * ṭanbir bi-riqqah wa-ʿtabir bi-l-mashnūqī*): with puns on *ālātī* ("musician," from *ālah* "(musical) instrument"; also, "tool, penis"), *riqqī* ("gentle"; also interpretable as a relative adjective from *riqq* "tambourine"), and *ṭanbir* ("to play the tambourine"; also "to rub oneself against boys").

400 "All great Arab physicians whose works have been preserved warned against eating beef and recommended mutton. According to al-Rāzī, almost all meats, with the exception of mutton, cause illnesses" (Ashtor, "Diet," 130).

401 This sense of the word is discussed below, §11.20.5.

402 See §11.14.8.

403 *rafrāfah*: the word is not attested in the lexica, but, according to an informant, is used in the countryside today to refer to a feast held at the time specified, rather than a dish.

404 See the discussion of the implied logical subject at §§11.5.3 and 11.14.2.

405 Here al-Shirbīnī invokes the second meaning of the verb, "to resolve, determine."

406 The verb is employed with and without the following preposition *ʿalā*.

407 Al-Shirbīnī plays with the ambiguity of the conjunction *wa-* ("and"), which may denote synonymity (in which case *yaʿzim* and *yuḍif* would both be understood in the basic sense of "invite/play host to") or contrast (in which case *yaʿzim* should be understood in its other sense of "to determine (to do something)"); he also puns on the various

senses of the root *ḍ-y-f* "to add, attach, join, annex" (hence *yanḍāfu* "to be added, be attached, be annexed (in the grammatical sense)") and *iḍāfah* "addition, annexation" on the one hand, and *ḍiyāfah* ("hospitality") and *ḍayf* ("guest") on the other. The grammatical usage of *iḍāfah* is further exploited below.

408 The second verbal noun, *ḍuyūf,* is a red herring, being merely the plural of *ḍayf* "guest."

409 On "annexation" (*iḍāfah*) in grammar, and the comic uses to which al-Shirbīnī puts it, see n. 194. In this passage, al-Shirbīnī focuses on another aspect of "annexation," namely, that the first noun, being definite by virtue of its position in the construction, may not end in *tanwīn* ("nunation," the endings *un, an, in,* from *nūn,* name of the letter *n*), the sign of the indefinite noun.

410 "puzzle word" (*muʿammā*): a form of riddle "solved . . . by combining the constituent letters of the word or the name to be found" (G. J. H. van Gelder, "Muʿammā," in *EAL*).

411 See above n. 108.

412 *Ṭāfiyah* is apparently a colloquial metathesis of literary *ṭāʾifah*; on al-Shirbīnī's deconstruction of the word, see n. 109.

413 I.e., take the word خذ ("take"), omit the dots above the letters so that it becomes حد and insert, in the empty (*fārigh*) space between the two letters, the word ما ("water" with omission of final *hamz*), and you get حماد (Ḥammād).

414 The name Shaḥātah (شحاته) (literally "begging") is explained as consisting of شُح ("avarice, miserliness"), followed by ا (the letter *alif,* the word *wālif* being interpretable as either equivalent to *wa-alif* ("and an *alif*") with elision of the glottal stop for the meter, or as an active participle meaning "friendly, familiar"), and finally by the letters ت and ه, together forming تِه, masculine singular imperative of the verb تاه "to lose one's way"; thus شح + ا + ته = شحاته.

415 Here it is the shapes and not the sounds of the letters that unlock the sense: thus, the name أحمد (Aḥmad) is envisioned as consisting of a ben tree (the أ), beneath which a worshipper bows down (the letter ح in its

initial form ﺣ), while clasping a pearl (the letter م in its medial form ﻤ), which is displayed (literally, suspended) in a bird's beak (the letter ذ).

416 I.e., instead of the formal reflex *hādhāka*; cf. n. 301.

417 See vol. 1, n. 258.

418 In fact, while all these "facetious plurals" share the root *kh-b-z*, the first two have no clear meaning, while the third means "bakers" and has no clear semantic connection to *khubbayz*; and, in fact, *khubbayz*, as a collective or mass noun, is unlikely to form a plural.

419 In other words, the word should be read in the verse as *khubbayza* (= *khubbayzah*, a feminine noun), which is in fact the standard colloquial form; however, in inscribing the verse, the author has disguised the colloquialism by pretending that the *a* represents the literary accusative ending.

420 Al-ʿAynī built the ʿAyniyyah *madrasah* in Cairo (still standing, opposite the house of Zaynab Khātūn, behind al-Azhar) but died before the Mamluk sultan Qāyitbāy came to power in 872/1468; there is no evidence that he ever lived in Dimyāṭ. A unique feature of the ʿAyniyyah was the Anatolian glazed-tile mosaic (destroyed during restoration in 1980) of the prayer niche, and this may explain al-Shirbīnī's characterization of the mosque; Ibrahim and O'Kane note that al-ʿAynī, who was originally from ʿAyntāb (modern Gaziantep) in southeastern Anatolia, "may have tried to underline his non-native origins by stylistic means, in order thus to stress his affinities with the ruling class" (Ibrahim and O'Kane, "Madrasa," 268).

421 The cotton teaser prepares cotton for stuffing mattresses, etc., or renews it after it has become compressed from use, by pulling a handful of cotton against the wire "string" of his bow and then releasing the string, thus fluffing the cotton. He usually works very fast, and it is the speed with which he grabs, processes, and crams the wool into the mattress that suggests the figurative use of the verb.

422 According to a *ṣaḥīḥ* ("sound," i.e., accurate and reliable) Tradition, these words were spoken by the Prophet to encourage his weary and hungry followers on a cold day as they dug the earthwork that

allowed the Muslims to defend Medina and defeat the Meccans at the Battle of the Ditch (al-Bukhārī, *al-Ṣaḥīḥ*, *TIF*, 2871).

423 *Nadīf*, verbal noun of *anduf*, relates to the latter as *tajrīf* to *yujarrif* in the earlier use of the same construction; see n. 385.

424 See al-Shaʿrānī, *Laṭāʾif*, 668.

425 On the dropping of *-an*, see n. 385; al-Shirbīnī's assertion that the word نديف is to be read here as a diminutive, i.e., *nudayf*, "for the sake of the rhyme" is puzzling, since other line-final syllables *must* be realized as *-īf*; see, for example, *yaḥīf* in the third line (there being no verbal form **yuḥayf*), and *līf* in the fourth line (there being no word **layf*). If it is contended that *īf* is an acceptable near-rhyme for *ayf* and that all rhyme words capable of taking a diminutive form should be treated as diminutives (e.g., one should read *nuḥayf* for *nuḥīf* in the opening line) and that, despite the difficulties (e.g., verbal nouns such as *nadīf* do not normally form diminutives), al-Shirbīnī's assertion that *ayf* is the default rhyme nevertheless remains entirely arbitrary, because these forms are identical metrically; thus the assertion has been ignored on the grounds that it probably represents no more than comic obfuscation.

426 The glottal stop with which first-person singular imperfect verbs begin is frequently elided when preceded by an open syllable in modern Egyptian (Mitchell, *Introduction*, 36); similar forms occur elsewhere in the Ode: *wa-hurru* (§11.6), *wa-baṭṭiṭu* (§11.21), *wa-bīʿū* (§11.37), and, again, *wa-luffū* (§11.38). As usual, al-Shirbīnī's presentation of the standard colloquial form as though it were a literary form adapted for the sake of the meter is unconvincing (see vol. 1, p. liii).

427 On such intensifiers, see n. 385.

428 *wa-baṭṭiṭu, wa-ḍarriṭu, wa-barbiṭu*: these three words are written in the manuscripts without initial *alif*, thus signaling the same elision described in the case of *w-aluffu* above (§11.20.5).

429 The basic sense of *ṭaḥīn* as a concrete noun is "flour," but the word is also used in the countryside to refer to harvested wheat as a foodstuff stored in the house to be ground as needed; the essence of

al-Shirbīnī's question seems to be "What is the connection between a change in the nature of a thing and a change in its name?" Throughout the passage, al-Shirbīnī mimicks and perhaps mocks the concerns and language of scholastic theologians and philosophers.

430 The feast with which Ramadan ends.

431 *Maṭyab* and *maḥsan* (in the following line) are colloquialized forms *mā aṭyaba* and *mā aḥsana*, "verbs of surprise or wonder" (*afʿāl al-taʿajjub*), and the particle *a-yā* clearly is used here in an exclamatory sense to reinforce this usage; however, al-Shirbīnī insists on interpreting the particle as though it is being used in its more usual vocative sense, and so supplies a missing addressee, "people."

432 Perhaps *Zahr al-kimām fī qiṣṣat Yūsuf ʿalayhi l-salām* (*The Flowers in the Calyces on the Story of Yusuf, Peace Be upon Him*) by the mystic Ibrāhīm ibn Yaḥyā al-Awsī (687–751/1288–1350) (cf. *GAL*, 2:265, *Suppl.*, 2:377–78).

433 The celebrated treatise *Al-Qānūn fī al-ṭibb* (*The Canonical Work on Medicine*) by Ibn Sīnā (Avicenna). In his chapter on leprosy, Ibn Sīnā says, "If hot weather combines with bad food such as fish, jerked meat, coarse meats, donkey meat, or lentils, it is likely that leprosy will result, as happens frequently in Alexandria" (*Al-Qānūn*, 3:612).

434 I.e., without the inflectional endings of literary Arabic.

435 Al-Shirbīnī uses the term farcically here, as there is no real connection between the supposedly corresponding items.

436 See §11.10.11 for more on palindromes.

437 This definition is not, in fact, that given above.

438 *ʿalā l-nadā*; literally "at the dew."

439 I.e., "he is generous," "he has no generosity," and "generosity is the companion of excellence."

440 Cf. n. 153.

441 See vol. 1, n. 258.

442 *ʿalā rukbah wa-nuṣṣin*: literally "on a knee and a half."

443 Al-Shirbīnī is wrong: the poet in fact (see next note) meant "Prepare yourself for action!" (see Ibn Manẓūr, *Lisān*, s.v. *h-m-m*).

444 The pre-Islamic ʿAbd al-Masīḥ ibn ʿAmr al-Ghassānī (see, e.g., Ibn Ḥamdūn, *Al-Tadhkirah*, 8:11).

445 Of the *shimār*, Lane says, "The full sleeves . . . are sometimes drawn up, by means of a cord, which passes round each shoulder and crosses behind, where it is tied in a knot" (Lane, *Manners*, 32).

446 The form used in the verse is colloquial.

447 The literary reflex of the same word.

448 This parodies the *khuṭbat al-naʿt*, the second and more standardized of the two sermons delivered during the Friday prayer service, including all the main elements of the latter and much of its typical phrasing, and may be compared with Lane's translation of a sermon of this type from the second decade of the nineteenth century (Lane, *Manners*, 87–90). In both, the preacher begins with praise of God and His Prophet (Lane, 87: "Praise be to God, abundant praise, as He hath commanded . . ."; al-Shirbīnī: "Praise be to God, to whom for sure all praise is owed"), moves on to the exhortation and warning of the believers (Lane, 88: "O people, reverence God by doing what He hath commanded and abstain from that which He hath forbidden and prohibited"; al-Shirbīnī: "My people, why do I behold you of sweet rice with honey all unaware . . . . [H]ave nothing to do with foods that are coarse . . . ."), and moves via prayers for the victory of the ruler and the confusion of his enemies (Lane, 89: "Aid el-Islam . . . by the preservation of thy servant . . . our master the sultan . . . . O God, frustrate the infidels and polytheists . . . ."; al-Shirbīnī: "O God, bring us after dispersal all together, and grant victory, support, and safety to Sultan Sugar-Candy . . . And destroy, O God, the reprobates three . . .") to end with Q Anʿām 6:90 (Lane, 89: "Verily God commandeth justice . . . . He admonisheth you that ye may reflect"; al-Shirbīnī: "He exhorteth you . . . that you may reflect").

449 I.e., the Kaaba, at Mecca.

450 The same words are attributed elsewhere to the pre-Islamic poet Taʾbbaṭa Sharrā and to Aḥmad ibn al-Ṭayyib al-Sarakhsī (d. 286/899) (van Gelder, *Dishes*, 109 and 151 n. 3).

451 On the topos of mutton as the lord of foods, see Finkel's discussion of a Mamluk *Rangstreit* pitting King Mutton against Sultan Sugar Cane; in the same article Finkel provides a translation of this passage from *Hazz al-quḥūf*. Goody, writing on Finkel's article, comments that "the conflict between meat and vegetables . . . is a class war" (Goody, *Cooking*, 133).

452 Q Hūd 11:61.

453 This parodies the "chain of authority" (*isnād*) that establishes the reliability of a Tradition; the names, some of which have occurred earlier, are either apparently meaningless (Sahlab, Mahlab, Zinṭāḥ) or comically absurd (Naṭṭāḥ "Head-Butter"; Qalīl al-Afrāḥ, "Having-Few-Joys").

454 Q Shuʿarāʾ 26:227; the same verse occurs in Lane's example (*Manners*, 88).

455 Compare Lane, *Manners*, 88: "O God, do thou also be pleased with the four Khaleefehs."

456 The fig and the olive are mentioned in Q Tīn 95:1 and the pomegranate in Anʿām 6:99 and elsewhere; the peach (*khawkh*) is not mentioned in the Qurʾan.

457 Compare Lane, *Manners*, 88: "And be Thou well pleased, O God, with the six who remain of the ten noble and just persons who swore allegiance to Thy Prophet Mohammad."

458 From *qirmiz* "cochineal," hence "the scarlet (dish)."

459 I.e., the Prophet Muḥammad.

460 Q Naḥl 16:90.

461 The poet was an unnamed cousin of Sharaf al-Dawlah, an ʿUqaylid ruler of Mosul (d. 453/1061) (see Ibn al-ʿAdīm, *Zubdat al-ḥalab*, 215).

462 I.e., Muḥammad ibn Saʿīd al-Būṣīrī (608/1213 to 694/1294–95) (see Glossary).

463 See al-Būṣīrī, *Dīwān*, 240.

464 The *ṭurṭūr* is a high, conical hat. A fatwa concerning the Muṭāwiʿah dervishes written in 1782 by Shaykh ʿAlī l-Ṣaʿīdī l-ʿAdawī refers to their wearing "palm leaf hats and *ṭarāṭīr* on which they put shells and feathers and bits of cloth, etc." (al-Ṭawīl, *Al-Taṣawwuf*, 1:85).

465 And thus resembles the end of a palm branch where it sprouts from the tree, another meaning of *qaḥf*. ʿĀlī Muṣṭafā, writing in 1599, describes the caps of the peasants as having "the shape of buckets emptied of their water" (Tietze, *Description*, 42).

466 "Un bonnet haut, couvert de drap et doublé de coton qu'on enveloppait d'un grand morceau de toile fine" (Raymond, *Artisans*, 1:325 n. 4).

467 From al-Shirbīnī's account, it seems that *libdah* (literally "(piece of) felt") was a generic term; that the *qaḥf*, the *ṭurṭūr*, and the "*libdah* that resembles a European hat" were specific styles thereof; and that all the latter were associated with Sufis and had strong negative associations at the time al-Shirbīnī wrote, being considered outmoded and uncouth. Despite al-Shirbīnī's emphasis on the outmodedness of the *libdah*, the term was in use in the early nineteenth century to denote "a white or brown felt cap" worn under the tarboosh or, among the very poor, on its own (Lane, *Manners*, 32). The *libdah* that is still in use in Lower Egypt has the form of a roughly conical cap of coarse brown wool, though it is apparently now worn only by peasants, among whom it is the "signe de majorité et de respectabilité" (Berque, *Histoire*, 30).

468 See vol. 1, §7.41.

469 Abū Nuwās: these verses do not occur in his collected works, and the attribution is dubious.

470 "furrow": i.e., "[are used to] plow," etc.

471 I.e., "and do not abuse him by reference to the latter and say to him 'you buffalo-cow' (*yā jāmūsah*)!"

472 Today an "earthenware tub for kneading dough, similar to a *maguur* . . . but smaller" (Hinds and Badawi, *Dictionary*, 796).

473 In fact, the literary rather than colloquial form of the same word, cf. *ṣalāt il-laqqān* "[Christian] ceremony of washing the feet" (Hinds and Badawi, *Dictionary*, 796).

474 In fact, the root of *yaluqqu* is *l-q-q*, while that of *laqqānah* is *l-q-n*.

475 I.e., he drops the glottal stop from the standard literary form *malʾānah* (modern Egyptian *malyānah*).

476 A recipe is to be found in Khawam, *Cuisine*, 170. It resembles what today is called *mahallabiyyah* or *nisha*, i.e., blancmange.

477 The literary feminine singular relative pronoun.

478 The incident is recorded by both Yāqūt (*Udabāʾ*, 3:138) and Ibn al-Jawzī (*Al-Adhkiyāʾ*, 249). Yāqūt and Ibn al-Jawzī attribute the first fragment, attributed here to Abū l-ʿAtāhiyah, to ʿAlī ibn al-Jahm; that by al-Maʿarrī is from his *Saqṭ al-zand* (229).

479 The forenoon prayer is not compulsory and is performed from approximately half an hour after sunrise until midday.

480 Al-Shirbīnī implies that the name Waṭīf (root *w-ṭ-f*) derives from *ṭ-w-f* (root of *aṭwāf*, and also, below, *ṭawāf*) by metathesis.

481 See §11.9.6.

482 "Then enter the dome," etc: the comparison of the beloved's backside to a dome and the exploitation in the same context of the association of domes with buried holy men are commonplaces (see, e.g., vol. 1, §5.2.16).

483 A synonym of *laban*, in the latter's primary sense.

484 The substitution of *ghalw* for *ghaly* is also a solecism, in that the former belongs to the root *gh-l-w*, which denotes "exceeding normal limits, becoming expensive," etc., whereas it is the latter, which belongs to the root *gh-l-y*, that denotes "boiling."

485 See references to *khubz* above, §§11.19.3, 11.19.7.

486 I.e., because it is diminutive and hence hypercoristic.

487 Cf. Abū Nuwās, *Dīwān*, 3:126.

488 Ibn al-Fāriḍ, *Dīwān*, 343; the following line reads "That my hearing may witness the one I love, should he remain aloof, his phantom conjured by those words of blame, rather than by dreams."

489 From the description, *mafrūkat al-laban* resembled today's *Umm ʿAlī*, which is a "dessert of filo pastry, raisins and butter cooked in hot milk" (Hinds and Badawi, *Dictionary*, 37), but cf. *mafrūkah*, "type of fine maize couscous, usually eaten with milk and sugar" (ibid., 653, specified as rural).

490 See n. 385.

491 Though included in Ibn al-Fāriḍ's collected works (p. 380), these lines are attributed more authoritatively to Bahā' al-Dīn Zuhayr (581–656/1186–1258) (see Zuhayr, *Poetical Works*, 107 transl. 124, and al-Muḥibbī, *Nafḥat al-rayḥānah*, 4:368).

492 *fatt*; here and in the discussion that follows, Shirbīnī uses *fatt* and *taftīt* interchangeably to designate the dish that is today called *fattah* (cf. Hinds and Badawi, *Dictionary*, 638 "dish, consisting of hot broth or the like ... poured over crumbled bread"; *fattit ʿads* "bread in lentil soup," etc.).

493 See §11.19.2.

494 See §11.27.2.

495 Q Muṭaffifīn 83:1; thus the verb *ṭaffafa*, of which *taṭfīf* and *muṭaffif* are, respectively, the verbal noun and active participle, has two contradictory senses (cf. Lane, *Lexicon*, 857).

496 What follows is a summary of the account of the martyrdom of al-Ḥusayn ibn ʿAlī Ṭālib (d. 61/680), grandson of the Prophet, as given in *Al-Kawākib al-durriyyah fī tarājim al-ṣūfiyyah* (1:100–104) by ʿAbd al-Raʾūf ibn Tāj al-ʿĀrifīn ibn ʿAlī ibn Zayn al-ʿĀbidīn ibn Yaḥyā ibn Muḥammad al-Munāwī (952–1031/1545–1621), a leading religious scholar and Sufi of the day. The work is also known as *Ṭabaqāt al-Munāwī* (*al-Munāwī's Biographical Dictionary*), and it is under this title that al-Shirbīnī introduces a direct quotation below. It is difficult to understand al-Shirbīnī's reasons for including this long, serious digression; conceivably the answer lies in the reference at the end of the passage (§11.31.14) to a difference of opinion concerning the resting place of al-Ḥusayn's head in Cairo, which implies that the issue was of concern to his contemporaries.

497 I.e., Sulaymān ibn Aḥmad al-Ṭabarānī (260–320/873–971), a leading compiler of collections of Traditions (al-Ziriklī, *Al-Aʿlām*, 3:121), though this excerpt was not found.

498 Al-Munāwī, *Al-Kawākib*, 1:102; see n. 496.

499 From al-Ṭabarānī, with minor differences (al-Ṭabarānī, *Al-Muʿjam*, no. 2814).

500 Ibn Saʿd, *Al-Ṭabaqāt*, 6:419, with differences.

501 Abū Yaʿlā, *Al-Musnad*, 2:176.

502 Abū Nuʿaym: probably Abū Nuʿaym al-Iṣfahānī (d. 430/1038), author of *Ḥilyat al-awliyāʾ*, is meant, but this story was not found there.

503 The tenth day of the month of Muharram, observed as a voluntary fast; hence the date of al-Ḥusayn's martyrdom was, according to the Gregorian calendar, October 10, 680.

504 I.e., the caliph Yazīd (r. 60–64/680–683).

505 Q Kahf 18:9.

506 Al-Shirbīnī refers presumably to al-Mashhad al-Ḥusaynī, or Jāmiʿ al-Ḥusayn, near al-Azhar mosque, which remains one of Cairo's most important shrines; however, al-Ṣāliḥ Ṭalāʾiʿ originally intended the mosque that bears his name and stands outside Bāb Zuwaylah to serve this purpose.

507 Apparently a noncanonical version of the "sound" Tradition that says, "No contagious disease, no evil omens, and the righteous augur—the fair word—pleases me." The sense would seem to be that all events, including illness, are to be attributed to God's direct intervention and not to other natural or supernatural forces.

508 Al-Shirbīnī repeats himself, seemingly having forgotten that he has already introduced the phrase.

509 Abū l-ʿAbbās Aḥmad ibn ʿAlī al-Būnī (d. 622/1225) was an influential writer on the esoteric sciences, with numerous works to his name, including many that are pseudonymous. The source of this quotation has not been identitifed.

510 "ewe": in the Arabic, *faṣīl* ("young camel"), a word also meaning "gap, divide"; for further similar anecdotes, see van Gelder, *Dishes*, 41.

511 I.e., *Mawāqiʿ al-nujūm wa-maṭāliʿ ahillat al-asrār wa-l-ʿulūm* (*GAL*, 1:443, *Suppl.*, 1:795 (19)).

512 On the depiction by Arab historians of the Umayyad caliphs as gluttons, see Van Gelder, *Dishes*, 26–27.

513 Al-Walīd was a famous bacchic poet; for these lines, see al-Walīd, *Shiʿr*, 45.

514 Q Ibrāhīm 14:15.

515 The name is given to several dishes (see van Gelder, *Dishes*, 70, and Rodinson, "*Ma'mūniyya* East and West").

516 *fisīkh*: use of the colloquial form here (versus *fasīkh*) seems justified in view of the etymology that al-Shirbīnī gives below.

517 Q Zukhruf 43:71, referring to Paradise.

518 See vol. 1, §5.2.2.

519 Q Dukhān 44:29.

520 Nuṣayb ibn Rabāḥ (d. ca. 108/726) (see, with differences, *Shiʿr Nuṣayb ibn Rabāḥ*, 130).

521 In fact the roots are unrelated: *b-k-y* "to weep," *b-k-k* "to ooze, exude."

522 See vol. 1, §5.2.2.

523 See §11.18.5.

524 I.e., drinks, as pigeons do, by sipping with their heads lowered, and not as do most other birds, which raise their heads and let the water run down their throats.

525 I.e., the Citadel of Cairo, on which work was initiated by Ṣalāḥ al-Dīn (Saladin) beginning in 1176. In al-Shirbīnī's day, the Citadel housed the Ottoman governor, various administrative offices and functional establishments, including the mint, and the barracks of two of the seven military corps stationed in Egypt (the Janissaries and the ʿAzab) (Raymond, *Artisans*, 1:1, 2, 10, 26).

526 These large structures, consisting of one or more conical towers several meters high, remain prominent features of the rural landscape.

527 "waterwheel jars" (*qawādīs*): Hinds and Badawi, *Dictionary*, 690, illus. 975.

528 Cf. Q Nūr 24:60.

529 "As for the number of visitors to a modestly sized bathing establishment, for the Ottoman period this has been estimated at between fifty and sixty people a day" (Warner, "Taking the Plunge," 51–52).

530 The employment of beardless boys in bathhouses was discouraged but widespread (Warner, "Taking the Plunge," 62).

531 In reality, the roots are *ḥ-w-m* and *ḥ-m-m*, respectively.

532 Q Ḥajj 22:19.

533 Q Ghāfir 40:18.

534 "he is diminished" (*inkhafaḍa*): meaning also "he is pronounced with an *i*."

535 I.e., invariable colloquial *Abū* has been used instead of literary *Abī*.

536 See §11.26.10.

537 I.e., they dropped *bi-* and the genitive marker *-i* that should be attached to the noun (according to literary rules). The author should perhaps also mention that they dropped the definite article (*-l-*) and explain the presence of the *Abū* of *Abū Shaʿnīf*.

538 *shaʿnafah*: meaning unknown.

539 In the literary language, a verb may be followed immediately by its verbal noun for emphasis (see n. 148); *faṭāyir*, however, is not a verbal noun but, as the author goes on to state, the plural of *faṭīr*, a concrete noun. Al-Shirbīnī appears to be assimilating to the literary construction a different, distinct colloquial construction, which allows, at least in a few set phrases, the use of a concrete noun of the pattern CaCāyiC (such as *faṭāyir*) to similar effect, e.g., *ʿamal ʿamāyil* ("he did terrible things"). The expression *qashar qashāyir*, however, is his own, jocular, invention.

540 Properly speaking, *faṭāyir* is the plural of the unit noun *faṭīrah* and means "pieces (or cakes) of *faṭīr*," while *faṭīr* is a collective/mass noun and means "many-layered flaky pastry" in general. Similarly, *khamīr* is a mass noun and *ḥamīr* a simple plural.

541 Abū Qays ibn Rifāʿah (a contemporary of the Prophet Muḥammad; dates unknown).

542 A misquotation of a line usually attributed to the mystic poet al-Ḥusayn ibn Manṣūr al-Ḥallāj (244–309/857–922): "I am the one I love and the one I love is I / We are two souls incarnated in a single body" (see, e.g., Ibn Khallikān, *Wafayāt*, 2:141).

543 From his *Tarjumān al-ashwāq*, 42 (translation 139).

544 The poet compares himself and his beloved to a *ḥarf mushaddad*, a doubled consonant represented by a single letter distinguished by a special sign (*shaddah*).

545 Locusts and fish are eaten without being ritually slaughtered (G.-H. Bousquet, "Dhabīḥa," in *EI2*); the description "dead or alive" here apparently alludes to their nonslaughtered status rather than implying that fish and locusts may be eaten alive; thus the meaning is equivalent too "in any (edible) state."

546 Presumably referring to the Ḥaydariyyah, an originally Iranian antinomian Sufi movement founded by Quṭb al-Dīn Ḥaydar, who died ca. 618/1221–22 (Karamustafa, *Friends*, 3); on the Ḥaydarīs in Mamluk Egypt, see Sabra, *Poverty*, 28–31.

547 Islamic law requires that, in order to clarify the paternity of any children she may be carrying, a woman must wait for a specified period following divorce or death before remarrying.

548 Transmogrification into a living creature would imply the waiting period at the end of which return to the original marriage is possible, i.e., that for divorce (three menstrual cycles); that into an inanimate object, the waiting period at the end of which return is not possible, i.e., that for death (four months and ten days).

549 Ibn al-Rūmī, *Dīwān*, 809 (lines 1–3); sometimes also attributed to Abū l-Ḥasan ʿAlī ibn Faḍḍāl (d. 479/1086) (e.g., al-Zamakhsharī, *Rabīʿ al-abrār*, 1:446).

550 These and the following verses do not appear in al-Shāfiʿī's collected works. "Little Dog" and "Frayed" are puns on two famous names from pre-Islamic lore, Kulayb ("Little Dog") and his brother Muhalhil ("Ragged"), nickname of ʿAdī (or Imruʾ al-Qays) ibn Rabīʿah, so called because "he made poetry ragged, i.e., thin" (*halhala l-shiʿr, ay araqqahū*) (see Ibn Qutaybah, *Al-Shiʿr*, 297), which is taken by some to mean that he wove poetry finely (see Thomas Bauer, "al-Muhalhil ibn Rabīʿa", in *EAL*); he is said to have been the first to compose a *qaṣīdah* ("a polythematic poem with identical meter and rhyme," ibid.).

551 "he also said": in fact the verses are by ʿAbd Allāh al-Ḥumayḍī al-Andalusī (d. 488/1095) (see, e.g., Ibn Khallikān, *Wafayāt*, 4:283).

552 Attributed to Muslim ibn Ibrāhīm Abū l-Faḍl al-Sulamī al-Bazzāz (d. 455/1063), known as al-Shuwayṭir, in al-Ṣafadī, *Al-Wāfī*, 25:549.

553 Q Ḥujurāt 49:10.

554 All three of the slave girl's quotations are from Q Āl ʿImrān 3:134.

555 No such saying is to be found in the Christian scriptures; the words are attributed to Jesus by Ibn Qutaybah (*ʿUyūn*, 2:268) in some later sources and to al-Ḥasan al-Baṣrī (21–110/642–728) by al-Jāḥiẓ (*Al-Bayān*, 3:164).

556 Al-Ghazzī, *Al-Zubdah*, 57.

557 The story is told by the poet's grandson, ʿAlī Sibṭ Ibn al-Fāriḍ, in his biography of Ibn al-Fāriḍ (see Homerin, *Ibn al-Fāriḍ*, 47).

558 Al-Shaʿrānī reports that Yūsuf al-ʿAjamī al-Kūrānī (d. 768/1367) "was in the habit of educating his novices by a strange method: He did everything to thwart their natural inclinations in order to break down their willpower" (Winter, *Society and Religion*, 93).

559 "the Feast of the Slaughtering" (ʿĪd al-Naḥr): i.e., the Feast of the Sacrifice (ʿĪd al-Aḍḥā).

560 In modern Egypt, the word appears to apply specifically to a room built on top of a house, hence the figurative sense in which the plural *ʿalālī* is used by al-Shirbīnī and still today (cf. Hinds and Badawi, *Dictionary*, 598).

561 *Fī* can be used with a variety of locative and other functions in addition to its basic sense of "in, inside." Thus, in the two phrases *fī l-tall* and *fī l-jabal*, the preposition is used in a more generalized sense than in the phrase *fī l-dār*.

562 A crisis arose between the Mamluk and Safavid empires in the autumn of 913/1507, when the Safavids invaded a Mamluk vassal state in southeastern Anatolia. For the verses, see Ibn Ṭūlūn, *Mufākahat al-khillān*, 288, and al-Ghazzī, *Al-Kawākib*, I/297 (the reply is not found in these sources).

563 See al-Muḥibbī, *Khulāṣah*, 1:106, where these lines are said to have been written on Nebuchadnezzar's sword.

564 I.e., to slaughter for the feast.

565 *Dhibbān* is the literary reflex of colloquial *dibbān*.

566 The last form is unattested in modern Egyptian.

567 Q Ḥajj 22:73.

568 I.e., *Laṭāʾif al-minan* ("The Subtle Blessings"); see al-Shaʿrānī, *Laṭāʾif*, 295.

569 I.e., the imperfect preformative is *yi-*, as in modern Egyptian, rather than *ya-*, as in literary Arabic.

570 I.e., *yaʿuffu*; al-Shirbīni is, however, misinformed: the literary imperfect of the verb in this sense is *yaʿiffu*.

571 Al-Shirbīnī omits the second word of the phrase (*bi-ḥālu* "all") from the commentary.

572 *Akhadhtuhu* is the literary reflex of *khadtū*.

573 I.e., by the Prophet Muḥammad, who ascended into the heavens on his Night Journey (*al-Isrāʾ*); see Q 17, Sūrat al-Isrāʾ.

574 I.e., Paradise, Riḍwān being the guardian thereof. However, the reference is made even more apt by the fact that a park called the Garden of Riḍwān Bey existed and was "without peer in Cairo" according to Shalabī (*Siyāḥatnāmah*, 599).

575 I.e., the Prophet Muḥammad; see Q Qamar 54:1.

576 Shirbīn produced at least three distinguished scholars and Sufis before Yūsuf al-Shirbīnī's day, according to ʿAlī Mubārak (*Al-Khiṭaṭ*, 1:127–28): Muḥammad al-Shirbīnī, who lived on the eve of and predicted the Ottoman conquest (see al-Shaʿrānī, *Lawāqiḥ*, 2:118); Shams al-Dīn al-Khaṭīb al-Shirbīnī; and the latter's son ʿAbd al-Raḥmān ibn al-Khaṭīb al-Shirbīnī (al-Muḥibbī, *Khulāṣat al-athar*, 2:378).

577 "do not use it for its appointed purposes" (*wa-lam yaṣrifhā fī maṣārifihā*): the phrase evokes the *maṣārif al-zakāh*, i.e., the eight classes of alms recipient specified in Q Tawbah 9:60. Thus, the implication is that such nouveaux riches ignore their obligation to use their wealth to help those who are worse off.

578 "Divine Tradition": a communication to the Prophet by God that is not in God's precise words (and therefore not a part of the Qur'an).

579 These verses do not appear in his published works.

580 The relative merits of boys without and with beards are much debated in verse from Abbasid times, if not earlier; see, e.g. (for Abū Nuwās) Ibn Manẓūr, *Akhbār*, 9892.

581 The next three poems have already appeared (in different order) in al-Shirbīnī's earlier treatment of this theme, see **vol. 1, §§7.39–40**.

582 “another”: the grammarian Muḥammad ibn Yūsuf ibn Ḥayyān al-Andalusī (d. 745/1344) (see al-Ṣafadī, *Al-Wāfī*, 5:273–74).

583 The first hemistich is by Abū Firās al-Ḥamdānī (320–57/932–68) (*Dīwān*, 34); see further vol. 1, n. 248.

584 Perhaps Fakhr al-Dīn Abū Bakr Muḥammad al-Ḥakkāk al-Ṣūfī (fl. 752/1351), a Syrian mystic (*GAL Suppl.*, 2:3).

585 On this rhetorical device, see vol. 1, n. 279; al-Shirbīnī means, jokingly, that “crone” and “virgin” occur in the opposite of chronological order.

586 Bashshār ibn Burd (ca. 95–167/714–784) (*Dīwān*, 4:117).

587 *The Westward Migration of the Banū Hilāl* (*Taghrībat Banī Hilāl*): one of the cycles of the *Sīrat Banī Hilāl* epic, which describes the movement of the originally Arabian Banū Hilāl tribe from Egypt to Tunis (see G. Canova, “Banū Hilāl, romance of,” in *EAL*); parts of the epic are still recited in Egypt.

588 “Some say he used to teach . . . he knew . . . he possessed knowledge . . . he used to instruct . . .,” etc: the basic sense of *ʿarīf* in common usage is “monitor in a school, who hears the students rehearse their lessons” (Lane, *Lexicon*, 2016). Al-Shirbīnī, however, exploits the tri-consonantal root *ʿ-r-f*, with its connotations of “knowledge” and “teaching” to string together a list of further, improbable, instructional roles for the *ʿarīf*, before getting around to this basic sense.

589 Q Māʾidah 5:38.

590 “if there is doubt (*shubhah*)”: “In attempting to avoid as much as possible imposition of the severe *ḥadd* penalties . . . the jurists appealed to a prophetic Tradition instructing the believers to ‘avert the *ḥadd* penalties by means of ambiguous cases’” (E. K. Rowson, “Shubha,” in *EI2*).

591 The first line is by Abū l-ʿAlāʾ al-Maʿarrī (363–449/973–1058) (*Al-Luzūmiyyāt*, 1:391), the reply by ʿAlam al-Dīn al-Sakhāwī (d. 643/1245) (see al-Ṣafadī, *Al-Wāfī*, 7:110).

592 Amputation of the hand for theft is one of the *ḥadd* punishments, i.e., one of those specifically prescribed in the Qurʾan.

593 Al-Shirbīnī seems to imply that the two words are synonymous, though, in formal terms, *jāmiʿ* is more correctly applied to a large

mosque used for collective prayer, while *masjid* is applied to a smaller mosque.

594 Typically, the worshipper removes his slippers on entering the mosque and places them near him while praying.

595 Major ritual impurity (*janābah*) is "caused by marital intercourse . . . [or] any *effusio seminis*" (Th. W. Juynboll, "Djanāba," in *EI2*), and one in this state cannot perform a valid prayer (*ṣalāt*), enter a mosque, or perform a number of rites.

596 Al-Būṣīrī was of rural origin and spent several years as a financial official in the Delta town of Bilbays.

597 A district called al-Rukn al-Mukhallaq ("The Perfumed Corner") lay south of Bāb al-Futūḥ (Raymond, *Marchés*, 86), and this street was probably located there.

598 "slippers as red as your face": apparently a popular joke, see vol. 1, §3.17.

599 Al-Būṣīrī plays with the colloquial expression *ʿala qafa min yishīl*, literally "on the necks of those who would carry them off," i.e., "there for the taking." On *qafā* ("back of the neck, nape") in insults, see vol. 1, n. 28.

600 Like other verses in mixed colloquial-classical style attributed to him by al-Shirbīnī, this is not included in al-Būṣīrī's works.

601 Al-Būṣīrī puns on *dukhūl*, literally "entering" but used here in the specialized sense of "fine singing, singing in tune," and its opposite, *khurūj* ("exiting; singing out of tune").

602 See Ibn Khallikān, *Wafayāt*, 2:98ff.

603 In Iḥsan ʿAbbās's edition of Ibn Khallikān, the name of this otherwise apparently unknown individual is given as Jamāl al-Dīn Maḥmūd ibn ʿAbd Allāh *al-Irbilī*. He may be Jamāl al-Dīn Muḥammad ibn ʿAbd Allāh al-Badīhī, man of letters, poet, and musician, who died in Cairo in 656/1258 and was therefore a contemporary of Ibn Khallikān (see al-Ṣafadī, *Al-Wāfī*, 26:275–76, where he is not called al-Irbilī but is said to have grown up in Mosul, which is not far from Irbil).

604 As al-Shirbīnī explains below, the verses exploit lines from a poem by Abū Nuwās that flatters the caliph by referring to the custom

by which camels used to bring riders to a holy sanctuary, such as that at the Prophet's tomb in Medina, were released from further service. Thus the poet compares his visit to Ibn Khallikān's office to that of a poet to his master and a visitor to the Prophet's tomb in Medina, and he compares his stolen slippers to the now emancipated camel on which he made this pilgrimage. Abū Nuwās's verses are to be found, with some differences, in Abū Nuwās, *Dīwān*, 1:127.

605 I.e., if ʿIwaḍ is "recompense," as his name implies, for a pair of slippers, he can be no better than such himself.

606 *Muqaylī* is the diminutive of *maqlī* ("fried").

607 On this colloquial use of *laff* (literally "to wrap"), see §11.7.10.

608 See Marzolph and van Leuwen, *Arabian Nights Encyclopedia*, 1:405–6, where the story is described as belonging to "the core corpus" of the *Nights*.

609 I.e., with both Ibn ʿAbbās and his father, ʿAbbās.

610 The barber never does get around to saying how much of the day has elapsed, as his interminable sentence takes off in other directions.

611 The second month of the Hijri year.

612 Equivalent to AD 12 April 1352, though this was a Wednesday, not a Friday.

613 "the era of Our Lord Adam . . . of Alexander the Greek and . . . of the Persian reckoning": these three dating systems for the pre-Islamic period are described in some detail by al-ʿĀmirī (Rowson, "A Muslim Philosopher," 61–67). However, according to al-ʿĀmirī, the time elapsed between the creation of Adam and the first year of the Hijra (the era of Adam) amounts to either 6215 or around 4280 Persian years (depending on the method of calculation used) rather than the barber's 7000. The era of Alexander dates from the latter's arrival in Jerusalem (historically, 313), when he ordered the Jews to begin a new era, and thus the number of years elapsed before the Hijra should equal 935 years versus the barber's 320 years. The Persian era also dates from the creation of Adam.

614 Q Anbiyāʾ 21:7.

615 "the Aswan Mug" (*al-kūz al-aswānī*): Dozy (*Supplément* s.v. *kūz*) quotes Lane's comment in his translation: [the Aswan Mug] "seems to imply that the person thus named was always like a mug, with open mouth, and insensible as flint to rebuke," referring to *aswānī*, meaning "flint."

616 Q Āl ʿImrān 3:134. The sense is completed in verse 136: "The reward of such will be forgiveness from their Lord," etc.; cf. the use of the same verse above (§11.35.13).

617 Q ʿAnkabūt 29:8.

618 Q Nūr 24:61.

619 A conflation of two lines by al-Zubayr ibn ʿAbd al-Muṭṭalib, uncle of the Prophet Muḥammad (see Ibn Sallām al-Jumaḥī, *Ṭabaqāt*, 205).

620 The names (which rhyme in the Arabic) are a mixture of the ordinary—though linked to low-status trades—such as ʿAkrashah, Saʿīd, Ḥāmid, ʿUkāshah, and the eccentric, such as Zaytūn ("Olives"), Big-Mouth (Dalīʿ al-Fāmī, presumably a distortion of *dalīʿ al-fam*), Salawṭaḥ (cf. *salṭaḥ* "to lie down flat, stretch out" (Hinds and Badawi, *Dictionary*, 509; cf. Lane, *Lexicon*, 1406 s.v. "islanṭaḥ")), Suwayd ("Little Black"), and Sheep-Larks (*Qunbur al-Khirfān*).

621 Kharā-Lḥas: i.e., Kharā Ilḥas (for the meter).

622 I.e., bright red.

623 Meaning, perhaps, that his wife is bound to get along somehow, and he need not worry about her himself.

624 Ibn Sabuʿ al-imām al-khaṭīb Abū l-Rabʿ Sulaymān al-Sabtī is mentioned by Ḥājjī Khalifah as the author of a work named *Shifāʾ al-ṣudūr* (Ḥājjī Khalīfah, *Kashf al-ẓunūn*, col. 1050); he is also quoted by al-Suyūṭī (*Al-Itqān*, 4:226) and mentioned several times by al-Damīrī (*Ḥayawān*).

625 The convention of ending a book with "miscellaneous anecdotes" is old, being present already in, e.g., al-Jāḥiẓ's *Mufākharat al-jawārī wa-l-ghilmān* (al-Jāḥiẓ, *Rasāʾil*, 4:125–38). Such anecdotes appear to have a structural purpose, touching on several of the themes of the book; in this case some are at the expense of grammarians, and the

theme of disillusionment with the world, which recalls complaints of neglect with which the book opens, recurs.

626 Q Nisā' 4:86.

627 A less elaborate version of the same story appears in the *Kitāb al-Manẓūm wa-l-manthūr* of Aḥmad ibn Abī Ṭāhir Ṭayfūr (d. 280/893), where, however, the protagonist is a certain Salāmah ibn Fulayḥ and the caliph is al-Mahdī (Borg, "Lust," 158).

628 Zayd and ʿAmr (who makes an appearance below) are names used in examples of grammatical points memorized by schoolchildren, such as "ʿAmr struck Zayd," where ʿAmr stands for the subject of the verb and Zayd for the object; under this convention Bakr is usually the third actor, introduced when needed.

629 In Arabic, vowels are called *ḥarakāt* (literally "motions"); desinential inflection often consists of the addition of short vowels to the verb or noun.

630 "active participle" (*fāʿil*): meaning both "doer, actor" (in both the basic sense and that of "active partner in intercourse, fucker") and "active participle."

631 Al-Shirbīnī switches to the technical terminology of Qur'anic recitation, alluding to the *madd muttaṣil* (a long open vowel of two to six beats that links two words) and the *madd munfaṣil* (a long vowel occurring within a word and closed with a glottal stop) (see Nelson, *Art*, 25).

632 The "stranger" here is the food that has not been eaten, and the funeral is that held by his relatives for a man who has left his homeland and is presumed to have died (usually called "the prayer for the absent dead" (*al-ṣalāh ʿalā al-mayyit al-ghā'ib*)).

633 It is forbidden to sell meat from an animal that was not in healthy condition when slaughtered.

634 The utterance of the formula *bism illāh al-raḥmān al-raḥīm* ("In the name of God, the Merciful, the Compassionate").

635 The formula *ḥayya ʿalā l-ṣalāh ḥayya ʿalā l-falāḥ* ("Come to prayer! Come to prosperity!"), which occurs in the call to prayer; it is not, however, supposed to be used when slaughtering.

636 I.e., the Kaaba.

637 Q Naḥl 16:7.

638 Q Ḥijr 15:46; the reference in the original context is to the gardens of Paradise.

639 The incident is reported in various sources, with minor differences and with the verses from which these lines are extracted attributed to various poets (see, e.g., al-Khaṭīb al-Baghdādī, *Tārīkh*, 14:196; al-Masʿūdī, *Murūj*, 4:23).

640 al-Ḥarīrī: these lines are not found among al-Ḥarīrī's works, and the attribution is dubious.

641 al-Būṣīrī: these lines are not found among al-Būṣīrī's works, and the attribution is dubious.

642 "a pipsqueak that from the beaten path departs" (*ka-l-ziblati fī l-tayyār*): the line is reminiscent of the modern saying *ziblah wi-tqāwiḥ it-tayyār* (literally "a dung pellet, and it goes against the stream"), meaning "he's a nobody and he's out to change the world" (Hinds and Badawi, *Dictionary*, 365).

643 A variant of the name Muḥammad.

Glossary

'abā'ah "a long, wide garment made of wool with different-colored stripes, which the country people use as something to lie on in summer and as a cover in winter" (§11.7.10).

'Abd al-Malik (r. 65–86/685–705) fifth caliph of the Umayyad dynasty.

'Abd al-Wahhāb al-Sha'rānī (897–973/1491–1565) a leading Egyptian Sufi of his time.

'Abd Qays an eastern Arabian tribe.

'Ablah cousin and beloved of 'Antarah (q.v.).

Abū l-'Atāhiyah Abū l-'Atāhiyah Ismā'īl ibn al-Qāsim (131–211/748–826), a poet of Baghdad known for his pious and censorious verse.

Abū Ḥāmid al-Ghazālī (450–505/1056–1111), theologian, jurist, mystic, and religious reformer, author of *Iḥyā' 'ulūm al-dīn* (*The Revival of the Religious Sciences*).

Abū Ḥanīfah al-Nu'mān (ca. 81–150/700–67), celebrated religious scholar of Iraq, after whom the Hanafi school of law is named.

Abū Nu'aym Aḥmad ibn 'Abd Allāh Abū Nu'aym al-Iṣfahānī (336–430/948–1038), author of *Ḥilyat al-awliyā' wa-ṭabaqāt al-aṣfiyā'* (*The Adornment of the Saints and Classes of the Pure*), a biographical dictionary of early Islamic pious people, renunciants, and mystics.

Abū Nuwās Abū Nuwās al-Ḥasan ibn Hāni' al-Ḥakamī (ca. 130–98/ca. 747–813), one of the most famous poets of the Abbasid "Golden Age," especially in wine poetry and the love lyric. Though Abū Nuwās spent his most brilliant years in the service of the caliph al-Amīn, popular imagination has linked him with Hārūn al-Rashīd, al-Amīn's father. This popular Abū Nuwās is also the focus of numerous comic or instructive anecdotes.

Abū Ṣīr name of several villages, the one in the central Delta, on the eastern bank of the eastern branch of the Nile, probably being the one referred to in *Brains Confounded*.

Abū ʿUbaydah Abū ʿUbaydah Maʿmar ibn al-Muthannā (d. 209/824–25), philologist and historian of pre-Islamic and early Arabic history and culture.

Abū Yaʿlā Abū Yaʿlā Aḥmad ibn ʿAlī ibn al-Muthannā al-Mawṣilī al-Tamīmī (d. 307/919–20), an early and highly reputed transmitter of Traditions.

Ād and Thamūd ancient tribes of Arabia, both mentioned in the Qur'an as having been wiped out by disasters in punishment for misdeeds (in ʿĀd's case, by a violent storm (Q Aʿrāf 7:65, Hūd 11:58, etc.) or a drought (Q Hūd 11:52), in Thamūd's by an earthquake (Q Aʿrāf 7:78) or a thunderbolt (Q Fuṣṣilat 41:13, 17)).

ʿAdnān according to traditional Arab genealogy ʿAdnān was the ancestor of the Northern Arabs, that is, those who inhabited the Hijaz and Najd and spoke Arabic proper, as distinct from the Arabs of the Yemen, who descended from Qaḥṭān and spoke a related language. Both ʿAdnān and Qaḥṭān descended from Sām ibn Nūḥ (Shem son of Noah).

Aḥmad al-Sandūbī Aḥmad ibn ʿAlī al-Sandūbī (d. 1097/1686), a scholar and teacher at al-Azhar (see vol. 1, p. xiii).

ʿĀʾishah bint Abī Bakr (d. ca. 58/677–78) the favorite wife of the Prophet Muḥammad.

ʿAlī (ibn Abī Ṭālib), the Imam first cousin and son-in-law of the Prophet Muḥammad and fourth rightly guided caliph (d. 40/661). A highly venerated figure among Sunni as well as Shiʿi Muslims, he has become the attributive source of a vast number of maxims. None of the four sayings attributed to ʿAlī in this work is to be found in the standard collections.

al-Aʿmash Abū Muḥammad Sulaymān ibn Mihrān al-Aʿmash (60–148/679–765), traditionist and transmitter of one of the fourteen canonical readings of the Qur'an.

al-Amīn al-Amīn Muḥammad (170–198/878–813), a son of Hārūn al-Rashīd; as a full-blooded Hashemite (descendant of the Prophet's ancestor Hāshim), he succeeded to the caliphate on the latter's death but was later overthrown by an older brother, al-Ma'mūn ʿAbd Allāh, the son of a slave.

Anṣinā Antinoe, in the district of Mallawī, near Asyūṭ, site of the tomb of Antinous, favorite of the Roman emperor Hadrian, who drowned nearby.

ʿAntar see *ʿAntarah.*

ʿAntarah (or ʿAntar) ʿAntarah ibn Shaddād al-ʿAbsī (fl. second half of the sixth century AD); pre-Islamic poet and hero of the folk epic *Sīrat ʿAntar.*

antithesis (muqābalah, ṭibāq) technically *muqābalah,* refers to a compound form of antithesis in which "there is more than one term on each side of the antithesis" (W. P. Heinrichs "Rhetorical Figures" in *EAL*, 2:659, s.v. *muṭābaqah*), whereas *ṭibāq* refers to "the inclusion of two contraries in one line or sentence" (ibid.); al-Shirbīnī, however, seems to use *ṭibāq* as a synonym of *muqābalah.*

ʿArab a woman's name, used conventionally for the Beloved.

ʿAshūrāʾ the tenth day of the month of Muḥarram, observed as an optional fast and celebration.

al-Aṣmaʿī Abū Saʿīd ʿAbd al-Malik ibn Qurayb al-Bāhilī al-Aṣmaʿī (122–213/740–828?), the most celebrated of the early philologists and collectors of Bedouin poetry and language.

ʿAsqalān a city in southwestern Palestine, now called al-Majdal.

aṭwāf courses of dung cakes laid in a spiral; a fire is lit inside the resulting igloo-like structure to dry out the dung in preparation for its use as fuel.

ʿawāʾid ("customary dues") gratuities paid to officials in return for the performance of various services and counted among the *maẓālim* (q.v.) (see Raymond, *Artisans*, 1:124 and passim).

al-ʿawnah see *corvée.*

al-ʿAynī Abū Muḥammad Maḥmūd ibn Aḥmad ibn Mūsā Badr al-Dīn al-ʿAynī (762–855/1361–1451), Mamluk scholar and bureaucrat.

ʿayniyyah a poem with *ʿayn* as rhyme consonant.

al-Azhar the mosque of al-Azhar: founded in 361/972, the mosque became Egypt's preeminent institution of learning (sometimes referred to as a mosque-university) during the Ottoman period (vol. 1, p. lvi).

Bāb al-Naṣr "The Gate of Victory," a gate in Cairo's northeast city wall.

Bāb Zuwaylah Cairo's eastern gate, at the end of al-Ghūriyyah street, named after the Berber tribe al-Zawīlah, who were quartered nearby when the gate was built by the Fatimids in 485/1092.

al-Badawī, Aḥmad (596/1199–1200 to 675/1276), a widely venerated saint whose shrine is at Ṭanṭā, in the Delta, eponym of an antinomian, largely rural socio-mystical movement, the Aḥmadiyyah (unrelated to the modern Pakistan-based Ahmadiyya movement).

Baḥīrā a monk encountered by the Prophet Muḥammad when he accompanied a trade caravan from Mecca to Syria as a boy; according to Muslim tradition, Baḥīrā recognized the Prophet's status, while, according to the Arab and Greek Christian traditions, he "became [Muḥammad's] inspirer and involuntary accomplice . . . in the composition of the Qur'an" (A. Abel, "Baḥīrā," in *EI2*).

bailiff (shādd and *mashadd)* a village official responsible for the maintenance of law and order and, in particular, for the payment by the peasants of their taxes.

Banū l-ʿAbbās the Abbasids, the descendants of the Prophet's uncle al-ʿAbbās ibn ʿAbd al-Muṭṭalib; they formed the third caliphal dynasty, taking power in 132/750.

Banū Umayyah the Umayyad dynasty, which ruled the Muslim world from 41/661 to 132/750.

Banū ʿUqbah a subtribe of Judhām/Judām (al-Maqrīzī, *Al-Bayān*, 18; Murray, *Sons*, 25).

al-Baqīʿ the oldest Muslim cemetery in Medina.

al-Barmakī, Jaʿfar (150–87/767–803), member of the celebrated "Barmecide" family of leading officials at the court of Hārūn al-Rashīd.

basīsah a sweet pastry made with corn (maize) flour.

al-Basūs, War of the most famous of the *Ayyām al-ʿArab* ("Battle-days of the Arabs"), conflicts between tribes that provided the occasion for much of the heroic poetry of pre-Islamic Arabia.

bawshah according to al-Shirbīnī, the *bawshah* is a vessel used for cooking fava beans, wheat groats, and *bīsār* (q.v.); today, a rounded earthenware vessel for storing water, milk, clarified butter, etc. (Behnstedt and Woidich, *Glossar*, 40).

Bayn al-Qaṣrayn literally Between the Two Palaces, a stretch of the street called al-Qaṣabah (today al-Muʿizz li-Dīn illāh Street); a main thoroughfare of medieval Cairo, originally a ceremonial ground between the Eastern and Western palaces of the Fatimids.

Birkat al-Fīl literally, the Pond of the Elephant, the second largest of the thirteen major ponds or lakes in Cairo in al-Shirbīnī's day (Shalabī, *Siyāḥatnāmah*, 374–75).

bīsār/bisārah fava beans mashed with *mulūkhiyyā* (Jew's mallow).

bisāriyah small fry of several species of Nile fish.

The Blue Ocean and Piebald Canon (Al-Qāmūs al-azraq wa-l-nāmūs al-ablaq) a fictitious dictionary (see vol. 1, n. 127).

The Brilliant Poem (Al-Badīʿiyyah) that is, *The Brilliant Sufficient Poem on the Sciences of Rhetoric and the Charms of the Badīʿ Style* (*Al-Kāfiyah al-Badīʿiyyah fī ʿulūm al-balāghah wa-maḥāsin al-badīʿ*), a poem in praise of the Prophet Muḥammad by al-Ṣafī al-Ḥillī (q.v.) that uses each of the major rhetorical tropes in turn.

al-Bukhārī Abū ʿAbd Allāh Muḥammad ibn Ismāʿīl al-Bukhārī (194–256/810–870), renowned collector of Traditions, best known for his *Al-Jāmiʿ al-Ṣaḥīḥ* (*The Reliable Collection [of Traditions]*), a compilation of Traditions meeting the highest criteria of authenticity.

Būlāq the port on the Nile west of Cairo and separated from it, in al-Shirbīnī's day, by agricultural land.

Būlāq al-Takrūr a suburb of al-Jīzah (today called Būlāq al-Dakrūr).

al-Būnī Abū l-ʿAbbās Aḥmad ibn ʿAlī ibn Yūsuf al-Būnī al-Qurashī al-Ṣūfī (d. 622/1225 in Cairo), a scholar of Maghribī origin and author of several books on the esoteric sciences.

al-Burdah see *al-Būṣīrī*.

būrī a kind of gray mullet.

al-Būṣīrī Muḥammad ibn Saʿīd al-Būṣīrī (608/1213 to 694/1294–95), a poet whose long panegyric of the Prophet entitled *The Mantle*

(*Al-Burdah*) was immensely popular; few of the verses attributed to al-Būṣīrī by al-Shirbīnī are included in his published works.

carat (qirāṭ, pl. qarārīṭ) a twenty-fourth part; village lands were divided into lots, each equal to one twenty-fourth of the whole.

caudal paronomasia (jinās mudhayyal) repetition of homophonic elements (paronomasia) with the appendage of an additional dissimilar element, as in the saying *al-ʿār dhull al-ʿārif* ("Shame is the humiliation of the discerning") (al-Ḥillī, *Al-Badīʿiyyah*, 63).

Chosroes (Kisrā Anūshirwān; Persian Khusraw Anūshirwān*)* a Sassanid emperor (r. AD 521–79).

the Christian of the village (naṣrānī l-balad) informal designation of the *ṣarrāf* (village tax collector), reflecting the dominance by Christians of the administrative and financial professions. ʿAbd al-Raḥīm states that the *ṣarrāf*'s functions included the assessment of the taxes (in terms of sown and fallow land, the latter being untaxed) and the assignment of the tax obligation on each parcel (ʿAbd al-Raḥīm, *Al-Rīf*, 43–46, 160); the *ṣarrāf* also maintained registers showing what each cultivator owed and how much each had paid.

Companions (of the Prophet) those Muslims who had contact with the Prophet Muḥammad during his lifetime. They are particularly honored as transmitters of Traditions.

copper piece (jadīd) see *silver piece (nuṣṣ).*

the corvée (al-ʿawnah) compulsory labor on the tax farmer's demesne (*ūsyah/wisiyyah*); cf. *al-sukhrah.*

al-Damīrī Kamāl al-Dīn Muḥammad ibn Mūsā l-Damīrī (745–808/1344–1405), author of several works on zoology, including a *Greater* and a *Lesser Life of Animals* (*Ḥayāt al-ḥayawān al-kubrā* and *al-ṣughrā*)—alphabetical encyclopedias listing etymologies of the names of animals, references to animals in the Qur'an, Traditions, and poetry, their uses in medicine, and so on.

al-Danaf, Aḥmad a popular archetype of robbers from early Islamic times who also appears as a leader of a band of forty rogues in *The Thousand and One Nights* (*Alf laylah wa-laylah*) and as the hero of a popular fifteenth-century romance, *Sīrat Aḥmad al-Danaf.* While his epithet is given by some scholars as *al-Danif*, meaning "the Sick," in Egypt today, where he remains a figure of the popular imagination, it is pronounced *al-Danaf*, possibly meaning "Sweetie-pie."

dārah a children's game of tag (see §§10.9, 11.19.5).

Day of Escape (yawm al-hurūbah) Lane, writing in the 1830s, says, in reference to urban weddings, "On the morning after the marriage . . . if the bridegroom is a young man, [a friend] generally takes him and several friends to an entertainment in the country, where they spend the whole day. This ceremony is called 'el-huroobeh' or the flight. Sometimes the bridegroom himself makes the arrangements for it; and pays part of the expenses, if they exceed the amount of the contributions of his friends; for they give nukoot [*nuqūṭ* 'gifts of money'] on this occasion. Musicians and dancing-girls are often hired to attend the entertainment" (Lane, *Manners*, 174).

Day of the Divine Decree (yawm al-qadr) more usually referred to as "the Night of the Divine Decree"; the night during Ramadan on which the Qur'an was first revealed to the Prophet; its precise date is not known, though it is generally taken to be that before the twenty-seventh day. Many believe that, on that night, those who are vigilant will be rewarded by having their prayers granted and their sins forgiven.

Dayr al-Ṭīn ("The Mud Monastery") perhaps the village of that name south of Old Cairo (Ramzī 1:77); see also *al-Ṣābūnī, Bridge of* below.

demesne (wisiyyah; also, in formal contexts, *ūsyah)* a private, tax-exempt grant of land sometimes made to a tax farmer in compensation for expenses occurred in the performance of his duties. The *wisiyyah* varied from one-quarter to one-half of the entire tax farm ('Abd al-Raḥīm, *Al-Rīf*, 96–100; Shaw, *Financial*, 22–23, 57–58).

dervish (faqīr, pl. fuqarā') literally "poor man," that is, one who is "poor in God," a conventional term for a Sufi mystic; al-Shirbīnī uses the term mainly of mendicant rural dervishes.

dhikr literally "mentioning" or "naming" (of God), which, ritualized in various forms (with or without music, silently or audibly, accompanied, or not, by bodily movement), has become the central ceremony of most Sufi orders and groups.

Dimyāṭ Damietta, a town on the Mediterranean, at the mouth of the eastern branch of the Nile and, in al-Shirbīnī's day, Egypt's second city and its most important port for commerce with the eastern Mediterranean, handling the greater part of Egypt's rice exports (Raymond, *Artisans*, 1:166). Al-Shirbīnī's contemporary Wansleben says of it that, "Next to Cairo it is the greatest, most beautiful, the richest, the most populous, and the fullest of Merchants of all Egypt" (Wansleben, *Present State*, 67).

al-Dīrīnī, ʿAbd al-ʿAzīz (d. 697/1297–98), a Sufi reported to have been "possessed of magnificent states, noble conditions, famous miracles, and numerous written works, in the fields of commentary, jurisprudence, language, and Sufism, and much well-known verse . . . . His residence was in the countryside near Cairo" (al-Shaʿrānī, *Lawāqiḥ*, 1:172).

emir (amīr) "commander," a title given high-ranking military officers. By al-Shirbīnī's time, most tax farmers were emirs.

fālūdhaj a sweet dish made of wheat or starch with water and honey (Lane, *Lexicon*) or of almonds and sugar (Rodinson, *Recherches*, 149).

faqīh see *pastor.*

faqīr see *dervish.*

faqr see *poverty.*

al-Farazdaq ("the Lump of Dough") nickname of the poet Hammām ibn Ghālib (d. 110/728 or 112/730).

farḍ ("duty") in Islam, "a religious duty or obligation, the omission of which will be punished and the performance of which will be rewarded" (Th. W. Juynboll, "Farḍ," in *EI2*).

Fātiḥah opening chapter of the Qur'an.

faṭīrah (pl. faṭīr, faṭāyir) a round or square of many-layered flaky pastry.

feddan (faddān, pl. fadādīn) a surface measure equal today to 4,200 square meters or 1.038 acres.

fiqī see *pastor.*

fisā l-kilāb a plant, "white pigweed"; literally "dog's fart."

foot soldiers (mushāh) the term *mushāh*, sometimes coupled with *jidʿān* ("brave lads"), appears to refer to the village's own armed forces, ready to take part in the raids and fighting for which the countryside was notorious.

Friend(s) of God see *God's Friends.*

ghafīr village guard or constable. "They prevented thefts and other crimes and gave warning of Bedouin attacks. They guarded the *multazim*'s [tax farmer's] house and the harvest and they watched the dykes to prevent their being tampered with out of season" (Rivlin, *Policy*, 29).

the Ghawāzī a Gypsy group that traditionally makes its living from dancing and other entertainment.

al-Ghawrī, Qānṣawh (r. 906–22/1501–16), penultimate sultan of the Burjī Mamluk dynasty.

the Ghuzz a term loosely applied, in al-Shirbīnī's time, to any troops of Turkic origin (from *Oğuz*, a group of Turkic tribes that moved west from Mongolia in the eighth century AD and were ultimately incorporated into the Muslim armies).

God's Friends, Friend(s) of God (wulāh, sg. walī) persons to whom God has vouchsafed esoteric knowledge "by transmission from Muḥammad, through a chain of elect masters, and also by direct inspiration" (Trimingham, *Sufi Orders*, 141, also 133–35).

ḥadd the *ḥadd* punishments are those specified in the Qur'an, including amputation of the hand for theft.

al-Ḥājj title of a man who has made the pilgrimage to Mecca.

al-Ḥajjāj al-Ḥajjāj ibn Yūsuf (41–95/661–714), Umayyad general and governor, famous for his harsh rule and chaste language.

al-Ḥākim bi-Amr Allāh (r. 386–411/996–1021), sixth caliph of the Fatimid dynasty.

al-Ḥalabī Nūr al-Dīn ibn Burhān al-Dīn ibn ʿAlī ibn Ibrāhīm ibn Aḥmad ibn ʿAlī ibn ʿUmar al-Qāhirī al-Shāfiʿī al-Ḥalabī (975/1567–68 to 1044/1635), author of a biography of the Prophet entitled *Insān al-ʿuyūn* (*The Pupil of the Eyes*), generally known as *Al-Sīrah al-ḥalabiyyah* (*Al-Ḥalabī's Biography*).

ḥālūm a kind of salted cheese.

hamziyyah a poem whose rhyme consonant is the letter *hamzah* (glottal stop, transliterated as ').

ḥarām "forbidden by religion."

Ḥarām (tribe) see *Saʿd.*

al-Ḥarīrī Abū Muḥammad al-Qāsim ibn ʿAlī l-Ḥarīrī (446–516/1054–1122), poet and man of letters, best known for his collection of fifty narrations in rhymed prose interspersed with verse (*maqāmāt*), in which he frequently uses puns and riddles.

harīsah "Any of a number of sweet confections made with flour, clarified butter and sugar" (Hinds and Badawi, *Dictionary*, 904).

Hārūn al-Rashīd (r. 170–93/786–809) fifth caliph of the Abbasid dynasty.

al-Ḥasan (d. 49/669–70), older son of Fāṭimah, the Prophet Muḥammad's daughter and only surviving child, and of ʿAlī ibn Abī Ṭālib, the prophet's cousin; on his father's death, al-Ḥasan conceded the caliphate to Muʿāwiyah.

Ḥassān ibn Thābit Ḥassān ibn Thābit ibn Mundhir al-Khazrajī al-Anṣārī (d. 54/674), a poet who supposedly lived sixty years before the coming of Islam and sixty years after the coming of Islam and was the Prophet's most prominent laureate.

Hijra the "migration" of the Prophet from Medina to Mecca; the Islamic (*hijrī*) calendar starts from the beginning of that year (18 July 622).

Hind a woman's name, used conventionally for the Beloved.

the House of Binding (Dār al-Shadd) "a building which was maintained by the [bailiff] as a hotel for visitors in the village and as the headquarters of the *multazim* [tax farmer] and his agents. The *Fellahin* were provided with suitable quarters at the *Dar al-Shadd* until their accounts were settled, and the payments which they made in kind were stored there until they were disposed of" (Shaw, *Financial*, 55–56); the quarters would be for peasants from outlying villages under the authority of a single bailiff.

al-Ḥumaydī ʿAbd al-Raḥmān ibn Muḥammad al-Ḥumaydī, a poet and physician and shaykh of the Cairo book trade. Although he does not give his dates, al-Khafājī (979–1069/1571–1659) includes him in his biographical dictionary of his contemporaries (al-Khafājī, *Rayḥānat al-alibbāʾ*, 2:114–16), and he would thus have been a (probably older) contemporary of al-Shirbīnī, who appears also to have been a bookseller (see vol. 1, p. xxii).

Hurbayṭ a village, since disappeared, on the eastern branch of the Nile.

al-Ḥurr ibn Yazīd al-Tamīmī a Muslim general sent by the caliph Yazīd to prevent the Prophet Muḥammad's grandson al-Ḥusayn from reaching al-Kūfah during the struggle over the succession to the caliphate following the death of Muʿāwiyah. Al-Ḥurr, however, joined al-Ḥusayn's forces and died with him on the battlefield.

al-Ḥusayn (d. 61/680), younger son of Fāṭimah, daughter and only child of the Prophet Muḥmmad and wife of ʿAlī ibn Abī Ṭālib; following the death of the caliph Muʿāwiyah, al-Ḥusayn briefly contested the succession of the latter's son, Yazīd, and was killed in battle at Karbalāʾ, in Iraq.

al-Ḥusayniyyah a residential neighborhood of Cairo, northeast of Bāb al-Futūḥ.

Iblīs Satan.

Ibn ʿAbbās ʿAbd Allāh ibn ʿAbbās (d. ca. 68/687–88), cousin of the Prophet, renowned as a recorder of Traditions, and a scholar of jurisprudence and Qurʾanic exegesis.

Ibn Abī Burdah, Bilāl (d. ca. 126/744), a judge and governor of Basra; of his approach to judging he said, "If two men come to me with a dispute, I decide in favor of the one I find the less tedious."

Ibn Adham Ibrāhīm Ibn Adham ibn Manṣūr (d. 161/778), seen by Sufis as a prototype and predecessor; Ibn Adham went bareheaded and barefoote gave his inheritance away, sought learning, fought the Greeks, and lived by the labor of his own hands.

Ibn Aktham, Yaḥyā (d. 242/857), chief justice of the Abbasid caliph al-Maʾmūn and representative in *adab* literature of the "supposed inclination of judges towards forbidden homosexuality" (Rosenthal, "Male and Female," 30).

Ibn al-ʿArabī Abū ʿAbd Allāh Muḥammad ibn ʿAlī ibn Muḥammad ibn al-ʿArabī al-Ḥātimī al-Ṭāʾī (560–638/1165–1240), one of the greatest exponents of metaphysical Sufism and author of several hundred works of prose and verse.

Ibn al-ʿĀṣ, ʿAmr (d. ca. 42/663), a Companion of the Prophet Muḥammad and one of his leading military commanders, who led the conquest of Egypt (19–21/640–42).

Ibn al-Fāriḍ ʿUmar ibn ʿAlī ibn al-Fāriḍ (576–632/1181–1235), a celebrated Sufi poet whose tomb "became a gathering place for all of Cairo's classes and, by the seventeenth century, a mosque for weekly worship unsurpassed in all of Egypt" (Homerin, *Ibn al-Fāriḍ*, 93). His verses remain popular today.

Ibn al-Khaṭṭāb, ʿUmar (r. 13–23/634–44), the second rightly guided caliph.

Ibn al-Mudabbir, Aḥmad (d. 270/884), director of finance (*ʿāmil al-kharāj*) in Egypt, under the Abbasid caliph al-Mutawakkil (r. 232–47/847–61); Ibn al-Mudabbir "introduced a number of new taxes . . . such as the one on cattle fodder . . . as well as the monopoly on caustic soda . . . . Hence he became the most hated director of finance for centuries" (Gottschalk, "Ibn al-Mudabbir," in *EI2*).

Ibn al-Rāwandī Abū Ḥusayn Aḥmad ibn Yaḥyā ibn Isḥāq ibn al-Rāwandī (fl. third/ninth century), a freethinker whose writings survive mainly as fragments in the works of his critics and are primarily concerned with the rejection of prophecy and of the intervention of the divine in the lives of men.

Ibn al-Zubayr ʿAbd Allāh ibn al-Zubayr (d. 73/692), prominent member of the ʿAbd Shams clan of the tribe of Quraysh and younger relative of the Prophet Muḥammad who, from Mecca, led an anti-Umayyad movement during the reigns of Yazīd and ʿAbd al-Malik.

Ibn ʿAmr al-Asadī, Minhāl a Kufan transmitter of Traditions.

Ibn ʿArūs a poet of quatrains with a moralizing tone and a distinctive, easily memorized rhyme scheme (ABAB) and rhythm, which still form part of the Egyptian folk-wisdom tradition and are sometimes sung to preface performances of the folk epic *Sīrat Banī Hilāl*. Sources differ as to the origins of Ibn ʿArūs (Qinā in Upper Egypt or Tunis; al-Shirbīnī refers to him as a "Pole of the Maghrib") and his dates.

Ibn Daqīq al-ʿĪd, Taqī al-Dīn probably intended is Taqī al-Dīn Muḥammad ibn ʿAlī ibn Wahb ibn Muṭīʿ (or Abī l-Ṭāʿah) al-Quṣayrī (or al-Qushayrī) al-Manfalūṭī (625–702/1228–1302), a scholar of Tradition, professor of jurisprudence, and, at one point, chief judge of Egypt, who was also a poet and the scion of a distinguished family of scholars with whom he bore the sobriquet Ibn Daqīq al-ʿĪd ("Son of Flour-of-the-Festival").

Ibn Durayd Abū Bakr Muḥammad ibn al-Ḥasan ibn Durayd al-Azdī (223–312/838–933), a central figure of the linguistic scholarship of his time and author of *Al-Qaṣīdah al-maqṣūrah*, a pedagogical poem on words ending in *-ā*.

Ibn Ḥajar Ahmad ibn ʿAlī ibn Ḥajar al-ʿAsqalānī (773–852/1372–1449), Egyptian Traditionist, scholar, biographer, and historian.

Ibn Khālawayh Abū ʿAbd Allāh al-Ḥusayn ibn Aḥmad ibn Khālawayh al-Hamadhānī (d. 370/980–81), eminent grammarian and litterateur.

Ibn Khallikān Aḥmad ibn Muḥammad Abū l-ʿAbbās ibn Khallikān (608–81/1211–82), celebrated biographer, author of the multivolume *Obituaries of Noted Men* (*Wafayāt al-aʿyān*).

Ibn Muqlah Muḥammad ibn ʿAlī Ibn Muqlah (272/856–57 to 328/904) systematized the six basic cursive scripts of classical Arabic calligraphy. He was three times vizier under the Abbasids and died in prison, having had one hand and his tongue cut off.

Ibn Saʿd ibn Abī Waqqāṣ, ʿUmar (d. 66/686), an Umayyad general and son of a well-known Companion of the Prophet.

Ibn Sūdūn ʿAlī ibn Sūdūn al-Bashbughāwī (810–68/1407–64), author of several verse and prose pieces, both serious and humorous, are collected in an anthology entitled *Nuzhat al-nufūs wa-muḍḥik al-ʿabūs*. Al-Shirbīnī quotes several of his verses and parodies, as well as a lengthy prose piece ("Funayn's Letter") from the anthology and refers to him as a source of his own inspiration (see vol. 1, p. xxxv and §1.4).

Ibn ʿUmar ʿAbd Allāh ibn ʿUmar ibn al-Khaṭṭāb (10–73/613–692), son of the second caliph, noted for his piety and moral qualities.

Ibn Wāsiʿ, Muḥammad Muḥammad ibn Wāsiʿ ibn Jābir al-Azdī (d. 123/741), a traditionist of Basra.

Ibn Zāʾidah, Maʿn (d. 151/768), Umayyad and Abbasid governor, renowned for his generosity.

Ibn Ziyād, ʿUbayd Allāh (d. 67/686), Umayyad general, appointed governor of al-Kūfah by Yazīd in 60/679–80.

Imru' al-Qays Imru' al-Qays ibn Ḥujr, a poet of the sixth century AD, whose best known ode was one of those that, by tradition, are held to have been hung in the Kaaba at Mecca before the coming of Islam, and hence is known as his *muʿallaqah* ("suspended [ode]").

ʿInān (d. 226/841), a slave girl belonging to a Baṣran called al-Nāṭifī; she was renowned for the quickness of her repartee in verse, often displayed in joking contests with Abū Nuwās.

Inspector (kāshif, pl. kushshāf) official responsible for a minor province; the literal meaning of *kāshif* is "revealer, uncoverer." The duties of the Inspector in Ottoman Egypt consisted primarily of the maintenance of security and order, supervision of the exploitation of the land (including organization and monitoring of the irrigation system), and performance of imperial services (including payment of provincial garrisons and purchase of items required by the central authorities) (Shaw, *Financial*, 61). Wansleben comments that "a Cascief never ventures out in a Journy without a great train of Horse and Foot, and without expecting great matters" (*Present State*, 149), while Shalabī notes that the Nile flood cut them off from their districts during six months of the year, during which they appointed deputies, who traveled by boat to administer the areas (*Siyāhatnāmah*, 433) but that, "when the Nile recedes after three [*sic*] months leaving the land as mud, the peasants cast their seeds and put their feet on the land; then the hearts of the *kāshifs* and the officers and the tax-farmers are set at rest and they set off, with their troopers, to their provinces to sow their land" (idem, 434).

Inspector of Markets (muḥtasib) an official charged with the inspection of weights, measures, and prices and with maintaining public morality, who, as Lane noted in the Cairo of the 1830s, "occasionally [rode] about town, preceded by an officer who [carried] a large pair of scales, and followed by the executioners and numerous other servants" (Lane, *Manners*, 122).

inverted paronomasia (jinās maqlūb) that is, paronomasia in which the order of the homophonic elements is reversed, as in *āmālī* ("my hopes") versus *alāmī* ("my pains") (al-Ḥillī, *Al-Badīʿiyyah*, 67).

jawād a type of peasant shoe, synonymous, according to al-Shirbīnī, with *markūb* or *zarbūn* (kinds of slipper).

Jew's mallow see *mulūkhiyyā.*

Jibrīl the angel Gabriel.

al-Jisr district on the western bank of the Tigris at Baghdad, opposite al-Ruṣāfah and originally connected to the latter by a bridge (*jisr*) of boats.

al-Jīzah the settlement opposite Cairo on the west bank of the Nile (today usually spelled al-Guizah or Giza).

jubbah "long cloth coat of any color . . . , the sleeves of which reach not quite to the waist" (Lane, *Manners*, 30); it is open in front and usually worn over an under-robe.

Judām see *Judhām.*

Judhām (also Judām) a "Yemenite" (Qaḥṭānī) tribe that entered Egypt with the Muslim conquest and was present in the Delta (including the district of Hurbayṭ, close to Shirbīn) from at least the mid-eighteenth century. The name occurs three times in *Hazz al-quḥūf* to designate the opponents of the clan of Ḥarām and is thus apparently synonymous with Sa'd.

Juḥā protagonist of an enormous number of Egyptian (and other Middle Eastern) jokes and anecdotes, in which he often plays the role of the "wise fool."

al-Junayd Abū l-Qāsim ibn Muḥammad al-Junayd (d. 298/910), a key figure in the development of the moderate Baghdad school of Sufism.

Kafr Dundayṭ a village in the district of Mīt Ghamr in the modern governorate of al-Daqahliyyah.

Kafr Hurbayṭ see *Hurbayṭ.*

al-Kalbī, Ḥakīm ibn 'Ayyāsh (fl. second/eighth century), Syrian poet, best known for his satirical verse.

Karbalā' a city about sixty miles south-southwest of Baghdad.

the Khān of Abū Ṭaqiyyah complex of a depot, shops, and a hostelry built by the prominent merchant Ismā'īl Abū Ṭaqiyyah (fl. 1580–1625), the remains of which can still be seen in Khān Abū Ṭaqiyyah Street, directly behind the Qalāwūn complex on Bayn al-Qaṣrayn (q.v.).

al-Khānkah a town a few miles north of Cairo built around a Sufi hospice (*khānaqāh*) founded by the late seventh/thirteenth-century Mamluk sultan al-Malik al-Nāṣir Muḥammad ibn Qalāwūn.

kharāj land taxes; see also *māl (al-sulṭān)*.

Khawāmis, the name of the group that is the primary target of al-Shirbīnī's criticism of heterodox rural Sufi dervishes; vol. 1, pp. xlv–xlvi.

khayāl al-ẓill ("the shadow play") shadow plays, using leather cutouts on sticks held against a backlit screen, were popular entertainment, performed generally in colloquial Arabic with comic and often bawdy texts.

khushtanānak a sort of croissant made with butter and sugar and stuffed with almonds or pistachios.

kunāfah pastry made of vermicelli-like strands of dough, filled with pistachios or other nuts, and drenched in syrup.

kunyah a descriptive epithet consisting (for men) of the word *Abū* ("Father of") or (for women) of *Umm* ("Mother of"), followed by the name of the eldest son (in which case it is used as an honorific) or by a word denoting some characteristic of its bearer; thus, in the former case, a man with a son called Aḥmad may be known by the *kunyah* Abū Aḥmad (Father of Aḥmad), while, in the latter, the *kunyah* might also be translated as "He (or She) with . . . ," for instance, Abū Kirsh "The man with a (big) belly." Most of the *kunyah*s given by al-Shirbīnī are of the descriptive type, though not all of them yield a clear meaning.

kushshāf see *kāshif*.

kuttāb one-room school where children learn to recite the Qur'an, their ABCs, and arithmetic.

al-Lakhmī, Hishām ibn Ruqayyah Ibn ʿAbd al-Ḥakam (fl. third/ninth century), author of *Futūḥ Miṣr wa-akhbāruhā*, the earliest extant history of Islamic Egypt, drew on the reports of this person, who presumably accompanied ʿAmr ibn al-ʿĀṣ (q.v.) on the invasion of Egypt.

Laqqānah a village in the province of al-Buḥayrah, in the northwestern Delta.

lupine (turmus) the waxy yellow seeds of a leguminous plant of the genus *Lupinus*, still sold from street barrows as a snack.

Luqmān a legendary sage of pre-Islamic Arabia. Luqmān appears in the Qur'an (Q Yūsuf 12:31 and Raʿd 13:31) as a monotheist and a wise father giving advice to his sons and later became, in Islamic lore, the attributive author par excellence of wisdom literature.

al-Maʿarrī, Abū l-ʿAlāʾ Aḥmad ibn ʿAbd Allāh ibn Sulaymān Abū l-ʿAlāʾ al-Maʿarrī (363–449/973–1058), Syrian poet, prose writer, and skeptic.

al-Maḥallah (al-Kubrā) town in the central Delta and the center of Egypt's textile industry, in al-Shirbīnī's day as now.

al-Malik al-Ẓāhir Baybars (r. ca. 658–76/1260–77), one of the greatest of the first (Baḥrī) dynasty of Mamluk sultans, Baybars conducted campaigns against several Christian states, including the Franks in Palestine and the Armenians.

Mālik, the Imam Mālik ibn Anas ibn Mālik ibn Abī ʿĀmir ibn ʿAmr al-Aṣbaḥī (d. 179/795), author of the earliest codification of Muslim law (the *Kitāb al-Muwaṭṭaʾ*) and founder of one of the four canonical schools of law.

Mallawī a town in Upper Egypt, south of al-Minyā.

mamluk a white male slave, generally from the Caucasus or neighboring regions. Most of these were destined to be trained as soldiers in the household of one of the major officers of the army or for the state.

al-Maʾmūn (r. 198–218/813–33), seventh caliph of the Abbasid dynasty.

al-Manzalah a town southeast of Dimyāṭ, on Lake Manzalah, on Egypt's northeastern coast.

maqāmah a composition belonging to a literary genre usually consisting of "collections of short independent narrations written in ornamental rhymed prose . . . with verse insertions, a common plot-scheme, and two constant protagonists: the narrator and the hero" (R. Drory, "Maqāma," in *EAL*).

maqṣūrah a poem rhyming in *-ā*.

marjūnah a storage basket.

Marqaṣ a village in the district of Shubrākhīt, al-Buḥayrah.

Marṣafah a village near Banhā, north of Cairo.

master (ustādh/ustād) title by which peasants address and refer to the tax farmer of their village.

matrad (pl. matārid) "a vessel of red pottery, smaller than the *shāliyah*" (§11.16.2); cf. modern Egyptian *matrid* "an earthenware vessel similar in shape to a *maguur* [kneading bowl]" (Hinds and Badawi, *Dictionary*, 810–11).

al-Māturīdī, Shaykh Abū Manṣūr Muḥammad ibn Muḥammad ibn Maḥmūd al-Māturīdī al-Samarqandī (before 260/873 to ca. 333/944), a Hanafi theologian, jurist, and Qur'an commentator and founder of one of the main schools of Sunni systematic theology; his name refers to Māturīd, near Samarqand.

mawāliyā verse form characterized by colloquial features and consisting of four rhyming hemistiches in *basīṭ* meter.

maẓālim literally "injustices," unofficial levies that accompanied the creation of private, unofficial, tax farms on the backs of the official tax farms (Raymond, *Artisans*, 2/614–15) and that were "incessantly denounced, periodically abolished, but almost always re-instated" (ibid). Because most such levies were not catalogued or defined in the official tax registers (ibid, 135), the precise meaning of each is not always clear, and definitions in the secondary literature sometimes differ. Among the *maẓālim* were *ziyādāt al-kharāj* ("tax augmentations") (q.v.), *'awā'id* ("customary dues") (q.v.), *maghārim* ("obligations"), and *kulaf* ("charges"). Ibrāhīm describes the resulting "tax accumulation" of these levies as absorbing much of the rural income and as one of the main causes of malnutrition among the rural population (Ibrāhīm, *Al-Azamāt*, 103, 126).

miḥrāb the recess in the wall of a mosque that indicates the *qiblah*, or direction of Mecca, which Muslims face when performing the five formal daily prayers.

minqalah "mancala," a game of the "sowing games" family.

mishammar a kind of *faṭīr*, or cake of flaky pastry, to be eaten with cream, honey, aged cheese, etc.

mishsh seasoned, milk-based liquid culture in which cheese is fermented.

mu'allaqah one of the seven odes that were, according to tradition, written on cloth in letters of gold and suspended in the sanctuary of the

Kaaba in pre-Islamic Mecca and which, from early times, have been considered the best examples of pre-Islamic poetry.

Muʿāwiyah Muʿāwiyah ibn Abī Sufyān (r. 41–60/661–80), founder of the Umayyad caliphate.

mulūkhiyyā Jew's mallow (*Corchorus olitorius*), a leafy green vegetable.

al-Munāwī, ʿAbd al-Raʾūf ʿAbd al-Raʾūf ibn Tāj al-ʿĀrifīn ibn ʿAlī ibn Zayn al-ʿĀbidīn ibn Yaḥyā ibn Muḥammad al-Munāwī (952–1031/1545–1621), a leading religious scholar and Sufi of his time, author of the biographical dictionary of Sufis entitled *Al-Kawākib al-durriyyah fī tarājim al-sādah al-ṣūfiyyah*, also known as *Ṭabaqāt al-Munāwī*.

Muqawqis a title by which the Coptic patriarchs of Egypt were known to the Arabs and which, in Arab tradition, denotes "the individual who . . . plays the leading part on the side of the Copts and the Greeks at the conquest of Egypt" (K. Öhrnberg, "al-Muḳawḳis," in *EI2*).

muqaylī fried sprouted beans.

al-Mutanabbī, Abū l-Ṭayyib Aḥmad ibn al-Ḥusayn Abū l-Ṭayyib al-Mutanabbī (ca. 303–54/915–65), a renowned poet of the Abbasid age.

al-Muʿtaṣim (r. 218–27/833–42), eighth caliph of the Abbasid dynasty.

al-Mutawakkil (r. 232–47/847–61), tenth caliph of the Abbasid dynasty.

My Master (Sayyidī) title given eminent scholars and others, including those of earlier generations.

al-Nakhaʿī, Ibrāhīm Abū ʿImrān Ibrāhīm ibn Yazīd ibn Qays al-Nakhaʿī (50–96/670–715), a leading traditionist of his generation and authority for later jurists of various schools.

al-Nāṭifī see *ʿInān*.

Nayrūz a major festival formerly celebrated on the first day of Tūt, the first month of the Coptic year, at about the height of the Nile flood; from Persian *nō rōz* ("new day").

Niftawayh literally "tar-complexioned," the nickname of Abū ʿAbd Allāh Ibrāhīm ibn ʿArafah ibn Sulaymān ibn al-Mughīrah ibn al-Muhallab ibn Abī Ṣufrah al-ʿAtakī al-Azdī (244–323/858–935), influential grammarian and philologist, whose works are mostly lost.

pastor (faqīh (colloquially fiqī), pl. fuqahā') properly speaking, a *faqīh* is one learned in Islamic jurisprudence (*fiqh*). When speaking of the "ignorant *fuqahā'*" of the countryside, al-Shirbīnī seems to mean villagers who claim some learning (of dubious authority) and as such are the religious leaders of their villages. The anecdotes in the section "An Account of Their Pastors and of the Compounded Ignorance, Imbecility, and Injuries to Religion and the Like of Which They Are Guilty" (vol. 1, §4) imply that each village boasted one, who might also function as the village schoolteacher. Occasionally, *faqīh* is also used in its more formal sense.

the Pillar of the Columns (in the text ʿĀmūd al-Ṣawārī, elsewhere usually spelled ʿAmūd al-Sawārī) a red granite column on what were, in the seventeenth century, the outskirts of Alexandria; it was popularly supposed to mark the tomb of Pompey the Great and was known to English travelers as "Pompey's Pillar."

poverty (faqr) lack of material wealth and, in Sufi terms, awareness of inadequacy in relation to God; by the second half of the thirteenth century, the term had become synonymous with Sufism itself.

al-Qāḍī al-Fāḍil (529–96/1135–1200) ʿAbd al-Raḥīm ibn ʿAlī, known as al-Qāḍī al-Fāḍil ("the Virtuous Judge"), was a statesman, model of epistolary style, poet, and head of the chancery of Ṣalāḥ al-Dīn al-Ayyūbī (Saladin) from 566/1171.

al-Qādisiyyah site of the battle (between 14/635 and 16/637) southwest of al-Kūfah at which the Muslims won a decisive victory over the Sassanid army, opening the way to their conquest of Iraq.

qafqūlah "earthenware cooking pot or milk pot" (Behnstedt and Woidich, *Glossar*, 389, s.v. *gafgūl*).

qaḥf (1) the broad, deeply indented, thorny end of the palm frond where it joins the tree; (2) a type of peasant hat; (3) a peasant (as a coarse, unpolished person).

al-Qalyūbī, Shihāb al-Dīn Aḥmad ibn Aḥmad ibn Salāmah Shihāb al-Dīn al-Qalyūbī (d. 1069/1659), a writer on jurisprudence, geography, medicine, and the occult sciences, and author of belles lettres; see vol. 1, p. xxii.

al-Qarāfah the great cemetery complex of Cairo.

qaṭāyif "small pancakes stuffed with nuts or other sweet filling fried and moistened with syrup or honey" (Hinds and Badawi, *Dictionary*, 709).

Qāyitbāy, Sulṭān (r. 872–901/1468–96), Mamluk ruler of the Burjī dynasty.

Qiblah the direction the worshipper faces when performing the ritual prayer (*ṣalāh*).

quotation (iqtibās) the use of a quotation from the Qur'an in poetry; this rhetorical device "consists of the poet introducing into his poetry deliberately a word or a verse from the Mighty Qur'an, and is of three types: praiseworthy and accepted, permitted but vulgar, and rejected and despicable" (al-Ḥillī, *Al-Badīʿiyyah*, 326–27).

al-Quḥāfah a village in the province of al-Gharbiyyah.

qulqās a tuberous, starchy, taro-like root vegetable (*Colocasia antiquorum*).

Quraysh the tribe of the Prophet Muḥammad.

al-Quṣayr a port on the Red Sea, about three hundred miles south of Suez and a major point of embarkation for pilgrims traveling to Mecca.

Rashīd Rosetta, on the mouth of the western branch of the Nile, a major entrepôt for trade between Cairo and Alexandria.

restraint (iktifāʾ) a rhetorical device by which "a poet produces a line of verse whose rhyme-word is dependent [for the completion of the sense] on a word that is omitted and that must be borne in mind if the meaning is to be understood but which the poet does not mention because the words of the verse themselves imply it; he thus relies on what the reader can be expected to know naturally for the completion of the sense" (al-Ḥillī, *Al-Badīʿiyyah*, 105).

rolling and unrolling (laff wa-nashr) in rhetoric, "an enumeration of terms followed by an enumeration of predicates or comments" (W. P. Heinrichs, "Rhetorical Figures," in *EAL*).

al-Rūm Anatolia; literally "the Land of the [eastern] Romans," that is, the Byzantines.

al-Rumaylah a large open space in front of Cairo's Citadel.

al-Ruṣāfah a quarter of Baghdad on the eastern bank of the Euphrates.

al-Ṣābūnī, Bridge of (*qanāṭir al-Ṣābūnī*) a village called al-Ṣābūnī formerly existed south of Old Cairo between the districts of al-Maʿādī and

Dayr al-Ṭīn and was associated with an island of the same name (now called Jazīrat al-Dahab) (Ramzī 1:77); this bridge may have linked the two.

Saʿd (or Judhām/Judām) with Ḥarām, one of two feuding armed factions into which the peasants were divided (see vol. 1, n. 13).

al-Ṣafī al-Ḥillī ʿAbd al-ʿAzīz ibn Sarāyā Ṣafī al-Dīn al-Ḥillī (667/1278 to ca. 750/1349), a poet from Iraq who spent much time in Egypt at the courts of the last Ayyubids and first Mamluks.

the Ṣaʿīd Upper Egypt, usually defined as Egypt south of Cairo.

saint's feast (mawlid, pl. mawālid) typically, the celebration of the birthday of a Muslim holy man, often associated with the Sufi group founded by that saint. The early Ottoman period in Egypt saw an efflorescence of *mawlids* (Winter, *Society and Religion*, 178–80).

al-Ṣalībah literally "The Cross-Shaped (Street)"; a major street running west from the north end of the square below the Citadel.

al-Ṣāliḥ al-Ṭalāʾiʿ Abū l-Ghārāt Fāris al-Muslimīn al-Malik al-Ṣāliḥ Ṭalāʾiʿ ibn Ruzzīk al-Ghassānī al-Armanī (495/1101–2 to 556/1161), a Fatimid general and governor of Egypt.

Samannūd a town in the central Delta, on the western bank of the eastern (Dimyāṭ) branch of the Nile, about twenty-five miles from Shirbīn.

sanjak (ṣanjaq) (originally a Turkish term, *sancak*, literally "flag") one of a group of military grandees, ranging at various times from sixteen to thirty-six or even more, who were promoted out of the officer corps of the Ottoman army in Egypt to act as counselors (and counter-weights) to the viceroy and to occupy key positions in the Egyptian state apparatus.

sarkūj apparently an item of headwear or upper-body wear.

scholar (ʿālim, pl. ʿulamāʾ) a scholar learned in the religious sciences (such as Qurʾanic exegesis, jurisprudence, and prophetic traditions). Here, the term is used primarily of scholars associated with the mosque of al-Azhar, who often find themselves in conflict with the rural pastors known as *fuqahāʾ* (sg. *faqīh*, colloquially *fiqī*) (q.v.).

Shaʿbān the eighth month of the Islamic calendar, immediately preceding Ramadan.

al-Shāfiʿī, the Imam that is, Muḥammad ibn Idrīs al-Shāfiʿī (150/767–68 to 204/820), pupil of the Imam Mālik and founder of the school of law that, by the twelfth century AD, had become dominant in Lower Egypt and to which al-Shirbīnī belonged.

Shanashah a village, since disappeared, near Shirbīn.

al-Sharb one of Cairo's principal cloth markets.

sharif a descendant of the Prophet Muḥammad.

Shīḥah sister of the hero Abū Zayd in the epic romance of the Banū Hilāl (*Al-Sīrah al-Hilāliyyah*).

Shirbīn Yūsuf al-Shirbīnī's birthplace, on the northern bank of the eastern branch of the Nile (see vol. 1, p. xxi).

shovel-sledge (jarrāfah) a wooden, animal-drawn sledge used to clean and dredge canals and level fields. It is shaped like an equilateral triangle, with sides about three feet in length and a truncated front end from which descend two sides with raised edges.

Shubrā a village north of Cairo.

silver piece here translates *nuṣṣ* (pl. *anṣāṣ*), a silver coin minted in Egypt during the Ottoman period and the chief specie used for medium to large purchases; copper coins known as *jadīd*s were used for small local purchases, while gold coins were used for major purchases and transactions and foreign exchange (Pamuk, *Monetary History*, 66). The *nuṣṣ* remained the basic coin of Egypt until the coinage reform of Muḥammad ʿAlī, in 1834 (Pamuk, *Monetary History*, 95).

al-Sirw village on the east bank of the eastern branch of the Nile, in the district of Fāriskūr, al-Daqahliyyah, near Shirbīn.

sow thistle (juʿḍayḍ) *Sonchus oleraceus*, a weed whose stalks may be peeled and eaten.

subūʿ the seventh day after the birth of a child, on which it is customary for the mother to be visited by her friends, who take part in various rituals to ensure the good health of herself and her child (cf. Lane, *Manners*, 504–5).

Suʿdā a woman's name, used conventionally for the Beloved.

al-sukhrah compulsory labor on public works (especially the maintenance of the irrigation system); cf. *corvée* (*al-ʿawnah*).

Sulaymān Solomon.

Sulṭān Qizilbash ("Sultan Red-Hat") the Safavid ruler of Iran; from Turkish *kızılbaş*, in reference to the distinctive headgear of the followers of the Safavid shaykhs.

Sunnah ("custom") in Islam, an act approved because imitative of the practice of the Prophet.

surah chapter of the Qur'an.

surveyor (khawlī, pl. khawālī) "The [*khawlī*] . . . was responsible for determining exactly the limits of the village, the *Asar* [tax-paying] land of each cultivator, the nature and timing of the seeding and cultivation of each portion of the watered land, and the amount of tax owed by each cultivator. He was also charged with making sure that the waters in the irrigation canals were properly apportioned amongst the cultivated lands and that the irrigation canals and equipment of the village were kept in proper repair. The [*khawlī*] was elected by the cultivators and was their chief representative in the village administration" (Shaw, *Financial*, 54).

Suwayqat al-Sabbāʿīn a "little," that is, temporary, market west of Birkat al-Fīl (q.v.), southwest of Bāb Zuwaylah (q.v.).

al-Suyūṭī, al-Jalāl Jalāl al-Dīn Abū l-Faḍl ʿAbd al-Raḥmān ibn Abī Bakr al-Suyūṭī (848–911/1445–1505), one of the most prolific polymaths of medieval Arabic.

sycamore (jummayz) sycamore figs, the fruit of *Ficus sycamoris*, which resemble small pinkish figs with whitish pulpy flesh. A visitor to Egypt in the 1640s remarked that "it is the fruit of the poor, which costs them nothing except for the cooking" and notes that the fruit went untaxed, unlike that of other productive trees (Brémond, *Voyage*, 35).

Ṭalkhah chief town of the district of the same name in the province of al-Gharbiyyah, on the west bank of the eastern branch of the Nile.

tarjīl (pl. tarājīl) a type of peasant shoe, synonymous, according to al-Shirbīnī, with *markūb* or *zarbūn* (kinds of slipper) (q.v.).

tax collectors, tax-collection apparatus (dīwān) literally "council" or "bureau," the administration of Ottoman Egypt devolved through a series of *dīwāns*, with the High Dīwān (*al-dīwān al-ʿālī*) of the viceroy constituting the "principal executive and legislative council" (Shaw, *Financial*, 2). Under this was the Registration Bureau of the Sultan (*al-dīwān al-daftarī al-sulṭānī*) and its subdepartment, the Bureau of the Daybook (*dīwān al-ruznāmah*), which was responsible for the "administering of the imposition, registration and collection of taxes and revenues . . . and their disposition" (ibid, 338). Reflecting the informal usage of the time, al-Shirbīnī applies the term *dīwān* to the local administrative apparatus of the tax farmer, which mirrored the national-level *dīwān*.

tax farm (iltizām) the right to collect the taxes of an area of land, a right that, at this period, was purchased at auction; as Shalabī put it, "The *multazim* [tax farmer] who buys the village . . . has to come up with the tax . . . . and whatever is left over is his" (Shalabī, *Siyāḥatnāmah*, 191). Tax farmers also acted as local administrators, overseeing the maintenance of the irrigation system at the local level, approving acquisition and transfer of land by villagers, and nurturing agricultural prosperity generally. In 1658–60, a quarter century before al-Shirbīnī wrote, there were 1,714 *multazims*, over 90 percent of whom were emirs (military officers). The *iltizām* system was abolished beginning in the winter of 1813–14 as part of Muḥammad ʿAlī's reforms in favor of a state monopoly of tax collection (Raymond, *Artisans*, 2:612–18; Cuno, *Peasants*, 2:25–27, 33–47; Winter, *Egyptian Society*, passim).

Thamūd see *ʿĀd*.

thawb a "large, loose gown" or a "shirt" worn by women (Lane, *Manners*, 45).

al-Thawrī, Sufyān Sufyān ibn Saʿīd ibn Marzūq al-Thawrī (97/715–16 to 161/778), a celebrated transmitter of Traditions.

Tradition (of the Prophet Muḥammad) (ḥadīth, pl. aḥādīth) an account of his words or deeds to which he gave his tacit approval. Traditions supplement the ordinances found in the Qur'an and provide a model for the attitudes and comportment of the believer. They are categorized, based on the reliability of their chain of transmission, on a scale from *saḥīḥ* ("sound") to *ḍaʿīf* ("weak"); an account that lacks all credibility is dismissed as *mawḍūʿ* ("concocted") or as *khabar kādhib* ("a mendacious report"). Of the twenty-three claimed Traditions occurring in the book, nine are fundamentally "sound" (albeit two of them occur with minor variations from the canonical wording), nine are "weak," "concocted," or "mendacious," and the rest fall in between.

ṭūbār a kind of gray mullet (*Mugil capito*).

al-Ṭūr a town on the west coast of the Sinai Peninsula.

Ṭuways ("Little Peacock") nickname of Abū ʿAbd al-Munʿim ʿĪsā ibn ʿAbd Allāh (b. 10/632), a celebrated singer of Medina during the early days of Islam who was also known for the coincidence of events in his life with unhappy events, for "he was born on the day the Prophet (upon him peace and blessings) died, weaned on the day Abū Bakr [the first caliph] (may God be pleased with him) died, was circumcised on the day ʿUmar [ibn al-Khaṭṭāb, second caliph] (may God be pleased with him) was killed, and married on the day ʿUthmān [ibn ʿAffān, third caliph] (may God be pleased with him) was killed" (al-Iṣfahānī, *Al-Aghānī*, 4/39).

ʿūd the Arab lute.

urjūzah a poem in *rajaz* meter (LLSL | LLSL | LLSL, with a wide range of permissible variants), usually in rhymed couplets with different rhymes in each couplet, in which form it may be referred to as an *urjūzah muzdawijah*. "On account of [the *muzdawijah*'s] easy rhyming scheme, it proved particularly suitable for long narrative and didactic poems" (W. Stoetzer, "rajaz," in *EAL*) such as Ibn Mālik's versified grammar, *Al-Alfiyyah*. Al-Shirbīnī uses this meter for the two long poems with which he summarizes volumes one and two, respectively, of his book.

vizier (wazīr) "minister," a title borne by some Ottoman governors of Egypt (Davies, *Lexicon*, 130).

Wādī al-Tīh a valley in Sinai, at the head of the Gulf of ʿAqabah.

wajbah the duty, imposed on the villager, of providing the tax farmer (*multazim*) and other officials and their entourages and animals with food (§§11.3.9–11).

al-Walīd ibn Yazīd (r. 125–26/743–44) eleventh caliph of the Umayyad dynasty and a poet.

waqf an endowment, often made for charitable purposes such as the upkeep of a mosque.

al-Wāthiq (r. 227–32/842–47) ninth caliph of the Abbasid dynasty.

wheat groats (kishk) hulled wheat cooked with sour milk, formed into balls, and dried.

Yāsīn the thirty-sixth Surah of the Qur'an.

Yazīd (r. 60–64/680–83) second caliph of the Umayyad dynasty.

al-Zāhidī, Imam Najm al-Dīn Abū l-Rajā' Mukhtār ibn Maḥmūd ibn Muḥammad al-Zāhidī l-Ghazmīnī l-ʿArramānī (362–428/972–1037), a Hanafi jurisprudent.

Zayd, Sultan Zayd ibn Muḥsin (b. 1015/1607), founder of the Dhawū Zayd dynasty of rulers of Mecca.

Zubaydah cousin and wife of the Abbasid caliph Hārūn al-Rashīd and mother of his successor, al-Amīn Muḥammad (q.v.).

al-Zukhruf the forty-third Surah of the Qur'an.

zummārah a cane or wood pipe with reed.

Bibliography

ʿAbd al-Raḥīm, ʿAbd al-Raḥīm ʿAbd al-Raḥmān. *Al-Rīf al-miṣrī fī l-qarn al-thāmin ʿashar*. Cairo: Maktabat Madbūlī, 1986.

Abū l-ʿAtāhiyah. *Ashʿāruhu wa-akhbāruhu*. Edited by Shukrī Fayṣal. Damascus: Maktabat Dār al-Mallāḥ, n.d. Photomechanical repr. of ed. Damascus: Maṭbaʿat Jāmiʿat Dimashq, 1965.

Abū Firās al-Ḥamdānī. *Dīwān*. Edited by ʿAlī al-ʿUsaylī. Beirut: Manshūrāt Muʾassasat al-Aʿlamī, 1998.

Abū Nuwās, al-Ḥasan ibn Hāniʾ. *Dīwān Abī Nuwās al-Ḥasan ibn Hāniʾ al-Ḥakamī*. Edited by Ewald Wagner and Gregor Schoeler. 7 vols. Cairo and Wiesbaden: Franz Steiner/Beirut and Berlin: Klaus Schwarz, 1958–2006 (vols. 6–7: indexes). The second edition of vol. 1 (2001) has been used.

Abū Yaʿlā, Aḥmad ibn ʿAlī ibn al-Muthannā al-Tamīmī. *Al-Musnad*. Edited by Ḥusayn Salīm Asad. 15 vols. Beirut: Dār al-Maʾmūn li-l-Turāth, 1410/1989.

Ahlwardt, Wilhelm. *The Divans of the Six Ancient Arabic Poets*. London: 1870, reprinted Osnabrück: Biblio, 1972.

Aḥnaf, ʿAbbās al-. *Dīwān*. Edited by ʿĀtikah al-Khazrajī. Cairo: Dār al-Kutub al-Miṣriyyah, 1954.

ʿAjlūnī, Ismāʿīl ibn Muḥammad. *Kashf al-khafāʾ wa-muzīl al-ilbās ʿammā shtahara mina l-aḥādīth ʿalā alsinat al-nās*. 2 vols. Beirut: Dār al-Kutub al-ʿIlmiyyah, 1988.

Ālātī, Ḥasan al-. *Tarwīḥ al-nufūs wa-muḍḥik al-ʿabūs*. Cairo: Jarīdat al-Maḥrūsah, 1889.

Alf laylah wa-laylah. Edited by al-Shaykh Qiṭṭah al-ʿAdawī. Cairo: Maṭbaʿat Bulaq, 1836. Offset, reprint edition, Beirut: Dār Ṣādir, n.d.

Alf laylah wa-laylah min al-Mubtadaʾ ilā l-Muntahā: ṭabʿah muṣawwarah min ṭabʿat Barislaw bi-taṣḥīḥ Maksīmīliyānūs ibn Hābikhṭ. 2nd ed. Cairo: Dār al-Kutub al-Miṣriyyah, 1998.

ʿĀlī, Muṣṭafā *see* Tietze, Andreas.

ʿĀmilī, Bahāʾ al-Dīn al-. *Al-Kashkūl*. Beirut: Dār al-Kitāb al-Lubnānī, 1983.

Amīn, Aḥmad. *Qāmūs al-ʿādāt wa-l-taqālīd wa-l-taʿābīr al-Miṣriyyah*. Cairo: Maṭbaʿat Lajnat al-Taʾlīf wa-l-Tarjamah wa-l-Nashr, 1953.

ʿAntarah ibn Shaddād. *Sharḥ Dīwān ʿAntarah ibn Shaddād*. Edited by ʿAbd al-Munʿim ʿAbd al-Raʾūf Shalabī. Cairo: al-Maṭbaʿah al-Tijāriyyah al-Kubrā, n.d.

Arberry, A. J. *The Seven Odes: The First Chapter in Arabic Letters*. London: George Allen and Unwin, 1957.

———. *The Koran Interpreted*. Oxford World's Classics. Oxford: Oxford University Press, 1982.

Armbrust, Walter. *Mass Culture and Modernism in Egypt*. Cambridge Studies in Social and Cultural Anthropology 102. Cambridge: Cambridge University Press, 1996.

Ashtor, Eliyahu. "An Essay on the Diet of the Various Classes in the Medieval Levant." In *Selections from the Annales, Sociétés, Économies, Civilisations*, edited by Robert Forster and Orest Ranum, 125–62. Baltimore and London: Johns Hopkins University Press, 1975.

Aubaile-Sallenave, Francoise. "Al-Kishk: The Past and Present of a Complex Culinary Practice." In *Culinary Cultures of the Middle East*, edited by Sami Zubaida and Richard Tapper, 105–39. London and New York: I. B. Tauris, 1994.

ʿAyyāshī, Abū Salim al-. *Al-Riḥlah al-ʿAyyāshiyyah (Māʾ al-mawāʾid)*, edited by M. Hajji. 2 vols. Rabat: n.p., 1977.

Baer, Gabriel. "Fellah and Townsman in Ottoman Egypt: A Study of Shirbini's Hazz al-Quḥūf." *Asian and African Studies* [Jerusalem], 8 (1972): 221–56.

———. *Fellah and Townsman in the Middle East: Studies in Social History.* London: Frank Cass, 1982.

———. "Shirbīnī's Hazz al-Quḥūf and its Significance." In Gabriel Baer, *Fellah and Townsman in the Middle East: Studies in Social History.* London: Frank Cass, 1982.

Baqlī, Muḥammad Qindīl al-, ed. *Qaryatunā l-Miṣriyyah qabla l-thawrah – 1.* Cairo: Dār al-Nahḍah al-ʿArabiyyah, n.d. [1963].

Bashshār ibn Burd, Abū Muʿādh. *Dīwān.* Edited by Muḥammad al-Ṭāhir Ibn ʿĀshūr. 4 vols. Algiers and Tunis: al-Sharikah al-Waṭaniyyah/ al-Sharikah al-Tūnusiyyah, 1976.

Bayḍāwī, ʿAbd Allāh ibn ʿUmar ibn Muḥammad al-Shīrāzī al-. *Anwār al-tanzīl wa-asrār al-taʾwīl.* 2 vols. Beirut: Dār al-Kutub al-ʿIlmiyyah, 1999.

Bayhaqī, Aḥmad ibn al-Ḥusayn al-. *Kitāb al-zuhd al-kabīr.* Edited by ʿĀmir Aḥmad Ḥaydar. Beirut: Dār al-Janān wa-Muʾassasat al-Kutub al-Thaqāfiyyah, 1987.

Behnstedt, Peter, and Manfred Woidich. *Die ägyptisch-arabischen Dialekte* . Vol. 4, *Glossar Arabisch-Deutsch.* Wiesbaden: Dr. Ludwig Reichert Verlag, 1994.

Behrens-Abouseif, Doris. *Egypt's Adjustment to Ottoman Rule: Institutions, Waqf and Architecture in Cairo (16th and 17th Centuries).* Leiden: E. J. Brill, 1994.

Berque, Jacques. *Histoire sociale d'un village égyptien au XXème siècle.* Paris: Mouton, 1957.

Blanc, Haim. "La Perte d'une forme pausale dans le parler arabe du Caire." *Mélanges de l'Université Saint Joseph* 48 (1973–74): 376–90.

Borg, Gert. "Lust and Carnal Desire: Obscenities Attributed to Arab Women." *Arabic and Middle Eastern Literatures* 3, no. 2 (2000): 149–64.

Bosworth, Clifford Edmund. *The Mediaeval Islamic Underworld: The Banū Sāsān in Arabic Society and Literature.* 2 vols. Leiden: E. J. Brill, 1976.

Brémond, Gabriel. *Voyage en Égypte de Gabriel Brémond 1643–45.* Edited by Georges Sanguin. Collection des voyageurs occidentaux en Egypte 12. Cairo: Institut Français d'Archéologie Orientale, 1974.

Bukhārī, Muḥammad ibn Ismāʿīl ibn Ibrāhīm al-. *Al-Jāmiʿ al-musnad al-ṣaḥīḥ al-mukhtaṣar min umūr rasūl Allāh ṣallā Allāh ʿalayh wa-sallam wa-sunanih wa-ayyāmih.* 3 vols. Stuttgart: Islamic Thesaurus Society, 1421/2000–2001.

Burckhardt, John L. *Arabic Proverbs; or the Manners and Customs of the Modern Egyptians Illustrated by Their Proverbial Sayings Current in Cairo.* 3rd ed. London: Curzon Press, 1972.

Būṣīrī, Sharaf al-Dīn Abū ʿAbd Allāh Muḥammad ibn Saʿīd al-. *Dīwān.* Edited by Muḥammad Sayyid Kīlānī. Cairo: Muṣṭafā al-Bābī al-Ḥalabī, 1973.

Cachia, Pierre. *The Arch Rhetorician or the Schemer's Skimmer: A Handbook of Late Arabic badīʿ Drawn from ʿAbd al-Ghanī an-Nabulsī's Nafaḥāt al-Azhār ʿalā Nasamāt al-Asḥār, Summarized and Systematized by Pierre Cachia.* Wiesbaden: Harrassowitz, 1998.

———. *Popular Narrative Ballads of Modern Egypt.* Oxford: Clarendon Press, 1989.

Çelebi *see* Shalabī, Awliyā.

Coppin, Jean. *Voyages en Égypte de Jean Coppin, 1638–1646.* Edited by Serge Sauneron. Collection des voyageurs occidentaux en Egypte 4. Cairo: Institut Français d'Archéologie Orientale, 1971.

Crecelius, Daniel, and Abd al-Wahhab Bakr. *Al-Damurdāshī's Chronicle of Egypt 1688–1755: al-Durrah al-muṣānah fī akhbār al-Kinānah.* Leiden: E. J. Brill, 1991.

Cuno, Kenneth M. *The Pasha's Peasants: Land, Society and Economy in Lower Egypt, 1740–1858.* Cairo: American University in Cairo Press, 1994.

Damīrī, Kamāl al-Dīn Muḥammad ibn Mūsā al-. *Ḥayāt al-ḥayawān al-kubrā.* 2 vols. Cairo: Muṣṭafā al-Bābī al-Ḥalabī, 1978.

Davies, Humphrey. *A Lexicon of 17th-Century Egyptian Arabic.* Orientalia Lovaniensia Analecta 225. Leuven: Peeters, 2013.

———. *Seventeenth-Century Egyptian Arabic: A Profile of the Colloquial Material in Yusuf al-Shirbīnī's "Hazz al-quḥūf fī sharḥ qaṣīd Abī Shādūf."* PhD diss. University of California, Berkeley, 1981. Available from ProQuest Dissertations & Theses Global (order no. 8200073). http://search.proquest.com/docview/303007733.

———. *Yūsuf al-Shirbīnī's Kitāb Hazz al-Quḥūf bi-Sharḥ Abī Shādūf ("Brains Confounded by the Ode of Abū Shādūf Expounded")*, Volume 1: Arabic text. Orientalia Lovaniensia Analecta 141. Leuven: Peeters, 2005.

———. *Yūsuf al-Shirbīnī's Brains Confounded by the Ode of Abū Shādūf Expounded,* Volume 2: *English translation, Introduction, and Notes.* Orientalia Lovaniensia Analecta 166. Leuven: Peeters, 2007.

Dols, Michael W. *Majnūn: The Madman in Medieval Islamic Society.* Oxford: Clarendon Press, 1992.

Dozy, R. *Supplément aux Dictionnaires Arabes.* 2 vols. Leiden: E. J. Brill, 1881. Offset, Beirut: Librairie du Liban, 1968.

Dunne, Bruce W. "Sexuality and the 'Civilizing Process' in Modern Egypt." PhD diss., Georgetown University, 1996.

EAL = *Encyclopedia of Arabic Literature.* Edited by Julie Scott Meisami and Paul Starkey. 2 vols. London and New York: Routledge, 1998.

EI2 = *Encyclopaedia of Islam.* 2nd ed. Edited by P. Bearman, Th. Bianquis, C. E. Bosworth, E. von Donzol, and W. P. Heinrichs. Leiden: E. J. Brill, 1960–2009.

Finkel, Joshua. "King Mutton, a Curious Egyptian Tale of the Mamluk Period. Edited from a Unique Manuscript, with Translation, Notes, Glossary and Introduction." *Zeitschrift für Semitistik* 8 (1932): 122–48 and 9 (1933–34): 1–18.

Fīrūzābādhī, Muḥammad ibn Yaʿqūb al-. *Al-Qāmūs al-muḥīṭ wa-l-qābūs al-wasīṭ fī al-lughah.* 2nd ed. 4 vols. Cairo: al-Maktabah al-Ḥusayniyyah al-Miṣriyyah, 1344/1925–26.

Fischer, Wolfdietrich. *Die demonstrativen Bildungen der neuarabischen Dialekte.* The Hague: Mouton, 1959.

GAL = Brockelmann, Carl. *Geschichte der arabischen Litteratur, I–II.* Leiden: E. J. Brill, 1943, 1949; Suppl. I–III, Leiden: E. J. Brill, 1937–42.

GAS = Sezgin, Fuat. *Geschichte des arabischen Schrifttums, II.* Leiden: E. J. Brill, 1984.

Ghazzī, Badr al-Dīn Muḥammad al-. *Al-Zubdah fī sharḥ al-Burdah.* Edited by ʿUmar Mūsā Bashā. Algiers: al-Sharikah al-Waṭaniyyah li-l-Nashr wa-l-Tawzīʿ, 1972.

Ghazzī, Najm al-Dīn Muḥammad ibn Muḥammad al-. *Al-Kawākib al-sā'irah bi-a'yān al-mi'ah al-'āshirah*. Edited by Khalīl al-Manṣūr. 2 vols. Beirut: Dār al-Kutub al-'Ilmiyyah, 1997.

Ghuzūlī, 'Alā' al-Dīn 'Alī ibn 'Abd Allāh al-Bahā'ī al-. *Maṭāli' al-budūr fī manāzil al-surūr*. 2 vols. Bulaq: 1299–1300/1882–83.

Gonzales, Antonius. *Voyage en Egypte du Père Antonius Gonzales 1665–1666*. Edited by Charles Libois. Collection des voyageurs occidentaux en Egypte 19. Cairo: Institut Français d'Archéologie Orientale, 1977.

Goody, Jack. *Cooking, Cuisine and Class: A Study in Comparative Sociology*. Cambridge: Cambridge University Press, 1982.

Greene, Daniel. "An Egyptian Rabbi Trickster." *Journal of American Folklore* 79 (1966): 608–30.

Guillaume, A. *The Life of Muhammad: A Translation of Isḥāq's Sīrat Rasūl Allāh*. Karachi: Oxford University Press, 1967.

Ḥājjī Khalīfah (Kātib Çelebi). *Kashf al-ẓunūn 'an asāmī l-kutub wa-l-funūn*. Edited by Şerefettin Yaltkaya and Rifat Bilge. 2 vols. Istanbul: Maarif Matbaası, 1941–43.

Hanna, Nelly. "The Chronicles of Ottoman Egypt: History or Entertainment." In *The Historiography of Islamic Egypt (c. 950–1800)*, edited by Hugh Kennedy, 237–50. Leiden: Brill, 2001.

———. "Culture in Ottoman Egypt." In *The Cambridge History of Egypt*, edited by M. W. Daly, 2:87–112. Cambridge: Cambridge University Press, 1998.

Ḥarīrī, Abū Muḥammad al-Qāsim ibn 'Alī ibn Muḥammad ibn 'Uthmān al-. *Maqāmāt al-Ḥarīrī*. 3rd ed. Bulaq: Dār al-Ṭibā'ah al-'Āmirah, 1288/1871.

Ḥasan, Muḥammad 'Abd al-Ghanī. *Al-Fallāḥ fī l-adab al-'arabī*. Cairo: Dār al-Qalam, 1965.

Ḥassān ibn Thābit. *Dīwān*. Edited by Walīd 'Arafāt. Beirut: Dār Ṣādir, 1974.

Hilāl, 'Imād. *Al-Baghāyā fī Miṣr: Dirāsah tārikhiyyah ijtimā'iyyah (min 1834–1949)*. Cairo: al-'Arabī li-l-Nashr wa-l-Tawzā', 2001.

Ḥillī, Ṣafī al-Dīn al-. *Sharḥ al-Kāfiyah al-Badī'iyyah fī 'ulūm al-balāghah wa-maḥāsin al-badī'*. Edited by Nasīb Nashāwī. Damascus: Majma' al-Lughah al-'Arabiyyah bi-Dimashq, 1982.

Hinds, Martin, and El-Said Badawi. *A Dictionary of Egyptian Arabic: Arabic-English*. Beirut: Librairie du Liban, 1986.

Höglmeier, Manuela. *Al-Ǧawbarī und sein Kašf al-asrār: Ein Sittenbild des Gauners im Arabisch-islamischen Mittelalter (7./13. Jahrhundert): Einführüng, Edition und Kommentar*. Berlin: Klaus Schwarz, 2014.

Homerin, Th. Emil. *From Arab Poet to Muslim Saint: Ibn al-Fāriḍ, His Verse, and His Shrine*. Columbia: University of South Carolina Press, 1994.

Howarth, Herbert, and Ibrahim Shukrallah. *Images from the Arab World: Fragments of Arab Literature Translated and Paraphrased with Variations and Comments*. London: Pilot Press, 1944.

Ḥusayn, Ṭāhā. *Al-Ayyām*. 2 vols. Cairo: Dār al-Maʿārif, 1953.

Ibn ʿAbd al-Ḥakam, Abū l-Qasim ʿAbd al-Raḥmān. *The History of the Conquest of Egypt, North Africa and Spain = Futūḥ Miṣr wa-akhbāruhā*. Edited by Charles C. Torrey. New Haven: Yale University Press, 1922.

Ibn Abī l-Ḥadīd, ʿAbd al-Ḥamīd ibn Hibatallāh. *Sharḥ Nahj al-balāghah li-l-Sharīf al-Raḍī*. Edited by Muḥammad al-Faḍl Ibrāhīm. 20 vols. Cairo: Dār Iḥyāʾ al-Kutub al-ʿArabiyyah, 1963.

Ibn Abī ʿAwn. *Tashbīhāt*. Edited by M. ʿAbd al-Muʿīd. London: Luzac, 1950.

Ibn al-ʿAdīm, Kamāl al-Dīn Abū l-Qāsim ʿUmar ibn Aḥmad. *Zubdat al-ḥalab min tārīkh Ḥalab*. Edited by Khalīl al-Manṣūr. Beirut: Dār al-Kutub al-ʿIlmiyyah, 1996.

Ibn al-ʿArabī, Muḥyī l-Dīn Abū ʿAbd Allāh Muḥammad ibn ʿAlī. *Dīwān*. Beirut: Dār al-Kutub al-ʿIlmiyyah, 1996.

———. *Tarjumān al-ashwāq*. Edited by Reynold A. Nicholson. London: Royal Asiatic Society, 1911.

Ibn Dāniyāl, Shams al-Dīn Muḥammad. *Three Shadow Plays*. Edited by Paul Kahle with a critical apparatus by Derek Hopwood. Cambridge: Trustees of the E. J. W. Gibb Memorial, 1992.

Ibn Durayd, Abū Bakr Muḥammad ibn al-Ḥasan. *Dīwān*. Edited by ʿUmar Ibn Sālim. Tunis: al-Dār al-Tūnusiyyah li-l-Nashr, 1973.

Ibn al-Fāriḍ, Abū Ḥafṣ (Abū l-Qāsim) ʿUmar ibn Abī l-Ḥasan ʿAlī ibn al-Murshid ibn ʿAlī. *Dīwān Ibn al-Fāriḍ*. Edited by ʿAbd al-Khāliq Maḥmūd. Cairo: ʿAyn li-l-Dirāsāt wa-l-Buḥūth al-Insāniyyah wa-l-Ijtimāʿiyyah, [1995].

Ibn Ḥajar al-ʿAsqalānī, Aḥmad ibn ʿAlī. *Al-Durar al-kāminah*. Hyderabad: Dāʾirat al-Maʿārif al-ʿUthmāniyyah, 1929–31.

———. *Tahdhīb al-Tahdhīb*. Hyderabad: Maṭbaʿat Majlis Dāʾirat al-Maʿārif al-Niẓāmiyyah, 1907.

Ibn Ḥamdūn, Muḥammad ibn al-Ḥasan. *Al-Tadhkirah al-Ḥamdūniyyah*. Edited by Iḥsān ʿAbbās and Bakr ʿAbbās. 10 vols. Beirut: Dār Ṣādir, 1996.

Ibn Ḥanbal, Aḥmad. *Al-Musnad*. 6 vols. Cairo: Muʾassasat Qurṭubah, n.d.

Ibn Ḥijjah al-Ḥamawī, Abū Bakr Taqī al-Dīn. *Thamarāt al-awrāq*. Edited by Muḥammad Abū l-Faḍl Ibrāhīm. Cairo: Maktabat al-Khānjī, 1971.

Ibn Hishām, Muḥammad ibn ʿAbd Allāh. *Al-Sīrah al-nabawiyyah*. Edited by Ṭāhā ʿAbd al-Raʾūf Saʿd. Cairo: Maktabat al-Kulliyyāt al-Azhariyyah, 1974.

Ibn al-Jawzī, ʿAbd al-Raḥmān ibn ʿAlī. *Kitāb al-adhkiyāʾ*. Edited by Muḥammad ʿAbd al-Raḥmān ʿAwaḍ. Beirut: Dār al-Kitāb al-ʿArabī, 1986.

Ibn Khallikān, Aḥmad ibn Muḥammad Abū l-ʿAbbās Shams al-Dīn al-Barmakī al-Irbīlī. *Wafayāt al-aʿyān*. Edited by Iḥsān ʿAbbās. Beirut: Dār al-Thaqāfah, 1997.

Ibn Qayyim al-Jawziyyah, Muḥammad ibn Abī Bakr. *Al-Ṭibb al-nabawī*. Shubrā, Cairo: Dār al-Taqwā li-l-Nashr wa-l-Tawzīʿ, 2003.

Ibn Qutaybah, Abū Muḥammad ʿAbd Allāh ibn Muslim. *Al-Shiʿr wa-l-shuʿarāʾ*. Edited by Aḥmad Muḥammad Shākir. Cairo: Dār al-Maʿārif, 1966.

———. *ʿUyūn al-akhbār*. 4 vols. Cairo: Dār al-Kutub, 1925–30.

Ibn Manẓūr, Jamāl al-Dīn Muḥammad ibn Mukarram. *Akhbār Abī Nuwās*. Edited by Ibrāhīm al-Abyārī as an appendix to Abū al-Faraj al-Iṣfahānī's *Kitāb al-aghānī*, vols. 29–30. Cairo: Dār al-Shaʿb, 1979.

———. *Lisān al-ʿArab*. Accessed at http://www.baheth.info/.

Ibn al-Rūmī (Abū l-Ḥasan ʿAlī ibn ʿAbbās ibn Jurayj). *Dīwān*. Edited by Ḥusayn Naṣṣār. 6 vols. Cairo: al-Hayʾah al-Miṣriyyah al-ʿĀmmah li-l-Kitāb, 1973–81.

Ibn Sa'd (ibn Manī' al-Zahawī), Muḥammad. *Kitāb al-ṭabaqāt al-kabīr.* Edited by 'Alī Muḥammad 'Umar. 11 vols. Cairo: Maktabat al-Khānjī, 1421/2001.

Ibn Sallām al-Jumaḥī, Muḥammad. *Ṭabaqāt fuḥūl al-shu'arā'.* Edited by Maḥmūd Muḥammad Shākir. Cairo: Dār al-Ma'ārif, 1952.

Ibn Sīnā, al-Ḥusayn ibn 'Alī. *Al-Qānūn fī l-ṭibb.* Edited by Sa'īd al-Laḥḥām. 4 vols. Beirut: Dār al-Fikr, 1994.

Ibn Sūdūn (al-Bashbughāwī), 'Alī, *see* Vrolijk, Arnoud.

Ibn Ṭūlūn, Shams al-Dīn Muḥammad ibn 'Alī. *Mufākahat al-khillān.* Beirut: Dār al-Kutub al-'Ilmiyyah, 1998.

Ibn al-Zubayr (al-Qāḍī al-Rashīd), Aḥmad ibn al-Rashīd. *Kitāb al-dhakhā'ir wa-l-tuḥaf.* Edited by Muḥammad Ḥamīdallāh. Kuwait: Maṭba'at Ḥukūmat al-Kuwayt, 1959.

Ibrahim, Laila, and Bernard O'Kane. "The Madrasa of Badr al-Din al-'Ayni and Its Tiled Mihrab." *Annales Islamologiques* 24 (1988): 253–68.

Ibrāhīm, Nāṣir Aḥmad. *Al-Azamāt al-ijtimā'iyyah fī Miṣr fī l-qarn al-sābi' 'ashar.* Cairo: Dār al-Āfāq al-'Arabiyyah, 1998.

Ibshīhī, Muḥammad ibn Aḥmad al-. *Al-Mustaṭraf fī kull fann mustaẓraf.* 2 vols. Cairo: Muṣṭafā al-Bābī l-Ḥalabī, 1371/1952.

Idrīs, Yūsuf. *Al-Farāfīr.* Cairo: Maktabat Ghurayyib, 1977.

Imru' al-Qays. *Dīwān.* Edited by Muḥammad Abū l-Faḍl Ibrāhīm. 4th ed. Cairo: Dār al-Ma'ārif, 1984.

Irwin, Robert. *The Arabian Nights: A Companion.* London: Penguin Books, 1995.

———. "'Alī al-Baghdādī and the Joy of Mamluk Sex." In *The Historiography of Islamic Egypt (c. 950–1800)*, edited by Hugh Kennedy, 45–57. Leiden: Brill, 2001.

'Īsā, 'Alī. *Al-Lughāt al-sirriyyah.* Alexandria: Maṭba'at al-Intiṣār, n.d.

Iṣfahānī, Abū l-Faraj al-. *Kitāb al-aghānī.* 24 vols. Cairo: Dār al-Kutub/al-Hay'ah al-Miṣriyyah al-'Āmmah li-l-Kitāb, 1927–74.

Jabartī, 'Abd al-Raḥman al-. *'Ajā'ib al-āthār fī l-tarājim wa-l-akhbar.* 4 vols. Bulaq: al-Maṭba'ah al-Amīriyyah, 1880.

Jāḥiẓ, 'Amr ibn Baḥr al-. *Al-Bayān wa-l-tabyīn.* Edited by 'Abd al-Salām Muḥammad Hārūn. 4 vols. Cairo: Maktabat al-Khānjī, 1968.

———. *Al-Ḥayawān*. Edited by ʿAbd al-Salām Muḥammad Hārūn. 8 vols. Cairo: Muṣṭafā al-Bābī al-Ḥalabī, 1965–69.

———. *Rasāʾil al-Jāḥiẓ*. Edited by ʿAbd al-Salām Muḥammad Hārūn. 4 vols. Cairo: Maktabat al-Khānjī, 1965/1348.

Jarīr ibn ʿAṭiyyah. *Dīwān bi-sharḥ Muḥammad ibn Ḥabīb*. Edited by Nuʿmān Muḥammad Amīn Ṭāhā. 3rd ed. 2 vols. Cairo: Dār al-Maʿārif, 1986.

Jurjānī, ʿAbd al-Qāhir. *Dalāʾil al-iʿjāz*. Edited by Maḥmūd Muḥammad Shākir. Maktabat al-Khānjī: Cairo, 1984.

Karamustafa, Ahmet T. *God's Unruly Friends: Dervish Groups in the Islamic Later Middle Period 1200–1550*. Salt Lake City: University of Utah Press, 1994.

Kern, F. "Neuere ägyptische Humoristen und Satiriker." *Mitteilungen des Seminars fur Orientalische Sprache*, Section 2 (1906): 31–73.

Khafājī, Aḥmad ibn Muḥammad ibn ʿUmar al-. *Rayḥānat al-alibbāʾ*. Edited by ʿAbd al-Fattāh Muḥammad al-Ḥulw. 2 vols. [Cairo]: Maṭbaʿat ʿĪsā al-Bābī l-Ḥalabī, 1967.

Khaṭīb al-Baghdādī, Aḥmad ibn ʿAlī ibn Thābit al-. *Tārīkh Baghdād*. 14 vols. Cairo: Maktabat al-Khānjī, 1349/1931.

Khawam, René R. *La cuisine arabe*. Paris: Albin Michel, 1970.

Khayrī, Badīʿ, and Najīb al-Rayḥānī. "Kishkish Bak ʿUḍw fī l-Barlamān." *Majallat al-nāqid* (17 February 1929). Reprinted in Ḥasan Darwīsh, *Badīʿ Khayrī: al-azjāl al-badīʿiyyah wa-l-alḥān al-rayḥāniyyah*. Cairo: al-Majlis al-Aʿlā li-l-Thaqāfah, 2001.

Kumayt ibn Zayd, al-. *Dīwān*. Beirut: Dār Ṣādir, 2000.

Lane, Edward William. *Account of the Manners and Customs of the Modern Egyptians*. 5th ed. London: John Murray, 1860. Offset, Cairo: American University in Cairo Press: 2003.

———. *An Arabic-English Lexicon*. 8 vols. London: Williams and Norgate, 1865. Offset, Beirut: Maktabat Lubnān, 1968.

Le Cerf, Jean. "Littérature dialectale et renaissance arabe moderne." *Bulletin d'Études Orientales* 11, no. 11 (1932): 179–258.

Maʿarrī, Abū l-ʿAlāʾ al-. *Al-Luzūmiyyāt*. Edited by Amīn ʿAbd al-ʿAzīz al-Khānjī. Cairo: Maktabat al-Khānjī, n.d. [1924].

Maghribī, Yūsuf ibn Zakariyyā ibn Ḥarb al-. *Dafʿ al-iṣr ʿan kalām ahl Miṣr.* Introduction and notes by ʿAbd al-Salām Aḥmad ʿAwwād. Moscow: Dār Nashr al-ʿIlm, 1968.

Maqqarī, Aḥmad ibn Muḥammad al-. *Nafḥ al-ṭīb min ghuṣn al-Andalus al-raṭīb.* Edited by Iḥsān ʿAbbās. 8 vols. Beirut: Dār Ṣādir, 1968.

Maqrīzī, Taqī al-Dīn Aḥmad ibn ʿAlī ibn ʿAbd al-Qādir ibn Muḥammad al-. *Al-Bayān wa-l-iʿrāb ʿammā fī Miṣr min al-Aʿrāb.* Cairo: 1961.

———. *Kitāb al-khiṭaṭ al-maqriziyyah al-musammā bi-l-Mawāʿiẓ wa-l-iʿtibār bi-dhikr al-khiṭaṭ wa-l-āthār.* 2 vols. Cairo: al-Maṭbaʿah al-Amīriyyah, 1853. Offset, Beirut: Dār Ṣādir, n.d.

Marmon, Shaun. *Eunuchs and Sacred Boundaries in Islamic Society.* New York: Oxford University Press, 1995.

Marzolph, Ulrich. *Arabia Ridens.* 2 vols. Frankfurt: Vittorio Klostermann, 1992.

Marzolph, Ulrich, and Richard van Leuwen, eds. *The Arabian Nights Encyclopedia.* 2 vols. Santa Barbara: ABC Clio, 2004.

Masʿūdī, Abū l-Ḥasan ʿAlī ibn al-Ḥusayn al-. *Murūj al-dhahab wa-maʿādin al-jawhar.* Edited by Muḥammad Muḥyī l-Dīn ʿAbd al-Ḥamīd. 4 vols. Cairo: al-Maktabah al-Tijāriyyah al-Kubrā, 1958.

Maydānī, Abū l-Faḍl Aḥmad ibn Muḥammad al-Nīsābūrī al-. *Majmaʿ al-amthāl.* 2 vols. Cairo: al-Maṭbaʿah al-Khayriyyah, 1321/1892.

Mehren, A. F. *Et Par Bidrag til Bedømmelse af den nyere Folkelitteratur i Ægypten.* Copenhagen: Bianco Lunos, 1872 (summary in French, 23–24).

Michel, Nicolas. "Les Dafatir al-Gusur, source pour l'histoire du réseau hydraulique de l'Egypte Ottomane." *Annales Islamologiques* 19 (1995): 151–68.

Mitchell, T. F. *An Introduction to Egyptian Colloquial Arabic.* London: Oxford University Press, 1956.

Moreh, Shmuel. *Live Theatre and Dramatic Literature in the Medieval Arab World.* New York: New York University Press, 1992.

Mubārak, ʿAlī. *Al-Khiṭaṭ al-tawfiqiyyah al-jadīdah.* Cairo: al-Maṭbaʿah al-Amīriyyah, 1887–89.

Mubarrad, Abū l-ʿAbbās Muḥammad ibn al-Yazīd al-. *Al-Kāmil*. Edited by Muḥammad Abū l-Faḍl Ibrāhīm. 8 vols. Cairo: Dār Nahḍat Miṣr, 1981.

Mufaḍḍaliyyāt, Al-. Edited by Aḥmad Muḥammad Shākir and ʿAbd al-Salām Muḥammad Hārūn. Cairo: Dār al-Maʿārif, n.d.

Muḥibbī, Muḥammad Amīn ibn ʿAbd Allāh al-. *Khulāṣat al-athar fī aʿyān al-qarn al-ḥādī ʿashar*. 4 vols. Cairo: 1284/1867–68. Offset, Beirut: Dār Sadir, n.d.

. *Nafḥat al-rayḥānah wa-rashḥat ṭilāʾ al-ḥānah*. 5 vols. Cairo: ʿIsā l-Bābī l-Ḥalabī, 1967–69.

———. *Qaṣd al-sabīl fī mā fī l-lughah al-ʿarabiyyah min al-dakhīl*. Edited by ʿUthmān Maḥmūd al-Ṣīnī. 2 vols. Riyadh: Maktabat al-Tawbah, 1994.

Munāwī, ʿAbd al-Raʾūf al-. *Fayḍ al-Qadīr: sharḥ al-Jāmiʿ al-ṣaghīr min aḥādīth al-baṣīr al-nadīr*. 6 vols. N.p.: Dār al-Fikr, n.d.

———. *Al-Kawākib al-durriyyah fī tarājim al-sādah al-ṣūfiyyah aw Ṭabaqāt al-Munāwī al-kubrā*. Edited by ʿAbd al-Ḥamīd Ṣāliḥ Ḥamdān. 4 parts in 2 vols. Cairo: al-Maktabah al-Azhariyyah li-l-Turāth, 1994.

Murray, G. W. *Sons of Ishmael: A Study of the Egyptian Bedouin*. London: Routledge, 1935.

Mutanabbī, Abū l-Ṭayyib Aḥmad ibn al-Ḥusayn al-. *Sharh dīwān al-Mutanabbī*. Edited by ʿAbd al-Raḥmān al-Barqūqī. 4 vols. Cairo: al-Maktabah al-Tijāriyyah al-Kubrā, 1938.

Nadīm, ʿAbd Allāh al-, ed. *Al-Aʿdād al-kāmilah li-Majallat al-Ustādh*. 2 vols. Cairo: al-Hayʾah al-Miṣriyyah al-ʿĀmmah li-l-Kitāb, 1994.

———. "Al-Waṭan" in *Akhbār al-adab* 217 (September 2003, 13–16).

Nelson, Kristina. *The Art of Reciting the Qurʾan*. Austin: University of Texas Press, 1985. Reprinted Cairo: American University in Cairo Press, 2001.

Newmark, Peter. *About Translation*. Multilingual Matters 74. Clevedon, UK: Multilingual Matters, 1996.

Nicolle, David, and Angus McBride. *The Mamluks 1250–1517*. Men-At-Arms 259. Botley, UK: Osprey Publishing, 1993.

Nīsābūrī, al-Ḥasan ibn Muḥammad ibn Ḥabīb al-. *ʿUqalāʾ al-majānīn*. Edited by Fāris al-Kīlānī. Cairo: al-Maṭbaʿah al-ʿArabiyyah, 1924.

Nuṣayb ibn Rabāḥ. *Shiʿr Nuṣayb ibn Rabāḥ*. Edited by Dāwūd Sallūm. Baghdad: Maktabat Marwān al-ʿAṭiyyah, 1967.

OLA 141 = Shirbīnī, Yūsuf al-. *Yūsuf al-Shirbīnī's Kitāb Hazz al-quḥūf bi-sharḥ qaṣīd Abī Shādūf*. Vol. 1, *Arabic Text*. Edited by Humphrey Davies. Orientalia Lovaniensia Analecta 141. Leuven: Peeters, 2005.

Omri, Mohamed-Salah. "Adab in the Seventeenth Century: Narrative and Parody in al-Shirbini's Hazz al-Quhuf." *Edebiyat* 11, no. 2 (2000): 169–96.

Pamuk, Şevket. *A Monetary History of the Ottoman Empire*. Cambridge: Cambridge University Press, 2000.

Perry, Charles. "Būrān: Eleven Hundred Years in the History of a Dish." In *Medieval Arab Cookery, Essays and Translations,* edited by Charles Perry et al., 239–50. London: Prospect Books, 2006.

Pertsch, Wilhelm. *Katalog der Orientalischen Handschriften der Herzoglichen Bibliothek zu Gotha*. Leipzig: Landesbibliothek Gotha, 1859–93.

Raḍī, al-Sharīf al- *see* Ibn Abī l-Ḥadīd.

Rāghib al-Iṣfahānī, Abū l-Qāsim al-Ḥusayn ibn Muḥammad al-. *Muḥāḍarāt al-udabāʾ wa-muḥāwarāt al-shuʿarāʾ wa-l-bulaghāʾ*. Bulaq: Maṭbaʿat Ibrāhīm al-Muwayliḥī/Jamʿiyyat al-Maʿārif, 1287/1870–71.

Ramzī, Muḥammad. *Al-Qāmūs al-jughrāfī li-l-bilād al-Miṣriyyah min ʿahd qudamāʾ al-Miṣriyyīna ilā sanat 1945*. Cairo: Maṭbaʿat Dār al-Kutub al-Miṣriyyah, 1953–54.

Raymond, André. *Artisans et commercants au Caire au XVIIIème siècle*. 2 vols. Damascus: Institut Français d'Etudes Arabes, 1973–75. Reprinted Cairo: Institut Français d'Archéologie Orientale, 1999.

———. *Les marchés du Caire*. Cairo: Institut Français d'Archéologie Orientale, 1979.

Rivlin, Helen Anne B. *The Agricultural Policy of Muhammad Ali in Egypt*. Cambridge, MA: Harvard University Press, 1961.

Rodinson, M. "*Maʾmūniyya* East and West." In *Medieval Arab Cookery, Essays and Translations,* edited by Charles Perry et al., 183–97. London: Prospect Books, 2006.

———. *Recherches sur les documents arabes relatifs à la cuisine*. Paris: Librairie Orientaliste Paul Geuthner, 1950.

Rosenthal, Franz. *Gambling in Islam*. Leiden: E. J. Brill, 1975.

Rowson, Everett K. "Al-ʿĀmirī." In *History of Islamic Philosophy*, edited by Seyyed Hossein Nasr and Oliver Leaman. New York: Routledge, 1996, 1:216–21.

———. "Cant and Argot in Cairo Colloquial Arabic." *Newsletter of the American Research Center in Egypt* 122 (Summer 1983): 13–24.

———. "Male and Female: Described and Compared." In *Homoeroticism in Classical Arabic Literature*, edited by J. W. Wright and Everett K. Rowson. New York: Columbia University Press, 1997.

———. *A Muslim Philosopher on the Soul and Its Fate: Al-ʿĀmirī's Kitāb al-Amad ʿalā l-abad*. New Haven: American Oriental Society, 1988.

Ṣabbāgh, Mikhāʾīl ibn Nīqūlā ibn Ibrāhīm. *Al-Risālah al-tāmmah fī kalām al-ʿāmmah wa-l-manāhij fī aḥwāl al-kalām al-dārij*. Edited by H. Thorbecke. Strassburg: Karl J. Trübner, 1886.

Sabra, Adam. *Poverty and Charity in Medieval Islam: Mamluk Egypt 1250–1517*. Cambridge: Cambridge University Press, 2000.

Ṣabrī, ʿUthmān. *Riḥlah fī l-Nīl*. Alexandria: ʿUthmān Ṣabrī, 1965.

Ṣafadī, Ṣalāḥ al-Dīn Khalīl ibn Aybak al-. *Aʿyān al-ʿaṣr*. Edited by Nabīl ʿAmshah et al. Damascus: Dār al-Fikr, 1988.

———. *Al-Ghayth al-musajjam fī sharḥ Lāmiyyāt al-ʿajam*. 2 vols. Beirut: Dār al-Kutub al-ʿIlmiyyah, 1975.

———. *Ikhtirāʿ al-khurāʿ*. Edited by Fārūq Islīm. Damascus: Ittiḥād al-Kuttāb al-ʿArab, 2000.

———. *Kitāb nuṣrat al-thāʾir ʿalā l-mathal al-sāʾir*. Edited by Muḥammad ʿAlī Sulṭānī. Damascus: Maṭbūʿāt Majmaʿ al-Lughah al-ʿArabiyyah bi-Dimashq, 1972.

———. *Al-Wāfī bi-l-wafayāt*. 30 vols. Beirut, Wiesbaden, and Berlin: Franz Steiner and Klaus Schwarz, 1931–2005.

Sale, George. *The Koran: Commonly Called The Alcoran of Mohammed; Translated into English Immediately from the Original Arabic with Explanatory Notes, Taken from the Most Approved Commentators*. London: William Tegg, 1850.

Shāfiʿī, Muḥammad ibn Idrīs al-. *Shiʿr al-Shāfiʿī*. Edited by Mujāhid Muṣṭafā Bahjat. Mosul: University of Mosul, 1986.

Shalabī, Awliyā [= Çelebi, Evliya]. *Siyāhatnāmah Miṣr*. Translated by Muḥammad ʿAlī ʿAwnī. Cairo: Dār al-Kutub, 2003.

Shaʿrānī, ʿAbd al-Wahhāb al-. *Laṭāʾif al-minan wa-l-akhlāq fī wujūb al-taḥadduth bi-niʿmat Allāh ʿalā al-iṭlāq*. Cairo: ʿĀlam al-Fikr, 1976.

———. *Lawāqiḥ al-anwār fī ṭabaqāt al-akhyār (Al-Ṭabaqāt al-kubrā)*. Cairo: al-Maṭbaʿah al-ʿĀmirah al- Sharafiyyah, 1315/1897.

Sharīf al-Raḍī, al-. *Dīwān*. Edited by Maḥmūd Muṣṭafā Ḥalāwī. 2 vols. Beirut: Sharikat al-Arqam ibn al-Arqam, 1999.

Shaw, Stanford J. *The Financial and Administrative Organization and Development of Ottoman Egypt, 1517–1798*. Princeton, NJ: Princeton University Press, 1962.

Shoshan, Boaz. *Popular Culture in Medieval Cairo*. Cambridge: Cambridge University Press, 1993.

Spitta, Wilhelm. *Grammatik des arabischen Vulgärdialektes von Aegypten*. Leipzig: J. C. Hinrichs, 1880.

Suyūṭī, Jalāl al-Dīn ʿAbd al-Raḥman al-. *Al-Itqān fī ʿulūm al-Qurʾān*. Edited by Muḥammad Abū l-Faḍl Ibrāhīm. Cairo: al-Hayʾah al-Miṣriyyah al-ʿĀmmah li-l-Kitāb, 1975.

Ṭabarānī, Sulaymān ibn Aḥmad Abū al-Qāsim al-. *Al-Muʿjam al-kabīr*. Edited by Ḥamdī ʿAbd al-Majīd al-Salafī. 20 vols. Cairo: Dār al-Bayān al-ʿArabī, n.d.

Tanūkhī, Abū ʿAlī l-Muḥassin ibn ʿAlī al-. *Al-Faraj baʿd al-shiddah*. Cairo: Maktabat al-Khānjī, 1955.

Ṭawīl, Tawfiq al-. *Al-Taṣawwuf fī Miṣr ibbān al-ʿaṣr al-ʿUthmānī*. 2 vols. Cairo: al-Hayʾah al-Miṣriyyah al-ʿĀmmah li-l-Kitāb, 1988.

Taymūr, Aḥmad. *Al-Amthāl al-ʿāmmiyyah*. 4th ed. Cairo: Markaz al-Ahrām li-l-Tarjamah wa-l-Nashr, 1986.

———. *Muʿjam Taymūr al-kabīr li-l-alfāẓ al-ʿāmmiyyah*. Edited by Ḥusayn Naṣṣār. Vols. 1–3, 2nd ed. Cairo: Maṭbaʿat Dār al-Kutub wa-l-Wathāʾiq al-Qawmiyyah, 2002; vols. 4–6, 1st ed., Cairo: Maṭbaʿat Dār al-Kutub wa-l-Wathāʾiq al-Qawmiyyah, 2003.

Thaʿālibī, Manṣūr ʿAbd al-Malik ibn Muḥammad ibn Ismāʿīl al-. *Yatīmat al-dahr*. Edited by Muḥammad Muḥyī l-Dīn ʿAbd al-Ḥamīd. 4 vols. Cairo: Maktabat al-Ḥusayn al-Tijāriyyah, 1947.

Tietze, Andreas. *Mustafa ʿAali's Description of Cairo of 1599: Text, Translation, Notes*. Vienna: Verlag der Österreichen Akademie der Wissenschaften, 1975.

TIF = *Jamʿ jawāmiʿ al-aḥādīth wa-l-asānīd wa-makniz al-ṣiḥāḥ wa-l-sunan wa-l-masānid; al-kutub al-sabʿah al-matīnah fī aḥādīth al-sunnah al-sharīfah*. Vaduz: Thesaurus Islamicus Foundation, 2001.

Tifāshī, Aḥmad ibn Yūsuf al-. *Surūr al-nafs bi-madārik al-ḥawāss al-khams*. Edited by Iḥsān ʿAbbās. Beirut: al-Muʾassasah al-ʿArabiyyah li-l-Dirāsāt wa-l-Nashr, 1980.

Trimingham, J. S. *The Sufi Orders in Islam*. Oxford: Clarendon Press, 1971.

Ṭurṭūshī, Muḥammad ibn al-Walīd al-. *Sirāj al-mulūk*. Edited by Jaʿfar al-Bayātī. London: Riad El-Rayyes Books, 1990.

Van Gelder, Geert Jan, trans. *Classical Arabic Literature: A Library of Arabic Literature Anthology*. Library of Arabic Literature. New York: New York University Press, 2013.

———. *Of Dishes and Discourse: Classical Arabic Literary Representations of Food*. London: Routledge, 2000.

———. "The Nodding Noddles, or Jolting the Yokels: A Composition for Marginal Voices by al-Shirbīnī (fl. 1687)." In *Marginal Voices in Literature and Society*, edited by Robin Ostle, 49–67. Strasbourg: European Science Foundation/Maison Méditerranéenne des Sciences de l'Homme d'Aix-en-Provence, 2000.

———. *Sound and Sense in Classical Arabic Poetry*. Arabische Studien 10. Wiesbaden: Harrassowitz, 2012.

Vial, Charles. "Le Hazz al-Quhuf de al-Širbini est-il un échantillon d'adab populaire?" In *Rivages et déserts: hommage à Jacques Berque*, 170–81. Paris: Sindbad, ca. 1988.

Vollers, K. "Beiträge zur Kenntniss der lebenden arabischen Sprache in Aegypten." *Zeitschrift des Deutschen Morgenländischen Gesellschaft* 41 (1887): 365–402.

Vrolijk, Arnoud. *Bringing a Laugh to a Scowling Face: A Study and Critical Edition of "Nuzhat al-Nufūs wa-Muḍḥik al-ʿAbūs" by ʿAlī Ibn Sūdūn al-Bashbughāwī*. Leiden: Research School CNWS, 1998.

Walīd ibn Yazīd, al-. *Shiʿr al-Walīd ibn Yazīd*. Edited by Ḥusayn ʿAṭwān. Amman: Maktabat al-Aqṣā, 1979.

Wansleben, F. *The Present State of Egypt: Or, a New Relation of a Late Voyage into the Kingdom, Performed in the Years 1672 and 1673* by F. Vansleb [*sic*]. Translated by M. D., B. D. London: 1678. Reprinted Westmead, UK: Gregg International Publishers, 1972.

Warner, Nicholas. *Guide to the Gayer-Anderson Museum Cairo*. Cairo: Ministry of Culture/Supreme Council of Antiquities, 2003.

———. "Taking the Plunge: the Development and Use of the Cairene Bathhouse" in *Historians in Cairo: Essays in Honor of George Scanlon*, edited by Jill Edwards, 49–79. Cairo: American University in Cairo Press, 2002.

Wehr, Hans. *A Dictionary of Modern Written Arabic*. Edited by Milton J. Cowan. 4th ed. Wiesbaden: Otto Harrassowitz, 1979.

Winter, Michael. *Egyptian Society under Ottoman Rule 1517–1798*. London and New York: Routledge, 1992.

———. *Society and Religion in Ottoman Egypt: Studies in the Writings of ʿAbd al-Wahhāb al-Shaʿrānī*. The Shiloah Center for Middle Eastern and African Studies: Studies in Islamic Culture and History. New Brunswick and London: Transaction Books, 1982.

WKAS = Ullmann, Manfred, with Anton Spitaler. *Wörterbuch des Klassischen Arabischen Sprache*. Wiesbaden: Otto Harrassowitz, 1970–.

Woidich, Manfred. "Materialen zur Kenntnis des Kairenisch-Arabischen." In *Leermiddelen voor de studie van de Arabische taal en cultuur* 2, 19ff. Amsterdam: Instituut voor het Moderne Nabije Oosten/Universiteit van Amsterdam, 1990.

———. "Zum Dialekt von il-ʿAwāmra in der östlichen Šarqiyya (Ägypten)." Part 1, "Einleitung: grammatische Skizze und Volkskundliches." *Zeitschrift für Arabischen Linguistik* 2 (1979): 76–99.

Wright, W. A. *Grammar of the Arabic Language*. 3rd ed. Revised by W. Robertson Smith and M. J. de Goeje. 2 vols. Cambridge: Cambridge University Press, 1951.

Yāqūt ibn ʿAbd Allāh al-Rūmī al-Ḥamawī. *Muʿjam al-udabāʾ*. Edited by Aḥmad Farīd Rifāʿī. 20 vols. Cairo, 1936–38. Reprinted Beirut: Iḥyāʾ al-Turāth al-ʿArabī, n.d.

———. *Muʿjam al-buldān*. Edited by Farīd ʿAbd al-ʿAzīz al-Jundī. 7 vols. Beirut: Dār al-Kutub al-ʿIlmiyyah, 1990.

Zack, Liesbeth. *Egyptian Arabic in the Seventeenth Century: A Study and Edition of Yūsuf al-Maghribī's Dafʿ al-iṣr ʿan kalām ahl Miṣr*. Utrech: LOT, 2009.

Zamakhsharī, Maḥmūd ibn ʿUmar al-. *Rabīʿ al-abrār wa-fuṣūṣ al-akhbār*. Edited by ʿAbd al-Majīd Diyāb. 2 vols. Cairo: al-Hayʾah al-Miṣriyyah al-ʿĀmmah li-l-Kitāb, 1991–92.

Ziriklī, Khayr al-Dīn al-. *Al-Aʿlām: qāmūs tarājim li-ashhar al-rijāl wa-l-nisāʾ min al-ʿArab wa-l-mustaʿribīna wa-l-mustashriqīn*. 8 vols. Beirut: Dār al-ʿIlm li-l-Malāyīn, 1990.

Zuhayr, Bahāʾ al-Dīn ibn Muḥammad. *The Poetical Works [by] Behà-ed-din Zoheir*. Arabic text edited by Edward Henry Palmer. 2nd ed. Amsterdam: Oriental Press, 1971.

Further Reading

Abū Fāshā, Ṭāhir. *Hazz al-quḥūf fī sharḥ qaṣīdat Abī Shādūf*. Cairo: al-Hay'ah al-'Āmmah li-l-Kitāb, 1987. [A study, not a text edition.]

Amīn, Aḥmad. *Fayḍ al-khāṭir*. Vol. 3. Cairo: n.p., 1965, 101–6. [Notice under the title *Dumyah fī dimnah*. All the information on the countryside contained in the same author's *Qāmūs al-'ādāt wa-l-taqālīd wa-l-ta'ābīr al-miṣriyyah* (Cairo: Maṭba'at Lajnat al-Ta'līf wa-l-Tarjamah wa-l-Nashr, 1953) is also taken, without attribution, from *Hazz al-Quḥūf*.]

Abd al Raheim, Abd al Raheim A. "*Hazz al-Quhuf*: A New Source for the Study of the *Fallahin* of Egypt in the XVIIth and XVIIIth Centuries." *Journal of the Economic and Social History of the Orient* 18/3 (October 1975), 245–70. [Translation of the next.]

'Abd al-Raḥīm, 'Abd al-Raḥīm 'Abd al-Raḥmān. "Dirāsah naṣṣiyyah li-Kitāb *Hazz al-Quḥūf*." *al-Majallah al-Miṣriyyah li-l-Dirāsāt al-Tārīkhiyyah* 20 (1973): 287–316.

———. *Al-Rīf al-miṣrī fī l-qarn al-thāmin 'ashar*. Cairo: Maktabat Madbūlī, 1986.

'Abd al-Raḥīm, 'Abd al-Raḥīm 'Abd al-Raḥmān, and Wāṭārū Mīkī. "Village in Ottoman Egypt and Tokugawa Japan: A Comparative Study." *Studia Culturae Islamicae* 7. Tokyo: Institute for the Study of Languages and Cultures of Asia and Africa, 1977.

Baer, Gabriel. "Fellah and Townsman in Ottoman Egypt: A Study of Shirbini's Hazz al-Quḥūf." *Asian and African Studies* [Jerusalem] 8 (1972): 221–56.

———. "Shirbīnī's Hazz al-Quḥūf and Its Significance." In Gabriel Baer, *Fellah and Townsman in the Middle East: Studies in Social

History. London: Frank Cass, 1982. [An expanded version of the preceding.]

———. *Studies in the Social History of Modern Egypt*. Chicago and London: University of Chicago Press, 1969.

Baqlī (al-), Muḥammad Qindīl. *Qaryatunā al-miṣriyyah qabla al-thawrah – 1*, with introduction by Muḥammad ʿĪsā Ṭalʿat. Cairo: Dār al-Nahḍah al-ʿArabiyyah, n.d. [1963]. [A shortened and expurgated version of *Hazz al-quḥūf*.]

Ben Cheneb, M. "Al-Shirbīnī." In *EI1*.

Davies, Humphrey. "The Use of Middle Arabic in Yūsuf al-Shirbīnī's *Hazz al-Quḥūf bi-Sharḥ Qaṣīd Abī Shādūf*" in *Proceedings of the First International Symposium (Louvain-la-Neuve, 11–14 May 2004) on Middle Arabic and Mixed Arabic Throughout History: The Current State of Knowledge, Problems of Definition, Perspectives of Research*. Publications de l'Institut Orientaliste de Louvain. Louvain-la-Neuve; Institut Orientaliste de l'Université Catholique de Louvain, 2008.

———. "Yūsuf al-Shirbīnī." In *Essays in Arabic Literary Biography (1350–1850)*, edited by Joseph E. Lowry and Devin Stewart. Wiesbaden: Otto Harrassowitz, 2009.

———. "Yūsuf al-Shirbīnī's Hazz al-Quḥūf: Issues Relevant to Its Assessment as a Source for 17th-Century Egyptian Colloquial." *Al-Logha* 2 (November 2000): 57–78.

Dayfīz, Hamfirī (Humphrey Davies), and Madīḥah Dōs, eds. *Al-ʿĀmmiyyah al-miṣriyyah al-maktūbah: mukhtārāt min 1401 ilā 2009*. Cairo: al-Hayʾah al-Miṣriyyah al-ʿĀmmah li-l-Kitāb, 2013.

Ḍayf, Shawqī. *Al-Fukāhah fī Miṣr*. N.p.: n.d., 91–99.

Doss, Madiha. "The Position of the Demonstrative DA, DI in Egyptian Arabic: A Diachronic Inquiry." *Annales Islamologiques* 15 (1979): 349–57.

———. "Réflexions sur les débuts de l'écriture dialectale en Égypte." *Égypte/Monde arabe*, ser. 1, 27–28 (1996): 119–46.

El-Rouayheb, Khaled. *Before Homosexuality in the Arab-Islamic World, 1500–1800*. Chicago: University of Chicago Press: 2009.

Finkel, J. "King Mutton, a Curious Egyptian Tale of the Mamluk Period. Edited from a Unique Manuscript, with Translation, Notes, Glossary and Introduction." *Zeitschrift für Semitistik* 8 (1932): 122–48, and 9 (1933–34): 1–18. [Pages 132–36 contain a discussion and partial translation of *Hazz al-quḥūf*'s "sermon on different dishes" (§11.25.7–13).]

Goldziher, Ignaz. "Jugend- und Strassenpoesie in Kairo." *Zeitschrift des Deutschen Morgenländischen Gesellschaft* 33 (1874): 608–30.

Hamarneh, Walid. "Aḥmad Fāris al-Shidyāq." In *Essays in Arabic Literary Biography (1850–1950)*, edited by Roger M. A. Allen, Joseph Edmund Lowry, and Devin J. Stewart. Wiesbaden: Otto Harrassowitz, 2010. [Compares and contrasts al-Shidyāq, al-Shirbīnī, Ibn Sūdūn, and other humorous writers; *see* p. 323.]

Ḥamzah, ʿAbd al-Laṭīf. *Al-Adab al-Miṣrī min qiyām al-dawlah al-ayyūbiyyah ilā majīʾ al-ḥamlah al-firansiyyah.* Cairo: Maktabat al-Nahḍah al-Miṣriyyah, [1960?], 209ff. [Excerpts, with introduction.]

Hanna, Nelly. *Ottoman Egypt and the Emergence of the Modern World: 1500–1800.* Cairo: American University in Cairo Press, 2014.

Ḥasan, ʿAbd al-Jalīl. "Sawṭ al-ṣāmiṭīn yaʿlū." *Al-Kātib* (August 1994): 134–43. [Baer, *Significance*, 26: "One of the best articles on Hazz al-Quḥūf written in Egypt so far."]

Ḥasan, Muḥammad ʿAbd al-Ghanī. *Al-Fallāḥ fī l-adab al-ʿarabī.* Al-Maktabah al-Thaqāfiyyah 128. [Cairo]: Dār al-Qalam, [1965], 139–44.

Hathaway, Jane. *A Tale of Two Factions: Myth, Memory, and Identity in Ottoman Egypt and Yemen.* New York: State University of New York Press, 2003.

Howarth, Herbert, and Ibrahim Shukrallah. *Images from the Arab World: Fragments of Arab Literature Translated and Paraphrased with Variations and Comments.* London: The Pilot Press, 1944, 21–23. [Translation of the tale of the Persian *ʿālim* (see vol. 1, §§4.5–4.9)].

Kern, F. "Neuere ägyptische Humoristen und Satiriker." *Mitteilungen des Seminars fur Orientalische Sprache* (1906), Section 2, 37–42 and 64–65. [The first passage is a description of the work, the second a transcription and translation of an excerpt.]

Mehren, A. F. *Et par Bildrag til Bedømmelsa af den nyere Folkeliteratur I Aegypten.* Copenhagen, 1872, 37–71. [With résumé and glossary in French of words "peu usités dans la langue littéraire" (58–71).]

Mikhail, Alan. “A Dog-Eat-Dog Empire: Violence and Affection on the Streets of Ottoman Cairo.” *Comparative Studies of South Asia, Africa and the Middle East* 35, no. 1 (2015): 76–95.

Muḥassib, Ḥasan. *Qaḍiyyat al-fallāḥ fī l-qiṣṣah al-miṣriyyah*. Maktabah al-thaqāfīyah 256. Cairo: al-Hay'ah al-Miṣriyyah al-ʿĀmmah li-l-Ta'līf wa-l-Nashr, 1971, 15–22.

Musawi, Muhsin J. al-. *The Medieval Islamic Republic of Letters: Arabic Knowledge Construction*. Notre Dame, IN: Notre Dame University Press, 2015.

Nallino, C. A. *L'Arabo parlato in Egitto. Grammatica, dialoghi i raccolta di vocabuli*. Milan: Editore-Libraio della Real Casa, 1900.

Omri, Mohamed-Salah. “Adab in the Seventeenth Century: Narrative and Parody in al-Shirbini's Hazz al-Quhuf.” *Edebiyat* 11, no. 2 (2000): 169–96.

Peled, M. “Nodding the Necks: A Literary Study of Shirbini's *Hazz al-Quhuf*.” *Die Welt des Islams* 26 (1986): 57–75.

Rowson, E. K. “Al-Shirbīnī.” In *Encyclopedia of Arabic Literature*, edited by Julie Scott Meisami and Paul Starkey. 2 vols. London and New York: Routledge, 1998, 715.

Ṣāliḥ, Aḥmad Rushdī. *Funūn al-adab al-shaʿbī*. Cairo: n.p., 1956, 43.

Selim, Samah. *The Novel and the Rural Imaginary in Egypt, 1880–1985*. London: RoutledgeCurzon, 2004.

Spitta, Wilhelm. *Grammatik des arabischen Vulgärdialektes von Aegypten*. Leipzig: J. C. Hinrichs, 1880. [Texts VIII and X derive from *Hazz al-Quḥūf*; *see* Davies, 1981, *Profile*, 34–35.]

Van Gelder, Geert Jan. *Of Dishes and Discourse: Classical Arabic Literary Representations of Food*. London: Routledge, 2000 (a).

———. “The Nodding Noddles, or Jolting the Yokels: A Composition for Marginal Voices by al-Shirbīnī (fl. 1687).” In *Marginal Voices in Literature and Society*, edited by Robin Ostle. Strasbourg, 2000 (b), 49–67.

———. “Satire, Medieval.” In *EAL*, 693–95.

Vial, Charles. “Le *Hazz Al-Quhuf* de Al-Širbini est-il un échantillon d'*adab* populaire?” In *Rivages et déserts: hommage à Jacques Berque*. Paris: Sindbad, ca. 1988, 170–81.

Vollers, Karl. "Beiträge zur Kenntniss der lebenden arabischen Sprache in Aegypten." *Zeitschrift des Deutschen Morgenländischen Gesellschaft* 41 (1887): 365–402.

Von Kremer, Alfred. "Aus einem Briefe von Prof. Dr. von Kremer an Prof. Fleischer." *Zeitschrift des Deutschen Morgenländischen Gesellschaft* 9 (1855): 847. [GAL II, p. 278, has "ZDMG 10" by mistake.]

Vrolijk, Arnoud. *Bringing a Laugh to a Scowling Face. A Study and Critical Edition of "Nuzhat al-Nufūs wa-Muḍḥik al-ʿAbūs" by ʿAlī Ibn Sūdūn al-Bashbughāwī.* Leiden: Research School CNWS, 1998, 138–40. [Reviews and critiques findings of Davies, *Seventeenth-Century.*]

Zakariyyā Saʿīd, Naffūsah. *Taʾrīkh al-daʿwah ilā al-ʿāmmiyyah wa-āthāruhā fī Miṣr.* Alexandria: Dār Nashr al-Thaqāfah, 1964, 240–49.

Zaydān, Jirjī. *Tārīkh adab al-lughah al-ʿarabiyyah.* Vol. 3. Cairo: Maṭbaʿat al-Hilāl, 1931, 276–77.

Zubaida, Sami. "Hazz al-Quhuf: An Urban Satire on Peasant Life and Food from Seventeenth-century Egypt." In *Food Between the Country and the City Ethnographies of a Changing Global Foodscape*, edited by Nuno Domingos, José Manuel Sobral, and Harry G. West. London: Bloomsbury Academic, 2014.

Risible Rhymes

or

The Book to Bring a Smile to the Lips of Devotees of Proper Taste and Style through the Decoding of a Sampling of the Verse of the Rural Rank and File

by

God's Humble Slave

Muḥammad ibn Maḥfūẓ al-Sanhūrī

May God Excuse Him His Sins

Translated by
Humphrey Davies

Volume Editors
James E. Montgomery
Geert Jan van Gelder

Introduction

Muḥammad ibn Maḥfūẓ al-Sanhūrī's *Kitāb Muḍḥik dhawī l-dhawq wa-l-niẓām fī ḥall shadharah min kalām ahl al-rīf al-ʿawāmm* (*The Book to Bring a Smile to the Lips of Devotees of Taste and Proper Style through the Decoding of a Sampling of the Verse of the Rural Rank and File*), or, in our abbreviated rendering, *Risible Rhymes,* is known from a single manuscript (see Note on the Text). Its author, who is otherwise unknown[1] but whose roots must have been, on the evidence of his name, in the town of al-Sanhūr in al-Fayyūm, in Upper Egypt, describes it as having been written at the behest of "a certain witty friend," unnamed (§1.1). Work on the book began at the end of the month of Shaʿbān of 1058 (mid-September AD 1648) (§5.1).

The first task set for the author by the commissioner of the work is to "to decode a sampling of what the rural rank and file have said in verse" (§1.1). Al-Sanhūrī's response to this challenge occupies about forty percent of the book, in which he discusses ten samples of supposedly rural verse. The remainder of the book is divided into two sections, the first devoted to the presentation and elucidation of several "hints" (*ishārāt*) and "riddles" (*alghāz*)—each a kind of conventional literary puzzle—while the last consists of a "wrangle" (*mabḥath*), or critical discussion, devoted to an analysis of different explanations of the meaning of a single word in a line of verse by Abū l-Ṭayyib al-Mutanabbī.

The significance of al-Sanhūrī's work from the present perspective and the reason for its publication in this series alongside Yūsuf al-Shirbīnī's *Hazz al-quḥūf bi-sharḥ qaṣīd Abī Shādūf* (*Brains Confounded by the Ode of Abū Shādūf Expounded*)[2] lies not in its value as literature, which is limited, nor simply in its concern with "rural" verse, but in the occurrence in it, with commentary, of six verses that occur also in the section of Volume One of *Brains Confounded* headed "An Account of Their Poets and of Their Idiocies and Inanities," (§5) in addition to four more that do not. Verses occurring (with minor variants) in both books are those beginning *wa-llāhi wa-llāhi l-ʿaḍīmi l-qādirī* (al-Sanhūrī §2.1.1; al-Shirbīnī §5.5), *hibabu furni-bni ʿammī* (al-Sanhūrī §2.3.1; al-Shirbīnī §5.6), *sa'altu ʿani l-ḥibb* (al-Sanhūrī §2.5.1; al-Shirbīnī §5.7), *wa-qultu lahā būlī ʿalayya wa-sharshirī* (al-Sanhūrī §2.7.1; al-Shirbīnī §5.3); *raqqāṣu ṭāḥūninā* (al-Sanhūrī §2.8.1; al-Shirbīnī §5.8), and *ra'ayt ḥarīfī bi-farqillah* (al-Sanhūrī §2.9.1; al-Shirbīnī §5.9). The four verses that occur only in *Muḍḥik dhawī al-dhawq* are those beginning *tanāmū wa-ʿaynī ḍarrahā l-buʿdu wa-l-sahar* (§2.2.1), *wa-qultu lahā yā bint al-ajwādi rawwiḍī* (§2.4.1), *sa'altu llāha yajmaʿunī bi-Salmā* (§2.6.1), and *laqītuhā qultu sittī bqī taʿā bukrah* (§2.10.1). Naturally, the point, made in the Introduction to *Brains Confounded* (vol. 1, p. xxvii), that such verses are mock-rural productions created by educated writers to be made fun of in the *majlis* (literary salon) applies equally to this work. The question of whether *Brains Confounded* derives directly from *Risible Rhymes* or whether each work drew on a common stock of mock-rural verse and whether they therefore constitute elements of a genre otherwise, so far, lost to us is also discussed in the introduction to *Brains Confounded* (vol. 1, p. xxxvii).

In its treatment of the rural verses, *Risible Rhymes* superficially resembles *Brains Confounded.* It employs some of the formal comic devices found in the latter, such as the use of absurd words as mnemonics to represent meter (e.g., *mutanāqiṣun mutanāqiṣun mutanāqiṣun* (§2.1.3); cf. *Brains Confounded*'s *mutakhabbiṭun khābiṭun mutakhabbiṭun khubāṭ* (§5.2.1)) and references to a line of verse as stretching from one supposedly well-known place to another (e.g., "its length . . . is from Bedlam's hall to the hospice gate, and its breadth . . . from the Gate of the Chain to that of the Great Keep" (§2.1.3); cf. *Brains Confounded*'s "their length, at the very least, is from Alexandria to Rashīd, for sure, their breadth from Upper Egypt to Dimyāṭ, or more" (§5.2.1). The opening scene, in which "a man of taste and knowledge" and his companions arrive in the port of Rashīd, enter a mosque, and are accosted by "a man of the countryside . . . like some mordacious cur or mud-caked boar" who challenges them to a contest (§1.2, §1.3) is reminiscent of anecdotes in *Brains Confounded* such as that in which the Azharī shaykh Shihāb al-Dīn al-Qalyūbī finds himself in a village mosque and is challenged by "a man tall of stature, thick of leg" (§4.3) or that in which villagers subject a benighted scholar to examination by their local *fiqī* (village man of religion or pastor), who turns out to be "tall as a flagpole on a mountain and bulky and heavy in physique as the Pillar of the Columns, so that just looking at him was enough to make the skin crawl" (§4.2.2).

Risible Rhymes is, however, far in spirit from *Brains Confounded.* The commentary on the "rural" verse restricts itself to a mundane analysis focused on grammar and prosody in which, despite the presence of the comic devices referred to above, the poets' solecisms are taken and dealt with at face value, rather than as occasions for word-play and witty excursus. It is also repetitive and makes no digressions into other areas of life, deriving most of what comic force it may possess from invective rather than wit. Surprisingly, it fails to fulfill the promise of its title, in that the body of the text contains almost no reference, after the first scene, to the "country rank and file," and, even in that scene, the setting is specified as Rashīd, an important port rather than a village (§1.2). Given *Risible Rhymes*'s lack of both the satirical and parodic dimensions to the critique of mock-rural verse that are so well developed in *Brains Confounded*, the only substantive factor shared by the two works may be their contempt for the poetic production of uneducated, nonelite versifiers.

Neither the remaining "hints and riddles" nor the "wrangle" passages of *Muḍḥik dhawī al-dhawq*, whatever their merits—and certainly the critical approach, especially in the "wrangle" over al-Mutanabbī, is not without subtlety and interest—add much to our understanding of the "rural verse" genre. Both sections consist almost entirely of quotations from other writers; they may, indeed, be considered an almost comically extreme example of padding. They do, however, serve to remind us of the intense preoccupation with wordplay, grammar, and stylistics that dominated the discussion of poetry in their day and that shaped and made meaningful the mockery of "rural verse."

Note on the Text

This edition of *Muḍḥik dhawī l-dhawq wa-l-niẓām fī ḥall shadharah min kalām ahl al-rīf al-ʿawāmm* derives from an apparently unique manuscript preserved in Egypt's National Library.[3] The only ownership marks on the codex are the stamp of a *waqf* (religious endowment), indicating that it was once in the collection of the noted book collector and writer on language Aḥmad Taymūr Pasha (d. 1930) and the National Library's accession mark. The manuscript consists of 39 folios and appears to have been repaired and rebound.[4]

While English is the metalanguage of this series, in those sections of *Risible Rhymes* that consist of commentaries on texts (1 and 3), Arabic has been privileged, in the sense that the verses in question are reproduced in transliteration in the English text and precede (both when they first occur and in their further iterations within the commentary) their English translations. The reasons for doing so are set out in the Note on the Text to *Brains Confounded* (see vol. 1, p. lxviii).

One of the most conspicuous features of the text is the use of rhymed prose (*sajʿ*), which is pervasive in the passages written by the author, somewhat less so in the quotations from other writers. The translation attempts to include enough rhymes (or near rhymes or alliteration where full rhymes were not found) to signal its importance to the aesthetics of the text.

Notes to the Introduction

1 No Library of Congress authority was found for this name or for the title of the work.

2 Yūsuf al-Shirbīnī. *Brains Confounded by the Ode of Abū Shādūf Expounded.* Library of Arabic Literature. New York, NY: New York University Press, 2016.

3 Dār al-Kutub, Adab Taymūr 876.

4 I am indebted to Noah Gardiner for his assessment of the codex, based on a digital copy.

Risible Rhymes

Preamble

In the Name of God, the Merciful, the Compassionate

God bless Our Lord Muḥammad, his kin, and his Companions, and grant them peace! Thanks be to You, O God, who have bestowed sound taste on those of Your servants whom You desire and imparted to them the power to discriminate, through right understanding, between verse that's exquisite and that which is dire, just as You have singled out those whom You please for an intelligence barely flickering (the most to which any such may aspire) and given them a genius resistant to quickening, sealed against any seepage or transmission from those wellsprings that the conversion of scattered words into ordered verse inspire! And blessings and peace upon the most well-spoken of those who the *ḍād* pronounce,[1] the bravest of those who their enemies and opponents trounce (Muḥammad, sent to show humanity the clearest of ways) and upon his kin and his companions, those guiding stars, so long as sun shall rise and lightning blaze! 0.1

The Author Declares His Intention to Decode a Sampling of Rural Verse and to Follow This with a Sampling of Hints, Wrangles, and Riddles

1.1 To proceed: a certain witty friend whose company I enjoyed and the denial of whose wishes I made every effort to avoid once asked me to create a concoction of words, sweet both when strung on prosody's string and when dispersed,[2] that would serve to decode a sampling of what the rural rank and file have said in verse, making plain the meter of each example as well as its division into feet, and, indeed, everything else about it, including its length and thickness, while pointing out the shortcomings of the poet's intellect, as well as its sickness. Next, I was to follow this with a refined sampling of "hints" alluding to the poets of Islam and of wrangles and riddles that the work of master wordsmiths propose and pose, be they exquisitely framed in verse or prettily turned in prose, and thus guide us toward a happy conclusion and provide a solution for anything that lies beyond man's wit to fathom (being so far gone in delusion). I responded to his request—God set his feet and mine alike upon the path that's best!—and named my work *The Book to Bring a Smile to the Lips of Devotees of Taste and Proper Style through the Decoding of a Sampling of the Verse of the Rural Rank and File.*

A Certain Friend Arrives with His Party in Rashīd, and They Encounter a Local Poet

1.2 I therefore now declare—and in God lies all hope of help and success in any attempt at conceptualization and decision to say yes—that a certain friend, a man of taste and knowledge,[3] told me the story of how once he was making his way to the port of Rashīd, with, in his party, many a man of knowledge mature in thought and deed. One day, after alighting in that town and being welcomed by its people, they entered the mosque, each one's heart in pious concentration lost. Thinking of having something to eat, they discussed among themselves whom they might so commission, upon which one of them brought them the food, he being the one entrusted with that mission.

1.3 After they had sat down to feed, a man of the countryside passed by whom they failed to hail and to whom they paid no heed, causing him to turn back toward them like some mordacious cur or mud-caked boar. In his hand was a stick, thick and stout, over which he bent and on which he leant, saying "Salaam!"—to which all the response he got was ". . . aam!"[4] At this, he gazed on them with bulging eye and cried, "Each and every one of you's a cunt and deserves no better name than Runt!" Then he called out to them again and scolded, having by now the robe of decency not merely stripped off but folded, crying, "What is your trade, you billy goats, the youngest of whom's a faggot while the oldest's a maggot?" To this one of them, a man of sound taste, replied, "By God, 'you remain in your ancient error caught!'[5] We are but a company of poets seeking hospitality from the people of this port."

1.4 At his words, the man with fury became replete and began to froth, like a camel in heat. To the group he said, "You may be poets as you claim, but I'm the poet of this port, and it is I who over its folk hold sway—but who gave you, anyway, leave to stay in this town, when it belongs to me and I'm the one here to whom men allegiance own? By alighting here without my permission you have committed a violation and, in my view, deserve humiliation, not exaltation. You'll not eat your fill till you've paid your bill, or clapped your hands and danced to the rhythm, or sung my praises with a bit of highfalutin verse, or attacked me in a flyting of most base criticism, or I've lauded you, both your young and your old, or dissed you, be you insignificant or extolled."

A Sampling of the Verse of the Rural Rank and File

"By God, by God, the Moighty, the Omnipotent"

2.1.1 At this the company turned to look his way, all mocking him for the loathsome words they'd heard him say, concluding from what they saw that his case was dire. "You, brother poet," they said, "shall be the first to fire." So he pondered at length, telling them, "Halt, halt,[6] for sure!" and said this again and again, so dull his mind, so rigid his brain. Then he declaimed:[7]

wa-llāhi wa-llāhi l-ʿaḍīmi l-qādirī
huwa ʿāliman bi-sarāyirī wa-khabāyiṭī
in ʿāda qalbī dā l-mashūmu dhikirkamū
la-nuqaṭṭiʿū min muhjatī bi-ṣawābiʿī

By God, by God, the Moighty, the Omnipotent
He is cognizunt of my secrets and my clangers!
If this unlucky heart of mine should turn again to thoughts of youse
I'll cut it out of my heart with my fangers!

2.1.2 At this one among them rose and engaged in vociferation, saying, "Brother Poet, the path to success lies not in that direction. It would be more proper to say, at the end of the first line, *wa-ẓawāhirī* ('my patent errors') instead of *wa-khabāyiṭī* ('my clangers'), so that the words may have some merit and be with interpretation consistent, for the rhyme is with the letter *r*—be not then on your ignorance insistent!" This point the man conceded, acknowledging thereby that his help he needed. Then the other asked him, "Why did you not say, at the end of the second line, *wa-ẓawāfirī* ('and my fingernails') rather than *wa-ṣawābiʿī* ('my fangers'), and so your footsteps with the relics of the poets align?" The other, from his ignorance compounded, now shouted, "One thing is on another mounted, and the fingers are mounted on the nails, so the one for the other may substitute, you miscreant, you dissolute!" At this, the company mocked him and left him alone, abandoning him to his own devices and those of Satan, his patron. Let us now return to what we were about by way of a decoding of the poetry of this lout, who, from the portals of those of good taste and exquisite speech, must surely be driven out.

Thus we declare—and from God we seek aid and to Him we repair: this deficient verse is drawn from the ocean of madness[8] and consists of three feet: *mutanāqiṣun mutanāqiṣun mutanāqiṣun.*[9] A depiction of its scansion,[10] applied to the first hemistich,[11] would go: 2.1.3

wa-llāhi wa-l-	*lāhi l-ʿaḍī*	*mi l-qādirī*
mutanāqiṣun	*mutanāqiṣun*	*mutanāqiṣun*

This is its limping measure, which is anything but straight, while its length, as all may see, is from Bedlam's hall to the hospice gate, and its breadth, so complete, so broad in sweep, from the Gate of the Chain[12] to that of the Great Keep. As for the sense, it's beyond help, with regard to both wording and meaning, for, when pronounced *al-ʿaḍīm*, it's not an oath, for the latter is from *taʿḍīm* not *taʿẓīm*,[13] and if he uses it the oath nonbinding we must deem. Even if he meant by it something other than "held in awe," such a use would be repudiated, as being at odds with, and contrary to, the conventions of the law.

The poet's words *huwa ʿāliman* ("he is cognizunt"): the ending *an* here does not, according to the science of Arabic, compute, because *ʿāliman* should be, according to the rules of grammar, in the nominative[14]—over this there can be no dispute! 2.1.4

2.1.5 The poet's words in *ʿāda qalbī dā l-mashūmu dhikirkamū* ("If this unlucky heart of mine should turn again to thoughts of youse"): by putting an *a* after the second *k* correct grammar he has belied, and with his thinking on this point the robe of taste is folded and set aside. Moreover, having the verb in the perfect isn't any more correct—here the imperfect must be preferred, it being to either the present or the future that the reader is referred.[15] What the poet wants to say is "If this unlucky heart of mine should turn again to thoughts of you, I shall do to it this or that, or shall treat it thus and so."

2.1.6 The poet's words *la-nuqaṭṭiʿū min muhjatī bi-ṣawābiʿī* ("I'll cut it out of my heart with my fangers!") (or *bi-ẓawāfirī*, "with my fingernails"): this is something beyond the pale for any possessed of sound taste and insight hale because for him to cut out his heart with his fingers would be impossible, and the meaning has made no sense to any authority who is accessible. This demonstrates that the speaker of these words has no powers of ratiocination; in its absence, what he says is revoked without chance of cassation.

2.1.7 By Him, then, who has granted the eloquent the power of improvisation when uttering their verse in speech, and turned the chaste-tongued into chevaliers scattering poetry's tight ranks[16] when they storm the breach, this verse should be dropped from all collections; by it its author's price has been set according to the market rate, for how ignorant he is in both sense and sensibility, how undistinguished among the people of his race! Nevertheless we shall address, in the name of comradeship and ministration, as a favor and out of inclination, further verses the likes of this in terms of lowly position and tatty condition.

"You sleep while my eye by distance and insomnia's distressed"

2.2.1 Thus, among its likes are the words of that versifier of ignorance unrestricted, that glutton by bellyache afflicted, that go:

tanāmū wa-ʿaynī ḍarrahā l-buʿdu wa-l-sahar
wa-lā taʿlamū mā bī wa-lā ʿindakum khabar

You sleep while my eye by distance and insomnia's distressed
Though you know not from what I suffer, nor have you any news?

I declare: the meter of this verse is a concoction with fantasy replete, consisting of four mentally disordered feet, namely *khabūlun makhābīlun khabūlun makhābilū,*[17] while the scansion of the first hemistich is, as you see: 2.2.2

tanāmū	*wa-ʿaynī ḍar*	*rahā l-buʿ*	*du wa-l-sahar*
khabūlun	*makhābīlun*	*khabūlun*	*makhābilū*

Such is its scansion so brazenly abhorrent, in terms of all verse and prose aberrant. Its length is as short as that between the Chain of al-ʿArafshah[18] and one of its sprockets, its breadth from Daylam's Great Gate[19] to Hell's very floor (and «how wretched a fate!»).[20]

As for its meaning, my brother in knowledge, this is something with which the ears refuse to allow the mind to be impressed, because by "you sleep" in "you sleep while my eye by distance and insomnia's distressed," he wants to convey to those addressed a question—that is, "would you sleep?"—the interrogative particle being dropped for the sake of the meter, it being his intention that to his own everyday style of expression they should keep.[21] Likewise, through his words "though you know not from what I suffer, nor have you any news," he wants them to become fettered to his abjection and notable lack of glory, their heads bowed in sorrow and fully apprised of his perverted story, though none of that will ever come to pass. Indeed, he will not even for a second disturb their rest, for they are, before all others and quite specifically, at every hour and every instant, among the blessed, having nothing to do in their palaces but lie about on velvet cushions and recline, as silver goblets and flagons are passed around and glittering saliva 2.2.3

from the mouths of comely lads dilutes the wine,[22] while he stands on his hamlet's garbage dump in the worst of states, make no mistake, calling out to the one who watches his herd, "Fetch me the ox and the yoke!" with which two, when the other brings them to him and he's paired, he makes a third.

2.2.4 By Him who brought peace to the hearts of the Muslim nation and «taught Man what he knew not»[23] by way of eloquently expressed exposition and explanation, brought bodies and minds into companionate relation and guided whom He wished to the path of mature understanding and amelioration, he is, I swear, of very little brain, paralyzed of hand and shabby shoon, his verse as nasty as his get-togethers and as his every carious decaying bone!

"The soot of my paternal cousin's oven is as black as your kohl marks"

2.3.1 Similar to these verses in their inconsequentiality are the words of that poet who was excluded from the sciences of both tradition and rationality when of a pastoral he made delivery, one without parallel in wording, meaning, or use of simile:[24]

ḥibābu furni-bni ʿammī sūdu kuḥlātik
wa-ḥablu tawri-ibni khālī ṭūl midallātik
yā man ʿajantī qulaybī fī wuḥaylātik
yā raytanī qurṣa jillah bayna dayyātik

The soot of my paternal cousin's oven is as black as[25] your kohl marks
and my maternal cousin's ox-rope is long as the chains on your lovelocks.
O you who have kneaded my heart into your daubies
I wish I were a dung cake between your handies![26]

2.3.2 I declare: this pastoral is drawn from the ocean of what confusion may excrete[27] and consists of four disordered feet, namely, *mustakhbiṭun khābiṭan mustakhbiṭun khabṭan*,[28] while the scansion of its first hemistich goes:

hibābu fur	*ni-bni ʿam*	*mī sūdu kaḥ*	*lātik*
mustakhbiṭun	*khābiṭun*	*mustakhbiṭun*	*khabṭan*

This scansion is like the weak-sighted lurching of a man on the back of a blind she-camel perching. Its length is from the pond of Gharandal of the Little Mosque to the lowest foothold where the chasm gapes, its breadth from the graves of the Jews to the Isle of the Apes.[29]

Its semantics are strange, its constructions surprising because, with his words "The soot of my paternal cousin's oven is as black as your kohl marks," he seeks to make a comparison extrinsic to the thing's nature intrinsic, one hurtful to the sensibility of those possessed of insight and superiority, namely, when he says that it is as black as "your kohl marks." It is truly amazing that this wretch should compare the latter with soot; would that, in the comparison, some from an oven of his own he'd put—yet, in his footlingness and obscurity, he had to make the comparison with his paternal cousin's oven's sooty impurity! 2.3.3

His declaration "and my maternal cousin's ox-rope is like the chains on your lovelocks" make wounds out of words, for the lovelocks made by peasant women are generally a cubit[30] at their greatest extent[31]—and how thick-skinned his verse, given that, again, this ox doesn't mention an ox of his own, yet to it a rope, which he compares to lovelocks, he's lent! He is, I swear, one fit to be both «despised and discarded».[32] If you tell me that it's probable, with regard to his words "and my maternal cousin's ox-rope is like the chains on your lovelocks," that the rope may in fact have been short, I reply that it is your understanding that is severed and short, for the length of the ox rope known to the peasants extends some ten or twenty cubits in space; this makes the possibility you suppose both null and void, and the shortness of your understanding redounds to your disgrace. 2.3.4

Another example of the slow-wittedness of this poet, dozing in ignominy's vasty waste, is that, by addressing his beloved using the 2.3.5

borrowed figure of his paternal cousin's ox and its rope, he denies himself any possibility of his beloved finding his words to her taste. He also fails to mention, in his framing of this figure, any of the kinds of property that are his to deploy and that might soften his beloved's heart toward him, may God deprive him of every horseman and every foot soldier in his employ![33]

2.3.6 His words "O you who have kneaded my heart into your daubies" imply that this pot-bellied tub must have come across her in a kneading pit of daub and mud. He thus determined that she must be so in love with him that she'd ripped out his heart and placed it in the pit beneath her feet and was flipping it to right and to left, leaving to this dog whatever the south or north wind might blow his way, to snatch up in his teeth.

2.3.7 His words "I wish I were a dung cake between your handies!" give one to understand that he is lower than a dung cake in station, though the latter is among the most abject and degraded things in creation. Nay more, it gives one to understand that he is something that has been well and truly trodden beneath the hooves of the livestock and is with urine sodden. His hope is that he will be promoted to become a dung cake between his beloved's hands, this being appropriate to his way of thinking and personal and physical demands. Or it may be that he wanted to use a comparison that resembled him, that is, that of a cake of dung, given that he was bound by the fetters of love, his arm to his shank by its hobbles strung.[34]

2.3.8 By Him who has given to whomever of His creation He wills the finest of the pearls of this most precious of skills and polished the eye of his insight into the deduction of the inner meanings of the best of its spoken and unsaid production, this poet is certainly possessed, by his composition obsessed!

"And I said to her, 'O daughter of noble men, go into the garden!'"

2.4.1 Similar to this pastoral in its wretchedness and inconsequentiality, its silliness and prodigality, are the words of that other poet who said:

wa-qultu lahā yā binta l-ajwādi rawwiḍī
taray mā warā Ramaḍān ʾillā l-ʿīd

And I said to her, "O daughter of noble men, go into the garden
And you'll see naught after Ramadan but the Feast."[35]

I declare, the meter of this line of verse belongs to the class of the skinny underweight and consists of four feet, all fit to make one emaciate, namely, *hazūlun mahāzīlun hazūlun mahāzilū*,[36] and the scansion of the first hemistich therewith accords: 2.4.2

wa-qultu lahā	*yā binta l-aj*	*wādi rawwiḍī*
hazūlun mahā	*zīlun hazū*	*lun mahāzilū*

All proper feet from this scansion have been flayed, and it is in ugly and distorted form displayed. Its length is from that charlatan the Antichrist's den to where accursed Satan dwells among men, its breadth that between the houses of Thamūd and ʿĀd and the palaces of that wretch Shaddād ibn ʿĀd. Its meaning is of unknown interpretation, stripped of any possibility of explanation, incapable of being understood other than through the exigencies of deception and from the perspectives of forgery and falsification.

In this spirit we declare: this ignorant poet wished, by his words "I said to her, 'O daughter of noble men, go into the garden'" to obtain an assignation, that he might attain the one addressed, namely his beloved, who was the reason for his falling victim to all this ardor and infatuation. This, though, is an outcome of his imbecility and distraction both in his affairs and in his action, since, by rights, he ought to say to a woman "grant me an assignation, prithee!" and then only when in dandified state, with a knife at his waist, be it but a peeled withy.[37] 2.4.3

His words "And you'll see naught after Ramadan but the Feast" are intended to convey to his beloved that what follows the Fast must be the Feast; as though, through his meager understanding and execrable taste, not to mention his very makeup, sunk in oceans of inconsequentiality to its waist, and his mind, incapable of 2.4.4

grasping a topic or its implication, and through this lame language that excludes this verse from any possibility of interpretation, he had made of himself an object lesson beyond any prior, with consequences for him that could only be dire, for that what follows Ramadan must be the Feast is obvious and well known, may God place him in chains of ignominy until the Day of Doom!

2.4.5 By the Lord of the Kaaba, of the Maqām, of Zamzam, and of al-Ḥaṭīm then, this poet is fit indeed to be placed in a pillory with the devils and stoned and is become, for the havoc he has wreaked on the empire of love, one who reaps and has never sown, staked out on a chain of degradation whose length is seventy cubits by mensuration.[38]

"I ASKED AFTER THE BELOVED. THEY SAID, 'HE SKEDADDLED FROM THE SHACK!'"

2.5.1 Similar to such verse in its circumferential disgracefulness and nadiral shamefacedness, its blinding prattle and hurtful tattle, its darkness sombrous and condition tenebrous are the words of another, who said, in the form of a pastoral:[39]

sa'altu ʿalā l-ḥibbi qālū shatta mina l-tāyih
masaḥtu dimʿī bi-jillāyah wa-kirsāyih
wa-shiltu wajhī li-rabbī qultu mawlāyih
jāb lī rughayyif wa-ʿajjūrah wa-qattāyih

I asked after the beloved. They said, "He skedaddled from the shack!"
I wiped away my tears with a dung cake and a dung slab
And I lofted my face to My Lord, [and] said "My Master!"
He brought me a loaf, a melon, and a cucumber.[40]

2.5.2 I declare: this pastoral is weak in construction, and the one who composed it is vicious by constitution. It is drawn from that ocean that with false witness is replete[41] and consists of four pus-producing feet, namely *mustaqriḥun qāriḥun mustaqriḥun qarḥā*,[42] the scansion of the first hemistich being as follows:

sa'altu ʿa-l[43] *-ḥibbi qā* *lū shatta mi* *l-tāyih*
mustaqriḥun *qāriḥun* *mustaqriḥun* *qarḥā*

This scansion . . .[44] redounds only to his greater inconsequentiality, or he was a hungry, ulcerating, parasitical guest, an ignorant, barbarously-tongued, deformed, and vapid pest.

It follows that, by his question, he sought, beyond any doubt, something with which he might be fed, as may be inferred from his words that, in all their creativity and musicality, lie still ahead, to wit, "He brought me a loaf, a melon, and a cucumber." From these it may be deduced, with regard to his saying that "he lofted his head," that he was bold only where his hunger was concerned, not in offering prayers for the beloved nor in meeting him out of any love with which he might be supposed to have burned. Thus, he was content with the food that came his way and, after his initial question, had nothing that might indicate further curiosity to say. 2.5.3

By Him who has given to whom He pleases a mind capable of ratiocination and has raised whom He wishes to high station, if all the speaker of these words possesses is a sharp tongue, I should like it, root and branch, to sever, for with his verses he has left me incapable of sleep, may God disfigure his form among men forever! 2.5.4

"I asked God to join me together with Salmā"

The like of this pastoral, in its instinctual torpidity and innate stupidity, are the words in verse of another, the allusiveness of whose opening[45] is almost without equal, hard to rival, in terms of prosody beyond compare, free of anything to hurt the ear, quite without peer. The opening goes:[46] 2.6.1

sa'altu llāha yajmaʿunī bi-Salmā
fa-inna llāha yafʿalu mā yashā'ū

I asked God to join me together with Salmā
for God may do whatsoever He pleases.

2.6.2 This line belongs to the charming meter *wāfir*, preserved from metrical deviation[47] or phonetic contortion. The content is, with regard to sense, correct, with regard to constructions, direct. He follows it, however, with faulty lines leading to verses that veer far from correct confines. They are:

wa-yaṭraḥuhā wa-yaṭraḥunī ʿalayhā
shabīha l-zuqqi taḥmiluhu l-saqāʾū[48]
wa-yursilu man yuhazhizunā bi-lutfin
li-yanzila lī mina l-aʿḍāʾi māʾū
wa-yursilu baʿda dhā maṭaran ghazīran
yughassilunā wa-laysa bi-nā ʿanāʾū

And that He throw her down and throw me down on top of her
like the falcon (*zuqq*) carried by the hawkers (*saqāʾ*)
And send someone to jiggle us gently
that from my limbs may fall water
And then that He send a copious downpour
to wash us without lifting a finger.

2.6.3 I declare: these words belong to the ocean of ignorance and prodigality, and consist of four feet of inconsequentiality, namely *khamūlun khāmilun khamilun khamūlū*.[49] The application of these to the first hemistich is as follows:

wa-yaṭraḥuhā	*wa-yaṭra*	*ḥunī*	*ʿalayhā*
khamūlun khā	*milun kha*	*milun*	*khamūlū*

This scansion with none of that science's rules complies and is without meaning, unless all right doctrine on the matter be treated as lies. Its length is from north of Bāb al-Lūq, that low-class district,[50] to south of the Bridge of Carob and Grass,[51] while its breadth is from east of the Gate of the Smell of Rotten Meat,[52] that shabby portal, to west of the dwellings by the feather dumps that smell so awful.

2.6.4 Its meaning has no like and could only have been brought into being through a deficit in gallantry and excess of plummetry,[53] because, by his words "and that He throw her down and throw me down on top of her," he means that God should throw her down and then, on top of her, throw him, that he might have access to her quim—which is the vilest form of perverted chivalry and a degree of viciousness that deviates from all righteousness.

Then, the wretch, not satisfied with such words, goes on to make a comparison appropriate to peoples ill-omened when he says, "like the falcon carried by the hawkers,"[54] that is, like the *zuqq*, which is to say the *saqr* ("falcon"), while the *saqqāʾ* ("hawker") is the falcon's handler, he wanting to be like the falcon when launched at its prey—though what has he to do with such things, mired as he is in inconsequentiality and deceitful play? 2.6.5

By his words "And send someone to jiggle us gently without lifting a finger," he means, "When down on top of her I have been thrown, I want Him to send us someone to jiggle us gently together while I am thus prone, that the water may descend from my limbs"—which, of all calamities, is among the most sick. 2.6.6

By Him, then, who «causes death and gives life»[55] and «turns the green grass into black stubble»[56] after first making it quick, the only cure I have for this poet is the imposition of much exemplary punishment and much disease, and that to my shining unsheathed sword, which both his insides and outsides will jiggle, he submit, for he is in insignificance immured and nothing will budge him but "the fuel-filled pit."[57] 2.6.7

Next, having now talked of "throwing" and "sending" and "jiggling" and "descending," he sets about asking for "a copious downpour" to cleanse that swinish swain, and says "And after that send a copious downpour to wash us without lifting a finger." I declare: the poet wants continuous rain to be sent to cleanse him and his beloved without their exercising their own volition, may he remain forever bogged down on the highest pathways of perdition! 2.6.8

By Him to whom belongs all that's in the heavens or on Earth, the taste of the speaker of these words is, in my opinion, without worth, just as he is, let there be no doubt, deficient in chivalry, befuddled of nature inside and out. 2.6.9

"And I said to her, 'Piss on me and spray!'"

2.7.1 Among the likes of this poetry in woebegoneness, imbecility, and stupidity are the words of another such bumbler, who declaimed a contorted line of the sort that sticks firmly to the bottom of the tumbler, to wit:[58]

wa-qultu lahā būlī ʿalayyā wa-sharshirī
ṭawīlu l-qafā li-l-nāʾibāti ṣabūr

And I said to her, "Piss on me and spray!
One whose nape is broad endures the blows of fate!"

2.7.2 I declare: this line of verse is drawn from the ocean of boorish delirium and consists of four feet conducive to tedium, namely, *thaqīlun mathāqīlū thaqīlun mathāqilū*.[59] The scansion goes:

wa-qultu	*lahā būlī*	*ʿalayyā*	*wa-sharshirī*
thaqīlun	*mathāqīlū*	*thaqīlun*	*mathāqilū*

This scansion is beyond the pale for verse, stuffed with distractions perverse. Its length is from the soles of ʿŪj ibn ʿAnaq to the top of his head, its breadth from the miserable place where he first drew breath to the grave where they laid his carcass when dead.

2.7.3 Its content is derived from uncleanness and has been set down in tattiness and meanness, for his words, "And I said to her, 'Piss on me and spray!'," imply that, after being assailed by love's mighty blow and after his affairs, so ill-ordered, had been brought so low—despite which he still demanded union with his beloved and asked of her that she be not cold but grant him a kiss—he desired, when close by her, that she pour over his face, not rosewater, but piss. Likewise, as a result of the intensity of the disasters to which he was subjugated, he coined for himself a calamitous metaphor, as evidenced by his words "One whose nape is broad endures the blows of fate!"—may his person ne'er cease in ever-repeating misfortune and punishment to revolve and ne'er find peace! What the wretch means by his lame verse, taken as a whole, is that his endurance in the face of disasters is never to be ended; however, he is, in all cases, to be reprehended.

By Him, then, who provides relief to men at the end of their tether, and through His grace opens up for those of His creation whom He pleases broad avenues forever, the speaker of these words is verily one who on the paths of uncleanness has ceased to ambulate and is indeed a lout, stuck, immobile in his affairs, and a dunderpate![60] 2.7.4

"The rattle staff of our mill makes a sound like your anklets"

Similar to this verse in its harrowing lameness and grievous lack of moderation are the words of another in the form of a pastoral both painful to the body and agonizing to the organ of sensation, namely:[61] 2.8.1

raqqāṣu ṭāḥūninā yushbih li-khulkhālik
wa-ruḥiyyunā fī l-zarībah qālat ish ḥālak
illā wa-kallāf yaqūl lī yā ṣabī mālak
tawru-bni shaykhi l-balad ḥāluh mithāl ḥālak

The rattle staff of our mill makes a sound like your anklets
and our handmills in the pen said, "How are you?"
When suddenly a cowman says to me, "Lad, what's up with you?
The ox of the son of the shaykh of the village—his state is like yours!"

I declare: this pastoral is drawn from the ocean of nerves so ruffled they set one to prancing and consists of four feet fit to force one to dancing, namely *mustarqiṣun rāqiṣun mustarqiṣun raqṣā*,[62] its scansion being as follows: 2.8.2

raqqāṣu ṭā	*ḥūninā*	*yushbih li-khul*	*khālik*
mustarqiṣun	*rāqiṣun*	*mustarqiṣun*	*raqṣā*

This is a scansion designed to make one cavort, in its feet befuddled because cut short. Its length is from the four corners of the Earth to the last of the places animals call home or on it, grazing, roam, its breadth—I'll say it once only—from the ruined wells to the beginnings of the ends of the tall palace[63] and its cells.

2.8.3 Its meaning is stripped of any sense, devoid of any structure, liable to lead its composer into infamies and bring him only condolences and elegies, for by his words "The rattle staff of our mill makes a sound like your anklets" he means to say that the rattle staff of his mill makes a ringing sound that resembles that of his beloved's anklets to the ear—an example of his dim-wittedness, in that, in so doing, he combines wood with silver, which is something unpleasing to hear, for the sound of a mill's rattle staff strikes terror into the hearts of men, unlike that of the ringing of the beloved's anklets, which is beyond compare, a familiar sound, charming to listen to, of pleasant cheer.

2.8.4 Next, this low-natured poet, shabby of condition, not content with the above hateful sermon, conceived in his imagination an appalling thing—that the millstones were speaking to him—as one who, while gathering fuel by night, might find himself addressed by vermin![64] Thus he says "and our handmills in the pen said, 'How are you?'" by which this loathsome person means that, when his wounding words were given articulation, the millstones said to him, "How are you?" by way of interrogation. Then, when he took note that they had taken pity on his extraordinary state and comically strange fate, he introduced the particle of exception[65] and said, booted, as he had been, out of sublime dignity's doors, "When suddenly a cowman says to me, 'Lad, what's up with you? The ox of the son of the shaykh of the village—his state is like yours!'"

2.8.5 I declare: when this cowman, whom he mentions, became aware that the other was in great dismay, his affairs in disarray—that his state as a result of his insignificance and miserable plight was like that of the ox of the son of the shaykh of the village—said ox being ever associated with the horrors of exhaustion and adversity, unable to escape hard labor, now for the Muslims, now for the Christians, both by day and by night[66]—compared the state of the said ox to that at which the poet himself had arrived, such a comparison belonging to the category of the "comparison contrived." Verily, this poet has never ceased to befoul all free-running waters, thwarted and banished at beginning and at end, esoterically and exoterically[67] cast out and condemned![68]

2.8.6 By Him who grants gifts to whomever He wishes however He will, and rescues whomever He wishes however He wishes from hardship and ill, the sayer of these words is truly a brute and will go down forever in infamy for what he came up with—and «by the star when it plunges»,[69] "every man of what he sows will receive the fruit!"[70]

"I saw my beloved with a plaited whip driving oxen"

2.9.1 Comparable to this pastoral in the continuum of exuberant imbecility and brutality exponential, of disgusting taste and desire torrential, are the words of another in the form of a pastoral whose attributes are reprehensible and whose actuality is unconventional, as follows:[71]

ra'ayt ḥarīfī bi-farqillah yasūq tīrān
lū karru aṣfar ʿalā rāsuh ka-mā l-labsān
yā raytanī kuntu lū ḥidwah min al-ḥidwān
aw kāna shalqa ʿalā rāsī min al-kattān

I saw my beloved with a plaited whip driving oxen.
He has a cloth on his head yellow as mustard.
Would I were a pair of his sandals
or he a flaxen cord upon my head!

2.9.2 I declare: this pastoral comes from the ocean of corruption and consists of four feet full of bunkum, namely *mustakhrifun khārifun mustakhrifun kharfā*.[72] The scansion, as you can see, is:

ra'ayt ḥarī	*fī bi-far*	*qillah yasūq*	*tīrān*
mustakhrifun	*khārifun*	*mustakhrifun*	*kharfā*

This scansion is, in structure, aborted, in meaning, distorted, as though flushed from the loos in the form of hints and clues. Its length is from the apogee of the celestial sphere in its revolutions to the depths of the ocean floor with its convolutions, its breadth—too envenomed to be cured by any theriac—is that between the houses of Aleppo and the dwellings of Iraq.

2.9.3 Its meaning is beyond the power of any mind to assess, wounding to the hearts of any who manly qualities possess, for he intends, by his words "I saw my beloved with a plaited whip driving oxen," to paint a perfect picture of his beloved by making him a drover with a braided knout, to possess such a thing being his ultimate goal and desire devout.

2.9.4 Then, not content with this description distorted, he had to come up with a simile contorted, in the form of his words "He has a cloth on his head yellow as mustard" that compares what is on his head to the yellow flowers of plants of that kind, which is something in keeping with the baseness of that beast's mind.

2.9.5 Next, even that was as naught—may he remain in perdition's chains forever caught!—and he had to express the wish that he might be one of the other's sandals so that he could be on his two feet, and his walking through all the kinds of foulness might his credit complete, so he said, "Would I were a pair of his sandals!"

2.9.6 Thereafter he continues in optative mode by wishing his beloved might be on top of his head in the form of a flaxen cord—a condition he chooses of his own accord, as though there were, in his head, impulses driving him to commit bloopers and he wants to tie his head with this flaxen cord in the presence of his fighting men and his troopers,[73] causing him to say, "or he a flaxen cord around my head." May God then disfigure his flaccid person and bring about his end at the hands of a bailiff . . . ![74]

2.9.7 By Him who has made abject whomever He wishes by allowing him to utter of words the worst and exalted whomever He wishes by allowing him to bring to light the hidden beauties of the most exquisite verse, verily this poet is shabby of state, noxious of nimbus, utterly divested of any taste, to the day he meets his Maker eternally bumptious!

"I ran into her and said, 'My Lady, come tomorrow'"

Similar to these words in their disgusting disposition and blood-curdling constitution are the words of another in the form of a pastoral unfit to be listed in such poetry's roll call, indissolubly linked to all types of misfortune and pratfall, namely: 2.10.1

laqītuhā qultu sittī-bqī ta'ā bukrah
dūsī qafāyah anā ḥālī ṣibiḥ shuhrah
wa-jību lik 'aysh wa-jīb bīsāra fī nuqrah
wa-frish lakī tibn wa-'atghaṭṭā bi-dī l-wizrah

I ran into her and said, "My Lady, come tomorrow!
Tread on my nape—my state's become a byword—
And I'll bring you bread and I'll bring you *bīsār* in a hole
And I'll put down straw for you and cover myself with this towel."

I declare: this pastoral is at the top of the pile of such verses vile—after this we can no more provide, for it is commoner than defilement, constituted from all the different kinds of filth and concomitants of shabbiness already supplied—though the doorway of possibility is broad, and were we to open the gate to the whole horde, poetry of this sort would far exceed the holding capacity of any who at it looks and any who to it his ear has lent and would fill tome upon tome on days that are short and not of great extent.[75] We fear, however, enervating expatiation and exaggeratedly exhaustive investigation, as well as disgusted dismissal by those with noble spirits blessed and rejection by those of refined understandings possessed. After explaining, however, the meaning of this pastoral, we shall abrogate the concoction of craziness[76] that we have set forth above and replace it with a discussion of a refined sampling of the 2.10.2

poets of Islam and the princes of exquisite poetry whose mastery can be disputed by no man, providing examples of hints, wrangles, and riddles that in their verse recur, especially those that in the poetry of the paragon of eloquence among such poets, Abū l-Ṭayyib al-Mutanabbī, occur.

2.10.3 Let us now return to our immediate concern, which is to decode this pastoral both cold and hot,[77] whose composer's sole abode is Hell—and how wretched is he of whom an abode in Hell is the lot! Thus we declare: its meter is a sort of furious tramping and consists of four feet fit to send one ramping, namely *mustahwisun hāwisun mustahwisun hawsā*,[78] applied as follows:

laqītuhā	*qultu sit*	*tī-bqī ta'ā*	*bukrah*
mustahwisun	*hāwisun*	*mustahwisun*	*hawsā*

This scansion is mired in the consequences of the dirty deed, marred to make others take heed. Its length is from the privies of the houses of the polytheists to the borders of the salons of the infidels and atheists, its breadth from the channels of the whales to the furthest point on the Isle of Vales.[79]

2.10.4 Its meaning is immersed in procrastination, imbued with falsification, for by his words, "I ran into her and said, 'My Lady, come tomorrow,'" he means to say that his beloved should go to him, which is evidence of the dopiness by which, through his footlingness, he's benighted, for, when someone is in love and from his beloved disunited, it is *he* who makes every effort to go to him, be it over burning coal, that he may obtain from him his dearest goal (unless his request of the other was based on a promise the latter had earlier made, in which case responsibility for his broaching the topic should at the other's feet be laid).

2.10.5 In any case, it is our declaration that this person was in the clutches of Satan, who steered his thinking towards poetry that placed him in the parade of depravity, as evidenced by his words "Tread on my nape—my state's become a byword," meaning that his sole reason for asking her to come was that she might demonstrate she was a whore by drubbing his nape until it could take no more, for he was in a sorry state and a quarter of his patience was dissipated.

Then, not content with what he was suffering by way of distraction and etiolation, he decided she must be on the brink of hunger's crumbling bank rather than a party to his ardent emotion, so said "And I'll bring you bread and I'll bring you *bīsār* in a hole,"[80] his intention by so doing being that her appetite be satisfied and she not repelled and not intending thereby either to do her harm or to cause her hunger to be dispelled.[81] 2.10.6

Next, he goes on to mention, after eating, bed, and that he will bring her something on which the moths have fed, and says, "And I'll put down straw for you and cover myself with this towel." Thus, it appears that the only kind of bedding that this swindler, accursed among men, had to lay down for her was animal straw, may God have him chained, with nothing to hide his shame, to every door! 2.10.7

«By the Mount, and by a Book inscribed,»[82] what he says must be despised! His verses have filled my heart with gall, so may God assail him—verily he is perverted,[83] and that is all! 2.10.8

Look then, my brother! What have these flaccid, disordered minds, these mental faculties that by nature chase after every wording vile, in common with the noble minds of the poets of Islam and the refined ideas of the princes of poetry, endowed as they are with eloquent chasteness of speech and effectiveness of style? *They* are the masters of improvisation when they recite, *they* the brave knights in this field when they enter the fight. How many of poetry's hidden treasures have they brought to light! How many choice lines of verse, fresh as brides, have they uttered, causing delight! How often has chaste language opened to them its gate! How often the cups of eloquence among them circulate! Glory then to Him who granted them minds free of sin and bestowed on them gifts that mystic intuitions induce,[84] for «Whatsoever mercy God opens to 2.10.9

men, none can withhold, and whatsoever He withholds, none after Him can loose,»[85] there being no messenger to them after him, and if the eye of your insight be but with clarity furnished, the mirror of your thoughts well burnished, the secret with which they have been entrusted—of elegantly turned verse fit any beloved to woo—and of His gifts, will be revealed, likewise, to you.

A Sampling of Hints and Riddles

Let us then turn to our above-stated intention of presenting a sampling of their hints and witty riddles, along with their refined, elegant, and brilliant grammatical wrangles, and thus bring the book to a happy conclusion. 3.1

"O Scholars of Verse"

Thus we declare: the learned Ibn Hishām the Grammarian quotes in the first chapter, on "Riddles of the Meaning," of his *Lesser Riddles* (*al-Alghāz al-ṣughrā*)[86] (than which naught more original was ever penned, in days either of yore or closer to this end) two verses (the equal of which none other has come up with and than which naught more original ever was penned), which he attributes to the learned Ibn ʿUnayn, that writer so possessed of skill, eloquence, and ability to explain, namely: 3.2.1

> O Scholars of Verse, verily
>   there's a knotty problem I'm unable to unfetter,
> So tell me the name of a certain bird,
>   one half of which is an adverb, the other a letter.

Observe how, with a wit and lightness of touch that none could better, he combines the adverb and the letter! The answer to the riddle, O brother of those who know,[87] is the well-known birds called *warāshīn* ("wild doves"), for the first half of the name is an 3.2.2

adverb, namely *warā*,[88] the second, as may be plainly seen, a letter, namely *shīn*.[89]

"Avoid a friend who is like *mā*"

3.3.1 Similar in sense are the words of that master of similes telling and allusions compelling, Abū Muḥammad ʿAlī ibn Ḥazm al-Ẓāhirī:

> Avoid a friend who's like *mā* and leave the one
> who's like ʿAmr among men, be they of Arab or of foreign ore.
> An evil friend brings destruction, and my proof lies in the words,
> "Just as the front end of the lance chokes on gore."[90]

3.3.2 How witty his introduction into the latter verse of the quotation, through which he achieved glorious deeds, and elevation! The answer is that what he means by "a friend like ʿAmr" is one who to that which is not his right lays claim though he be forced to snatch it from the ember's burning flame, for "ʿAmr" takes the *wāw* in writing when in nominative or genitive declension[91] even though it isn't integral to its spelling, as per the preceding mention.[92]

3.3.3 This is why that other poet[93] is able to ascribe the adding of the latter to the former as an "injustice," saying:

> O you who foolishly claim descent from Sulaym,
> not a nail clipping of yours is of it.
> You are to Sulaym like a letter *wāw*
> that in some spellings of ʿAmr is wrongly added to it.

3.3.4 What is indicated by *mā* is the friend who pretends to greatness while forever letting you down, for the poet means either definite *mā*, which needs a relative clause and referent noun,[94] or interrogative *mā*, which loses a letter if attached to a preposition,[95] the latter having the greater right, as in the case of *bi-ma yarjiʿu l-mursalūn* («with what my envoys will return»)[96] or *fī-ma anta min dhikrāhā* («what have you to do with the mentioning of it?»)[97] and other Qurʾanic verses that men cite.

The probative quotation to which he refers and on which his words are based is the verse: 3.3.5

> And you will turn red by reason of the words I have broadcast,
> just as the front end of the lance chokes on gore (*ka-mā shariqat ṣadru l-qanāti mina l-damī*).

The verse is cited in Sībawayh's *Book*,[98] and its value as a citation lies in the verb, which, if the subject is feminine, should have a *t* attached to it, as in *qāmat Hind* ("Hind stood up"), while this will not do in the case of a masculine verb, such as *qāla Zayd* ("Zayd said"). Thus the attachment of a *t* to *shariqat* in *ka-mā shariqat ṣadru l-qanāti* ought not to be allowed, given *ṣadr*'s masculinity; *ṣadr*, however, by coming into close proximity with *qanāt* in a possessive construct, has become imbued with femininity.[99]

"Hie thee to men in positions of eminence"

Close to the preceding in sense and in probative utility are the words of another poet:[100] 3.4.1

> Hie thee to men in positions of eminence, for he who becomes
> a dependent of men of eminence himself becomes eminent,
> And beware lest you accept the friendship of one who is deficient,
> for then a portion of your high status will be diminished and you will be despised.
> The placing in the nominative of *abū man* and the placing in the genitive of *muzammal*
> prove my words, both the exhortation and the warning.

The poet's words "the placing in the nominative of *abū man*" refer to a sentence such as *ʿalimtu Zaydan abū man huwa* ("I learned who was Zayd's father"), with *ab* ("father") in the nominative, even though verbs of intellection and supposition[101] are prevented from governing the words that follow them only when the latter must take precedence in a clause.[102] One says *ʿalimtu zaydan qāʾiman* 3.4.2

("I learned that Zayd was standing"), and one is not allowed to use the nominative under any circumstances, while *li-naʿlama ayyu l-ḥizbayni aḥṣā*[103] («that We might know which of the two parties would better calculate») allows only the nominative, because the interrogative, in this case, takes literal precedence in the clause. Thus, what precedes the interrogative is not allowed to govern what follows because that would eject it from its position of precedence, and when "father" occurs adjacent to interrogative "who?" it acquires "prominence" from that. A yet more convincing argument than the foregoing is that, on this basis, they permit the use of the nominative for Zayd when it is equivalent to the *ab* ("the father of") that is annexed to the word that has prominence.[104]

3.4.3 The words of the poet "the placing in the genitive of *muzammal*" are an allusion to those of Imru' al-Qays[105] when he says:

> Thabīr, in the first onrush of its deluge, was like
> the chieftain of a tribe (*kabīru unāsin*) wrapped (*muzammalī*)
> in a striped mantle

because *muzammalī* ("wrapped") is an adjective describing *kabīru unāsin* ("the chieftain of a tribe"), which is, quite clearly, in the nominative; however, given that it is, with regard to the previous (genitively declined) word, in a state of contiguity, it too, quite rightly, has been placed in the genitive, by virtue of proximity.[106]

"What Is the Name of a Thing?"

3.5.1 It is similar, too, to the words of that master of instinctive elegance and natural eloquence, he who, in his enthusiasm for verse, is the brother of al-Miʿmār, namely the erudite Abū l-Ḥusayn al-Jazzār:[107]

> O Imam who is possessed of the lights of an intelligence
> by which are extinguished the lights of the sun,
> What is something with a name that may be given nominative
> and accusative endings,
> though it be solid of construction?

A landmark standing alone it is—if they raise it,
they raise it upright for the sake of the call.
They made it feminine, yet a form of it is known to be masculine,[108]
so behold the contradiction of things!
It is a container—now where is he who has the wit[109]
to shine a light on this obscure thing?

The answer is a minaret (*ma'dhanah*), because it has both raised sides and foundations erected (this statement cannot be contradicted) and is perfect and solid of construction.[110] It is also called a *manār*,[111] which is a "landmark standing alone" that, "if they raise it, they raise it upright for the sake of the call,"[112] which is to say "the call to prayer."[113] Thus, it is apparent that it is a feminine that belongs to the same class as a masculine and, on top of all that, is the container of a place.[114] 3.5.2

"My father I would give for the suns that turn away at sunset"

A hidden "hint" and quick-witted quip of which they tell concerns a certain king who bestowed generous favors on a certain poet and sent him home to his family joyful and blessed, along with two slaves to act as escorts, whom the king ordered to return, bearing some token that could serve as proof of the poet's safe arrival. Now, when the slaves had brought the poet to the halfway point on the road, they set upon him as though to kill him, so the man agreed with them that he would give them all he had with him, and they made him swear that he would put nothing of what had happened in writing for the king and thus point the finger at them and get them into trouble, and that he would not write a letter later and send it to him. He swore to them he would do what they asked and said, "When you meet with him, tell him, 'The sign of his safety, which saved him from being killed, are the words of Abū l-Ṭayyib al-Mutanabbī that go: 3.6.1

My father I'd give for the suns[115] that turn aside at sunset
wearing shifts of silk.'"

3.6.2 When they returned, they told this to the king, who had them seized. Asked about it, he said, "This line has no relevance, so I read the whole poem carefully and found in it:

The world made me thirst and, when I came to it
seeking water, rained disasters down upon me.
How can I expect the fates to release me,
once they have fastened in me their claws?"[116]

Then he had them put to the question, and they confessed to what they had done, so he punished them and returned to the poet the money and all that they had carried off. What a connoisseur, then, was this king to be able to understand his friend's allusion to al-Mutanabbī's ode, and what heights did he reach in restoring to the man the charity he had previously bestowed!

"Were it not for difficulties, all men would be lords"

3.7.1 Something else quite similar in form and not dissimilar in content, which "to none save those who know is intelligible"[117] and of whose significance only the pure in heart will be mindful, is the case of a man who was asked by someone intelligent to do something that would be to the latter's benefit and wrote a letter back to him saying, "Were it not for difficulties . . ." that is, excusing himself by saying, "Were it not that I face some difficulty with regard to the matter, I would indeed have been diligent." The other then sent him back a letter in which he said, as one from whose mouth pearls are heard, "Were it not for difficulties . . ." and added not a word. When the letter reached the first man, he took care of the second's business. Questioned about this, he said, "He alluded to the words of Abū l-Ṭayyib that go:[118]

Were it not for difficulties, all men would be lords.
Generosity makes destitute and destitution brings death."

How can one to verses of any other sort than these have recourse or go so far as to cast any further verses from the mold of the language of such versified discourse? I swear by God that taste is indeed a precious commodity and those who have it a well-guarded minority! Does morning wear a mantle that al-Mutanabbī has not figured with his exquisite conceits, do the Pleiades wear a necklace not fashioned by his glorious feats? For the reading of any eulogy to its charms other than one dictated by him would spring ever ask? Does musk emit aught other than a record of such of its graces as by him have been broadcast? 3.7.2

"O dwelling of 'Ātikah from which I depart"

3.8 Among further hints of this sort, which clothe with clarification what their wordings purport, is the tale of a man who used to accompany al-Manṣūr,[119] who never spoke unless asked a question and who, when he answered, never said more than was needed. Once, when they were out riding, they passed by the dwelling of 'Ātikah, which had been preserved, and al-Manṣūr asked, "Whose dwelling is this?" and the man replied, "This is the dwelling of 'Ātikah, of whom the poet[120] says:

O dwelling of 'Ātikah from which I depart
fearful of hostility, while yet the heart is with it charged."

The caliph then asked him, "Have you received the compensation that I commanded for you?" and the man said, "No." The caliph then ordered that it be given to him. When he was asked about this, he said, "This is a man who never speaks, under any circumstances, unless to say something pertinent, yet he added to his answer by quoting this line of verse. Thus I knew, without needing to look further afield, that to the following words of the poet in the same poem he appealed:

I see that you do what you say while others,
insincere of speech, say what they do not do."[121]

Observe the man's noteworthy articulation and how it was crowned with plentiful remuneration!

"She sent you ambergris"

3.9 One report,[122] transmitted on the authority of a certain litterateur, states that a certain refined singing girl presented a ball made of ambergris to al-ʿAzīz, son of al-Malik al-Nāṣir Ṣalāḥ al-Dīn ibn Yūsuf ibn Najm al-Dīn Ayyūb. They were keeping their liaison secret for fear of the sultan, so she sent him, by a servant, a ball of ambergris, and when he broke it open, lo and behold, he found a golden button. Not understanding what it meant, he sent it to al-Qāḍī l-Fāḍil asking him to look into the matter and reply to him with the answer, and the latter responded with the following admirable answer:

She sent you ambergris with, in its middle,
a button of gold finely soldered.
Button (*zirr*) and ambergris together mean
"Visit (*zur*),[123] like this, hidden in darkness!"

How tasteful, refined, and appealing that virtuous man of letters and perfect wit . . . .[124]

"An apple wounded by her front teeth"

3.10 Similar to this is the anecdote told concerning Ibn al-Jahm, who said, "I entered the presence of al-Mutawakkil, in whose hands was an apple that had been bitten into, given him by one of his slave girls. He said to me, 'Say something in verse before you take your seat, and you will receive a thousand dinars for each line.'" So Ibn al-Jahm recited the following verses than which, because of their enumeration of that apple's every charm, there are none more refined, being finer than yarn, and which go:[125]

An apple wounded by her front teeth
  is tastier to me than the world and all that's in it.
It was brought by a gazelle from a belle
  to ransom whom from harm and from evils I'd give my soul.
If I were dead and she called to me with her melodious voice,
  verily I would hurry from my grave to do her bidding.
Whiteness in redness, enveloped in precious fragrance
  —as though cut from the cheek of the one who gave it.

Ibn al-Jahm resumed, "He then ordered that I be given four thousand dinars."

"If, in all your days, one friend you find"

An example from poetry of the strange changes of meaning that can come about as a result of the altering of dots,[126] and of the pleasantries, embellished with every kind of marvelous marvel, that can result from such changes of spots, is what Vizier ʿAbbād[127] wrote to a friend of his, to wit: 3.11

If, in all your days, one friend you find,
  then that is all that one can ask for—yet where is he (*wa-ayna dhāka l-wāḥidū*)?

repeating at the bottom of the letter "*wa-ayna dhāka l-wāḥid*—change the dots and see!" When his friend read it, he was delighted to see how he had been characterized, because, when you change the dots on *ayna dhāka* ("where is he?"), it becomes *anta dhāka* ("you are he").

"I have not forgotten the time he visited me after his turning aside"

One refined riddle and amusing anecdote that people recount tells of a certain person who asked a friend of his, "How are you getting on with your beloved boy? Have you obtained from him the hoped-for joy?" to which the other replied, "He's being Abū Sufyān 3.12.1

al-Humām," to which the other responded, "Then seek help from the daughter of Bisṭām!" What the first meant by referring to Abū Sufyān was that the boy was like a rock, unyielding, because Abū Sufyān's given name was Ṣakhr ("rock"), while, by referring to Bisṭām's daughter,[128] the other meant Sulāfah, that is, "give him wine (*sulāfah*) to drink," Sulāfah being the daughter's given name.

3.12.2 A poet put this into verse, saying:

> I have not forgotten him since he visited after first turning aside,
> and I then spent the night as though boon companion to the full moon[129] on the Night of Power.
> He was Abū Sufyān at first, then Bisṭām's daughter caught fire
> in him, and together we spent the night till dawn.

How exquisite the casting by this master poet of that witty prose into the mold of verse!

"O you, 'Alī, who have risen to the summit of virtue"

3.13.1 Once a witty friend of mine, a brother devotee of taste and knowledge divine,[130] asked me to compose for him in verse a riddle to which the answer would be "hashish" and in which I would hint at the word using palindromes and *taṣḥīf*.[131] So I composed the following improvisation, cast in the form of an interrogation:

> O you, 'Alī, who have risen (*'alā*) to (*'alā*) the summit of virtue
> for sure (*yaqīnan*), give me an answer that will protect us (*yaqīnā*)
> To a question posed by an abject slave
> wandering lovelorn and exhausted through the universe!
> What is the name of a thing that, should half of its letters
> have their dots rearranged, would be a fetus in the bellies
> Or, if those of the whole, would be a low matter of which
> the sagacity of those who tread the Path has made me enamored,[132]

And if you should reverse, for sure,
its sound, meaningful first half[133]
Would become a trait of the vile, the devotees of ignorance
and that without a doubt in the eyes of the noble,
Or, should you reverse the last half and then make it indefinite
it is "a thing" in the eyes of those who speak Arabic featly.
Give me then the answer from your pearl-like poetry,
that it may appear to us as 'twere a precious necklace—
May you through virtue and eloquence forever ascend,
my dear one, in name and as a doughty fortress!

Observe then, O you whose success is plainly manifest and whose wings flutter in both East and West, the command of allusion displayed in the opening lines[134] and the perfect paronomasia to be found in their confines! The first example involves the verb and the preposition, namely *ʿalā* ("have risen") and *ʿalā* ("to"), the second comes about with the verbal noun and the verb, namely *yaqīnan* ("for sure") and *yaqīnā* ("will protect us"), in the vein of what preceded and was so sweetly pleaded. 3.13.2

As far as the solution to the riddle is concerned, حشيش (*ḥashīsh*) is four letters, and if you change the dots on half of it, that is, on حش (*ḥash*), you will find that it is still four letters, because the *shin* is worth three, and as such it becomes جنين (*janīn*: "a fetus").[135] And if you change the dots on the word as a whole, it becomes خسيس (*khasīs*: "vile"), which is a "low matter", according to proper reckoning. 3.13.3

My words حبّبتني به (*ḥabbabatnī bi-hi*: "of which . . . it has made me enamored") are the equivalent of حشيشة (*ḥashīshah*: "piece of hashish") if the dots are changed,[136] and, if you read the first half backwards, it becomes شُحّ (*shuḥḥ*: "stinginess"),[137] which is "a trait of the ignominious" in the eyes of the chivalrous and the magnanimous. Also, if you read the second half starting from the end, it becomes شي (*shay*: "thing"),[138] which dovetails neatly, and is the most indeterminate of all indeterminates, in the eyes of those who speak Arabic featly.[139] 3.13.4

A Wrangle over a Line by al-Mutanabbī

4.1 Let us now return to our stated intention of giving an account of the wrangles over the verse of him who was the best exponent of the most brilliant rhetorical formulation, who perfected a glorious competence in the deployment of grammar at his verses' declamation, who rendered the sword belt of speech more precious through the remolding of its golden nuggets and bumps and made poetry's gruel go down easier by providing his ink to smooth out its lumps—that imam of the poets of Islam's time, that holder of the rope by which poesy's princes are led in line, Abū l-Ṭayyib al-Mutanabbī—may God send clouds gravid with forgiveness to his grave!—who said:[140]

wa-staqbalat qamara l-samāʾi bi-wajhihā
fa-aratniya l-qamarayni fī-waqtin maʿā

And she faced the moon in the sky with her countenance,
thus showing me the two moons at one time together.

4.2 Thus we declare: that scholar in literature well versed, that man of understanding and intelligence, the wonder of Hamadān,[141] the paragon of Baysān, who takes his sobriquet from that city of learning and its gate, who has crowned with his poetry its homes, along with its domes, who combines vintage meanings with what is novel and distinguishes the vulgar from the noble, that sun of knowledge, that nonpareil of mystic comprehension, Shaykh Muḥammad ibn al-Sayyid Maḥmūd[142] (may God, in His affection, preserve his fire from extinction!), in his epistle (that work to bring to heart and eye delight) that he entitled *The Third, after the Two Stars That Burn Bright* (*Thālith al-nayyirayn*),[143] states the following:

> In his supercommentary on *The Extended* (*al-Muṭawwal*),[144] the Brilliant Reader[145]—may God overlook his mistakes and regard them as undone—says, concerning al-Mutanabbī's words "And she faced the moon in the sky with her countenance, thus showing me the two moons at one time together," that, by "the two moons," the poet meant the sun (this being "her countenance") and "the moon in the sky," meaning that her face, by virtue of its clearness and extreme limpidity, was, when she turned to the latter, imprinted with its image as an image is imprinted on a mirror; thus, when he looked at her face, the lover saw the sun and the moon at one time. The Brilliant Reader also quotes al-Tibrīzī[146] as saying, "He may have meant one moon plus another moon[147] because two moons can never come together on a night, and neither can the sun and the moon."[148] The Brilliant Reader further notes that "Our reading is more laudatory,[149] not to mention that 'the two moons' is customarily[150] taken to mean 'the sun and the moon.'" End of verbatim quote.[151] 4.3

Having sought first to understand from those who had looked into this matter—clever and dumb, grown men and young—their enthusiasm for what "the Reader" had struck from his flint and for his fire, their pining to be under his shade and follow the light from his tower, I said, "Caution, you there! Beware inattention, and distraction from the full moon by a 'bright star,'[152] for what that brilliant fellow brought to light is about to be eclipsed by my own repertoire! He is a lightning-bearing cloud that gives false hope of rain and will be put to flight by what's to come, for what 4.4

he states is a mere building of castles in the air,[153] a mendacious claim. The maker of these statements has nothing new to add: some are squirts squeezed from the udders of the she-camels of ʿAbdallāh ibn Hishām, that erudite scholar, others carrots from the garden of al-Damāmīnī, of Egypt and Syria alike the mentor.

4.5 "In sum, it is a morsel pre-chewed but neither digestible nor acceptable as food, for his statement regarding the imprinting of the image of the moon on her face as though it were a mirror (even if it be an ugly face in the eyes of the leading sages, as is clear from their books)[154] requires the likening of her face to a mirror using 'metaphor by allusion,' and this comes after he has already made her a sun by 'declarative metaphor.'[155] This cannot work unless something necessarily associated with the thing with which comparison is made—that thing being, in his conceptualization, the mirror—is also mentioned; yet there is nothing, either in this line of verse or in its immediate environs, that in any way points to any such necessarily associated thing, or anything else, and nothing calls, of necessity, for such a claim, as any investigation of the meaning will make plain. Likewise, mere mention of 'showing' is not enough to create a necessary association with 'mirror' such that the mind is transported from the one to the other.[156] Further, it is a condition of the metaphor by allusion that the associated thing with which comparison is made should not be incompatible with the thing compared; for example, if it were said that 'sweet life sank its claws [into something],'[157] the words would be almost beneath notice, while the incompatibility of 'sun-ness' with the visualization of the image in terms of 'mirror-ness' is clearer than that orb at its rising; that such an analogy should be a target for the literary shafts of that eloquent man[158] would be, than his firing off a shot at distant Capella, yet more surprising.

“And again, that ‘brilliant’ fellow’s statement requires that the ‘favoring’ in the line of verse be between the image of the moon[159] and the [real] sun, which is contrary to the familiar concept that currency in men’s minds has gained, and contradicts what he himself declared and at the beginning explained, when he says that ‘the poet meant the sun (this being “her countenance”) and the moon in the sky,’[160] even though there can be no doubt that the image of the moon is not the same as the moon itself. The invocation of customary usage in the case of an illusory ‘favoring’ such as this is objectionable and against convention. 4.6

“Yet more, what is mentioned in the verse is ‘the moon in the sky,’ not its reflection, and the real moon must be dealt with according to the rules of the real world. His assertion, however, requires that the latter be totally lost sight of in the poet’s words ‘thus showing me the two moons.’ What is intended by the reflection of the moon is a figure of speech, and what is intended by the sun is likewise a figure of speech, by virtue of ‘favoring.’ Yet, by token of the fact that it is invalid to say of the reflection of a man or the like ‘this is the man himself,’ so too is this invalid.[161] Furthermore, even if the interpretation that this is ‘favoring’ is accepted, the showing of the two moons ‘at one time together’ could still come about simply as a result of the beloved’s turning her face toward ‘the moon in the sky,’ because it would be possible, under such a condition, for the sight to take in both at one time, in the blinking of an eye,[162] as is the case with perceived objects that are directly in front of the optical rays emanating from the visual faculty, without, as should be obvious to any ‘brilliant’ mind, straining the laws of simultaneity. 4.7

“Would, then, I knew what impelled him to consider ‘the two moons’ as a way of saying ‘the sun plus the impression on that sun of the real moon,’ as he claims! Al-Mutanabbī’s 4.8

choice of the broader and more comprehensive *waqt* ('time') over *ān* ('an instant')[163] is, of these words that we have hung in your ear like a pendant,[164] the most effective confirmation and demonstration resplendent.

4.9 "In addition, to imagine the 'favoring' in this case—absent the pertinent rules and concomitants, of all shapes and sizes—is to disturb the order of the author's intended effects and the beauties of his harmonious arrangement and to imply that he was mouthing mere persiflage, with padding camouflaged, and, even worse, to insult him by accusing him of foolishness, in questioning, for example, his placing of the moon in a possessive construct with the sky. After all, had he said 'and with her countenance the shining moon she faced,' the 'favoring' would have been correct.[165] When, then, he insisted on placing the moon in a possessive construction with the sky, even though 'the moon' does not demand to be identified as being 'of the sky' in order to be understood as such, it may be deduced that he had an appropriate reason for so doing, namely, his claim that the face of his beloved was 'the moon of the earth,' by way of simple contrast.

4.10 "Also, the likening of the face of Mayy or Rabāb or Zaynab or Su'ād or Shabāb[166] to the clearly visible effulgent full moon is a custom on which the minds of the young Arabs of yore and the gallants of the deserts were firmly bent, given their habit of serenading them while wearing the robes of night and under its mantle and their stealing glances at the 'moons' of their faces under its tent, as their eloquent poet[167] eloquently expressed when he said:

The full moon promised to visit by night,
and, when he made good, I made good on my vows.[168]
I said, 'My Lord!' and 'Why prefer you the night
to the effulgent face of day?'

He answered, 'I do not like to change my rite—
and such is the rite of full moons at their rising.'

"Fie on thee! How many a peruser of collections of poetry holding within their boards the endeavors of pure-blooded, chaste-tongued Arabs has observed its stars[169] over barren deserts everywhere! How many a tome well-thumbed, full of plums, in the form of the verses of sublime souls, its virtues declare! In contrast, the comparison with the sun, from the perspective of what such souls do not find odd and of the paths their camels' hooves have already trod, is a supposition lame and worthy of blame; such a simile was not heard until after the rise of the sun of Islam,[170] so that it cannot be claimed to be appropriate to a eulogy, or to have vim or liberality. Al-Mutanabbī, on the other hand, was ever hell-bent on weaving his verses on the loom of those who wrapped themselves in the burnooses of desert tradition, too proud to descend to the low point reached by the limited talents allotted to the moderns as though in hostile opposition, though he may have committed slips in the heat of improvisation or while hunting the gazelles of amorous verse over its plateau in an attempt to relieve the lusts of the people of his age and to raise high the upper chambers of his own house and chateau.[171] 4.11

"If we were to descend, in all sincerity, from the ladder of critique regarding the laudatory nature of the comparison with the sun, we would still say that such an intent could never from such a well-ordered string be hung, because here any such would block that to which interest should naturally go and toward which the winds of longing and avidity briskly blow, namely, stripping the comparison of all elements of banality and distancing it from the censure of those critics who lack charity. This can happen only if the poet clothes it in new and eloquent clothing, such as a conceit woven out of a silk strangely spun, for 4.12

what is most strange is what is novel to the mind, furthest from what is hackneyed, the closest thing to which a smoothly pacing steed, if given its head, might run[172]—and the strangest thing that may be is the multiplication of an individual entity that is, in the view of all, circumscribed by being limited to a single exemplar within its own class, so as to bring it together with another similarly circumscribed entity,[173] and there can be no doubt that the visible coming together of one moon with another is stranger than the visible coming together of a moon with a sun. Indeed, the fact that the latter does occur coincidentally at the horizon weakens the impact of its strangeness in the eyes of the people of illumination.[174] «I swear by the glow of sunset» . . . «and the moon when it grows full»,[175] the sight of the sun and the moon in such a configuration ought not to be a goal that the likes of such a resourceful man of eloquence should strive to reach when seeking a way of imparting, to the strange, articulation.

4.13 "True, should their conjunction encompass some meaning exquisite and new, finer than all that déja vu—as when, like a sorcerer who deftly enchants people's eyes,[176] he[177] made to the Signs of the Last Hour allusion, accompanied by quotation, and dyed the garment of his literary works with the following verses, so brilliant at both their beginning and conclusion:

'Azzah let down her tresses.
Mayhap she desired to make the night last long.
'Sun and moon were brought together,'[178] when
the full moon rose wherever she slept.
After the ben tree of her figure appeared,
all said, 'A day of doom!'

"—it would rescue this simile from any overambition or glib facility.

"The fact of the matter is that all that al-Mutanabbī is attempting in this sublime bit of word play is the declarative metaphor of making the face of the beloved the 'moon of the earth' in contrast to the 'moon of the heavens' and making her turning of her face toward the latter the means by which two real moons became visible in the heavens of his imagination, and it's the same in the line of verse that comes earlier: 4.14

She loosened three tresses of her hair on a night that
made four nights visible.[179]

"Likewise, to return to the case before us, the poet says neither *fī layl* ('at night') nor *fī ān* ('at a determined time'), despite the fact that either would fit the meter and that both the preceding word is in harmony with the former and the following (namely *maʿā* ('together')) with the latter,[180] the reason being that 'night' does not fall within the orbit of strangeness nor 'a determined time' within that of keeping company. Thus the Learned Scholar[181] who provided the marginal commentary on this line was led by his general foolishness to follow the lead of those who interpret *waqt* ('time') as meaning 'at one time,' while, because of his specific foolishness, the Learned Scholar al-Tibrīzī interpreted it as 'on a night.' 4.15

"You two good friends of literature and loyalty,[182] halt, halt,[183] may you ever be possessed of fulfillment and a following! 'Beware the insight of the believer'[184] and of the true 'man of brilliance,'[185] who with the nectar of literature is intoxicated and on it fixated! Where am I to find the flame that accompanies the lantern of sagacity in its roaming! 4.16

"By Him who owns «what is in the Heavens»[186] and «what is below the Earth»,[187] who «knows both the secret and what is yet more dark»,[188] I found that this smear[189] 4.17

had left on my innermost thoughts a mark. My soul and yours[190] are mixed and joined, so every biting comment that hurts you hurts me. Methinks I hear you saying,[191] 'In your hand are two Indian swords, those of tongue and pen, that you have unsheathed—well-polished swords. What but an overstepping of the bounds of good manners[192] are your words, a challenge thrown down to grandfather and father? Where is respect for the sanctity of the forebears among the rabble of those who came after? They are spirits, and we are bodies. They are realities and we mere vestiges. They are suns, and we are full moons.[193] They are bellies, and we are backs.[194] Are they not our guides to an easy road? Are they not the leaders of the caravans of our high ambitions among the nations?' 'Indeed they are!' say I, 'and I am one of those!'[195] And yet the truth will out, as it is said (and how well he said who said!):

The telling of the truth—may all who speak it be held in high esteem—
Is something whose signs are implanted in men's minds.

4.18 "If then the Truth—glory and might be His!—be your guide, do not obey them, even should they strive to convince you:[196] I have presented you with firm rules, so take what's good and leave what's bad aside—the slips of shaykhs are like a mighty landslide. «By the sun and his morning brightness, and by the moon when she follows him»[197] my saying what I said above was not to offer our predecessors any slight, nor the flint of controversy strike; it was done because to promote the truth and establish it without doubt, to nurture it amongst literature's sons and make it sprout, calls for the rain storms of a minute analysis such as might pour down from 'the heaven of the returning rain'[198] and the keeping of a close watch on any

> flash of lightning that may flicker on the horizon of rebuke and disdain. «By the soul, and that which shaped it»,[199] I have here no stake other than this: God is the All-Forgiving, who «knows the thoughts in the breasts»[200] and has power over the secrets of the closed chambers. May the Guide show us the way by the light of the two moons of the Law and the Path[201] and lead us over the bridge of figurative expression to the safe haven of the truth and make us worthy of 'the word of self-restraint'[202] and save us from involvement in false complaint."

And I agree[203] with the words of the epistle's indicter,[204] lauder of 4.19
the Message and of its Honored Master.[205]

The Author Mentions the Date of Composition of the Work and Apologizes for Its Brevity

5.1 I plunged into this planting plot and canalized the channels of these planted lots[206] in the last days of Ennobled Shaʿbān,[207] without falsification, of the year 1058 of the Master of All Worlds' migration,[208] upon him the best of blessings and peace so long as trace still points to what once was but is now erased, and I watered that same trace from the spring of certain knowledge till it became, with that irrigation, as the pupil to the eye, from start to termination, its magnificent starry necklace scintillating like the full moon on the horizon, the constancy of its effulgence being in harmony with the indicators of its perfection.

5.2 This is the last of what we have consigned to these pages and my excuses for its brevity follow:

> I wrote it with no help to hand,
> so look upon it with indulgent eye,
> And, should you find a blemish, forgive—
> may you ever overlook the stumbler's blunders!
> From you my handwriting turns in shame,
> speaking as does one both wretched and confused.
> I came as a sick man, my powers weak.
> My lord, O my lord, be the one to help me to my feet!

We snatched a moment for it during a lull in the surging of the waves of the sea of impedimentation, despite the absence of any materials of ministration or kit made ready and for these endeavors fit, not to mention the length of time elapsed between me and my education and the interruptions to its application, my forgetfulness of how I was trained as a colt in the ring and once raced the dazzlingly white, so-prettily-standing steeds all over those lands—like a ball in Fate's vastness,[209] now in the cities, now in the countryside of blazing saxaul[210] brands.

But God's it is to command, and thanks be to Him 5.3
firstly and lastly, esoterically and exoterically
for the diversity of His gifts in every
generation.
And blessings and peace
upon His highest Messenger
glowingly, overflowingly
forever renewed with each and every
celestial revolution.
Amen Amen
—yet with just this I cannot be content
till after it a further thousand I have sent—
Amen Amen
Amen Amen Amen
Amen
Amen
The End

Notes

1 I.e., the Arabs, the consonant *ḍād* being regarded by the Arabs as unique to the language.

2 "when strung . . . and when dispersed": i.e., containing both poetry and prose (elements reversed in the translation for the rhyme).

3 Both *dhawq* ("taste") and *ʿirfān* ("knowledge") have mystical as well as literal connotations. Thus, in the usage of the Sufis, *dhawq* expresses "the ineffable and incommunicable nature of spiritual, amorous, contemplative, and cognitive experience" (Dennis Gril, "Dhawq," in *EI3*) while *ʿirfān* means "gnosis." Similarly in this paragraph, *ʿārif* may mean both "man of knowledge" and "one who has undergone mystical experiences" and so also elsewhere (e.g., §2.2.3, *yā akhā al-ʿirfān*, "(O) my brother in knowledge/gnosis"). This evocation of the world of mystical experience may perhaps be explained by the fact that most of the elite at this period belonged to Sufi orders; to write was thus, in effect, to address brother Sufis. Alternatively, the writer's use of such terms may be a way of teasing the reader by hinting at spiritual dimensions to the work that it does not, in fact, possess.

4 I.e., the visitors were so busy eating that their response of "Salaam!" came out in truncated form.

5 Cf. Q Āl ʿImrān 3:164 *wa-in kānū min qablu la-fī ḍalālin mubīn* «before that they were surely in manifest error.»

6 The words are intended to evoke one of the best known poems in Arabic, namely the "suspended" ode of the pre-Islamic poet Imruʾ al-Qays, which opens *qifā nabkī* ("Halt, my two companions, and let

us weep!"), though the use of the plural rather than the dual verb highlights the speaker's ignorance and lack of taste.

7 The same verse occurs in al-Shirbīnī, *Brains Confounded* (vol. 1, §5.5), with three differences: the spelling لا (*lā*) in the Arabic is a representation often found in Middle Arabic texts of the intensifying particle *la-*; the apparently first person plural form of the verb (*nuqaṭṭiʿ* versus *uqaṭṭiʿ*) is, in fact, first person singular, as in certain Egyptian dialects (see Blanc, *Nekteb-nektebu,* and Davies, *17th-Century Egyptian Arabic,* 114–15); the *alif* at the end of *nuqaṭṭiʿū* in the Arabic is a common orthography in nonstandard texts, generalized from the "otiose" *alif* found in other verb forms.

8 "is drawn from the ocean of madness" (*fa-min baḥr al-khurāʿ*): or, punning on another meaning of *baḥr*, "is drawn from the mad meter."

9 The meter is *kāmil,* with allowed variants; the Arabic spelling (*mutanāqiṣ*) is unusual, in that prosodic mnemonics are normally written with the implicit nunation realized as a final letter *nūn* (i.e., مُتَناقِصن) to allow complete representation of the syllabic count; in al-Sanhūrī's manuscript the nunation is suppressed throughout, as it is in the manuscripts of al-Shirbīnī. The mnemonic uses the root, *n-q-ṣ,* whose semantic range includes "lack," "deficiency," and "imperfection"; on the use of mnemonics formed from comically inappropriate roots to describe meters, as also in *Brains Confounded,* see the Introduction to the latter (vol 1, lix–lxi).

10 The line is set out in this way to demonstrate the division of the feet and its relation to the metrical mnemonic set out beneath it; see similarly *Brains Confounded,* vol. 2, §11.1.1.

11 "Hemistich" is normally *miṣrāʿ*, while *maṣraʿ* (used here, throughout, in such contexts; see §2.2.2 and §2.4.2) normally means "killing"; thus there may be a humorous evocation of the idea of "massacring" verse.

12 The Gate of the Chain, known today as Bāb al-ʿAzab ("the Gate of the Youth Levies"), is the main gate of Cairo's Citadel (Qalʿat al-Jabal).

13 "*al-ʿaḍīm* . . . is from *taʿḍīm* not *taʿẓīm*": the merging of *ẓ* and *ḍ* is widespread in Arabic dialects; overall, al-Sanhūrī seems to be saying that whether *al-ʿaḍīm* is from classical Arabic *ʿ-ḍ-m* (cf. *ʿaḍm* "winnowing

fork"), which would render the wording meaningless, or a result of the phonetic convergence mentioned above, the oath would be void.

14 "*ʿāliman* should be, according to the rules of grammar, in the nominative": see al-Shirbīnī, *Brains Confounded,* vol. 1, n. 260.

15 Al-Sanhūrī's objection is strange, as the use of the perfect (*al-māḍī*) following the conditional particle *in* is standard (see Wright, *Grammar* 2:14B).

16 Apparently meaning that the chaste speaker has the capacity to break verse into its components and reassemble it in the form of rhymed prose, which lacks the "tight" ordering of the former.

17 The mnemonic uses the root *kh-b-l,* whose semantic range covers "confusion" and "craziness."

18 ʿArafshah (or ʿArafsheh or ʿArabcheh) is a village in Iran's Zanjan province, which adjoins Daylam (see following note); the "chain" (*silsilah*) while referring, perhaps, to some feature of that place, also invokes the nonstandard meter of that name, which is related to the Iranian *dūbayt* meter (see Van Gelder, *Sound and Sense,* 126–27), even though the latter bears no relation to that of the verses quoted here.

19 Former name of present-day Iran's Gilan province; by its "Great Gate" may be meant the conspicuously large gate of Gilan's Rudkhan Castle, a Seljuq-era fortress of the Ismaili sect.

20 Q Baqarah 2:126 and passim.

21 I.e., it being his intention that his listeners should adopt his own vernacularisms, represented in this case by the omission of the interrogative particle.

22 I.e., the poets of the past enjoy the benefits of Paradise, happily oblivious to the faux pas of the poetaster under discussion.

23 Q ʿAlaq 96:5.

24 These verses occur also in al-Shirbīnī, *Brains Confounded,* with differences (vol. 1, §5.6).

25 *sūdu* ("is black as"): the form is strange: see al-Shirbīnī, *Brains Confounded* (vol. 1, §5.6.17).

26 *dayyātik* ("your handies"): apparently a plural, no longer attested, of colloquial *īd* ("hand"), see al-Shirbīnī, *Brains Confounded* (vol. 1, n. 284).

27 "the ocean of what confusion may excrete " (*baḥr khurāṭ al-takhlīṭ*): or, punning on another meaning of *baḥr*, "the meter of what confusion may excrete."

28 The mnemonic uses the root *kh-b-ṭ*, which includes in its semantic range such concepts as "striking," "trampling," "dust," "diabolical madness," and "sheep bloat" (*khubāṭ*).

29 Arab geographers mention such an island, in the Indian Ocean.

30 "cubit" (*dhirāʿ*): a unit—historically highly variable—of linear measurement (today standardized as 0.58 meters).

31 "at their greatest extent" (*bi-l-qiyās al-tāmm*): or, punningly, "to use an example of perfect analogy," referring to the fact that *kilām* ("wounds") and *kalām* ("words") have identical consonantal skeletons.

32 Q Isrāʾ 17:18.

33 On the employment by peasant leaders of fighting men, see al-Shirbīnī, *Brains Confounded*, Introduction (vol. 1, xlii–xliii).

34 The *shukl* (sg. *shikāl*) are "cords . . . by which a camel's fore shank and arm are bound together" (Lane, *Lexicon*) so that it can only hobble on three feet.

35 The fasting month of Ramadan is followed immediately by ʿĪd al-Fiṭr ("the feast of the breaking of the fast"); i.e., the beloved will, after a lean period, find a feast of love in the poet's arms.

36 The mnemonic uses the root *h-z-l*, which relates to "emaciation." The metrical table in fact divides the line into three rather than four feet, perhaps reflecting confusion as to how to deal with the breakdown of the meter at *binta l-aj*, which can be resolved only by eliding the hamzah (glottal stop) of *ajwād* (*binta l-ʾajwād* → *binta l-ajwād*); the meter is also irregular in the second hemistich.

37 "a peeled withy" (*ʿūdan muqashsharah*): this reading requires amendment of the Arabic text and the assumption that the writer regards *ʿūd* ("stick"), normally masculine in gender, as feminine; thus, the

translation is tentative. On the custom of substituting sticks for swords, see al-Shidyāq, *Leg Over Leg*, 1:179 (vol. 1, §1.12.2).

38 Cf. Q Ḥāqqah 69:32 «then in a chain of seventy cubits' length insert him».

39 These verses also occur in al-Shirbīnī, *Brains Confounded* (vol. 1, §5.7), with differences.

40 *tāyih ... kirsāyih ... mawlāyih ... qattāyih*: the representation of final *ah* as *ih* at the end of each hemistich indicates "pausal *imālah*," i.e., the raising of a final *a* following a "front" consonant such as *y* before a pause in speech, a phenomenon well documented in both Egyptian rural dialects and older Cairene Arabic (see Blanc, *Perte*, 4, and Davies, *Profile*, 81–85).

41 "the ocean that with false witness is replete" (*baḥr tazwīd al-tajrīḥ*): or, punning on another meaning of *baḥr*, "the meter ..." etc.

42 The mnemonic uses the root *q-r-ḥ*, which relates to "festering" and "ulceration."

43 *ʿa-l-ḥibbī ... mi-l-tāyih*: the colloquial contraction of *ʿala l-ḥibbi* to *ʿa-l-ḥibbi* and of *min al-tāyih* to *mi-l-tāyih* are required by the meter; see further al-Shirbīnī, *Brains Confounded*, vol. 1, n. 307.

44 "This scansion ..." (*hādhā l-tafʿīl ...*): in the manuscript, these words are followed by two blank pages; the lacuna appears to cover the discussion of the first line of the *mawāliyā,* and the text resumes with the discussion of the first hemistich of the second line; see further Note on the Text.

45 "the allusiveness of whose opening" (*barāʿat istihlālihi*): *barāʿat al-istihlāl* is a technical term from the science of rhetorical figures (*ʿilm al-badīʿ*) for the "making [of] one's opening indicative of one's intention, not by explicit statement but by subtle hinting" (Cachia, *Rhetorician*, 8), though the larger reference is not made clear here.

46 This and the three following lines are quoted, with considerable differences and without attribution, by Abū Hilāl al-ʿAskarī (d. after 395/1005), who cites them as an example of extreme laziness (al-ʿAskarī, *Dīwān al-maʿānī*, 1:197).

47 "metrical deviation" (*al-ziḥāf*): literally, "dragging," meaning certain permitted shortenings or elisions in the patterns of long and short

syllables forming a metrical foot (e.g., *fāʿilun* → *faʿilun*; *mutafāʿilun* → *mutfāʿilun* (i.e., *mustafʿilun*) or → *mufāʿilun*).

48 I.e., *saqqāʾū*, for the meter; in the commentary, the regular form (*saqqāʾ*) is used.

49 The feet are misleadingly divided (they should properly be given as *mukhāmilatun mukhāmilatun khamūlun*); in the Arabic text, in the application, below, of mnemonics to the first hemistich, these mnemonics are in fact divided into three columns, though this has been emended in the English to fit the distribution of the words of the verse. The root *kh-m-l* has associations of "inconsequentiality," "apathy," and "lethargy."

50 In the seventeenth century, Bāb al-Lūq, an area outside the precincts of the city of Cairo, housed slaughterhouses and tanneries (Raymond, *Artisans*, 1:312, 327) and was associated with prostitution and other low-status occupations (ibid., 2:609).

51 Two waterways—al-Khalīj al-Miṣrī and al-Khalīj al-Nāṣirī—traversed Cairo and were spanned by at least eighteen bridges (*qanāṭir*, sg. *qanṭarah*) (Pagano, *True Description*, 231–2; Raymond, *Caire*, 130); this particular bridge has not been identified and may be fictitious.

52 Perhaps a play on the name of a real gate of the Ottoman city, Bāb al-Kharq, "the Gate of Perfume" (now called Bāb al-Khalq).

53 "plummetry": the Arabic has *al-sanṭīr*, which yields no sense (*sanṭīr* means "psaltery"). It is assumed, therefore, that the intended word is *al-tasanṭīr*, verbal noun of colloquial *sanṭar* ("to collapse heavily").

54 "like the hawk carried . . . the hawker" (*shabīha l-zuqqi taḥmiluhu l-saqāʾū* [= *l-saqqāʾū*, for the meter]): an alternative reading of "like the wine (or water) skin (*al-ziqq*) carried by the wine pourer (or water carrier)" suggests itself, and the author's reading may be a tongue-in-cheek exercise in squeezing abstruse dictionary-based meanings from straightforward language.

55 Q Najm 53:44.

56 Q Aʿlā 87:4.

57 Cf. Q Burūj 85:5.

58 The same line of verse occurs, with one difference, in al-Shirbīnī, *Brains Confounded* (vol. 1, §5.2).

59 The mnemonic is based on the root *th-q-l*, which has connotations of "heaviness" and "boorishness."

60 "is indeed a lout, stuck, immobile in his affairs, and a dunderpate" (*innahu la-baqfun wāqifun fī-umūrihi wa-qafā*): a similar play on words is used by al-Shirbīnī in *Brains Confounded* (vol. 1, §5.3.15) in his commentary on the same line of verse.

61 The same verses occur, with differences, in al-Shirbīnī: *Brains Confounded* (vol. 1, §5.8).

62 The meter is *al-basīṭ*, although the metrical pattern of the word *ruḥiyyunā* does not actually fit any permitted variants; the mnemonic uses the root *r-q-ṣ*, meaning "to dance," triggered by the word *raqqāṣ* ("rattle staff"; literally, "dancer"); on the rattle staff, see al-Shirbīnī, *Brains Confounded* (vol. 1, n. 355).

63 Cf. Q Ḥajj 22:45: «How many a city We have destroyed in its evildoing, and now it is fallen down upon its turrets! How many a ruined well, a tall palace!»

64 The "gatherer of fuel by night" (*ḥāṭibu laylin*) is a conventional metaphor for "one who confuses in his speech . . . and in his affair: or one who speaks what is bad and what is good . . . for this person sees not what he collects in his rope . . . so he collects bad and good" (Lane, *Lexicon*, 594); thus the writer implies that, by making the millstones speak, the poet is presenting a grab bag of incoherent images.

65 I.e., the word *illā* ("except"), which here is followed by *wa-*, giving it the force of a conjunction indicating unexpected action.

66 The implication is that the son of the shaykh of the village owns its only ox and rents it out to the villagers.

67 "esoterically and exoterically" (*bāṭinan wa-ẓāhiran*): meaning either "according to all possible readings of the authoritative texts" or "in both a mystical and nonmystical sense"; see further n. 7.

68 Cf. Q Isrāʾ 17:18.

69 Q Najm 53:1.

70 A popular Tradition.

71 The same verses occur, with one difference, in al-Shirbīnī, *Brains Confounded* (vol. 1, §5.9).

72 The mnemonic is based on the root *kh-r-f,* which has connotations of "senility" and "foolish talk."

73 The association of peasants with warfare is stressed by al-Shirbīnī (see, e.g., *Brains Confounded,* vol. 1, §2.3).

74 "at the hands of a bailiff . . . [?]" (*ʿalā mashaddin bihi shadabah mina l-maḥmūdah*): an alternative reading of "at the hands of a *mashadd* (a kind of bailiff, see Glossary; or perhaps a *mushidd,* a 'well-mounted warrior') with a lopped-off branch (reading *shadhabah* for *shadabah,* for which no meaning is attested) of scammony" is possible but obscure; it seems likelier that the text is corrupt; note the similarity of consonantal skeleton between مشد به (which perhaps is to be read مشدبة) and the following شدبة.

75 I.e., the flood of bad verse would be so overwhelming that it would take little time to fill the tomes.

76 "the concoction of craziness" (*ikhtirāʿ al-khurāʿ*): perhaps a nod to the work by al-Ṣafadī of the same name (see al-Shirbīnī, *Brains Confounded,* vol. 1, xxxvi).

77 I.e., "both insipid and hard to swallow."

78 The mnemonic is based on the root *h-w-s*, which denotes "infatuation" and "being driven insane."

79 Unidentified and probably invented.

80 "in a hole" (*fī nuqrah*): in al-Shirbīnī's *Brains Confounded, nuqrah* refers most frequently to a hole or pit used for defecation (see *Brains Confounded*, vol. 1, §2.17, §3.25, etc.), and that may be what is meant here; presumably, a hole is required to provide privacy.

81 I.e., indifferent to whether the food was good or bad for her, his motive being simply to get her to meet with him.

82 Q Ṭūr 52:1–2.

83 Cf. Q Tawbah 9:30 *qātalahumu llāhu annā yuʾfakūn* («God assail them! How they are perverted!»).

84 The terminology is taken from the vocabulary of Sufism; see n. 7.

85 Q Fāṭir 35:2.

86 This work is unknown, and the riddle given is not found in Ibn Hishām's well-known *Grammatical Riddles* (*al-Alghāz al-naḥwiyyah*).

87 The terminology is again that of the mystics; see n. 7.

88 *warā*: according to modern practice, the word, which means "behind," should be spelled *warāʾ*; however, omission of the final *hamzah* (glottal stop) is typical of the orthography of the author's day and is required, in this instance, to make the word fit the answer to the riddle.

89 The thirteenth letter of the alphabet, transliterated *sh*.

90 "Just as the front end of the lance chokes on gore" (*ka-mā shariqat ṣadru l-qanāti mina l-damī*): the quotation is from a poem by al-Aʿshā Maymūn ibn Qays and is discussed further below (§3.3.5); see further Thaʿlab, *al-Ṣubḥ al-munīr*, 14:34.

91 The personal name ʿAmr is written with an unpronounced *wāw* in the nominative and genitive cases to distinguish it from the personal name ʿUmar, from which it would otherwise be indistinguishable if unvowelled (the author omits mention of the accusative, because a different rule applies there); the conceit is that ʿAmr lays claim to a *wāw* that does not belong to that name by right.

92 "as per the preceding mention" (*ka-mā marra*): i.e., "as indicated by the words 'one who lays false claim to riches that are not his own.'"

93 The following lines were written by Abū Nuwās to mock the poet al-Ashjaʿ ibn ʿAmr al-Sulamī (d. ca. 195/811), who, though born an orphan in Basra, falsely claimed to belong to the ancient Arab tribe of Sulaym (cf. Abū Nuwās, *Dīwān*, 2:76).

94 I.e., the conjunctive pronoun *mā*, in order to be definite, must be part of a relative clause (*ṣilah*) with a referent (*ʿāʾid*), as in *mā ʿindī min al-māl* ("what I have of money, the money that I have"), the implicit contrast here being with the less common indefinite *mā* (*mā l-mawṣūfah*), as in *marartu bi-mā muʿjibin laka* ("I passed by something pleasing to you") (see Wright, *Grammar*, 2:319); in this and the following case, the conceit is that *mā*, like an unreliable friend, lacks reliability and independent strength.

95 I.e., *mā* may, if attached to a preposition, be shortened, by omission of the letter *alif*, to *-ma*, as in the cases cited.

96 Q Naml 27:35.

97 Q Nāziʿāt 79:43.

98 ʿAmr ibn ʿUthmān ibn Qanbar Sībawayh (fl. second/eighth century) is regarded as "the creator of systematic Arabic grammar" (Meisami and Starkey, *Encyclopedia*, 1:718); his only work became so influential that it became known simply as Sībawayh's *Book*.

99 I.e., in the close relationship of the possessive construct, the gender of the first member of the phrase may be attracted into the gender of the second, because, as an Arab lexicographer puts it, speaking of the same example, "the *ṣadr* of the *qanāt* is a part of the *qanāt*" (see further Lane, *Lexicon*, s.v. *ṣadr*).

100 The verses are by Muḥammad ibn ʿAlī ibn Mūsā ibn ʿAbd al-Raḥmān Amīn al-Dawlah Abū Bakr al-Maḥallī (d. ca. 673/1275), a grammarian (al-Ṣafadī, *Wāfī*, 4:187–8; for the verses, 188).

101 E.g., *raʾā* ("to think, know"), *ʿalima* ("to know"), *ẓanna* ("to think, believe") (Wright, *Grammar*, 2:48D).

102 I.e., verbs such as *ʿalima* ("to know") cannot determine the case of a following embedded interrogative such as *man* ("who?") that would otherwise, by rule, occupy the initial position in a clause (*ṣadr al-kalām*) (just as one cannot say in English "I learned *whom* is Zayd's father"). In this case, however, because *abū man* is part of a possessive construct (*iḍāfah*), *man* annexes *abū,* and the rule is extended to the latter, even though it is not an interrogative and normally would not occupy initial position. In terms of the larger argument made in the preceding poem, the phrase *abū man* illustrates the point made in the first line, because *abū* has gained "elevation" (*rafʿ*) or, in grammatical terms "the state of being in the nominative," and "prominence" (*ṣadr*) or, in grammatical terms, "precedence, that is, the role of being the 'head' of an utterance," through its being "dependent on" (*muḍāfan li-*) or, in grammatical terms, annexed to, *man* in a possessive construct.

103 Q Kahf 18:12. Here the interrogative that must be in the nominative is *ayyu*; in other words, one cannot say *ayya* [accusative] *l-ḥizbayni*, and this is a clearer example of the rule, because here the interrogative actually occurs in initial position in the clause, and the issue is not complicated, as it is in the earlier example, by the presence of *abū* before *man*.

104 I.e., it is possible to say *ʿalimtu Zaydun abū man huwa*, with *Zayd* attracted into the nominative case by the force of the "eminence" of *man*; cf. Sībawayh's statement *wa-in shiʾta qulta qad ʿalimtu Zaydun abū man huwa* (*al-Kitāb*, 1:121).

105 The line is from the section of the poet's *muʿallaqah* ("suspended ode") describing a rain storm (al-Zawzanī, *Sharḥ*, 40).

106 I.e., *muzammal*, though logically nominative, is attracted into the genitive by the noun that immediately precedes it. In terms of the argument, *muzammalī* has lost the status it should have as an adjective describing *kabīru unāsin* ("the chieftain of a tribe") and been placed on the level of the relatively lowly "striped mantle."

107 These lines are found in al-Ṣafadī, *Wāfī*, 7:316, where they are attributed not to al-Jazzār but to ʿUmar ibn Muḥammad al-Sirāj al-Warrāq (d. ca. 695/1296) (al-Ṣafadī, *Wāfī*, 23:76–116); on changes to this line in the Arabic text, see Note on the Text, xiin5.

108 "yet a form of it is known to be masculine" (*wa-minhu qad ʿurifa l-tadhkīru*): or, punningly, "and from it reminders are known [to emanate]" (the relevance of which will appear in §3.5.2).

109 "vessel . . . wit" (*ẓarfun . . . ẓarfun*): punning on two meanings of *ẓarf*.

110 I.e., *maʾdhanah*, as a word, may occur in either the nominative case (*al-rafʿ*; literally "raising") or the accusative case (*al-naṣb*; literally "erecting") while, as a building, it "has raised sides and foundations erected"; at the same time, *mustaqirra l-bināʾ* ("solid of construction") may be taken, punningly, to mean "indeclinable," though the joke is weak here, as *maʾdhanah* is, in fact, declinable.

111 The word is masculine in gender and justifies the earlier statement that "some forms of it [i.e., the word meaning 'minaret'] are known to be masculine."

112 "A landmark standing alone—if they raise it, they raise it upright for the sake of the call" (*'alamun mufradun fa-in rafa'ūhū rafa'ūhū 'amdan li-ajli l-nidā'ī*): or, punningly, "a singular proper name—if they put it into the nominative case, they do so to make it straightaway into a vocative."

113 This justifies the punning reference to "reminders" above (n. 108).

114 Meaning, perhaps, that the minaret, as a structure, encloses or defines a certain space; also, punningly, "an adverb of place."

115 I.e., "the radiant women."

116 *aẓmatnī . . . makhālibā*: the tenth and seventh lines of the poem.

117 Cf. Q 'Ankabūt 29:43.

118 *lawlā l-mashaqqatu* etc.: from the poet's eulogy of Abū Shujā' Fātik (d. 350/961), a general of Egypt's Ikhshīdid dynasty (cf. al-Mutanabbī, *Dīwān*, 505, with differences); this is the forty-third line of the poem.

119 The incident reflects a story in which the caliph al-Manṣūr, while on a visit to Medina, asked for a guide familiar with "its ancient dwelling places and their remains" as "it is long since I visited the dwellings of my people, and I wish to refresh my memory of them" (al-Iṣfahānī, *Aghānī*, 10:107–8).

120 'Abdallāh ibn Muḥammad, known as al-Aḥwaṣ ("the Slit-Eyed") (40–105/660–724), a poet of Medina, who was once banished because of his affairs with women of high status.

121 In the source story, the official charged with paying the guide confesses that he has not done so.

122 The text of §3.9 and §3.10 is defective (see the Note on the Text); it has been recreated, in the case of the first anecdote (§3.9), using Ibn Khallikān's biography of al-Qāḍī l-Fāḍil (Ibn Khallikān, *Wafayāt*, 3:161) where a similar anecdote is told, and, in the case of the second (§3.10), using al-Zamakhsharī's *Rabī' al-abrār* (al-Zamakhsharī, *Rabī'*, 1:144).

123 "Button . . . Visit . . ." (*zirr . . . zur*): the two words appear identical when written without vowels and without *shaddah,* which indicates doubling of the *r*.

124 From this point until the translation resumes the text is fragmentary.

125 Al-Zamakhsharī (*Rabīʿ al-Abrār,* 1:144) attributes these verses to Ibn al-Jahm (d. 249/863), others (with variants) attribute them to Abū Tammām (ca. 189–232/805–45) or to Khālid ibn Yazīd al-Kātib (d. 262/876 or 269/883) or regard them as anonymous.

126 The ductus of some Arabic letters is common to more than one phoneme, the differences being marked by the use of one or more dots above or below the line (e.g., ص = *ṣ* while ض = *ḍ*, and ب = *b* while ت = *t*); *taṣāḥīf* (singular *taṣḥīf*) are changes, deliberate or in error, to the dots on the letters of one word that produce another, e.g., بنت/ثيب, *bint/thayyib* ("virgin/nonvirgin") or ريح/زنج, *rīḥ/zanj* ("wind/Negroes").

127 Perhaps meaning al-Ṣāḥib ibn ʿAbbād (326–85/938–95), the Būyid vizier famed for his literary brilliance.

128 I.e., the daughter of Bisṭām ibn Qays (d. 10/631–32), a warrior famed for his chivalry and courage.

129 A traditional metaphor for a beautiful person.

130 As elsewhere, the writer plays with Sufi terminology (see above, n. 7); the reference to hashish and to "those who tread the Path" (*al-sālikīn*) reinforce the association.

131 On taṣḥīf see above, n. 126; however, the first examples of word play in the poem (علا/علي, *ʿalā*, and يقينا/يَقِنَّا *yaqīnā*) are neither of *taṣḥīf* nor of palindromes but of paronomasia (see §3.13.2).

132 Presumably meaning that hashish is something "low" that the sagacity of the Sufis has nevertheless commended to him.

133 "its sound, meaningful first half" (*shaṭrahu l-awwala l-ṣaḥīḥa l-mubīnā*): the first half of حشيش, *ḥashīsh*, is حش, *ḥash*, which is "sound" because it contains no "weak" letters (i.e., *wāw* or *yāʾ*, letters that in certain environments undergo change) and can be regarded as meaningful if حش, *ḥash*, is reinterpreted as *ḥashsha*, "he cut".

134 "the command of allusion displayed in the opening lines" (*barāʿat istihlāl abyāt al-kalām*): see n. 131; perhaps the allusion is to "getting high."

135 I.e., each of the three "teeth" (i.e., raised tips) (*sinn*, pl. *asnān*) of which the letter ش is formed has the potential to become, and thus may be counted for these purposes as, a letter in its own right; *shīn*

consists of three *asnān,* and, if each *sinn* is repointed, may yield *n-y-n*; when these are added to the initial *ḥ* and the latter is repointed by the addition of a dot below, the resulting word is جنين, "fetus."

136 The number of "teeth" in each word (see preceding note) is seven, provided that the first *bā'* in the first word حبّبتني به, *ḥabbabatnī bihi,* which is doubled by the operation of the *shaddah*, is counted twice and provided that it is borne in mind that the final *yā'* of the first is written with a "tooth" when in nonfinal position; thus the diacritics could be distributed over the same ductus to produce the two different words (the first and last letters of each remaining unchanged).

137 شُحّ: only the consonantal skeleton is at issue: changes to the vowels and value (single or double) of consonants are discretionary.

138 شي: i.e., شيء ("thing"); the loss of the final *hamzah* ("glottal stop") is typical of the orthography of the time and does not imply its absence in pronunciation.

139 "the most indeterminate of all indeterminates, in the eyes of those who speak Arabic featly" (*ankar al-nakirāt 'ind al-mu'ribīn*): i.e., "thing" is the least specific way of referring to an object; at the same time, the author may be punning on the alternative sense of *shay'* as "penis" or "vulva," the alternative sense of *nakir* as "reprehensible," and the alternative sense of *mu'ribīn* as "those who speak explicitly"; the whole phrase might thus be translated alternatively as "the most reprehensible of all reprehensible things, as used by those who speak obscenely."

140 The line is taken from an encomium apparently written for one 'Abd al-Wāḥid ibn al-'Abbās ibn Abī l-Iṣba'; its opening line goes "O mounts of the beloved ones, my tears/ fall as hard upon my cheeks as do you[r hooves] when you stamp upon the crumbling rock" (*a-rakā'ibī l-aḥbābi inna l-admu'ā/taṭisu l-khudūda ka-mā taṭisna l-yarma'ā*) (al-Mutanabbī, *Dīwān*, 107–10; ninth line p. 108).

141 "the wonder of Hamadān" (*badī' Hamadān*): the writer flatters the soon-to-be-named "Shaykh Muḥammad ibn al-Sayyid Maḥmūd" by evoking the memory of Abū l-Faḍl Aḥmad ibn al-Ḥusayn al-Hamadhānī (358–98/968–1008), a writer of pyrotechnic linguistic skills, known as Badī' al-Zamān ("the Wonder of the Age").

142 Shaykh Muḥammad ibn al-Sayyid Maḥmūd: the identity of this writer remains unclear; a possibility is al-Sayyid Muḥammad ibn al-Sayyid Maḥmūd al-Ḥamīdī (or al-Ḥumaydī) mentioned by al-Muḥibbī in his biography of Shihāb al-Dīn ibn ʿAbd al-Raḥmān ibn Muḥammad (d. 1078) as one of the latter's teachers and described by him as "known as a descendant of the Prophet, chief judge of the army, and syndic of the Ottoman possessions" (*sharīf qāḍī l-ʿaskar wa-naqīb al-mamālik al-ʿUthmāniyyah*) (al-Muḥibbī, *Khulāṣat al-athar*, 2:232); al-Muḥibbī does not, however, provide a biography of al-Ḥamīdī.

143 *Thālith al-nayyirayn* (*The Third, after the Two Stars That Burn Bright*): by *al-nayyirayn* (literally "the two brightly lit things") the writer means "the sun and the moon" (on this rhetorical figure, known as "favoring," see Glossary), it being his claim that his epistle is as bright as either of the foregoing.

144 *The Extended* (*al-Muṭawwal*): the term is sometimes used to refer to a longer version of a work; a candidate in this case is al-Taftāzānī's commentary on al-Khaṭīb al-Qazwīnī's short textbook on the rhetorical sciences called *Talkhīṣ al-Miftāḥ* (*The Epitome of the Key*), of which al-Taftāzānī also wrote a shorter version, *al-Mukhtaṣar* (*The Abridgment*).

145 "the Brilliant Reader" (al-Almaʿī al-Qāriʾ): the writer apparently suppresses mention of this critic's real name, perhaps to minimize controversy, and instead refers to him using two ironically honorific epithets, "the Brilliant" (*al-almaʿī*) and "the Reader" (*al-qāriʾ*, meaning "reciter of the Qur'an").

146 al-Tibrīzī: Yaḥyā ibn ʿAlī al-Khaṭīb al-Tibrīzī (421–502/1030–1109) whose commentary on this line in his *al-Mūḍiḥ fī sharḥ shiʿr al-Mutanabbī* reads in full: "The two moons: he may mean by this two equal moons, because a face that is regarded as beautiful may be compared to the moon, and it is not usual for there to be more than one moon on any night; and by the moon that she showed him he may mean the sun, because the sun and the moon do not meet. People make the sun into a moon when they put it together with the moon that rises by night, at which point they make the

masculine preponderate over the feminine" (al-Tibrīzī, *al-Mūḍiḥ*, 3:317). Al-Tibrīzī seems to be saying here that, by "two moons," al-Mutanabbī means either the real moon plus the moon-like face of the beloved or the real moon plus the sun-like face of the beloved. Al-Tibrīzī also points out that, when people say "the two moons," they are using "favoring," in which case the masculine word *qamar* ("moon") subsumes the feminine word *shams* ("sun").

147 "one moon plus another moon" (*qamaran wa-qamaran*): i.e., Muḥammad ibn Maḥmūd understands al-Tibrīzī's "two equal moons" to mean "a moon of one sort plus a moon of another sort," i.e., "a real moon and a figurative moon, the latter being a human face" (see preceding note).

148 I.e., the end of the Brilliant Reader's quotation from al-Tibrīzī.

149 "Our reading is more laudatory" (*mā dhakarnāhu amdaḥ*): i.e., the Brilliant Reader claims that it is more fitting in a eulogy to compare the subject's face to a sun than to a moon as, on the surface, the poet seems to do.

150 "customarily" (*fī l-ʿurf*): i.e., according to the rhetorical figure known as "favoring" (see Glossary).

151 I.e., the end of Muḥammad ibn Maḥmūd's verbatim quotation from the Brilliant Reader. Hereafter, from §4.4 through the end of §4.18, the words are those of Muḥammad ibn Maḥmūd.

152 An allusion to "the Brilliant Reader"; throughout what follows, Muḥammad ibn Maḥmūd refers to the Brilliant Reader, sarcastically, as "that brilliant fellow," etc.

153 "a mere building of castles in the air" (*jadhbah bi-ghayr jādhibah*): literally, "a pull of drawn thread, or yarn, with no one to pull it."

154 The reference is unclear.

155 "'metaphor by allusion' . . . 'declarative metaphor'" (*al-istiʿārah bi-l-kināyah . . . al-istiʿārah al-taṣrīḥiyyah*): on the theory of metaphor in Arabic in general, see Meisami and Starkey, *Encyclopedia*, 2:522–4. Here Muḥammad ibn Maḥmūd appears to evoke the terminology of Yūsuf ibn Abī Bakr al-Sakkākī (555–626/1160–1229), a grammarian and rhetorician, who, in his influential *Miftāh al-ʿulūm* (*The Key to*

the Sciences), distinguishes between the metaphor by allusion (e.g., "death" in "death sank its claws into," where "sank its claws" alludes to the predator who is providing the underlying image; the author uses this same metaphor shortly hereafter) and "make-believe metaphor" (*al-istiʿārah al-takhyīliyyah*), here called "declarative metaphor" (*al-istiʿārah al-taṣrīḥiyyah*), which would have one believe, or declares, that there is a part of death that could be likened to claws. Thus, he is saying that the Brilliant Reader is subjecting one subject to two incompatible analyses, and the beloved's face cannot be likened, at the same time, to both a sun and a mirror.

156 In other words, al-Mutanabbī's use of the verb *arā* ("to show") is not enough to imply a mirror, even though the word *mirʾāh* is derived from the same root.

157 The writer evokes the standard metaphor of "death sinking its claws" into a person (see n. 155) by proposing an inappropriate change of subject.

158 I.e., al-Mutanabbī.

159 I.e., the image of the moon reflected in the beloved's face.

160 I.e., the Brilliant Reader has reversed his original assertion that it is the moon that is real and the sun that is figurative.

161 I.e., given that the poet has specified that he is referring to the real moon, it is invalid to claim that "the two moons" is an example of "favoring," because the latter can only be either consistently figurative or consistently nonfigurative.

162 I.e., there is no call for the Brilliant Reader's excessively elaborate figurative explanation, as it would be physically possible to see both the beloved's face and the actual moon at the same time.

163 The writer appears to contrast a "broader and more comprehensive" simultaneity with a narrower and less comprehensive one, as though the sight of the beloved facing the moon and thus providing a vision of two moons ought to be visible for a longer time than the brief flash of the sun as it is reflected in her face.

164 I.e., "that we have imparted to you as advice not to be forgotten."

165 I.e., if he had omitted mention of the sky, it would be possible to interpret "the two moons" figuratively; however, he did not, in fact, omit to mention it.

166 Generic names for beloved women.

167 The poem is attributed by ʿAbd al-Qāhir al-Jurjānī to Saʿīd ibn Ḥumayd, that is, Abū ʿUthmān Saʿīd ibn Ḥumayd ibn Saʿīd, a member of the chancellery under the Abbasid caliph al-Mustaʿīn (r. 248–51/862–66) (al-Jurjānī, *Asrār*, 291).

168 I.e., having previously vowed that he would, for example, give money to a charitable cause if his beloved made good on his promise, the lover discharged these obligations.

169 I.e., scintillating examples of the deployment of the image of "the full moon" in the sense of "the face of the beloved."

170 The implication is that pre-Islamic poetry could not be equaled by later verse.

171 I.e., to improve his own material circumstances.

172 "the closest thing to which a smoothly pacing steed, if being given its head, might run" (*wa-aqrabu li-an yubdhala tablīghu al-rahwān*): the translation is very tentative and depends on amending *al-rihān* in the manuscript to *al-rahwān*.

173 I.e., the simultaneous appearance of two moons constitutes a novel and arresting image, the moon being, by nature, unique.

174 See n. 7.

175 Q Inshiqāq 84:16 and 84:18. The writer apparently invokes these Qur'anic verses to confirm the possibility of sun and moon appearing together in the sky; the argument is weak, however, as *al-shafaq* in fact means the remains of daylight *after* the sun has set. The syntax is strange, and the text may be corrupt.

176 Cf. Q Aʿrāf 7:116 *saḥarū aʿyuna l-nās* («[and when they cast] they put a spell upon the people's eyes»).

177 Logically, "he" should mean al-Mutanabbī, but these jejune verses are certainly not by him and have not been found in other sources.

178 Cf. Q Qiyāmah 75:9; this is the quotation alluded to in the verse.

179 "She loosened three tresses . . ." (*arkhat thalātha dhawā'iba . . .*): this is the eighth line of the ode that contains *istaqbalat* etc. (al-Mutanabbī, *Dīwān*, 107 line 11), the point being that the poet has already, in the same poem, used the same kind of "declarative metaphor" (where "three tresses of her hair" equals "three nights") and the Brilliant Reader should have taken this into account in his discussion of the subsequent line.

180 Muḥammad ibn Maḥmūd seeks to refute the claim of al-Tibrīzī, quoted by the Brilliant Reader (§4.3), that the sight of "the two moons" occurred "on a night," and the preceding claim of the Brilliant Reader that the lover saw the sun and the moon "at one time," on the grounds that—even though the word *al-qamarayni* ("two moons"), which immediately precedes the temporal phrase, is compatible, logically and metrically, with *layl* ("night") and the word *maʿā* (i.e., *maʿan* with lengthening of the final syllable for the rhyme and meaning "together, simultaneously"), which follows it, is similarly compatible with *ān* ("a specific time")—al-Mutanabbī chose not to use either *layl* or *ān*, because the former is insufficiently "strange" (i.e., intriguing) and the latter invokes the idea of simultaneity but not that of accompaniment.

181 I.e., the Brilliant Reader.

182 Muḥammad ibn Maḥmūd addresses the Brilliant Reader and al-Tibrīzī.

183 "halt, halt" (*qifā qifā*): see n. 6 above; here the verb is, appropriately, in the dual.

184 "Beware the insight of the believer" (*iyyākumā wa-firāsat al-mu'min*): evokes a common hadith (more often given as *ittaqū firāsat . . .*) that continues *fa-innahu yanẓuru bi-nūri llāh* "for he sees with the light of God."

185 Muḥammad ibn Maḥmūd appropriates "the Brilliant Reader" sobriquet for himself.

186 Cf. Q Ṭā Hā 20:6 «to Him belongs all that is in the heavens and the earth and all that is between them, and all that is underneath the soil.»

187 Q Ṭā Hā 20:6.

188 Q Ṭā Hā 20:7; literally, «the secret and that which is yet more hidden.»

189 That is, this smear on al-Mutanabbī's reputation.

190 Muḥammad ibn Maḥmūd now addresses al-Mutanabbī.

191 Muḥammad ibn Maḥmūd reverts to addressing the Brilliant Reader and al-Tibrīzī.

192 "good manners" (*al-adab*): or, punningly, "literature."

193 I.e., we can only reflect their light.

194 Perhaps meaning, "they came first, and we came later."

195 "and I am one of those" (*wa-anā ʿalā*): an elliptical reference to *wa-anā ʿalā dhālikum mina l-shāhidīn* «I am one of those that bear witness thereunto» (Q Anbiyāʾ 21:56).

196 Cf. Q ʿAnkabūt 29:8 and similarly Luqmān 31:15 «but if they strive with thee to make thee associate with Me that whereof thou hast no knowledge, then do not obey them»; Muḥammad ibn Maḥmūd warns his readers against the fallacious arguments of "the Brilliant Reader" and al-Tibrīzī.

197 Q Shams 91:1–2.

198 Cf. Q Ṭāriq 86:11–12.

199 Q Shams 91:7.

200 Q Āl ʿImrān 3:119 and elsewhere.

201 I.e., the canon law of Islam and the mystic, or Sufi, path.

202 Q Fatḥ 48:26 (Pickthall, *Meaning*, 367).

203 Al-Sanhūrī abruptly endorses Muḥammad ibn Maḥmūd's opinions, and the work continues in his own voice to the end.

204 I.e., al-Shaykh Muḥammad ibn al-Sayyid Maḥmūd (see §4.2).

205 I.e., the Prophet Muḥammad.

206 I.e., "I started work on this book in . . ."; the irrigation image returns later in the passage ("and I watered").

207 The eighth month of the Islamic calendar; Shaʿbān 1058 H ran from 20 August to 20 September 1648 AD.

208 I.e., the departure of the Prophet Muḥammad from his native Mecca for Medina, where he was to establish the first Muslim state, in Year 1 of the Hegira.

209 "like a ball in Fate's vastness, now in the cities, now in the countryside" (*ka-l-kurati fī faḍāʾi l-qaḍā ṭawran bi-l-muduni wa-tāratan bi-rīfi . . .*): if, as here, one reads this enigmatic phrase as referring to the author as someone with little time for writing, one may suppose that al-Sanhūrī's career somehow required him to live in both the city and the countryside; it is tempting to speculate that he may have been a judge, shuttled from place to place at the behest of the authorities, and that the phrase *fī faḍāʾi l-qaḍā* is intended to be read not only as "in Fate's vastness" but also as "in the vastness of the judiciary."

210 Saxaul (*ghaḍā*) is a woody shrub or small tree, *Haloxylon ammodendron,* proverbial for the heat with which it burns.

Glossary

Abū l-Ḥusayn al-Jazzār (601/1204–5 to 679/1280–81) Yaḥyā ibn ʿAbd al-ʿAẓīm ibn Yaḥyā ibn Muḥammad ibn ʿAlī, Egyptian poet (al-Jammāl, *al-Adab al-ʿāmmī*, 191–200); often bracketed with al-Miʿmār (q.v.) because of their common plebeian origin.

Abū Muḥammad ʿAlī Ibn Ḥazm al-Ẓāhirī (384–456/994–1064) Andalusian polymath and prolific author, commonly referred to as Ibn Ḥazm.

Abū Nuwās (ca. 130–98/747–813) Abū Nuwās al-Ḥasan ibn Hāniʾ al-Ḥakamī, one of the most famous poets of the Abbasid Golden Age, especially in the fields of wine poetry and the love lyric.

Abū Sufyān al-Humām (d. 30/651) Ṣakhr ibn Ḥarb, better known as Abū Sufyān and nicknamed al-Humām ("the Generous"); a prominent leader of the Quraysh tribe in Mecca who initially opposed the Prophet Muḥammad but later accepted Islam.

ʿĀd see *Thamūd*.

al-Aʿshā (d. ca. 7/629) Abū Baṣīr al-Aʿshā Maymūn ibn Qays, a celebrated pre-Islamic poet.

ʿĀtikah daughter of the caliph Yazīd and granddaughter of Muʿāwiyah, founder of the Umayyad dynasty.

al-ʿAzīz al-Malik al-ʿAzīz I ʿUthmān ibn al-Nāṣir I Ṣalāh al-Dīn (r. 589–95/1193–98), Ayyubid ruler of Egypt, son of Ṣalāh al-Dīn (Saladin).

Bāb al-Lūq an area beyond the western limits of Ottoman Cairo; see also n. 50.

badīʿ rhetorical figures.

Baysān a town in northern Palestine.

bīsār a popular dish consisting of mashed fava beans (*fūl*) and "Jew's mallow" (*mulūkhiyyā*); for a detailed description, see al-Shirbīnī, *Brains Confounded*, vol. 2, §11.12.3.

al-Bisṭām Bisṭām ibn Qays (d. 10/631–32), a warrior famed for his chivalry and courage.

al-Damāmīnī (763–827/1362–1424) Badr al-Dīn Muḥammad ibn Abī Bakr al-Damāmīnī, also known as al-Badr al-Damāmīnī and Ibn al-Damāmīnī, Egyptian author of commentaries on and abridgments of works by authors in a variety of fields.

favoring (taghlīb) literally, "awarding of precedence": a stylistically elegant usage according to which the dual form of one noun is used to indicate both that noun and another with which it is closely associated, as for example, *al-qamarān* (literally, "the two moons"), meaning "the moon and the sun" and *al-aṣfarān* (literally, "the two yellow things"), meaning "gold and silver."

Hamadān an ancient city in western Iran, also spelled Hamadhān.

al-Ḥaṭīm a low, thick, semicircular wall of white marble opposite the northwest corner of the Kaaba between which and the Kaaba are said to lie the graves of Ismāʿīl and Hājar.

hints (ishārāt) as used here, the term refers to lines of verse that, precisely because they are apparently irrelevant to the matter at hand, push the addressee to find another, relevant, line within the same poem (see §3.1).

Ibn ʿĀd, Shaddād legendary son of the eponym of the tribes of ʿĀd. In one legend, Shaddād ibn ʿĀd built a city, called Iram of the Pillars, as an imitation of Paradise, and was then, as a punishment for his pride, destroyed by a tornado and the city buried in sand (W. Montgomery Watt, "Iram" in EI2).

Ibn Hishām (708–61/1309–60) ʿAbdallāh ibn Yūsuf ibn Hishām, known as Ibn Hishām al-Naḥwī (Ibn Hishām the Grammarian), a prolific Egyptian author, largely of pedagogical works on grammar.

Ibn al-Jahm (188–249/803–63) ʿAlī ibn al-Jahm, a poet at the Baghdad court of the Abbasid caliph al-Mutawakkil.

Ibn ʿUnayn (549–630/1154–1232) Muḥammad ibn Naṣr Allāh ibn Makārim ibn al-Ḥasan Ibn ʿUnayn, Syrian satirical poet and high government official under the Ayyubids.

Imruʾ al-Qays (6th century AD) Imruʾ al-Qays ibn Ḥujr, a pre-Islamic poet.

al-Malik al-Nāṣir Ṣalāḥ al-Dīn ibn Yūsuf ibn Najm al-Dīn Ayyūb (r. 564–89/1169–93) Ayyubid ruler of Egypt and Syria, known in English as Saladin.

al-Manṣūr (r. 136–58/754–75) second caliph of the Abbasid dynasty.

the Maqām (literally, "the Standing Place"): in the sanctuary at Mecca, a small open-sided building housing a stone on which the patriarch Ibrāhīm (Abraham) is said to have stood during the building of the Kaaba.

al-Miʿmār (fl. 7th/13th century) Ibrāhīm ibn ʿAlī al-Miʿmār, Egyptian satirical poet whose *mawāliyā*s are often built on puns; classified by contemporary critics as *ʿāmmī* ("of the common people") and *maṭbūʿ* ("natural," i.e., self-taught) but well regarded, despite his frequent violations of the rules of literary Arabic (al-Jammāl, *al-Adab al-ʿāmmī*, 185–9); often bracketed with Abū l-Ḥusayn al-Jazzār because of their common plebeian origin.

al-Mutanabbī, Abū l-Ṭayyib Aḥmad ibn al-Ḥusayn (303–54/915–65), a renowned poet of the Abbasid age.

al-Mutawakkil (r. 232–47/847–61) eleventh Abbasid caliph.

Night of Power (Laylat al-qadr) the night during the fasting month of Ramadan, usually taken to be that preceding the twenty-seventh day, on which the first of the revelations of the Qur'an was given to the Prophet Muḥammad; on this night, the gates of heaven are said to be opened and prayers sure of success.

pastoral (mawāliyā) the five *mawāliyā*s in this work are short poems in the *basīṭ* meter characterized by a mixture of colloquial and noncolloquial features and having as their theme love in a rural setting; as a genre, the *mawāliyā* has a long and varied history (see Pierre Cachia, "Mawāliyā," in *EAL*).

al-Qāḍī al-Fāḍil (529–96/1135–1200) ʿAbd al-Raḥīm ibn ʿAlī, known as al-Qāḍī al-Fāḍil ("the Virtuous Judge"): a statesman, model of epistolary style, poet, and head of chancery of Ṣalāḥ al-Dīn al-Ayyūbī (Saladin) from 566/1171.

Rashīd Rosetta, on the mouth of the western branch of the Nile, a major entrepôt for trade between Cairo and Alexandria; the city rose in importance during the seventeenth century following the decline of Fuwwah, which was ruined by the end of navigation on the Nile-Alexandria canal, ca. AD 1650 (Raymond, *Artisans*, 1:167).

riddles (alghāz) as used here, either the use of a name that brings to mind another name that has the intended meaning or of a question in the form of "What is the name of something that . . ." followed by clues to the name relying on metatheses or other variations on the consonantal skeleton of the word (see §3.1).

shaykh of the village (shaykh al-balad) headman or representative of the village vis-à-vis the state, responsible for the provision of certain services (such as that of an ox to turn waterwheels for raising water, see §2.8.5 below).

shīn thirteenth letter of the Arabic alphabet (ش).

Sībawayh (fl. second/eighth century) ʿAmr ibn ʿUthmān ibn Qanbar Sībawayh, regarded as "the creator of systematic Arabic grammar" (Scott and Meisami, *Encyclopedia*, 1:718); his only work became so influential that it was known simply as *Kitāb Sībawayh* (*Sībawayh's Book*).

supercommentary (ḥāshiyah) literally, "something stuffed (as a cushion)": a commentary on a commentary on an earlier work, usually "stuffed" into the margin of the commentary.

Thabīr a mountain near Mecca.

Thamūd and ʿĀd ancient tribes of Arabia, both mentioned in the Qurʾan as having been wiped out by disasters as punishment for misdeeds (in ʿĀd's case, by a violent storm (Q Aʿrāf 7:65, Hūd 11:58, etc.) or a draught (Q Hūd 11:52), in Thamūd's by an earthquake (Q Aʿrāf 7:78) or a thunderbolt (Q Fuṣṣilat 41:13, 41:17)).

al-Tibrīzī Yaḥyā ibn ʿAlī al-Khaṭīb al-Tibrīzī (421–502/1030–1109), author of several commentaries on the *dīwāns* of leading poets, including *al-Mūḍiḥ fī sharḥ al-Mutanabbī* (*The Clarifier concerning the Elucidation of al-Mutanabbī*).

Tradition (ḥadīth, pl. aḥādīth) an account of the Prophet's words or deeds to which he gave his tacit approval.

ʿŪj ibn ʿAnaq a giant, the Biblical "King Og" (B. Heller, "ʿŪdj b. ʿAnaḳ," in *EI2*).

wrangles (mabāḥith) discussions of knotty grammatical or stylistic points (see §4.1).

Zamzam a well within the enclosure of the Kaaba that was opened by the angel Jibrāʾīl (Gabriel) to save Hājar and her son Ismāʿīl from thirst.

Bibliography

Abū Nuwās, al-Ḥasan ibn Hāniʾ. *Dīwān Abī Nuwās al-Ḥasan ibn Hāniʾ al-Ḥakamī*. Edited by Ewald Wagner and Gregor Schoeler. 7 vols. Cairo and Wiesbaden: Franz Steiner, and Beirut and Berlin: Klaus Schwarz, 1958–2006 (vols. 6–7: indexes). The second edition of vol. 1 (2001) has been used.

Arberry, A. J. *The Koran*. Oxford: Oxford University Press, 1998.

al-ʿAskarī, Abū Hilāl al-Ḥasan ibn ʿAbdallāh. *Dīwān al-maʿānī*. 2 vols. Cairo: n.p. 1352/1933.

Blanc, Haim. "La Perte d'une forme pausale dans le parler arabe du Caire." *Mélanges de l'Université Saint-Joseph* 48 (1973–4): 376–90.

———. "The nekteb-nektebu imperfect in a variety of Cairene Arabic." *Israel Oriental Studies* 4 (1974): 206–26.

Cachia, Pierre. *The Arch Rhetorician or the Schemer's Skimmer: A Handbook of Late Arabic badīʿ Drawn from ʿAbd al-Ghanī an-Nābulsī's Nafḥat al-Azhār ʿalā Nasamāt al-Asḥār, Summarized and Systematized by Pierre Cachia*. Wiesbaden: Harrassowitz, 1998.

———. "The Egyptian Mawwal: Its Ancestry, Its Development, and Its Present Forms." *Journal of Arabic Literature* 8 (1977): 77–103.

Davies, Humphrey (1981). *Seventeenth-Century Egyptian Arabic: A Profile of the Colloquial Material in Yūsuf al-Shirbīnī's "Hazz al-quḥūf bi-sharḥ qaṣīd Abī Shādūf"*. Ph.D. diss. University of California, Berkeley. 1981. Available from ProQuest Dissertations & Theses Global (order no. 8200073). http://search.proquest.com/docview/303007733

———. *A Lexicon of 17th-Century Egyptian Arabic*. Orientalia Lovaniensia Analecta 225. Leuven: Peeters, 2013.

Ibn Khallikān, Aḥmad ibn Muḥammad. *Wafayāt al-aʿyān wa-anbāʾ abnaʾ al-zamān*. Edited by Iḥsān ʿAbbas. 8 vols. Beirut: Dār Ṣādir, 1972.

al-Idrīsī, Muḥammad ibn Muḥammad. *Nuzhat al-mushtāq fī ikhtirāq al-āfāq (Opus geographicum: sive "Liber AD eorum delectationem qui terras peragrare studeant")*. Edited by Enrico Cerulli, Alessio Bombaci, et al. Naples: Brill, 1970–.

al-Iṣfahānī, Abū l-Faraj. *Kitāb al-aghānī*. 24 vols. Cairo: Dār al-Kutub and al-Hayʾah al-Miṣriyyah al-ʿĀmmah li-l-Kitāb, 1927–74.

al-Jammāl, Aḥmad Ṣādiq. *al-Adab al-ʿāmmī fī Miṣr fī l-ʿaṣr al-mamlūkī*. Cairo: al-Dār al-Qawmiyyah li-l-Ṭibāʿah wa-l-Nashr, 1966.

al-Jurjānī, al-Qāḍī ʿAlī ibn ʿAbd al-ʿAzīz. *Asrār al-balāghah*. Edited by Hellmut Ritter. Istanbul: Wizārat al-Maʿārif, 1954.

Lane, Edward William. *An Arabic-English Lexicon*. 8 vols. London: Williams and Norgate, 1865. Offset: Beirut: Maktabat Lubnān, 1968.

Meisami, Julie, and Paul Starkey (eds.). *Encyclopedia of Arabic Literature*, 2 vols. London and New York: Routledge, 1998.

al-Muḥibbī, Muḥammad Amīn ibn ʿAbdallāh. *Khulāṣat al-athar fī aʿyān al-qarn al-ḥādī ʿashar*. 4 vols. Cairo: 1284/1867-68. Offset: Beirut: Dār Sadir, n.d.

al-Mutanabbī, Abū l-Ṭayyib. *Dīwān Abī l-Ṭayyib al-Mutanabbī*. Edited by ʿAbd al-Wahhāb ʿAzzām. Series: al-Dhakhāʾir 1. Cairo: al-Hayʾah al-ʿĀmmah li-Quṣūr al-Thaqāfah, n.d. [1995].

Pagano, Matheo, and Guillaume Postel. *The True Description of Cairo: A Sixteenth-Century Venetian View*. Translated and edited by Nicholas Warner. 3 vols. Oxford: The Arcadian Library with Oxford University Press, 2006.

Pickthall, Mohammed Marmeduke. *The Meaning of the Glorious Koran*. London: New English Library, 1963.

Raymond, André. *Artisans et commerçants au Caire au XVIIIème siècle*. 2 vols. Damascus: Institut Français d'Etudes Arabes, 1973–75. Reprinted Cairo: Institut Français d'Archéologie Orientale, 1999.

———. *Le Caire des Janissaires*. Paris: CNRS, 1995.

al-Ṣafadī, Khalīl ibn Aybak. *Al-Wāfī bi-l-wafayāt*. 30 vols. Beirut, Wiesbaden, and Berlin: Franz Steiner and Klaus Schwarz, 1931–2005.

al-Shidyāq, Aḥmad Fāris. *Leg over Leg*. Edited and translated by Humphrey Davies. 4 vols. Series: Library of Arabic Literature. New York: New York University Press, 2013–14.

Sībawayh, Abū Bishr ʿAmr ibn ʿUthmān ibn Qanbar. *Al-Kitāb*. Cairo: Dār al-Ṭibāʿah, 1318/1900–1901.

Thaʿlab, Abū l-ʿAbbās. *Al-Ṣubḥ al-munīr fī shiʿr Abī Baṣīr. Maymūn Qays ibn Jandal al-Aʿshā wa-l-Aʿshayayn al-ākharayn, maʿa sharḥ Thaʿlab Abī l-ʿAbbās*. Edited by Rudolf Eugen Geyer. Vienna: Adolf Holzhausens Nachfolger, 1928.

Tibrīzī, Yaḥyā ibn ʿAlī al-Khaṭīb al-. *Al-Mūḍiḥ fī sharḥ shiʿr al-Mutanabbī*. Edited by Khalaf Rashīd Nuʿmān. Series: Khizānat al-Turāth. 5 vols. Baghdad: Dār al-Shuʾūn al-Thaqāfiyyah al-ʿĀmmah, 2002.

Van Gelder, G. J. *Sound and Sense in Classical Arabic Poetry*. Wiesbaden: Harrassowitz, 2012.

Wright, W. A. *Grammar of the Arabic Language*. 3rd ed. Revised by W. Robertson Smith and M. J. de Goeje. 2 vols. Cambridge: Cambridge University Press, 1951.

Zamakhsharī, Maḥmūd ibn ʿUmar al-. *Rabīʿ al-abrār wa-fuṣūṣ al-akhbār*. Edited by ʿAbd al-Majīd Diyāb. Cairo: al-Hayʾah al-Miṣriyyah al-ʿĀmmah li-l-Kitāb, 1991–92.

Zawzanī, Abū ʿAbdallāh al-Ḥusayn ibn Aḥmad al-. *Sharḥ al-muʿallaqāt al-sabʿ*. Beirut: Dār Ṣādir and Dār Bayrūt, 1958.

Index

For all index headings, page numbers or section numbers referring to *Brains Confounded, Volume Two* appear first. Any page numbers or section numbers referring to *Risible Rhymes* appear after "**Risible**" in bold.

About the NYU Abu Dhabi Institute

The Library of Arabic Literature is supported by a grant from the NYU Abu Dhabi Institute, a major hub of intellectual and creative activity and advanced research. The Institute hosts academic conferences, workshops, lectures, film series, performances, and other public programs directed both to audiences within the UAE and to the worldwide academic and research community. It is a center of the scholarly community for Abu Dhabi, bringing together faculty and researchers from institutions of higher learning throughout the region.

NYU Abu Dhabi, through the NYU Abu Dhabi Institute, is a world-class center of cutting-edge research, scholarship, and cultural activity. The Institute creates singular opportunities for leading researchers from across the arts, humanities, social sciences, sciences, engineering, and the professions to carry out creative scholarship and conduct research on issues of major disciplinary, multidisciplinary, and global significance.

About the Translator

Humphrey Davies is an award-winning translator of Arabic literature from the Ottoman period to the present. Writers he has translated include Aḥmad Fāris al-Shidyāq, for the Library of Arabic Literature, as well as Elias Khoury, Naguib Mahfouz, Alaa Al Aswany, Bahaa Taher, Mourid Barghouti, Muhammad Mustagab, Gamal al-Ghitani, Hamdy el-Gazzar, Khaled Al-Berry, and Ahmed Alaidy. He has also authored, with Madiha Doss, an anthology of writings in Egyptian colloquial Arabic. He lives in Cairo.

The Library of Arabic Literature

For more details on individual titles, visit www.libraryofarabicliterature.org

Classical Arabic Literature: A Library of Arabic Literature Anthology
Selected and translated by Geert Jan van Gelder (2012)

A Treasury of Virtues: Sayings, Sermons, and Teachings of ʿAlī, by al-Qāḍī al-Quḍāʿī, with the *One Hundred Proverbs* attributed to al-Jāḥiẓ
Edited and translated by Tahera Qutbuddin (2013)

The Epistle on Legal Theory, by al-Shāfiʿī
Edited and translated by Joseph E. Lowry (2013)

Leg over Leg, by Aḥmad Fāris al-Shidyāq
Edited and translated by Humphrey Davies (4 volumes; 2013–14)

Virtues of the Imām Aḥmad ibn Ḥanbal, by Ibn al-Jawzī
Edited and translated by Michael Cooperson (2 volumes; 2013–15)

The Epistle of Forgiveness, by Abū l-ʿAlāʾ al-Maʿarrī
Edited and translated by Geert Jan van Gelder and Gregor Schoeler (2 volumes; 2013–14)

The Principles of Sufism, by ʿĀʾishah al-Bāʿūniyyah
Edited and translated by Th. Emil Homerin (2014)

The Expeditions: An Early Biography of Muḥammad, by Maʿmar ibn Rāshid
Edited and translated by Sean W. Anthony (2014)

Two Arabic Travel Books

Accounts of China and India, by Abū Zayd al-Sīrāfī

Edited and translated by Tim Mackintosh-Smith (2014)

Mission to the Volga, by Aḥmad ibn Faḍlān

Edited and translated by James Montgomery (2014)

Disagreements of the Jurists: A Manual of Islamic Legal Theory, by al-Qāḍī al-Nuʿmān

Edited and translated by Devin J. Stewart (2015)

Consorts of the Caliphs: Women and the Court of Baghdad, by Ibn al-Sāʿī

Edited by Shawkat M. Toorawa and translated by the Editors of the Library of Arabic Literature (2015)

What ʿĪsā ibn Hishām Told Us, by Muḥammad al-Muwayliḥī

Edited and translated by Roger Allen (2 volumes; 2015)

The Life and Times of Abū Tammām, by Abū Bakr Muḥammad ibn Yaḥyā al-Ṣūlī

Edited and translated by Beatrice Gruendler (2015)

The Sword of Ambition: Bureaucratic Rivalry in Medieval Egypt, by ʿUthmān ibn Ibrāhīm al-Nābulusī

Edited and translated by Luke Yarbrough (2016)

Brains Confounded by the Ode of Abū Shādūf Expounded, by Yūsuf al-Shirbīnī

Edited and translated by Humphrey Davies (2 volumes; 2016)

Light in the Heavens: Sayings of the Prophet Muḥammad, by al-Qāḍī al-Quḍāʿī

Edited and translated by Tahera Qutbuddin (2016)

Risible Rhymes, by Muḥammad ibn Maḥfūẓ al-Sanhūrī

Edited and translated by Humphrey Davies (2016)

A Hundred and One Nights

Edited and translated by Bruce Fudge (2016)

The Excellence of the Arabs, by Ibn Qutaybah
Edited by James E. Montgomery and Peter Webb
Translated by Sarah Bowen Savant and Peter Webb (2017)

Scents and Flavors: A Syrian Cookbook
Edited and translated by Charles Perry (2017)

Arabian Satire: Poetry from 18th-Century Najd, by Ḥmēdān al-Shwēʿir
Edited and translated by Marcel Kurpershoek (2017)

In Darfur: An Account of the Sultanate and Its People, by Muḥammad ibn ʿUmar al-Tūnisī
Edited and translated by Humphrey Davies (2 volumes; 2018)

War Songs, by ʿAntarah ibn Shaddād
Edited by James E. Montgomery
Translated by James E. Montgomery with Richard Sieburth (2018)

Arabian Romantic: Poems on Bedouin Life and Love, by ʿAbdallah ibn Sbayyil
Edited and translated by Marcel Kurpershoek (2018)

Dīwān ʿAntarah ibn Shaddād: A Literary-Historical Study, by James E. Montgomery (2018)

Stories of Piety and Prayer: Deliverance Follows Adversity, by al-Muḥassin ibn ʿAlī al-Tanūkhī
Edited and translated by Julia Bray (2019)

English-only Paperbacks

Leg over Leg, by Aḥmad Fāris al-Shidyāq (2 volumes; 2015)

The Expeditions: An Early Biography of Muḥammad, by Maʿmar ibn Rāshid (2015)

The Epistle on Legal Theory: A Translation of al-Shāfiʿī's Risālah, by al-Shāfiʿī (2015)

The Epistle of Forgiveness, by Abū l-ʿAlāʾ al-Maʿarrī (2016)

The Principles of Sufism, by ʿĀʾishah al-Bāʿūniyyah (2016)

A Treasury of Virtues: Sayings, Sermons, and Teachings of ʿAlī, by al-Qāḍī al-Quḍāʿī with the *One Hundred Proverbs* attributed to al-Jāḥiẓ (2016)

The Life of Ibn Ḥanbal, by Ibn al-Jawzī (2016)

Mission to the Volga, by Ibn Faḍlān (2017)

Accounts of China and India, by Abū Zayd al-Sīrāfī (2017)

A Hundred and One Nights (2017)

Disagreements of the Jurists: A Manual of Islamic Legal Theory, by al-Qāḍī al-Nuʿmān (2017)

What ʿĪsā ibn Hishām Told Us, by Muḥammad al-Muwayliḥī (2018)

War Songs, by ʿAntarah ibn Shaddād (2018)

The Life and Times of Abū Tammām, by Abū Bakr Muḥammad ibn Yaḥyā al-Ṣūlī (2018)

The Sword of Ambition, by ʿUthmān ibn Ibrāhīm al-Nābulusī (2019)

Brains Confounded by the Ode of Abū Shādūf Expounded, by Yūsuf al-Shirbīnī, with *Risible Rhymes* by Muḥammad ibn Maḥfūẓ al-Sanhūrī (2 volumes; 2019)

Printed and bound by CPI Group (UK) Ltd, Croydon, CR0 4YY

13/04/2025

14656574-0001